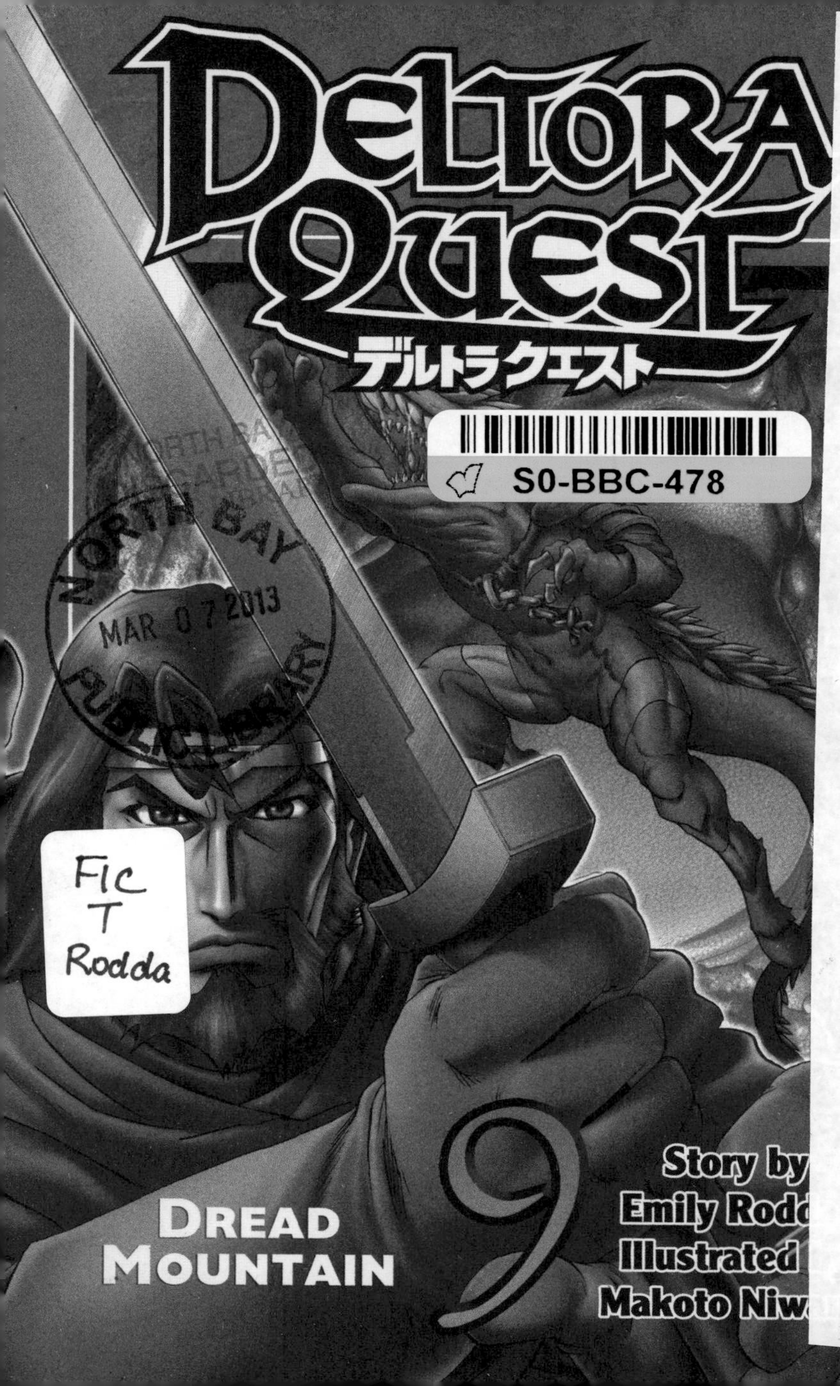
DELTORA QUEST
デルトラクエスト
9
DREAD MOUNTAIN
Story by
Emily Rodd
Illustrated
Makoto Niw
S0-BBC-478
NORTH BAY PUBLIC LIBRARY
MAR 07 2013
FIC
T
Rodda

Deltora Quest
デルトラクエスト

Volume 9: Character Introductions

Lief

In place of his father, he is on a journey to find the lost Seven Gems and restore peace and freedom to the Kingdom of Deltora, which has fallen into the hands of the Shadow Lord.

Barda

A former guard at the Palace of Del. He disguised himself as a beggar and hid in the city of Del for 16 years, in order to join Lief on his journey. A master swordsman.

Prin

A child of the legendary winged creatures, the Kin. She lives near the Dreaming Spring.

The Kin

Jasmine

Answering the wishes of her mother's spirit, she has joined Lief and Barda on their quest. She harbors an inexplicable hatred toward Doom.

Crenn

The Kin's elder. He worries about the future of his race.

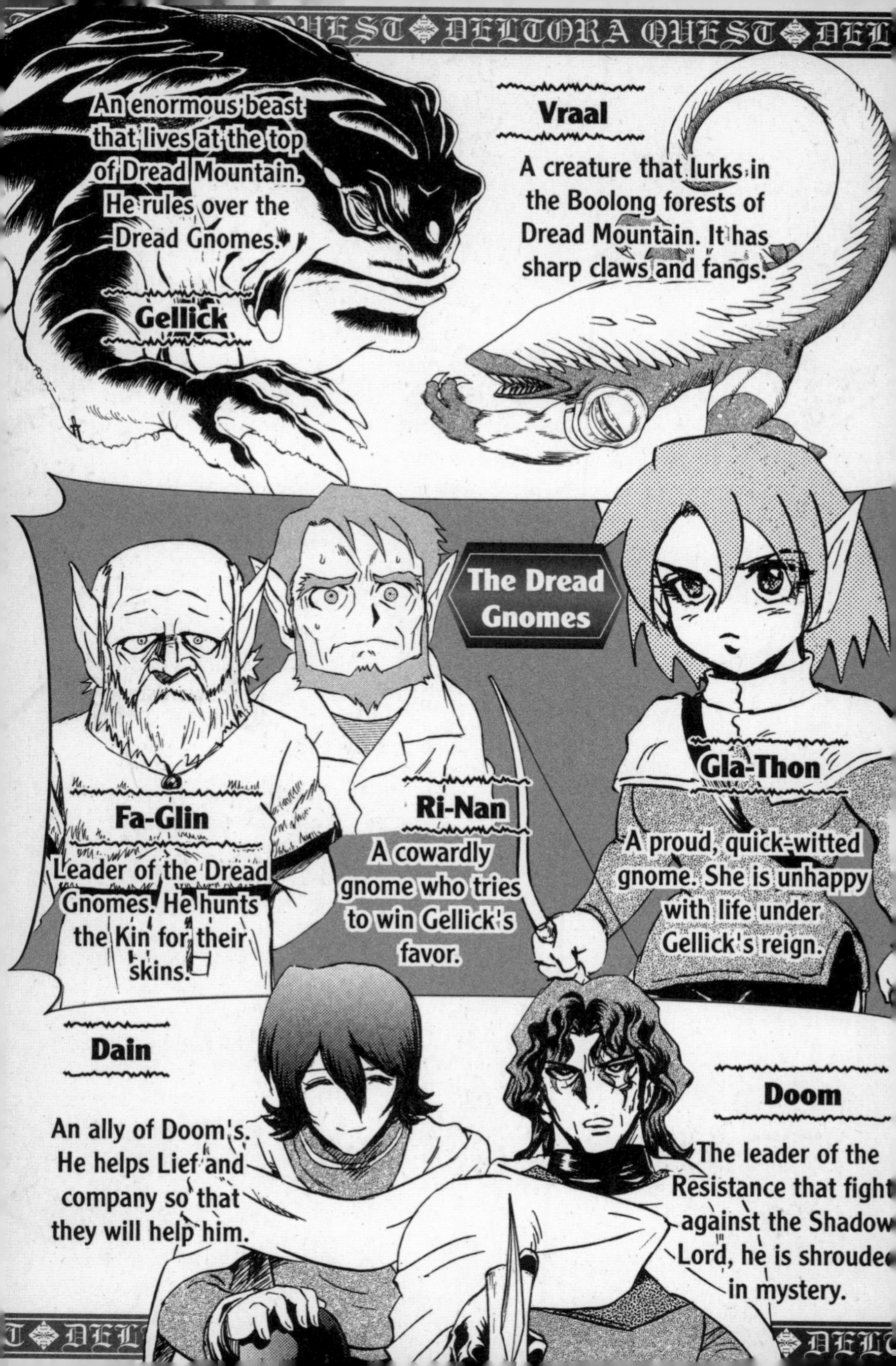
DELTORA QUEST
Vraal
A creature that lurks in the Boolong forests of Dread Mountain. It has sharp claws and fangs.
Gellick
An enormous beast that lives at the top of Dread Mountain. He rules over the Dread Gnomes.
The Dread Gnomes
Gla-Thon
A proud, quick-witted gnome. She is unhappy with life under Gellick's reign.
Ri-Nan
A cowardly gnome who tries to win Gellick's favor.
Fa-Glin
Leader of the Dread Gnomes. He hunts the Kin for their skins.
Doom
The leader of the Resistance that fight against the Shadow Lord, he is shroude in mystery.
Dain
An ally of Doom's. He helps Lief and company so that they will help him.

Synopsis

The Guardian of the Shifting Sands, created from the malice of the dead, awaited our heroes inside a giant pyramid of death. After defeating the Guardian and obtaining the fourth gem--the lapis lazuli--Lief purges the dead of their hate and narrowly escapes his own death.

⚜ ⚜ ⚜ ⚜ ⚜

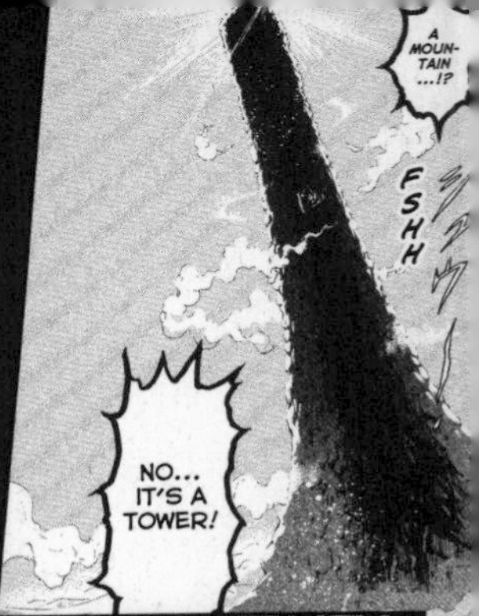
A MOUNTAIN ...!?
FSHH
NO... IT'S A TOWER!

On their way to Dread Mountain, Lief, Barda, and Jasmine come across the Dreaming Spring. There, they find the Kin. The Kin had been chased from their home on Dread Mountain by the gnomes there.

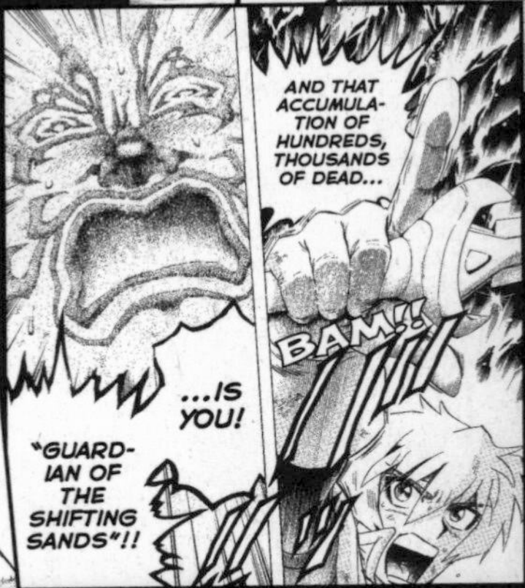
AND THAT ACCUMULATION OF HUNDREDS, THOUSANDS OF DEAD...
BAM!!
"GUARDIAN OF THE SHIFTING SANDS"!!
...IS YOU!

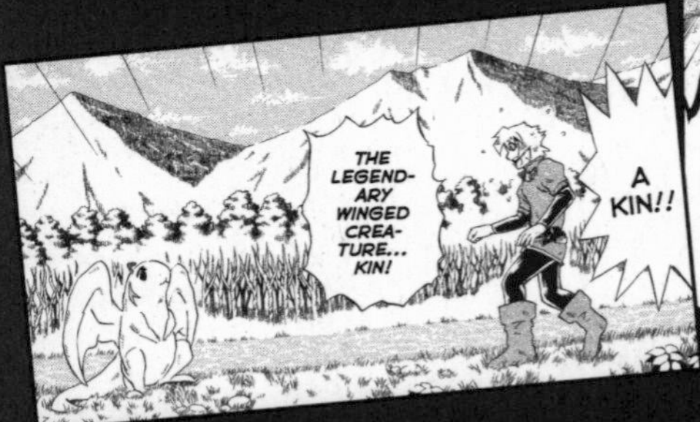
A KIN!!
THE LEGENDARY WINGED CREATURE... KIN!

Through the power of the Dreaming Spring, Lief learns that his parents are in grave danger, and he is ready to abandon everything and return to the City of Del. But Barda convinces him to renew his pledge to save Deltora and continue his quest.

Then our heroes discover a new mystery about Doom....

With the help of the Kin, the three friends take to the skies and journey to Dread Mountain, where they are sure to encounter formidable foes.

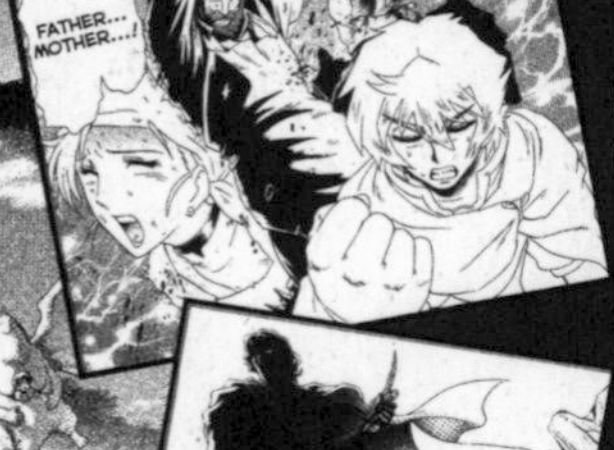
FATHER... MOTHER...!

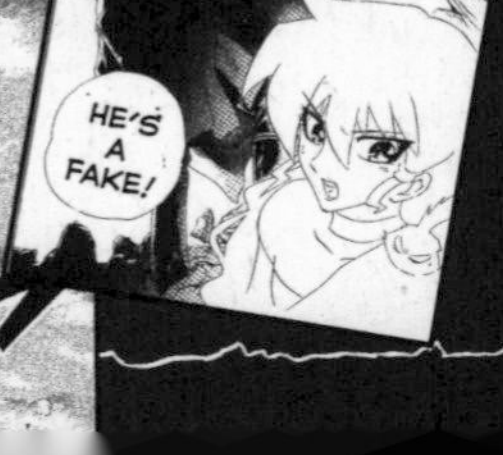
HE'S A FAKE!

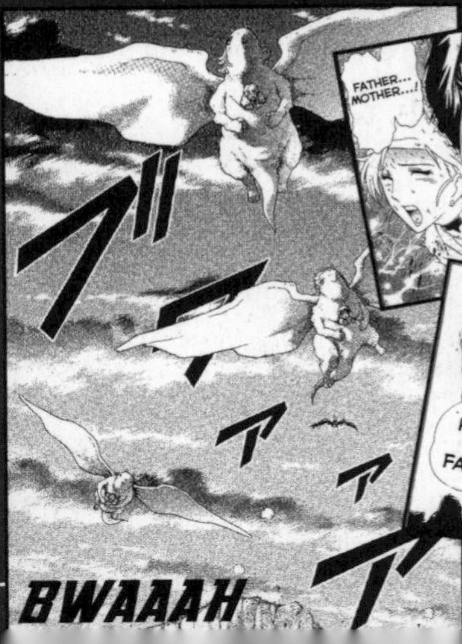
BWAAAH

Deltora Quest

DELTORA QUEST 9

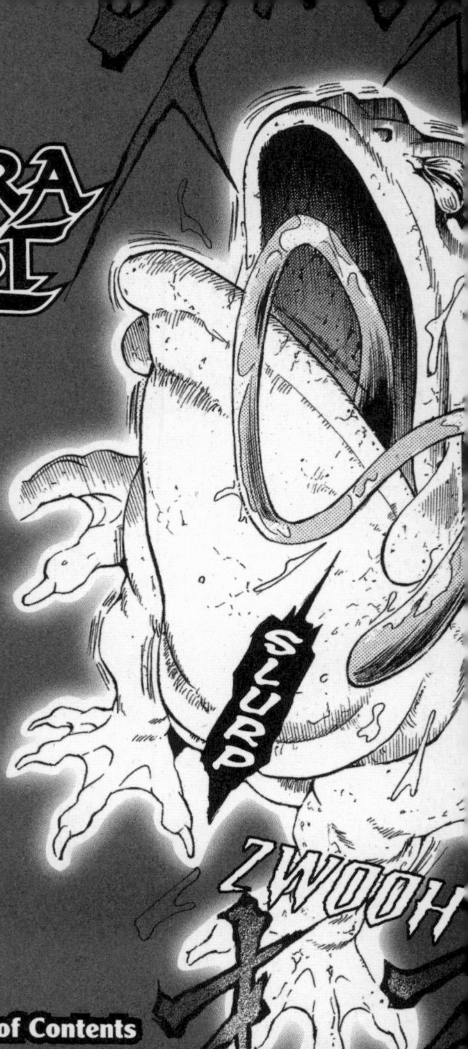
SLURP
ZWOOH

Volume 9: Table of Contents

DELTORA QUEST

デルトラクエスト

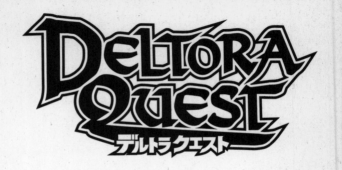

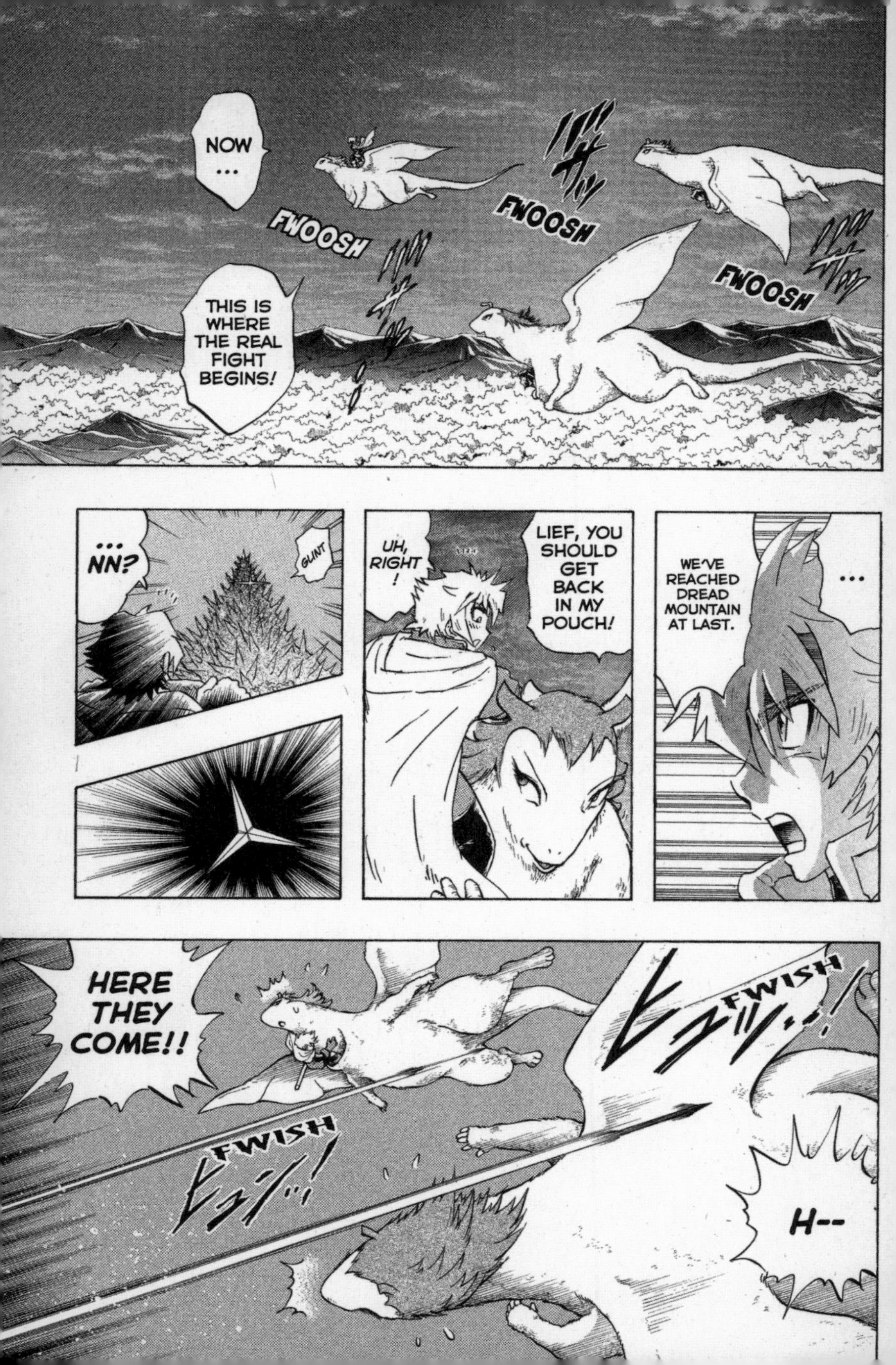
FWOOSH
FWOOSH
NOW...
FWOOSH
THIS IS WHERE THE REAL FIGHT BEGINS!
...
WE'VE REACHED DREAD MOUNTAIN AT LAST.
LIEF, YOU SHOULD GET BACK IN MY POUCH!
UH, RIGHT!
GLINT
...NN?
FWISH
H--
FWISH
HERE THEY COME!!

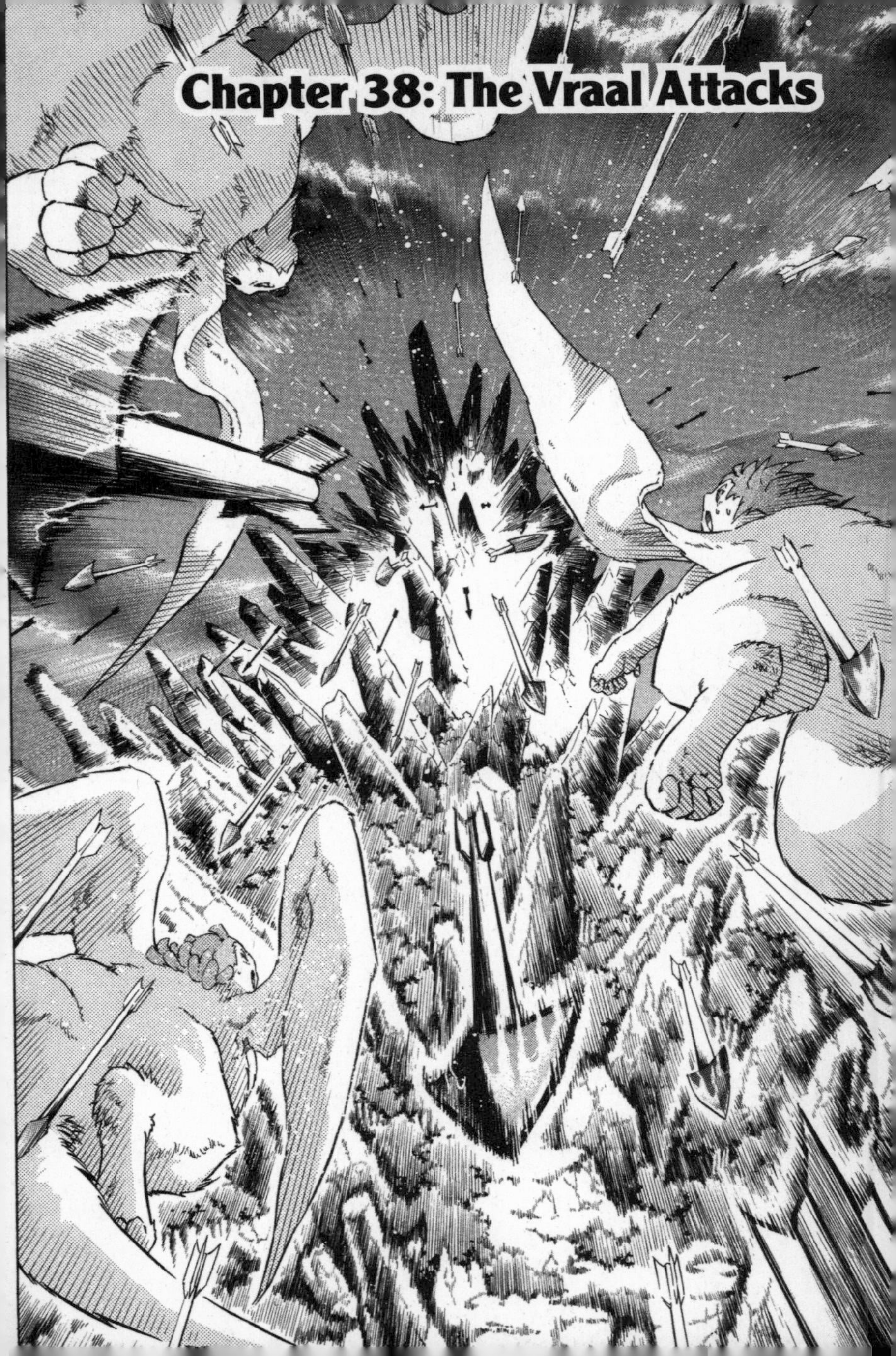
Chapter 38: The Vraal Attacks

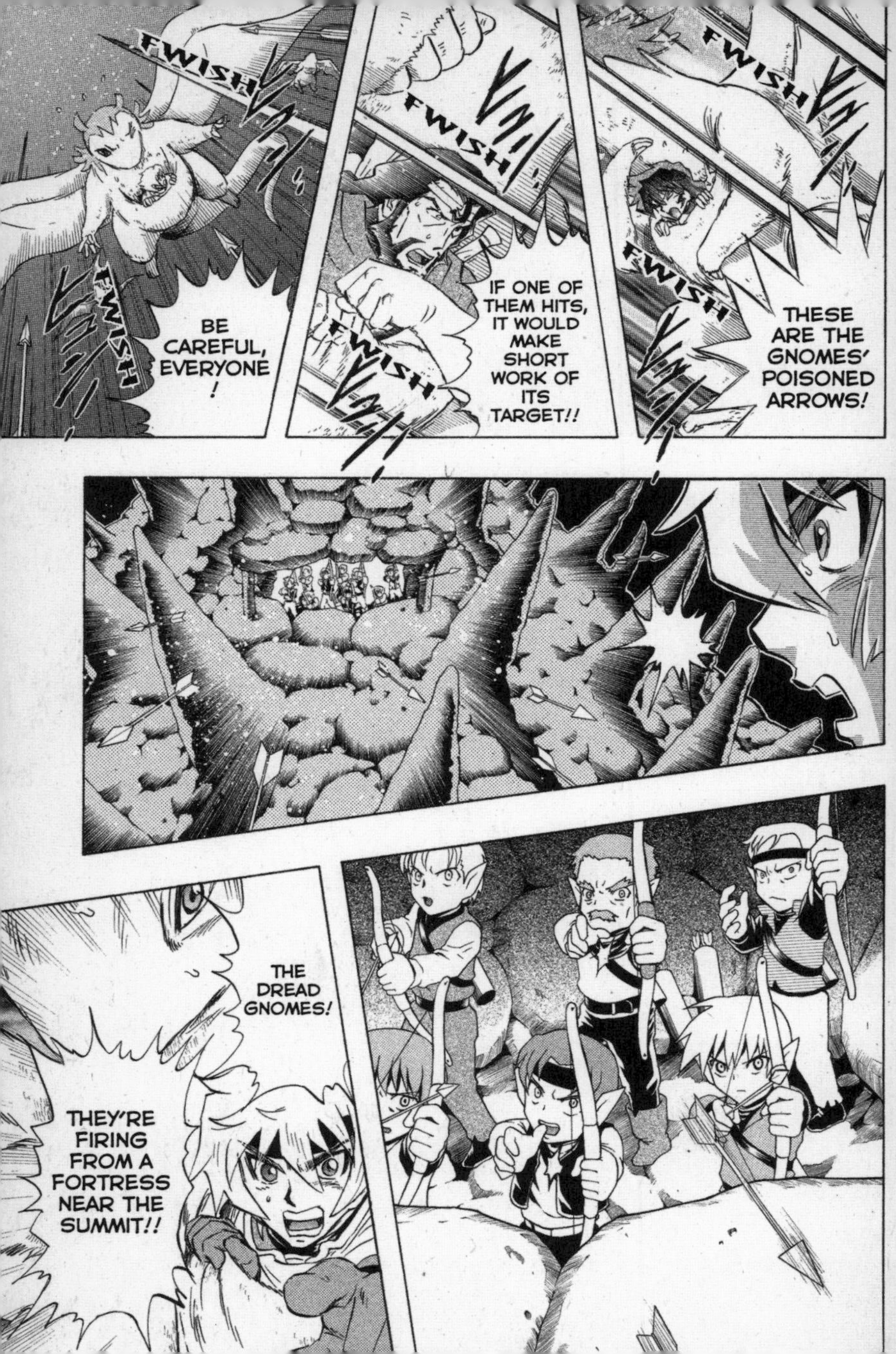
FWISH
FWISH
THESE ARE THE GNOMES' POISONED ARROWS!
FWISH
FWISH
IF ONE OF THEM HITS, IT WOULD MAKE SHORT WORK OF ITS TARGET!!
FWISH
FWISH
BE CAREFUL, EVERYONE!
THE DREAD GNOMES!
THEY'RE FIRING FROM A FORTRESS NEAR THE SUMMIT!!

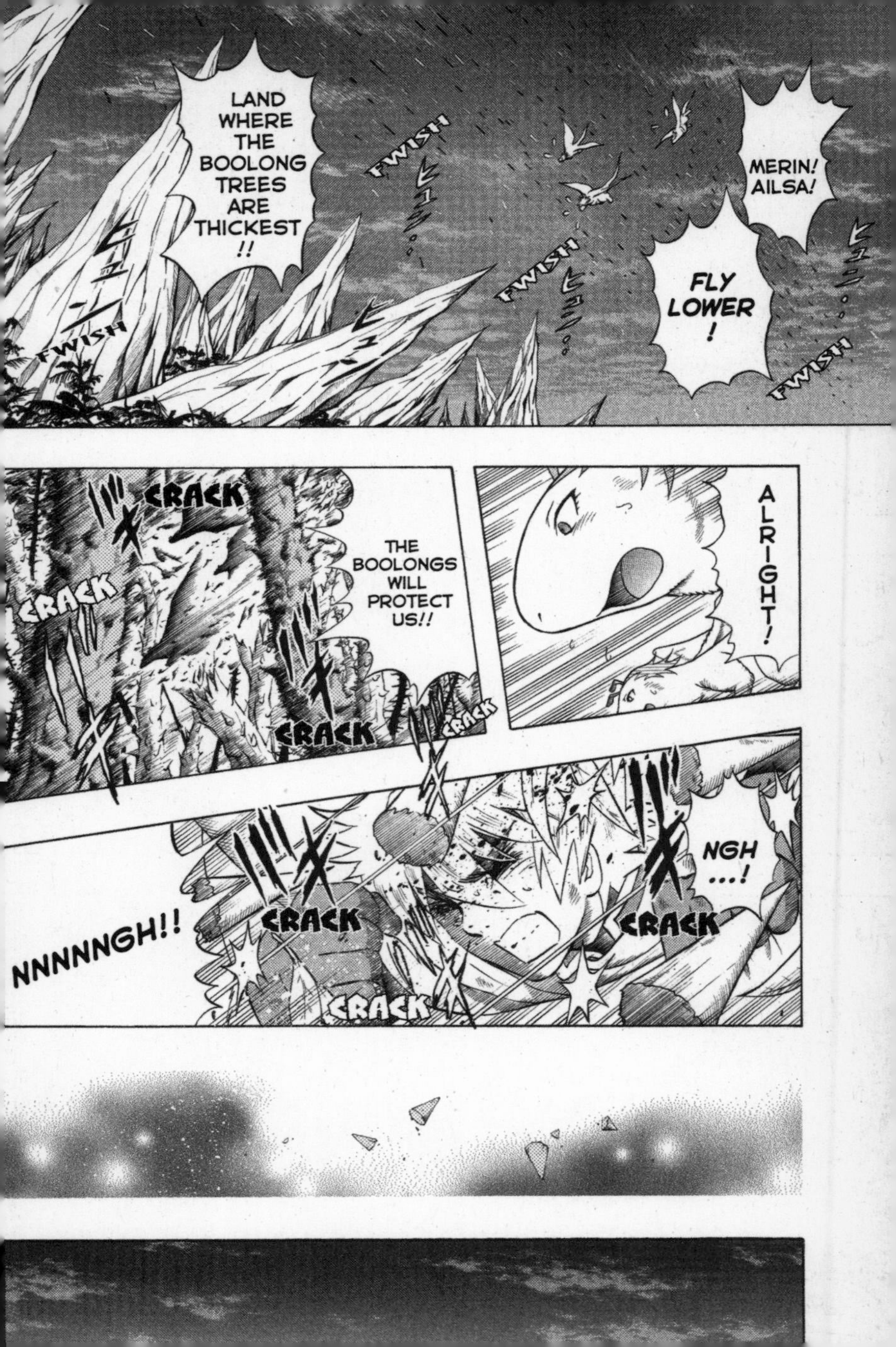
MERIN! AILSA!
FLY LOWER!
FWISH
FWISH
FWISH
LAND WHERE THE BOOLONG TREES ARE THICKEST!!
FWISH
ALRIGHT!
THE BOOLONGS WILL PROTECT US!!
CRACK
CRACK
CRACK
CRACK
NGH ...!
CRACK
CRACK
CRACK
NNNNNGH!!

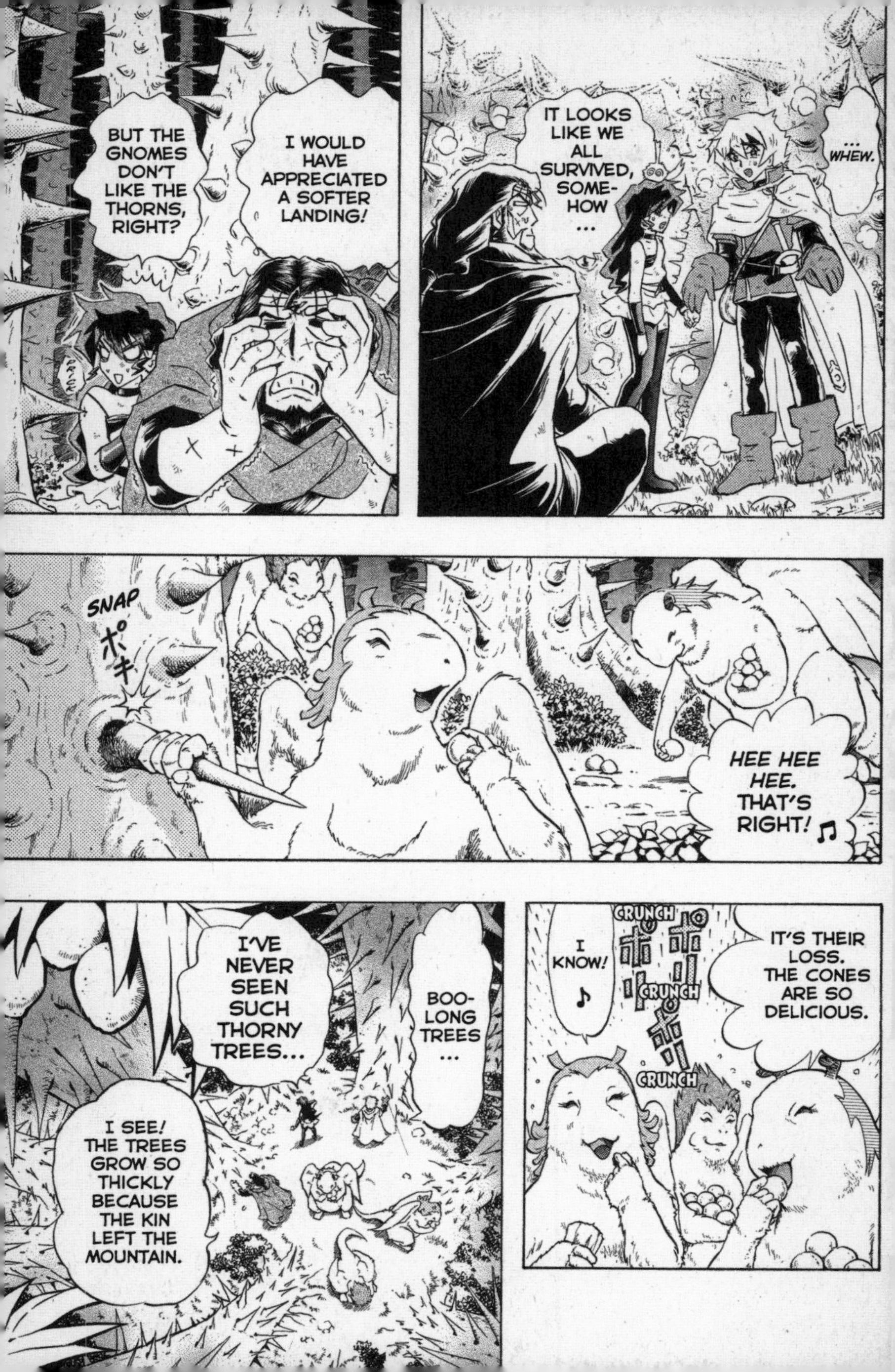
...WHEW.
IT LOOKS LIKE WE ALL SURVIVED, SOME-HOW...
I WOULD HAVE APPRECIATED A SOFTER LANDING!
BUT THE GNOMES DON'T LIKE THE THORNS, RIGHT?
HEE HEE HEE. THAT'S RIGHT! ♫
SNAP
ポキ
IT'S THEIR LOSS. THE CONES ARE SO DELICIOUS.
CRUNCH
CRUNCH
CRUNCH
I KNOW! ♪
BOO-LONG TREES...
I'VE NEVER SEEN SUCH THORNY TREES...
I SEE! THE TREES GROW SO THICKLY BECAUSE THE KIN LEFT THE MOUNTAIN.

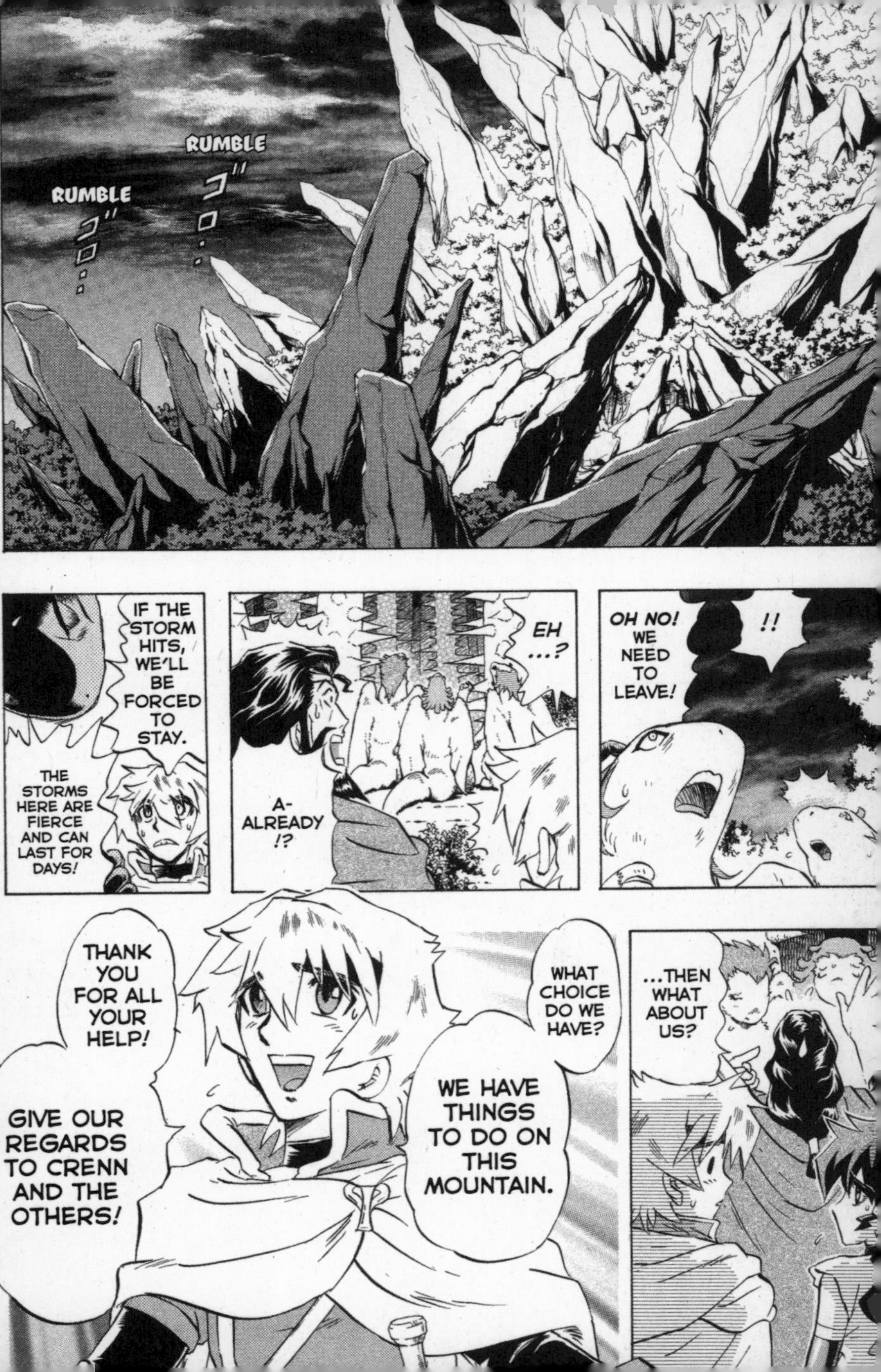
RUMBLE
ゴロ・・
RUMBLE
ゴロ・・
!!
OH NO! WE NEED TO LEAVE!
EH ...?
A-ALREADY !?
IF THE STORM HITS, WE'LL BE FORCED TO STAY.
THE STORMS HERE ARE FIERCE AND CAN LAST FOR DAYS!
...THEN WHAT ABOUT US?
WHAT CHOICE DO WE HAVE?
WE HAVE THINGS TO DO ON THIS MOUNTAIN.
THANK YOU FOR ALL YOUR HELP!
GIVE OUR REGARDS TO CRENN AND THE OTHERS!

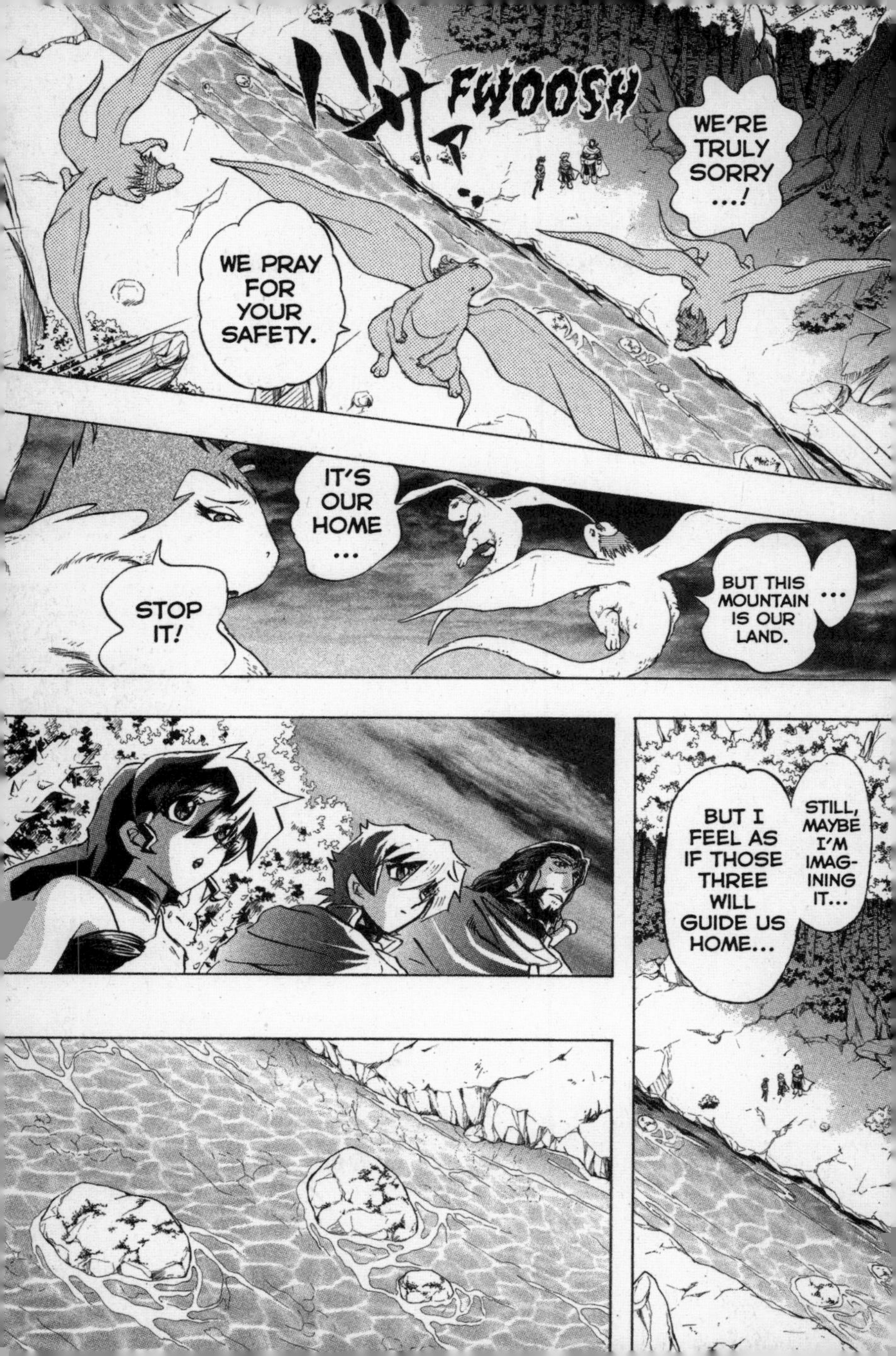
FWOOSH
WE'RE TRULY SORRY ...!
WE PRAY FOR YOUR SAFETY.
... BUT THIS MOUNTAIN IS OUR LAND.
IT'S OUR HOME ...
STOP IT!
STILL, MAYBE I'M IMAG-INING IT...
BUT I FEEL AS IF THOSE THREE WILL GUIDE US HOME...

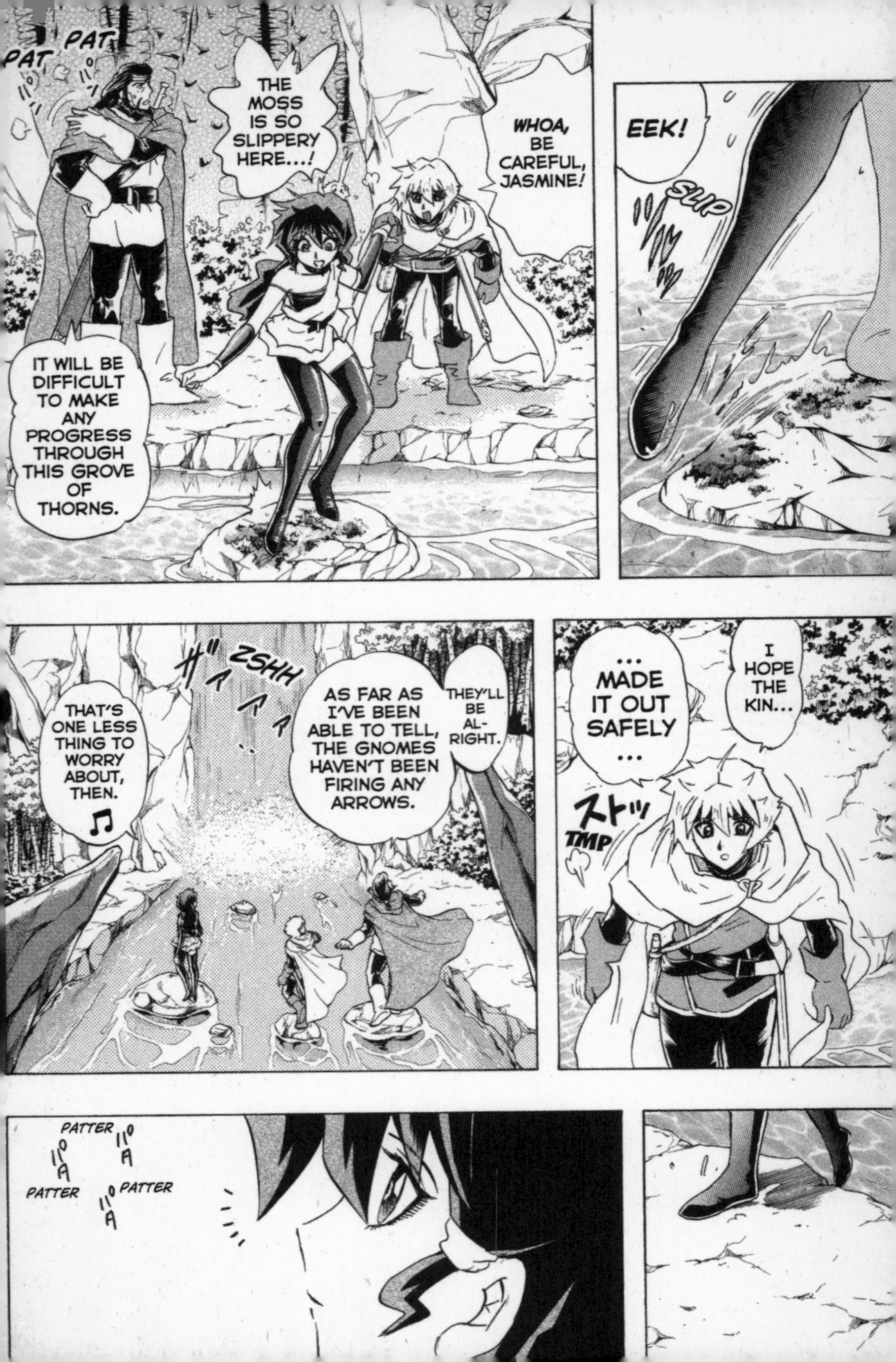
EEK!
SLIP
WHOA, BE CAREFUL, JASMINE!
THE MOSS IS SO SLIPPERY HERE...!
PAT PAT
IT WILL BE DIFFICULT TO MAKE ANY PROGRESS THROUGH THIS GROVE OF THORNS.
I HOPE THE KIN...
... MADE IT OUT SAFELY ...
TMP
THEY'LL BE AL-RIGHT.
AS FAR AS I'VE BEEN ABLE TO TELL, THE GNOMES HAVEN'T BEEN FIRING ANY ARROWS.
ZSHH
THAT'S ONE LESS THING TO WORRY ABOUT, THEN. ♫
PATTER
PATTER
PATTER

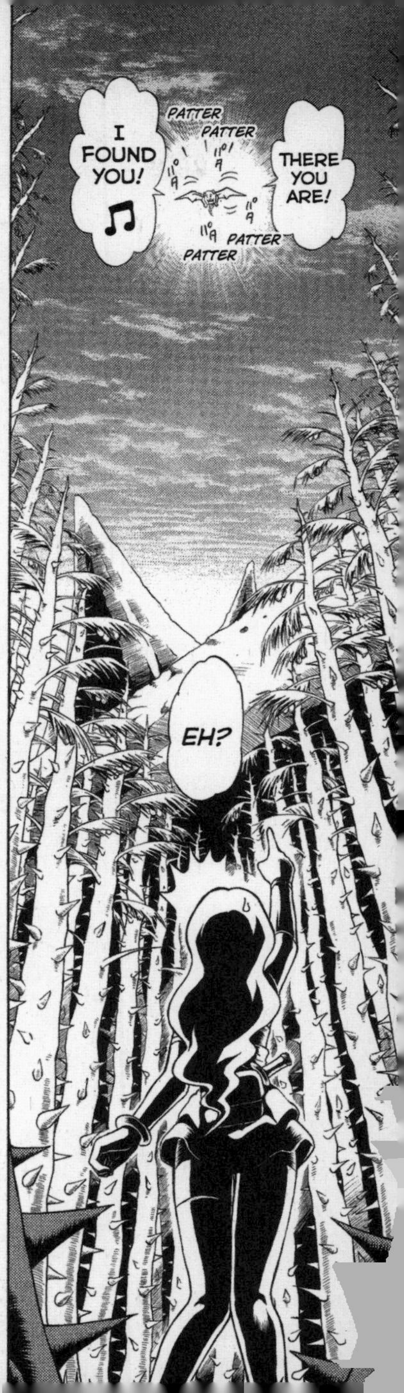
THERE YOU ARE!
PATTER PATTER
PATTER PATTER
I FOUND YOU! ♫
EH?

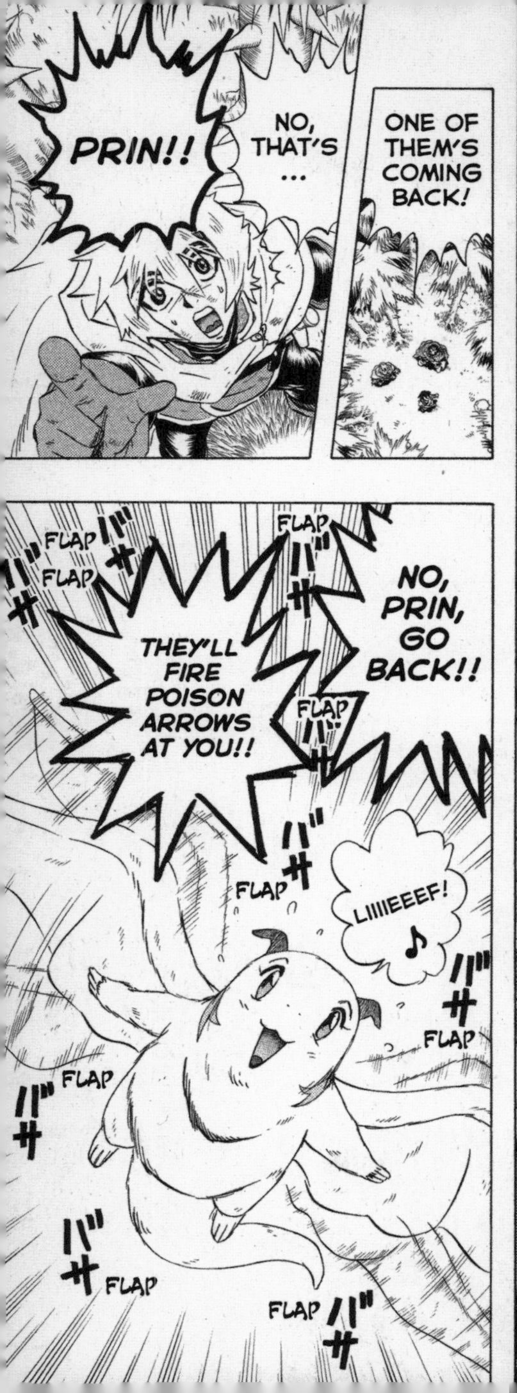
ONE OF THEM'S COMING BACK!
NO, THAT'S ...
PRIN!!
NO, PRIN, GO BACK!!
FLAP バサ
FLAP バサ
FLAP バサ
THEY'LL FIRE POISON ARROWS AT YOU!!
FLAP バサ
FLAP バサ
LIIIIEEEF! ♪
FLAP バサ
FLAP バサ
FLAP バサ
FLAP バサ

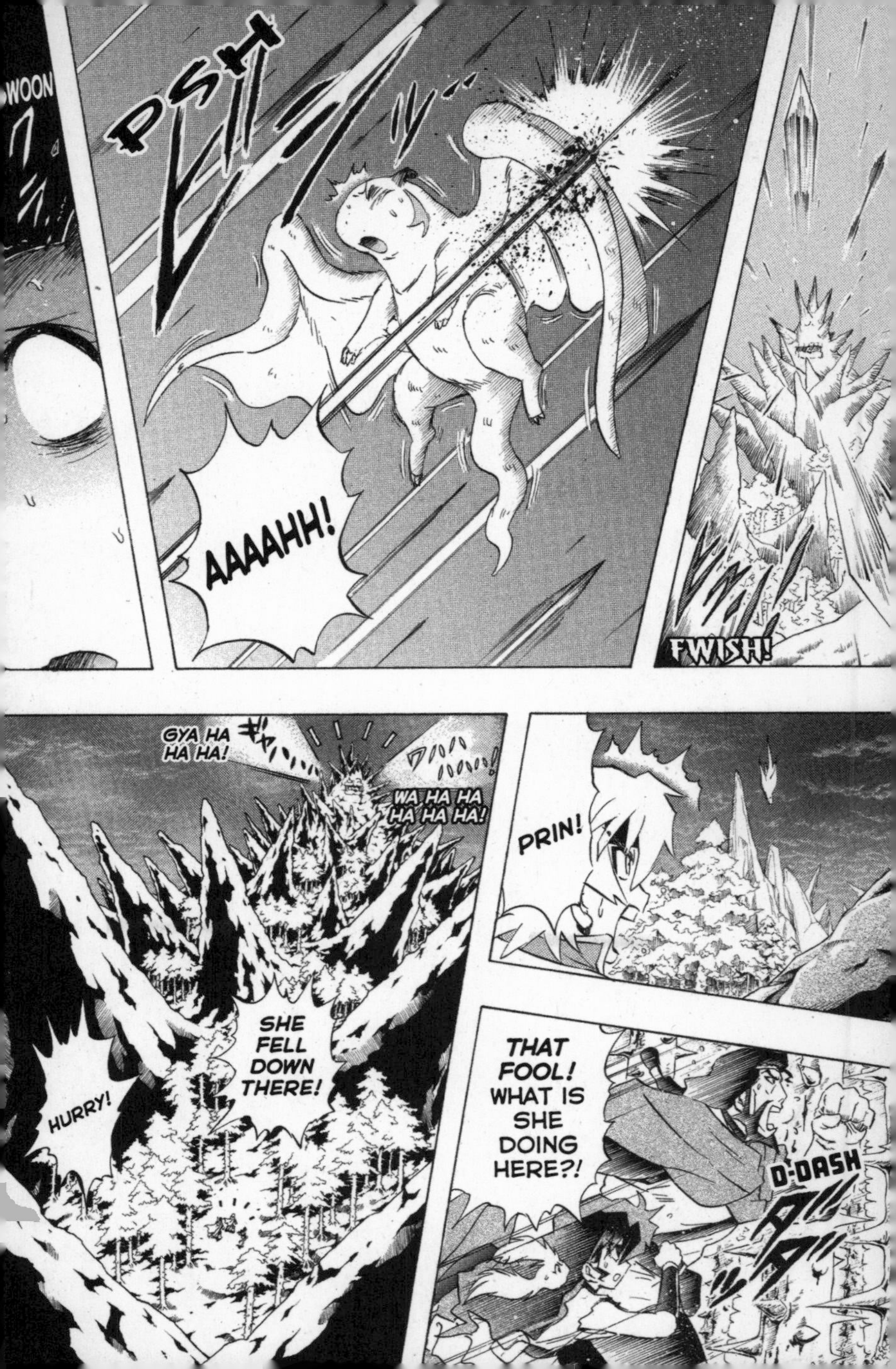
FWISH!
PSH
AAAAHH!
WOON
PRIN!
THAT FOOL! WHAT IS SHE DOING HERE?!
D-DASH
GYA HA HA HA!
WA HA HA HA HA HA!
SHE FELL DOWN THERE!
HURRY!

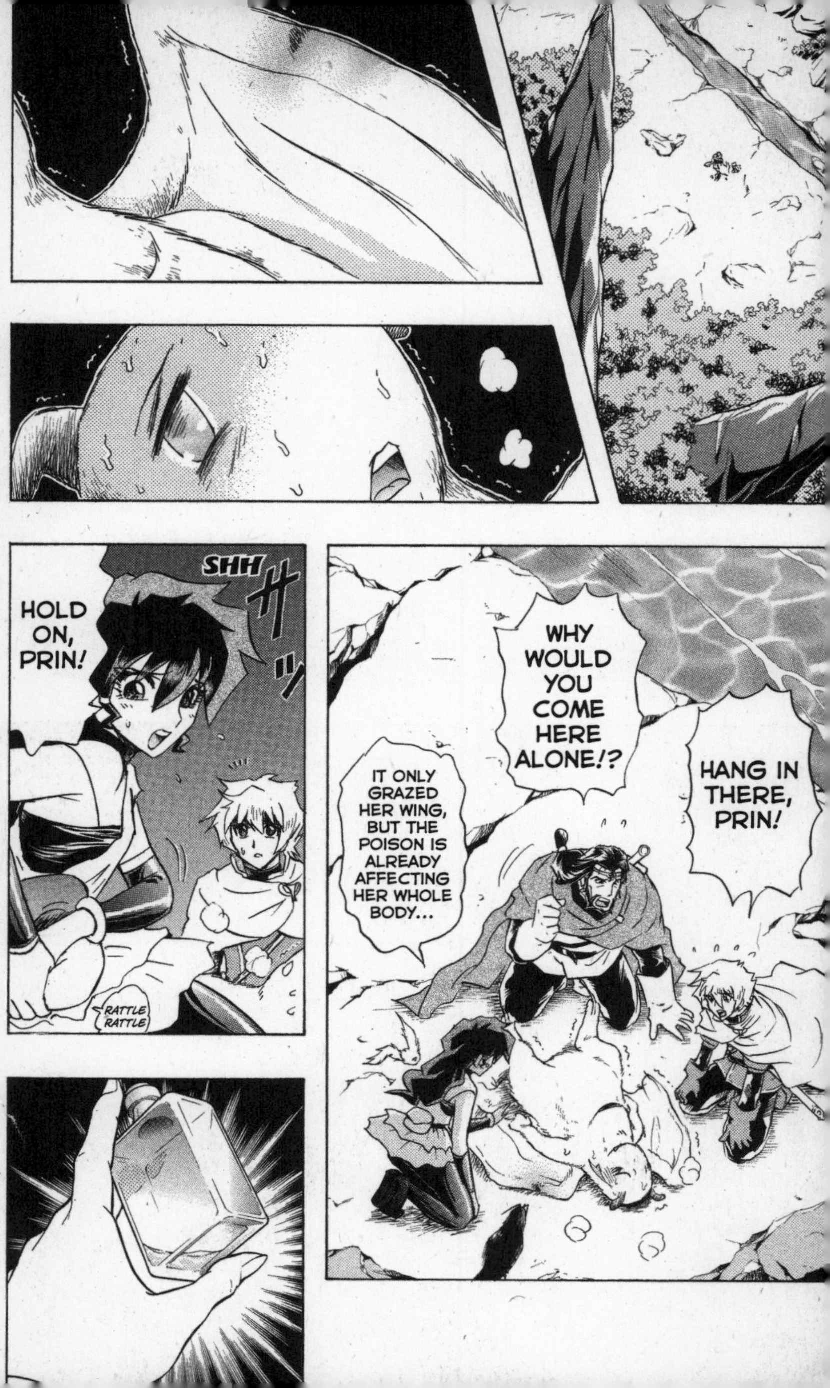
WHY WOULD YOU COME HERE ALONE!?
HANG IN THERE, PRIN!
IT ONLY GRAZED HER WING, BUT THE POISON IS ALREADY AFFECTING HER WHOLE BODY...
SHH
HOLD ON, PRIN!
RATTLE RATTLE

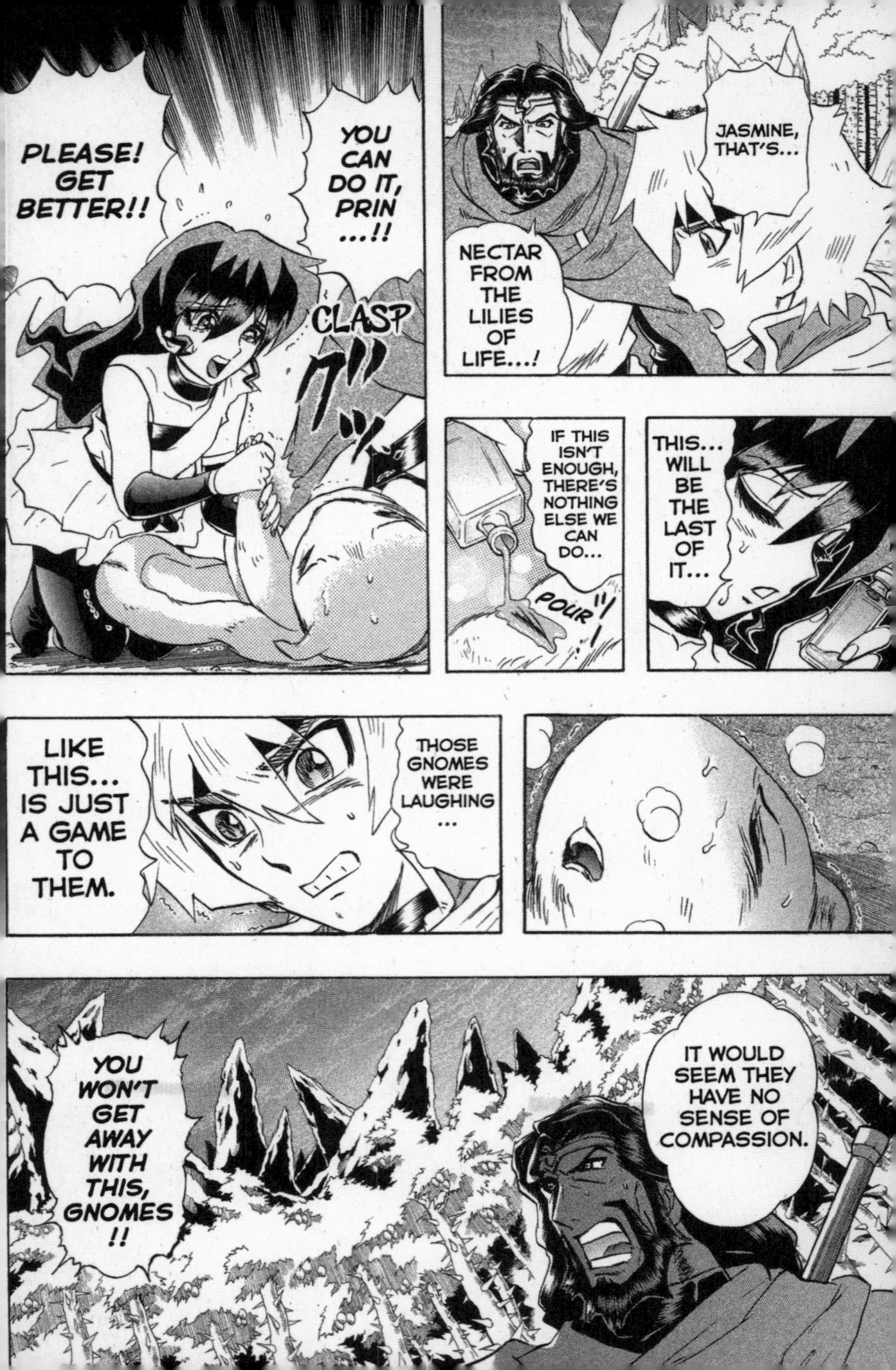
JASMINE, THAT'S...
NECTAR FROM THE LILIES OF LIFE...!
THIS... WILL BE THE LAST OF IT...
IF THIS ISN'T ENOUGH, THERE'S NOTHING ELSE WE CAN DO...
POUR
YOU CAN DO IT, PRIN ...!!
PLEASE! GET BETTER!!
CLASP
THOSE GNOMES WERE LAUGHING ...
LIKE THIS... IS JUST A GAME TO THEM.
IT WOULD SEEM THEY HAVE NO SENSE OF COMPASSION.
YOU WON'T GET AWAY WITH THIS, GNOMES !!

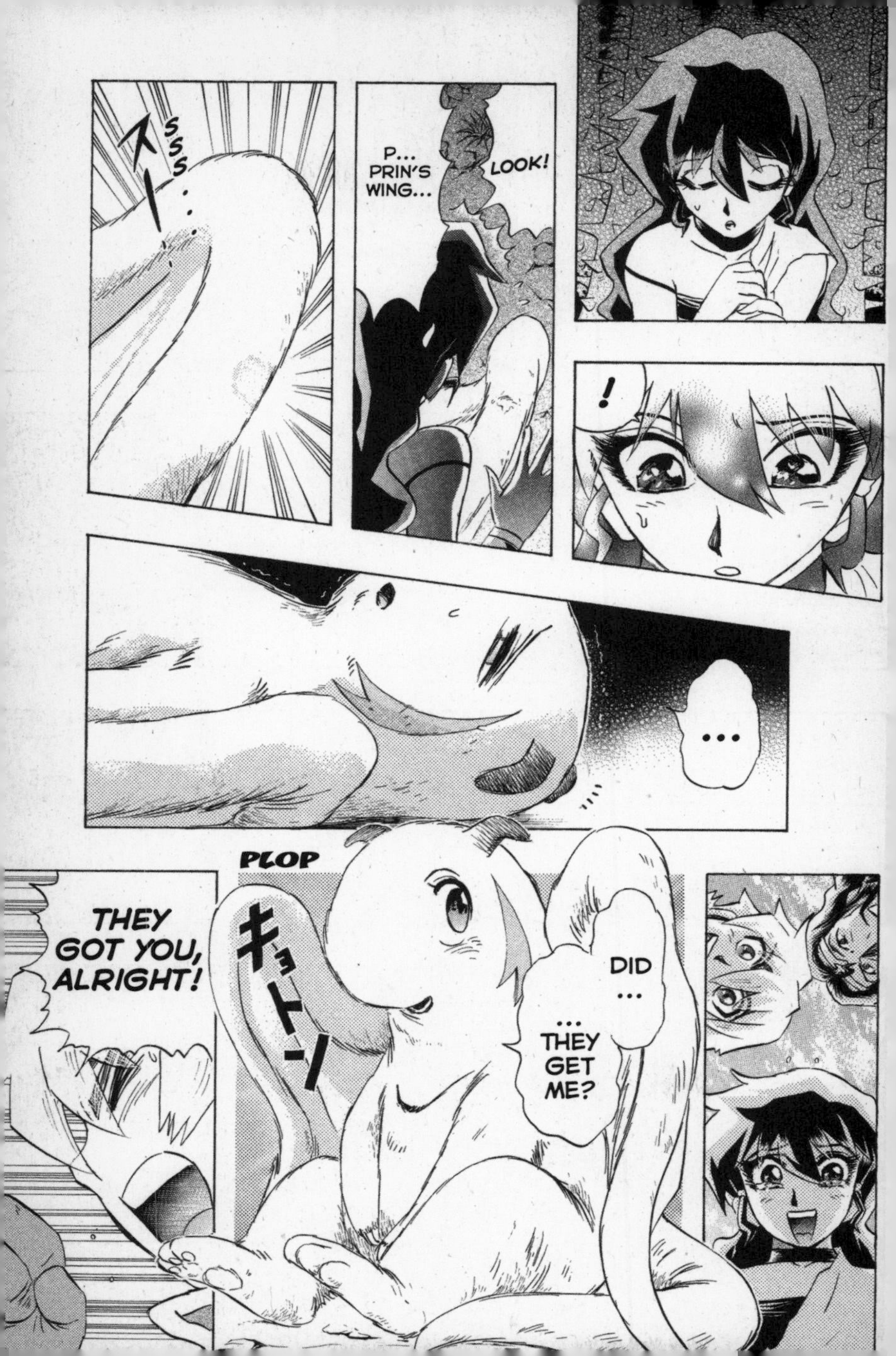

!
LOOK!
P... PRIN'S WING...
SSS...
スー
...
PLOP
DID ... ... THEY GET ME?
キョトーン
THEY GOT YOU, ALRIGHT!

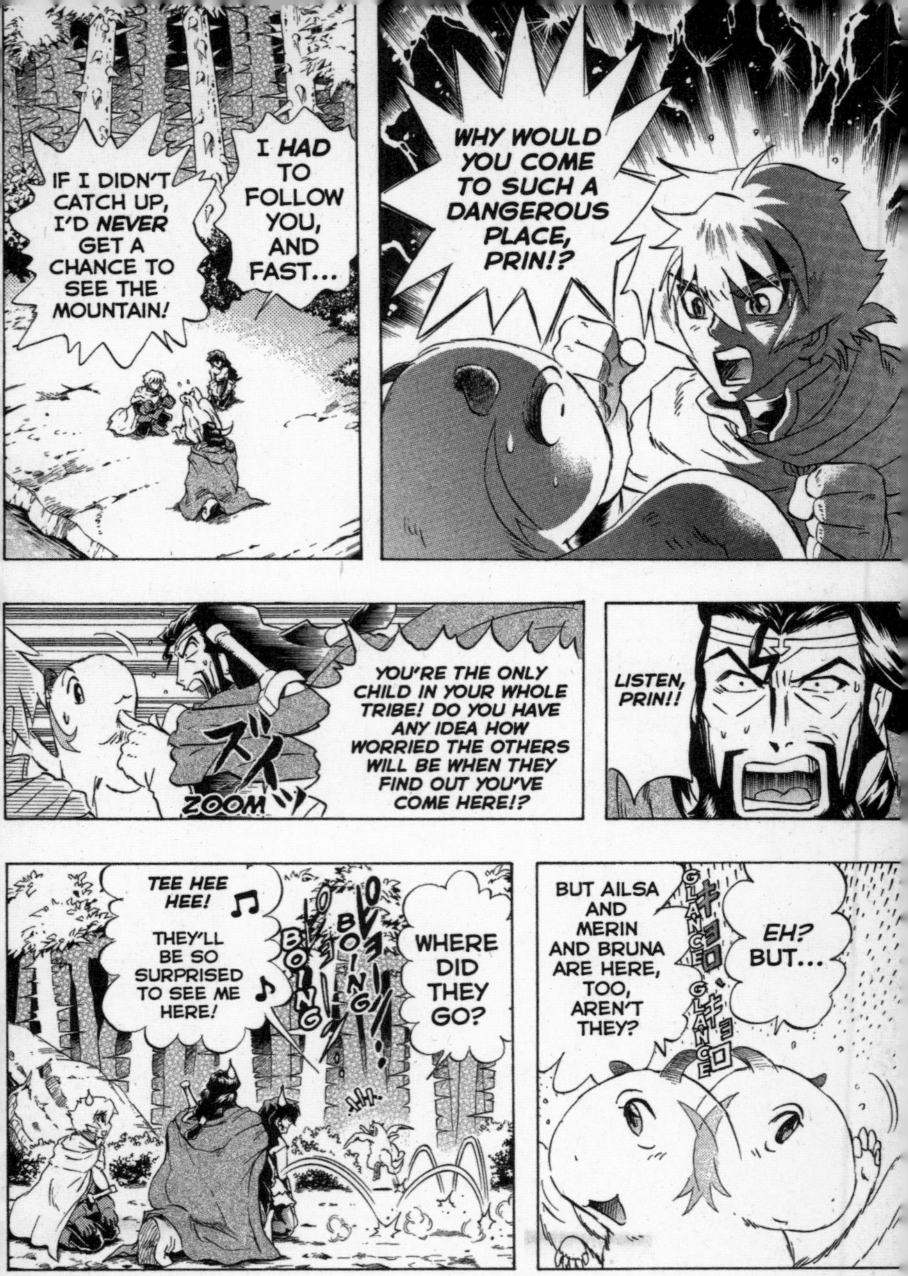
WHY WOULD YOU COME TO SUCH A DANGEROUS PLACE, PRIN!?
I *HAD* TO FOLLOW YOU, AND FAST...
IF I DIDN'T CATCH UP, I'D *NEVER* GET A CHANCE TO SEE THE MOUNTAIN!
LISTEN, PRIN!!
YOU'RE THE ONLY CHILD IN YOUR WHOLE TRIBE! DO YOU HAVE ANY IDEA HOW WORRIED THE OTHERS WILL BE WHEN THEY FIND OUT YOU'VE COME HERE!?
ZOOM
EH? BUT...
GLANCE GLANCE
BUT AILSA AND MERIN AND BRUNA ARE HERE, TOO, AREN'T THEY?
WHERE DID THEY GO?
BOING BOING
TEE HEE HEE! ♪
THEY'LL BE SO SURPRISED TO SEE ME HERE! ♪

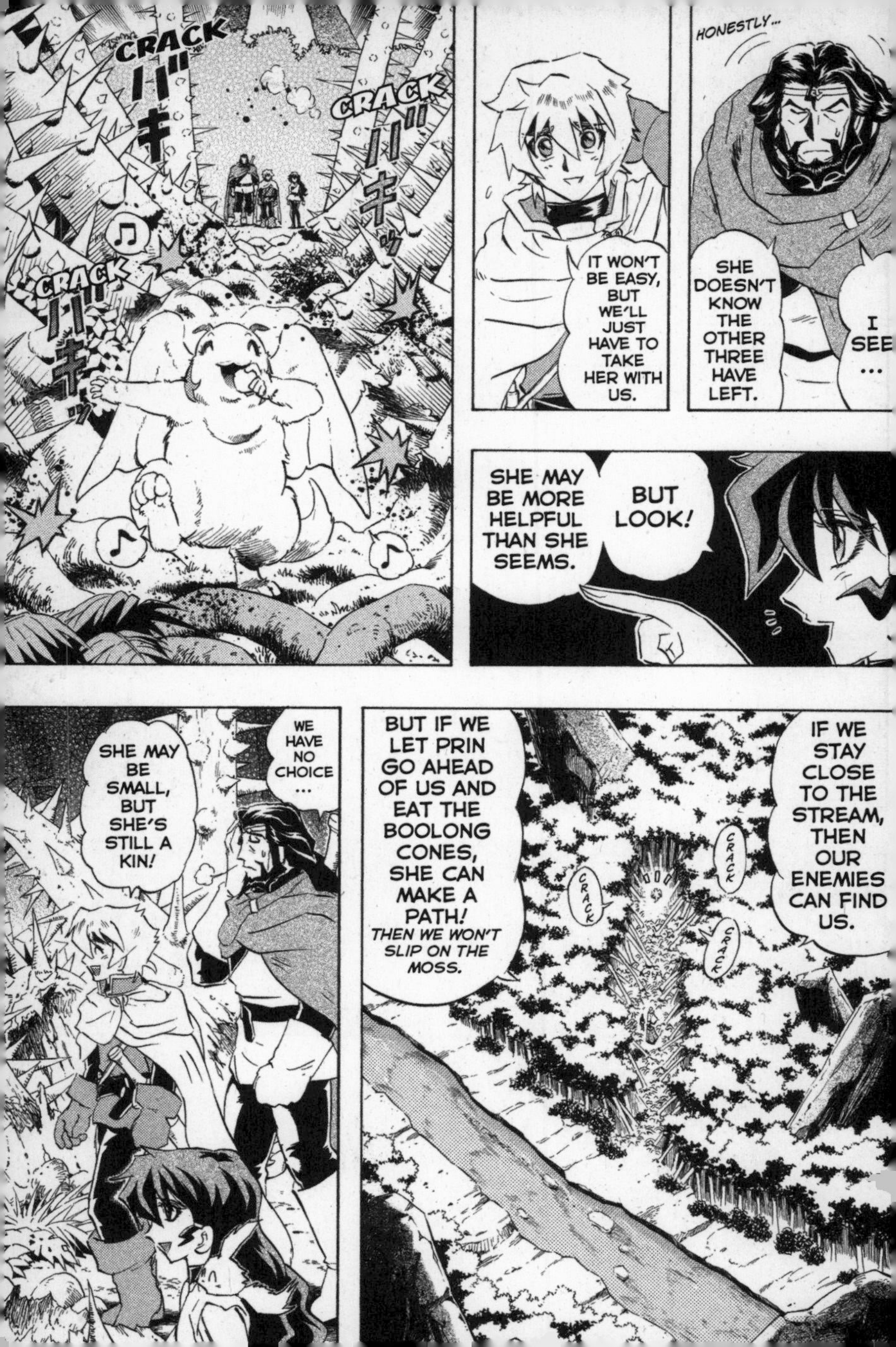
HONESTLY...
I SEE ...
SHE DOESN'T KNOW THE OTHER THREE HAVE LEFT.
IT WON'T BE EASY, BUT WE'LL JUST HAVE TO TAKE HER WITH US.
BUT LOOK!
SHE MAY BE MORE HELPFUL THAN SHE SEEMS.
CRACK
バキ
CRACK
バキ
CRACK
バキ
IF WE STAY CLOSE TO THE STREAM, THEN OUR ENEMIES CAN FIND US.
CRACK
CRACK
CRACK
BUT IF WE LET PRIN GO AHEAD OF US AND EAT THE BOOLONG CONES, SHE CAN MAKE A PATH!
THEN WE WON'T SLIP ON THE MOSS.
WE HAVE NO CHOICE ...
SHE MAY BE SMALL, BUT SHE'S STILL A KIN!

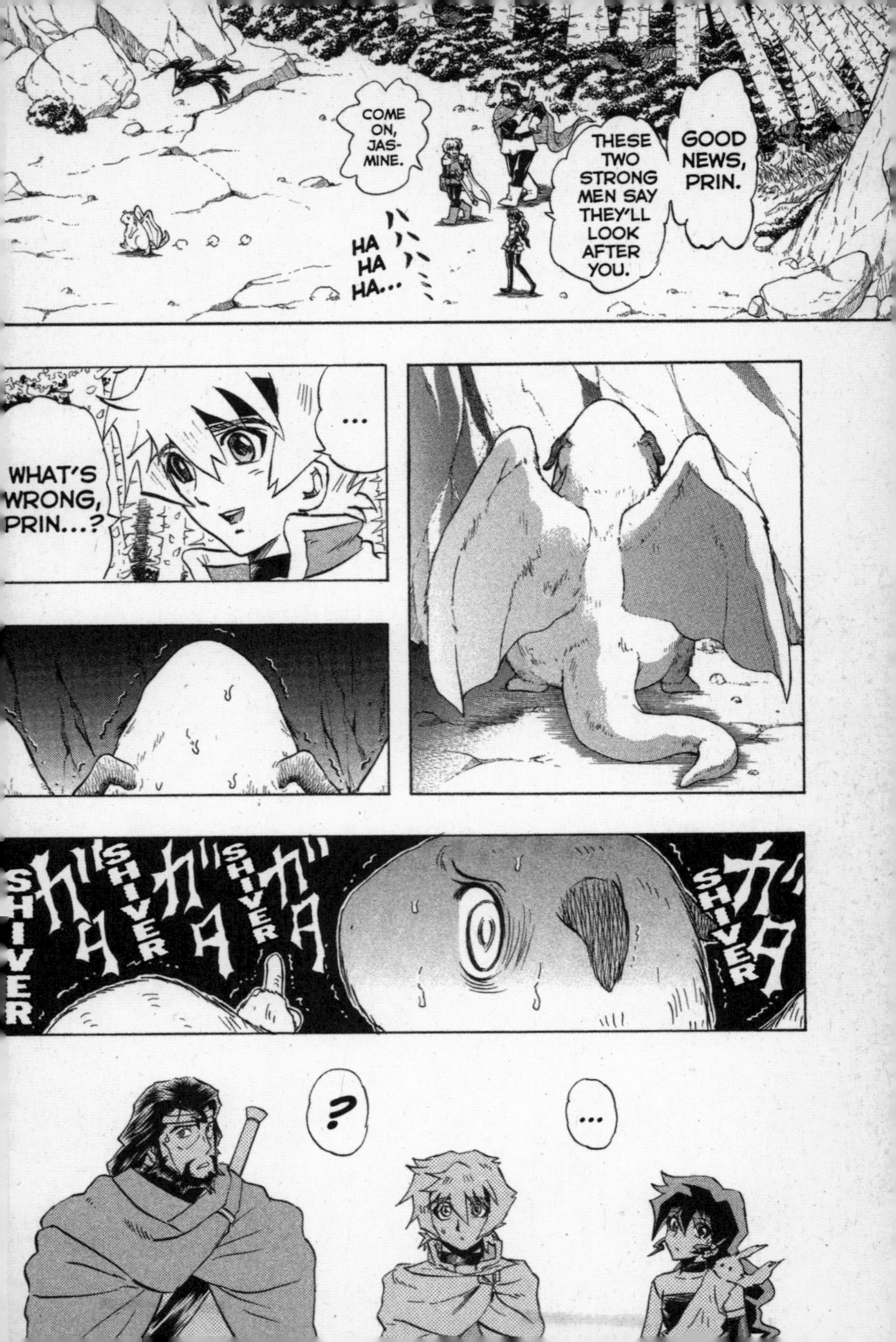
GOOD NEWS, PRIN.
THESE TWO STRONG MEN SAY THEY'LL LOOK AFTER YOU.
HA HA HA...
COME ON, JAS-MINE.
...
WHAT'S WRONG, PRIN...?
SHIVER
SHIVER
SHIVER
SHIVER
...
?

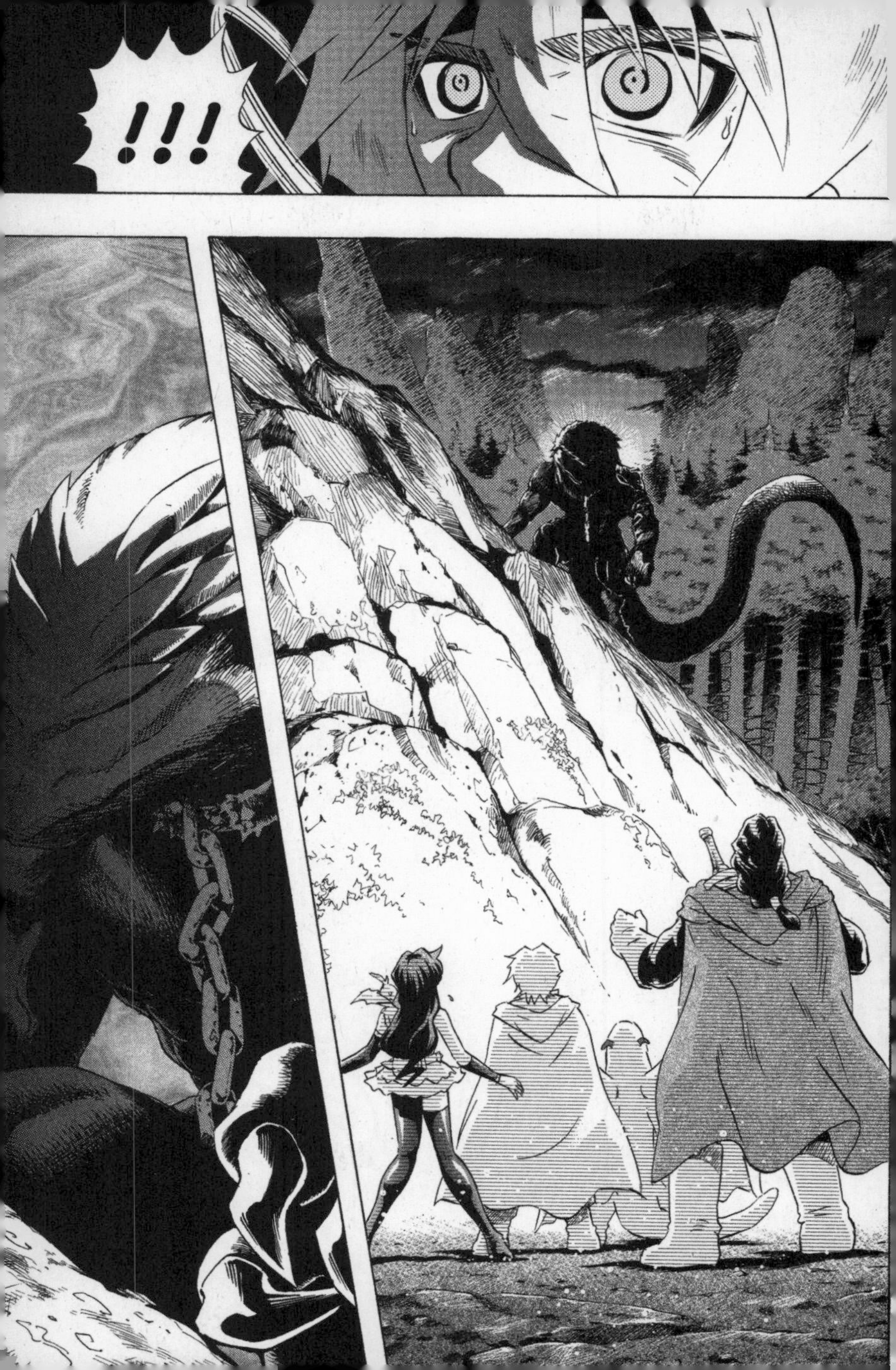
!!!

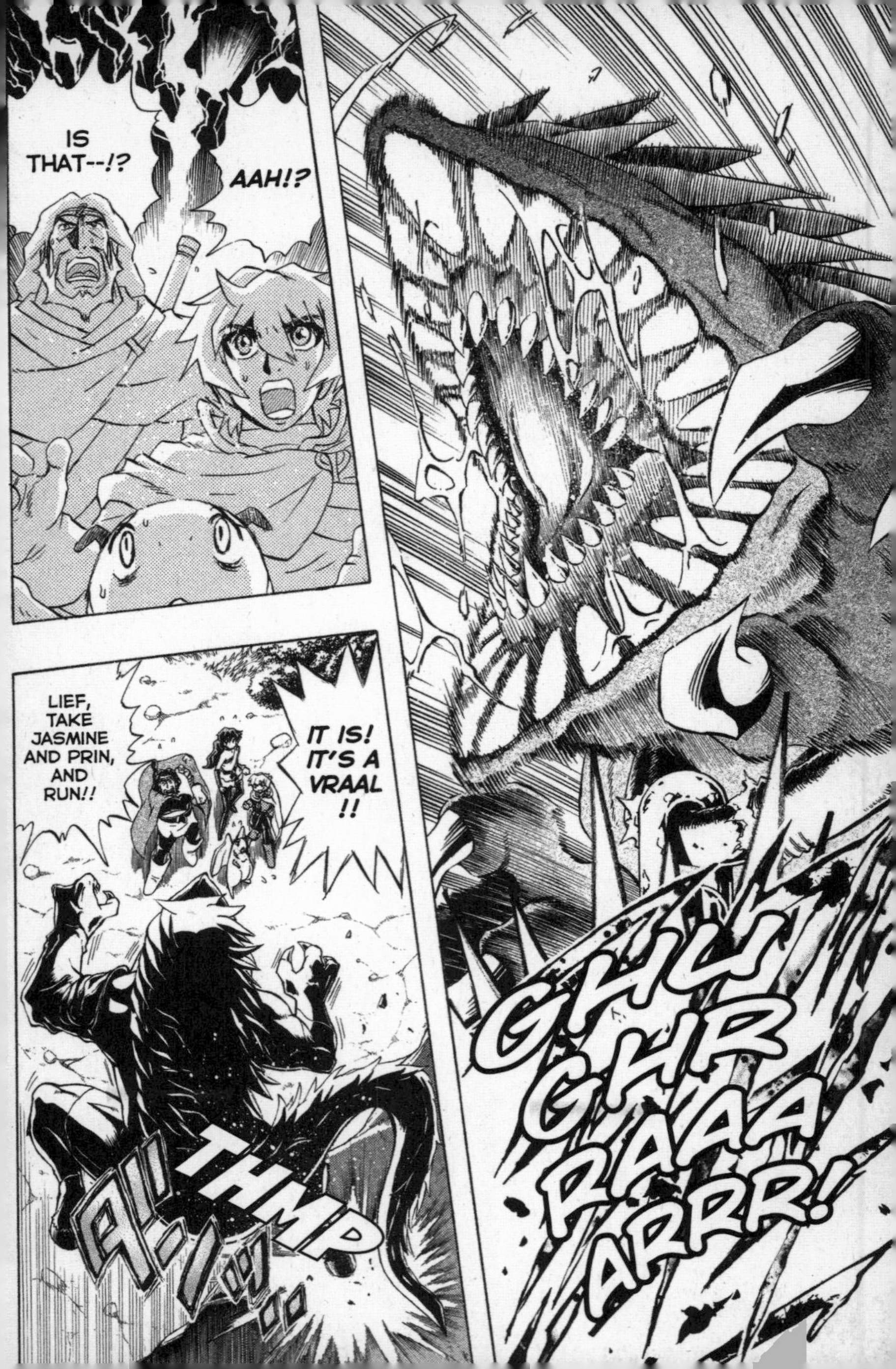
GHU GHR RAAA ARRR!
AAH!?
IS THAT--!?
IT IS! IT'S A VRAAL!!
LIEF, TAKE JASMINE AND PRIN, AND RUN!!
THMP

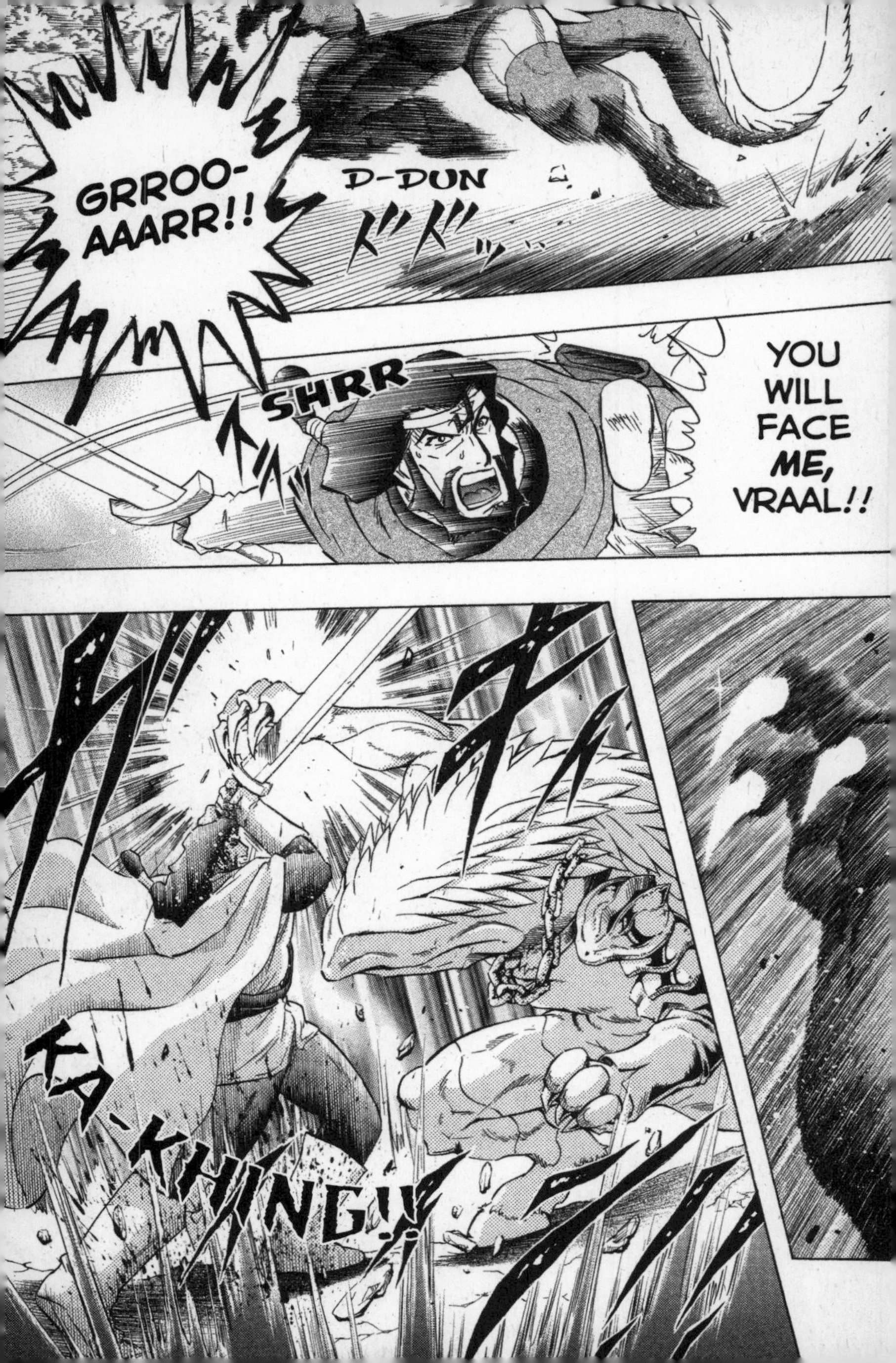

D-DUN
ドドッ
GRROO-AAARR!!
YOU WILL FACE ME, VRAAL!!
SHRR
KA-KHING!!

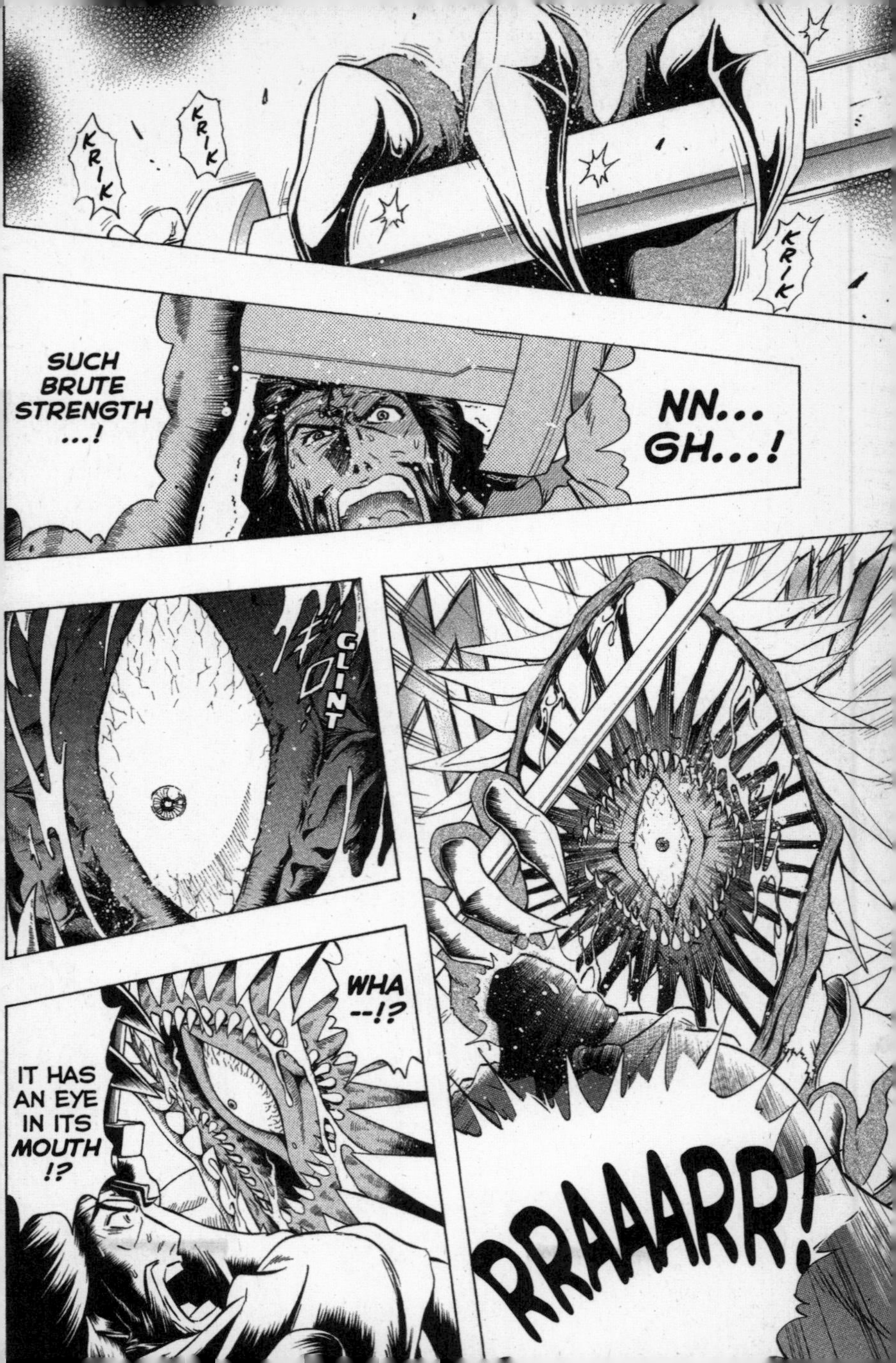
KRIK
KRIK
KRIK
NN... GH...!
SUCH BRUTE STRENGTH ...!
RRAAAARR!
GLINT
WHA --!?
IT HAS AN EYE IN ITS *MOUTH* !?

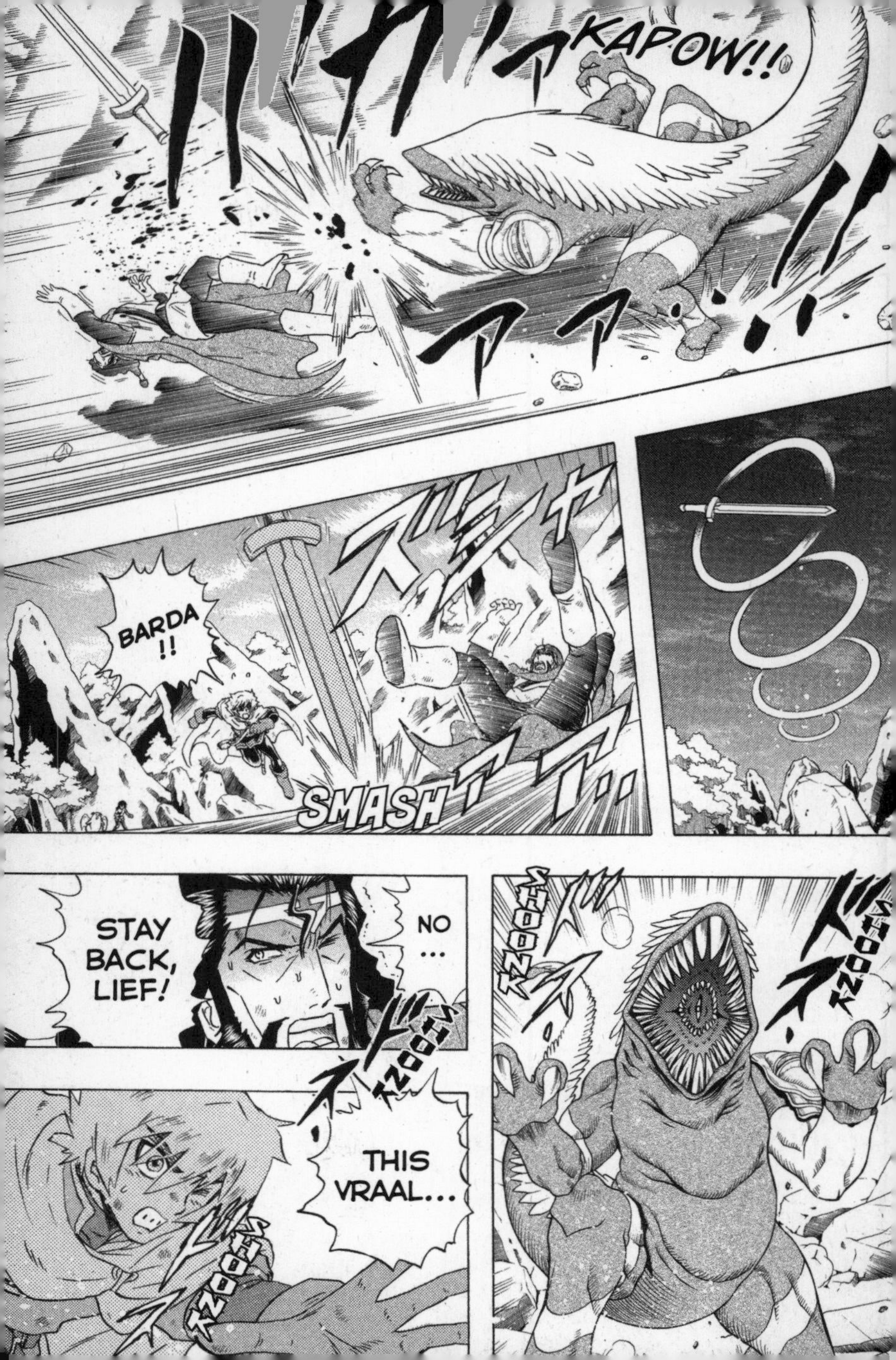
KAPOW!!
SMASH
BARDA!!
SHOONK
SHOONK
NO...
STAY BACK, LIEF!
SHOONK
THIS VRAAL...
SHOONK

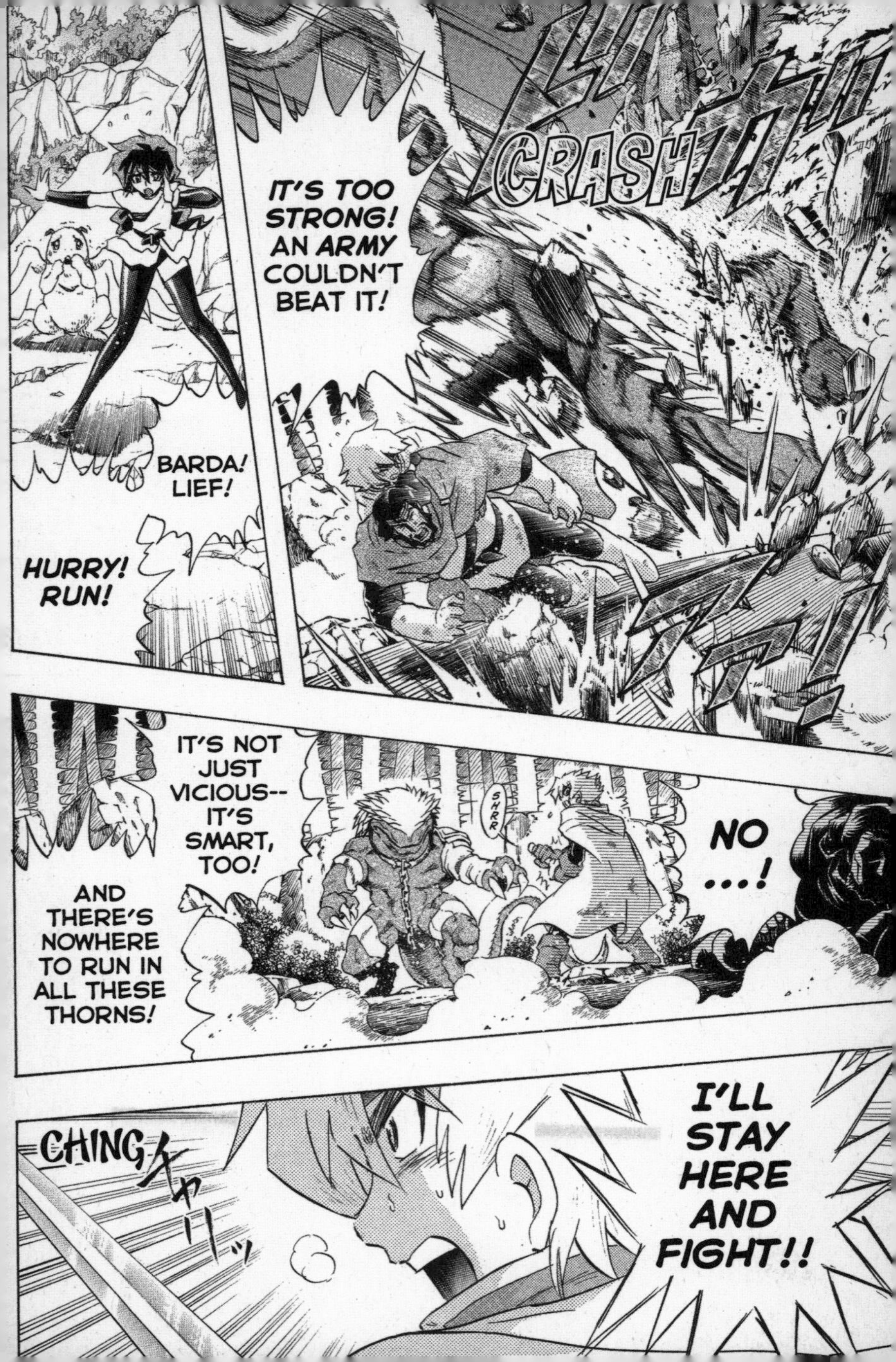
CRASH
IT'S TOO STRONG! AN *ARMY* COULDN'T BEAT IT!
BARDA! LIEF!
HURRY! RUN!
NO ...!
SHRR
IT'S NOT JUST VICIOUS-- IT'S SMART, TOO!
AND THERE'S NOWHERE TO RUN IN ALL THESE THORNS!
I'LL STAY HERE AND FIGHT!!
CHING

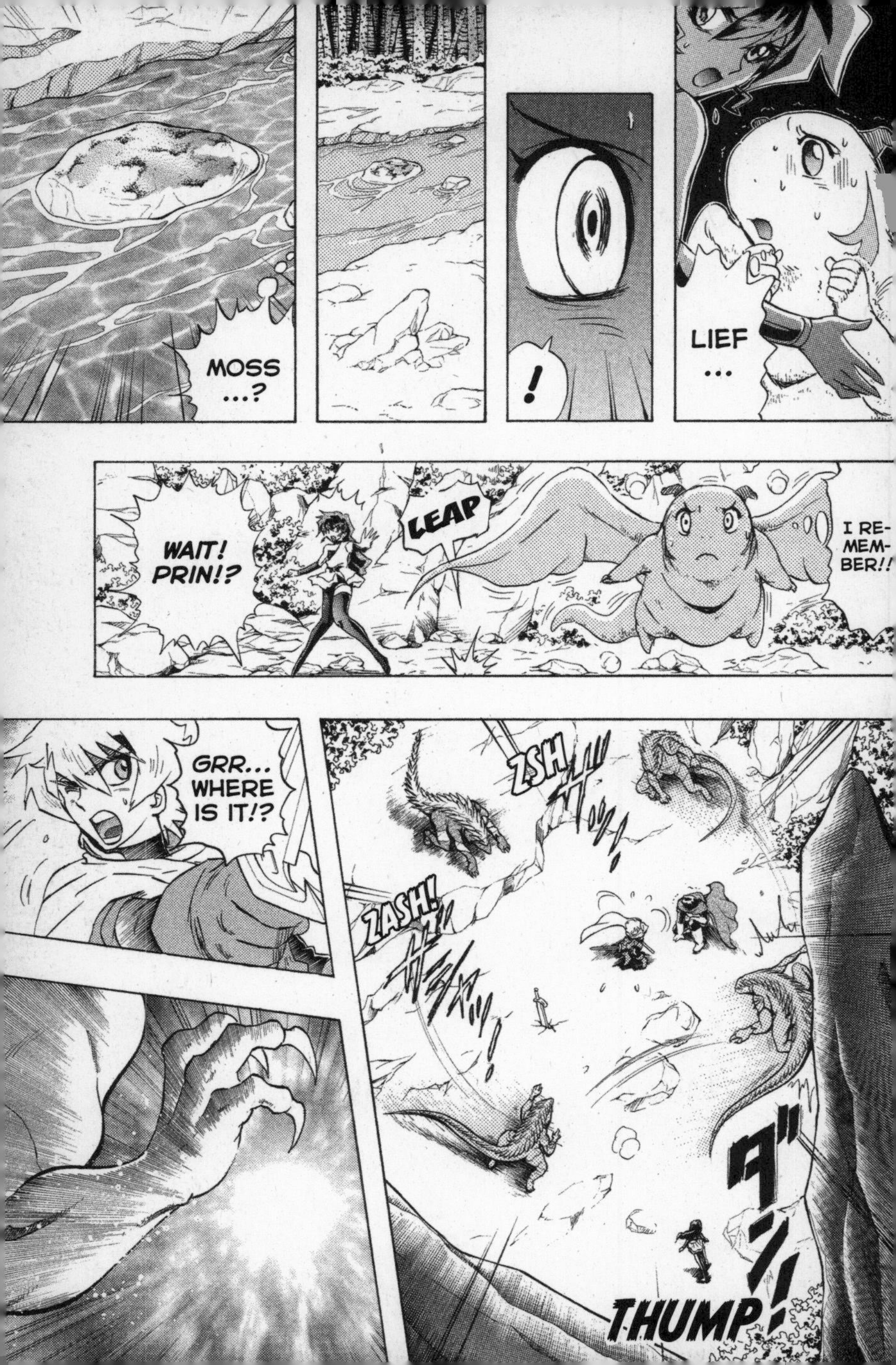
LIEF ...
!
MOSS ...?
I RE-MEM-BER!!
LEAP
WAIT! PRIN!?
ZSH
ZASH!
ダン
THUMP!
GRR... WHERE IS IT!?

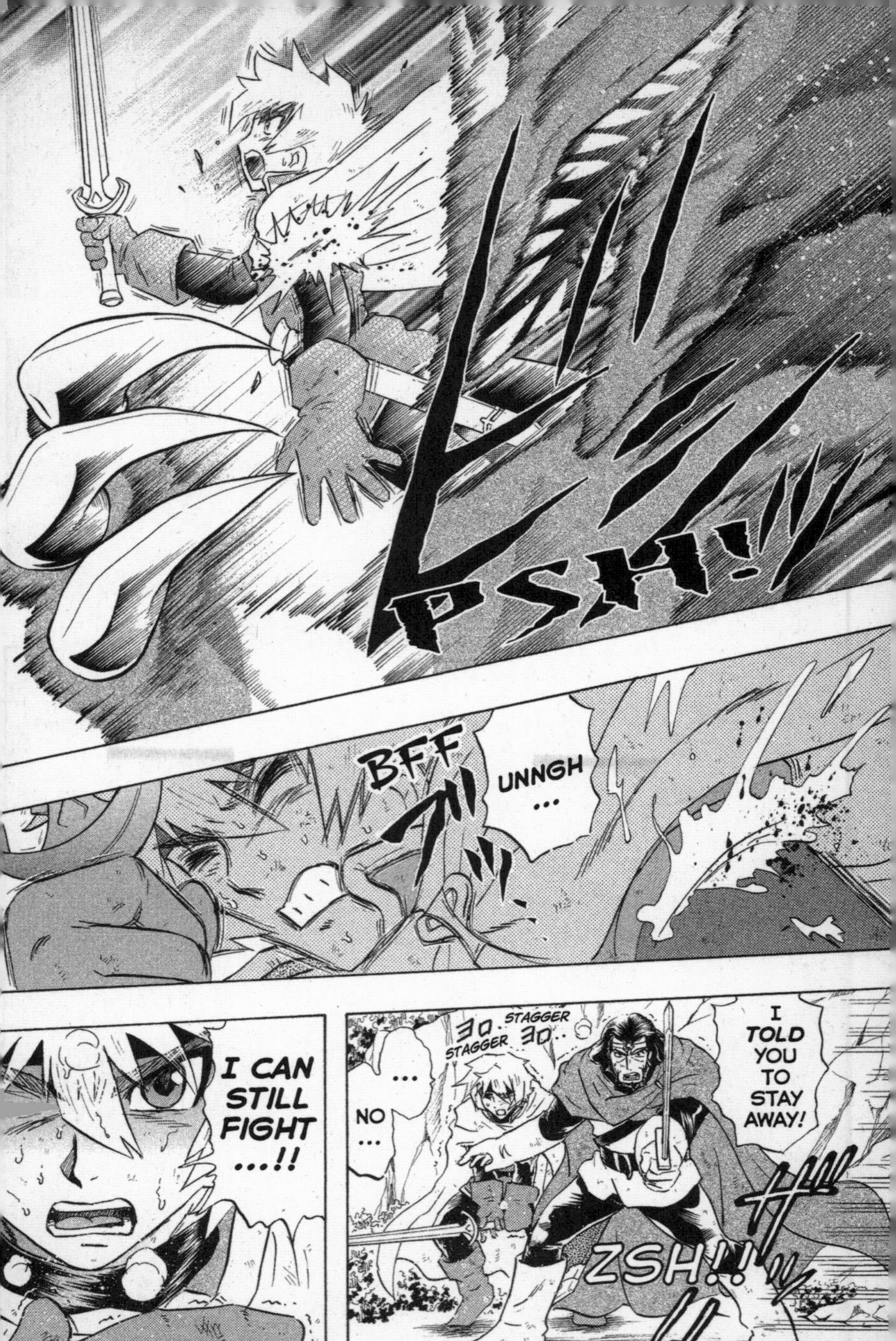
PSH!!
UNNGH ...
BFF
I TOLD YOU TO STAY AWAY!
STAGGER ヨロ
STAGGER ヨロ
... NO ...
ZSH!!
I CAN STILL FIGHT ...!!

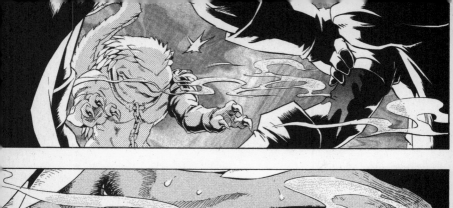

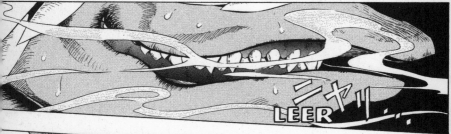

シャリ…
LEER
WHAT IS IT DOING ...?
...DON'T TELL ME IT'S REACTING TO THE SMELL OF YOUR BLOOD?
ジ…
INCH
ジ…
INCH
ジ…
INCH
RATTLE
!! A COLLAR ...?

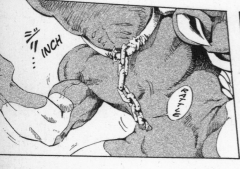

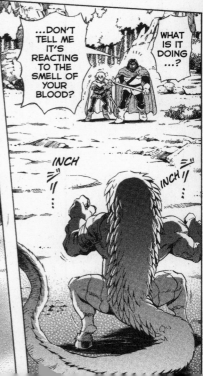

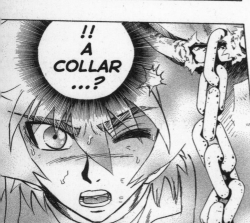

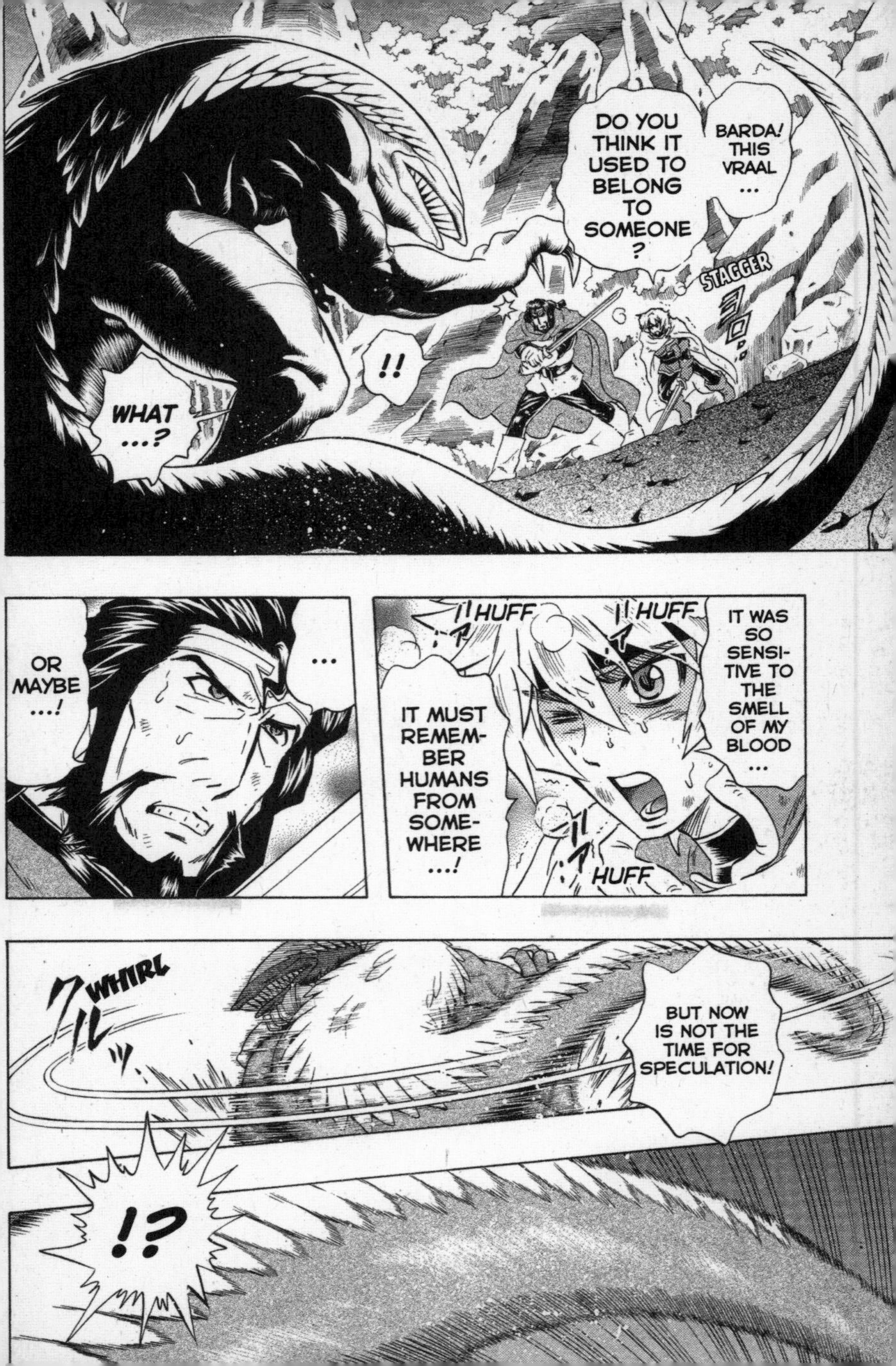
BARDA! THIS VRAAL ...
DO YOU THINK IT USED TO BELONG TO SOMEONE ?
STAGGER
!!
WHAT ...?
HUFF HUFF
IT WAS SO SENSITIVE TO THE SMELL OF MY BLOOD ...
IT MUST REMEMBER HUMANS FROM SOMEWHERE ...!
HUFF
...
OR MAYBE ...!
BUT NOW IS NOT THE TIME FOR SPECULATION!
WHIRL
!?

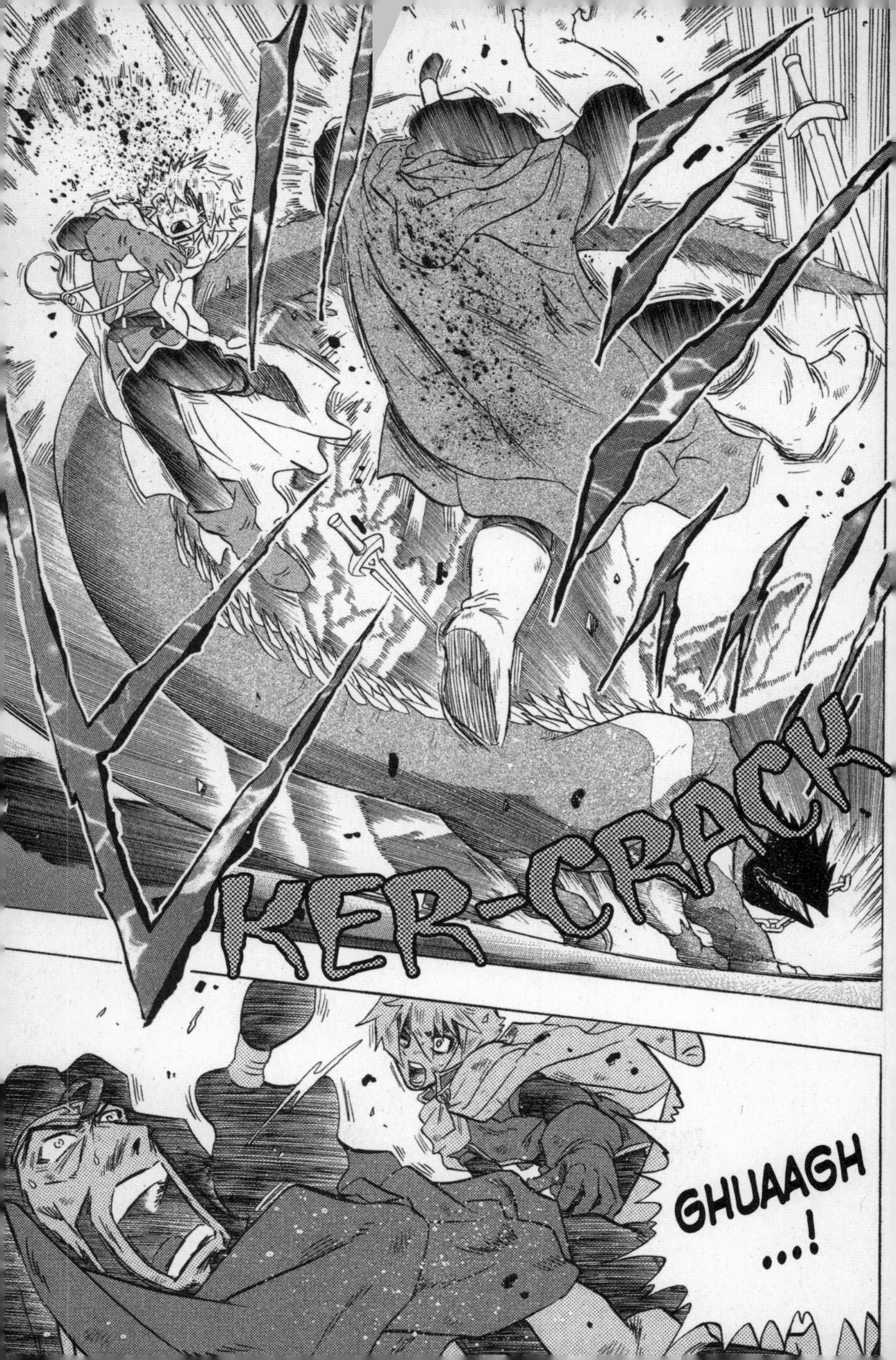
KER-CRACK
GHUAAGH ...!

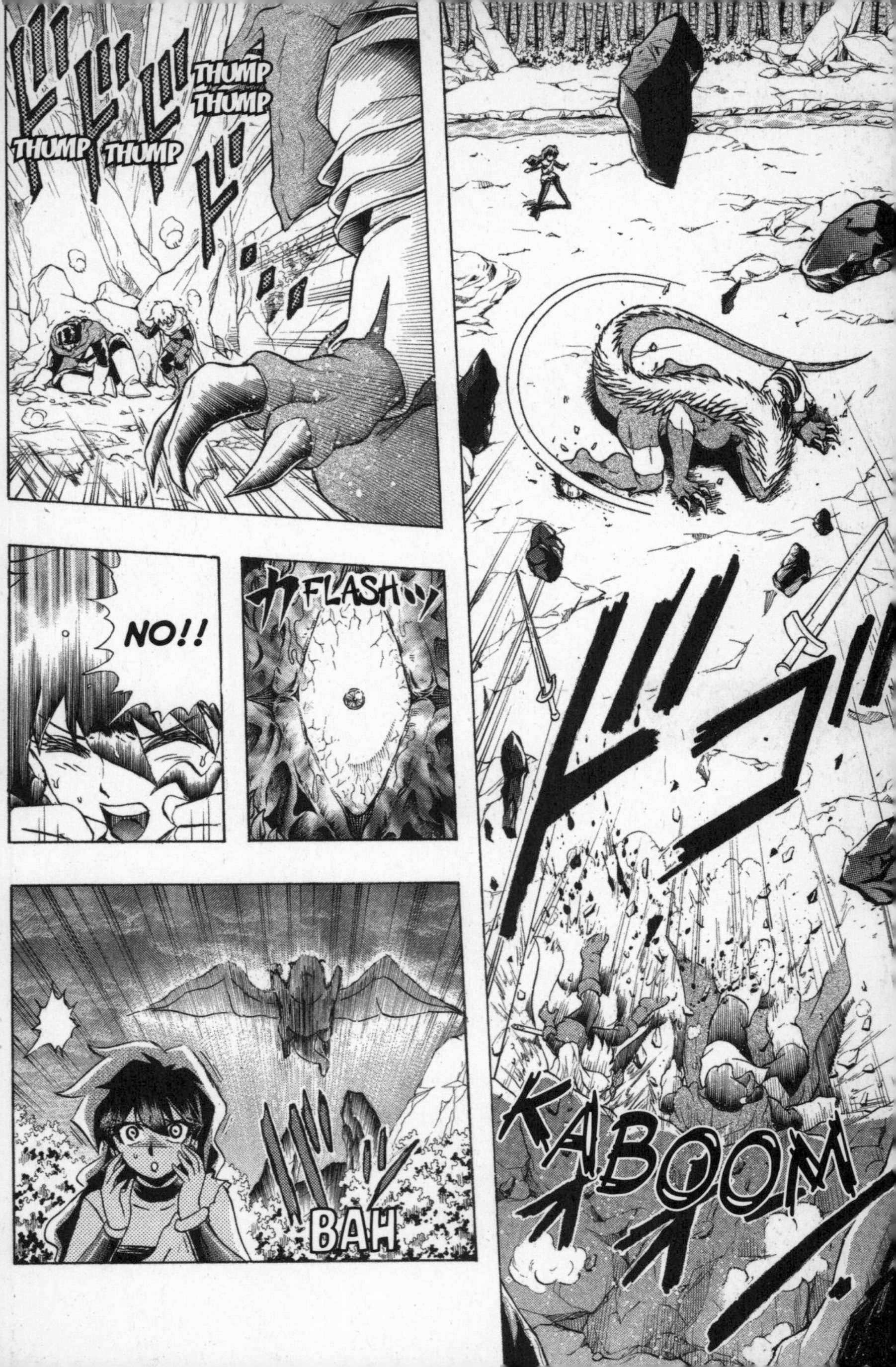
KABOOM
THUMP
THUMP
THUMP
THUMP
FLASH
NO!!
BAH

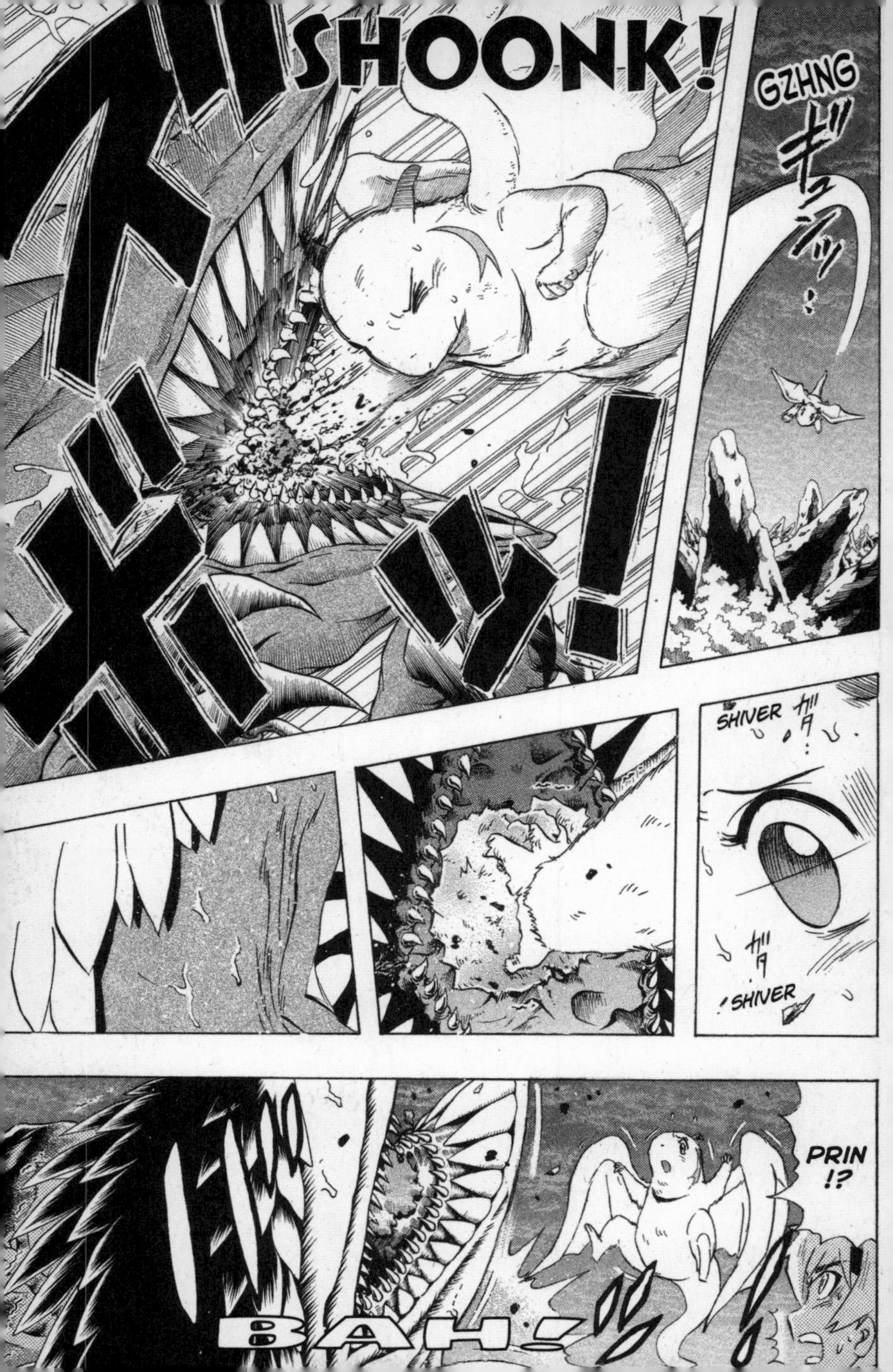
GZHNG
ギュンッ!
SHOONK!
SHIVER
ガタ
ガタ
SHIVER
PRIN
!?
BAH!

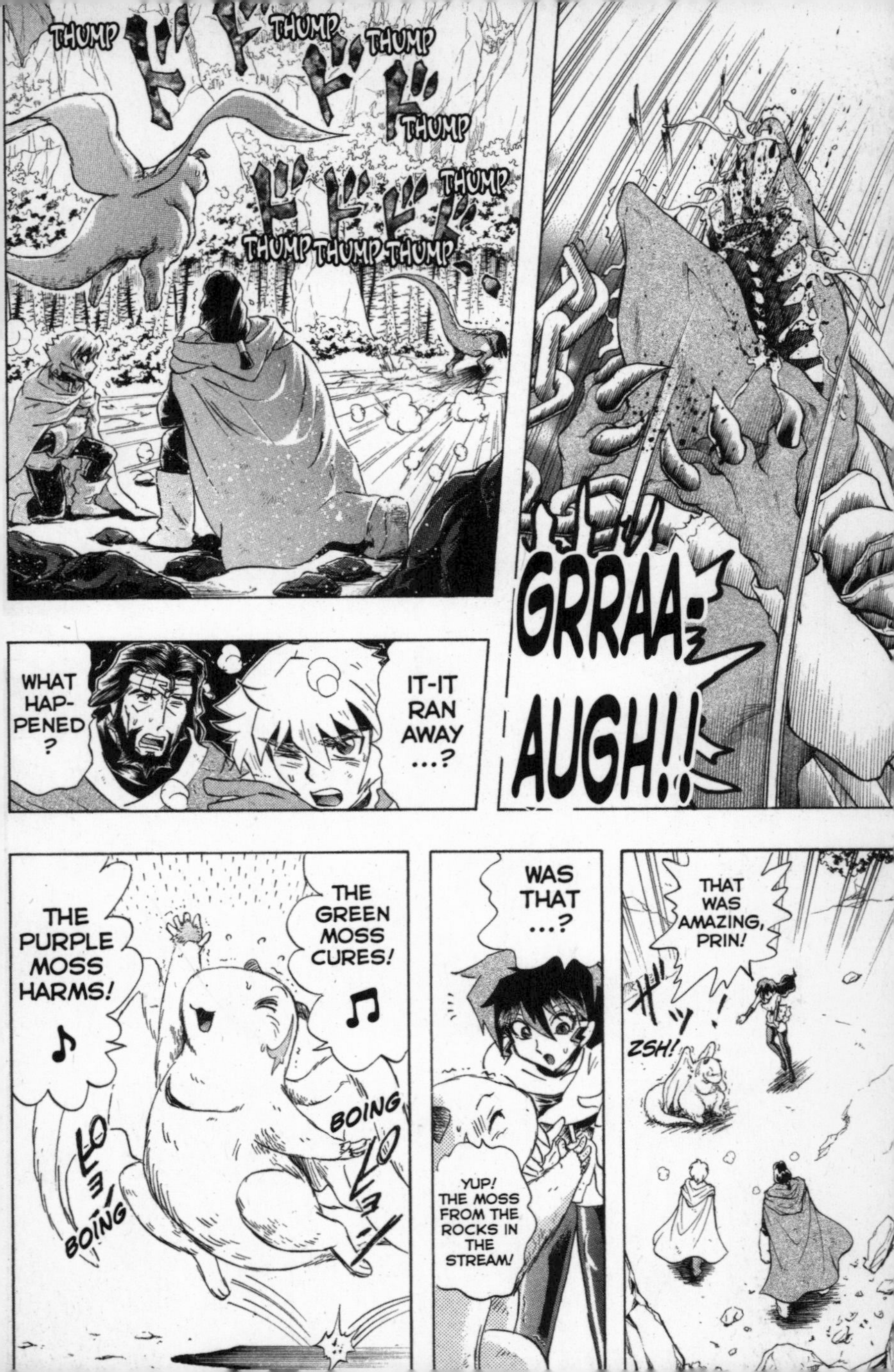
GRRAA-AUGH!!
THUMP
THUMP
THUMP
THUMP
THUMP
THUMP THUMP THUMP
IT-IT RAN AWAY...?
WHAT HAP-PENED?
THAT WAS AMAZING, PRIN!
ZSH!
WAS THAT...?
YUP! THE MOSS FROM THE ROCKS IN THE STREAM!
THE GREEN MOSS CURES! ♫
BOING
THE PURPLE MOSS HARMS! ♪
BOING

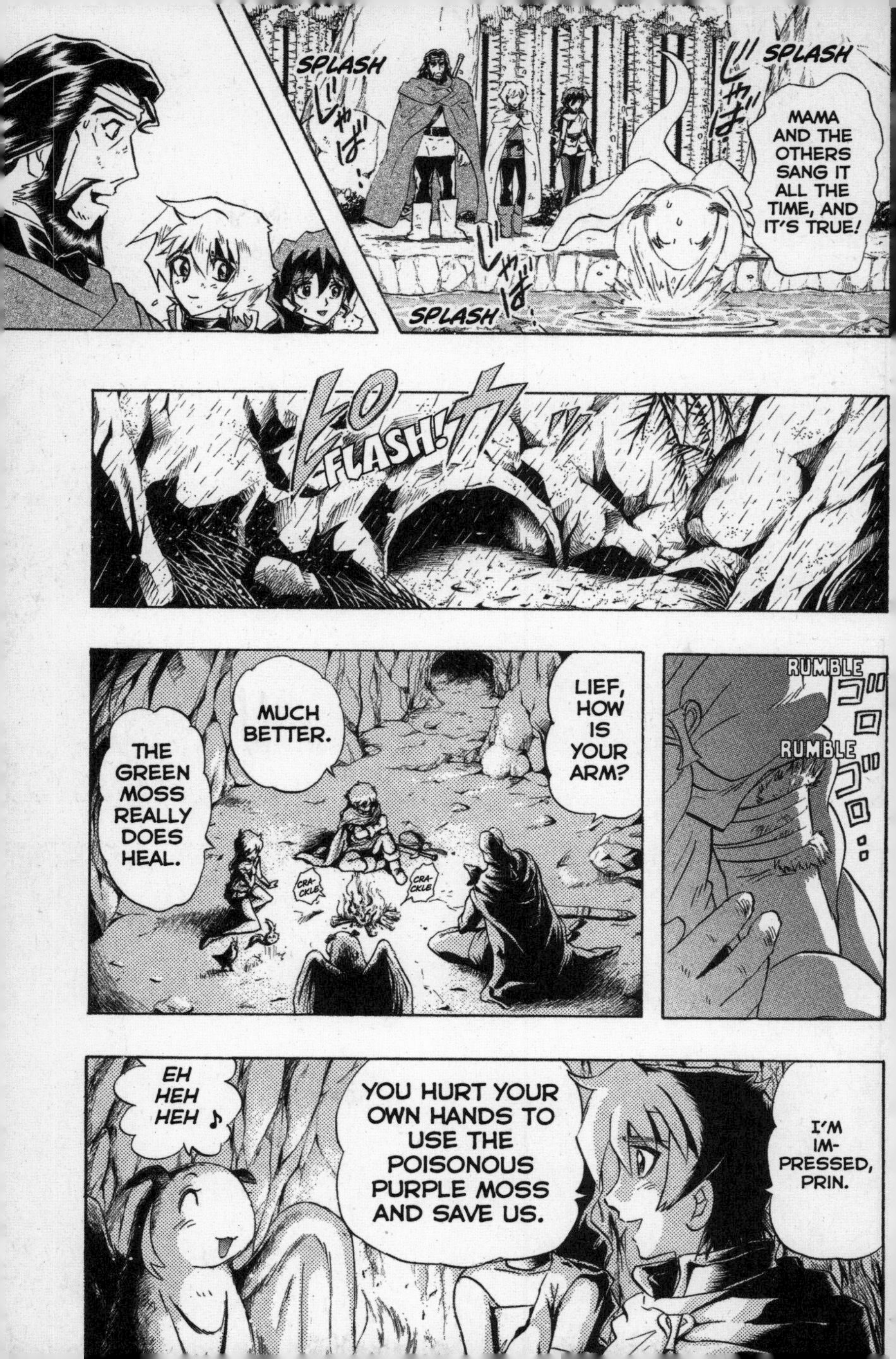
SPLASH
SPLASH
MAMA AND THE OTHERS SANG IT ALL THE TIME, AND IT'S TRUE!
SPLASH
FLASH!
RUMBLE
RUMBLE
LIEF, HOW IS YOUR ARM?
MUCH BETTER.
THE GREEN MOSS REALLY DOES HEAL.
CRA-CKLE
CRA-CKLE
I'M IM-PRESSED, PRIN.
YOU HURT YOUR OWN HANDS TO USE THE POISONOUS PURPLE MOSS AND SAVE US.
EH HEH HEH ♪

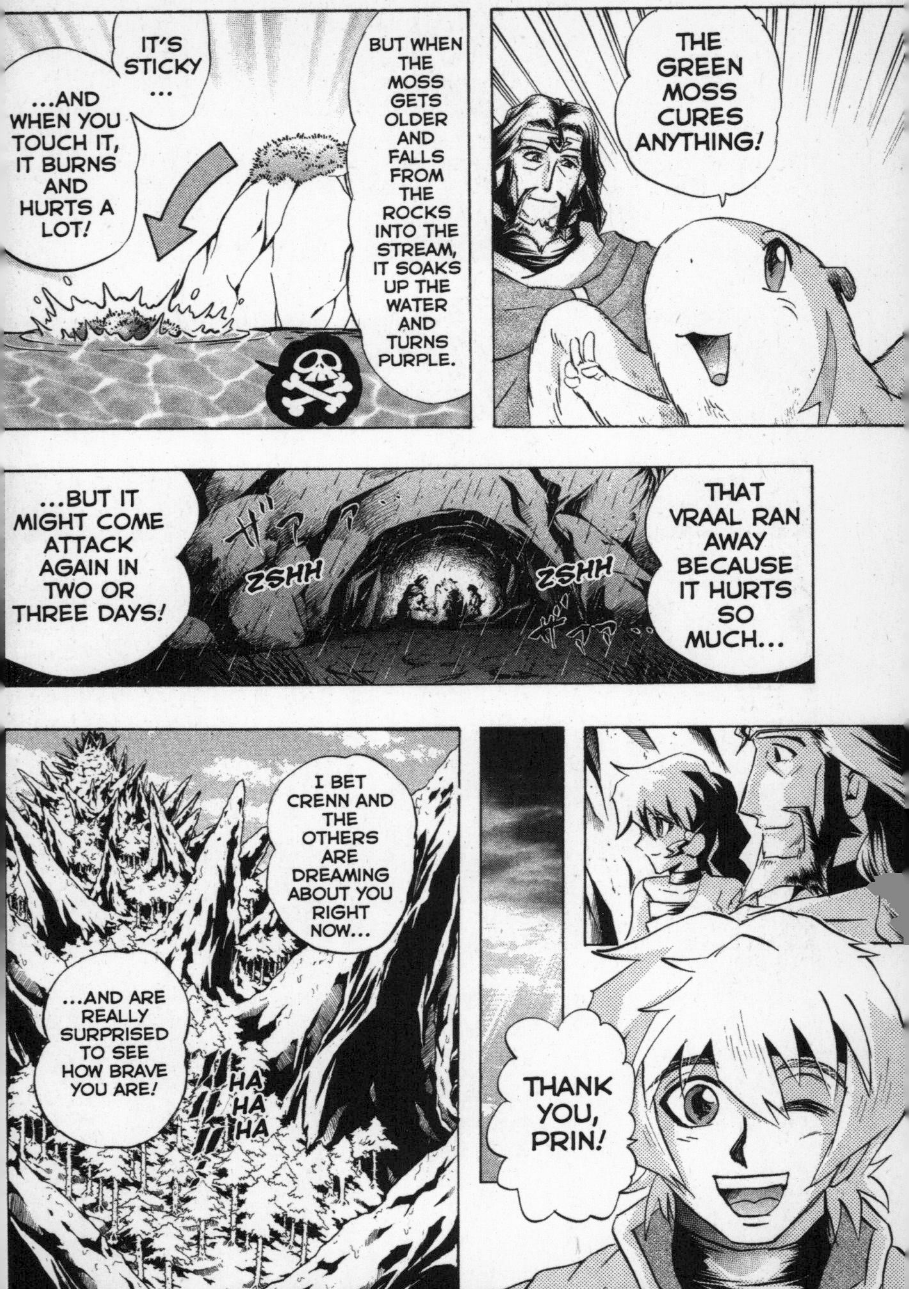
THE GREEN MOSS CURES ANYTHING!
BUT WHEN THE MOSS GETS OLDER AND FALLS FROM THE ROCKS INTO THE STREAM, IT SOAKS UP THE WATER AND TURNS PURPLE.
IT'S STICKY ...
...AND WHEN YOU TOUCH IT, IT BURNS AND HURTS A LOT!
THAT VRAAL RAN AWAY BECAUSE IT HURTS SO MUCH...
ZSHH
ZSHH
...BUT IT MIGHT COME ATTACK AGAIN IN TWO OR THREE DAYS!
THANK YOU, PRIN!
I BET CRENN AND THE OTHERS ARE DREAMING ABOUT YOU RIGHT NOW...
HA HA HA
...AND ARE REALLY SURPRISED TO SEE HOW BRAVE YOU ARE!

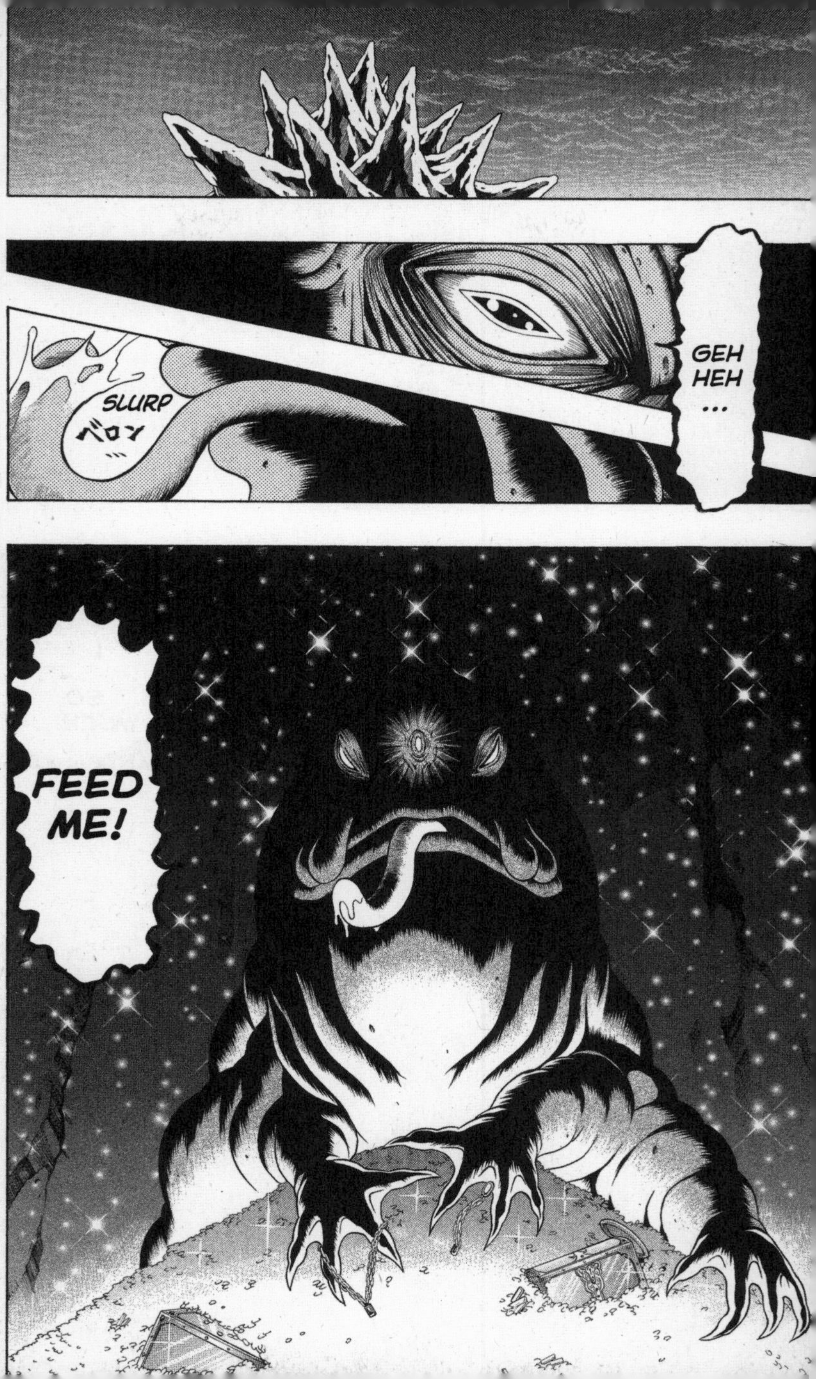
GEH HEH ...
SLURP
ベロッ
FEED ME!

DELTORA QUEST
デルトラクエスト

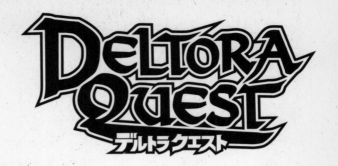

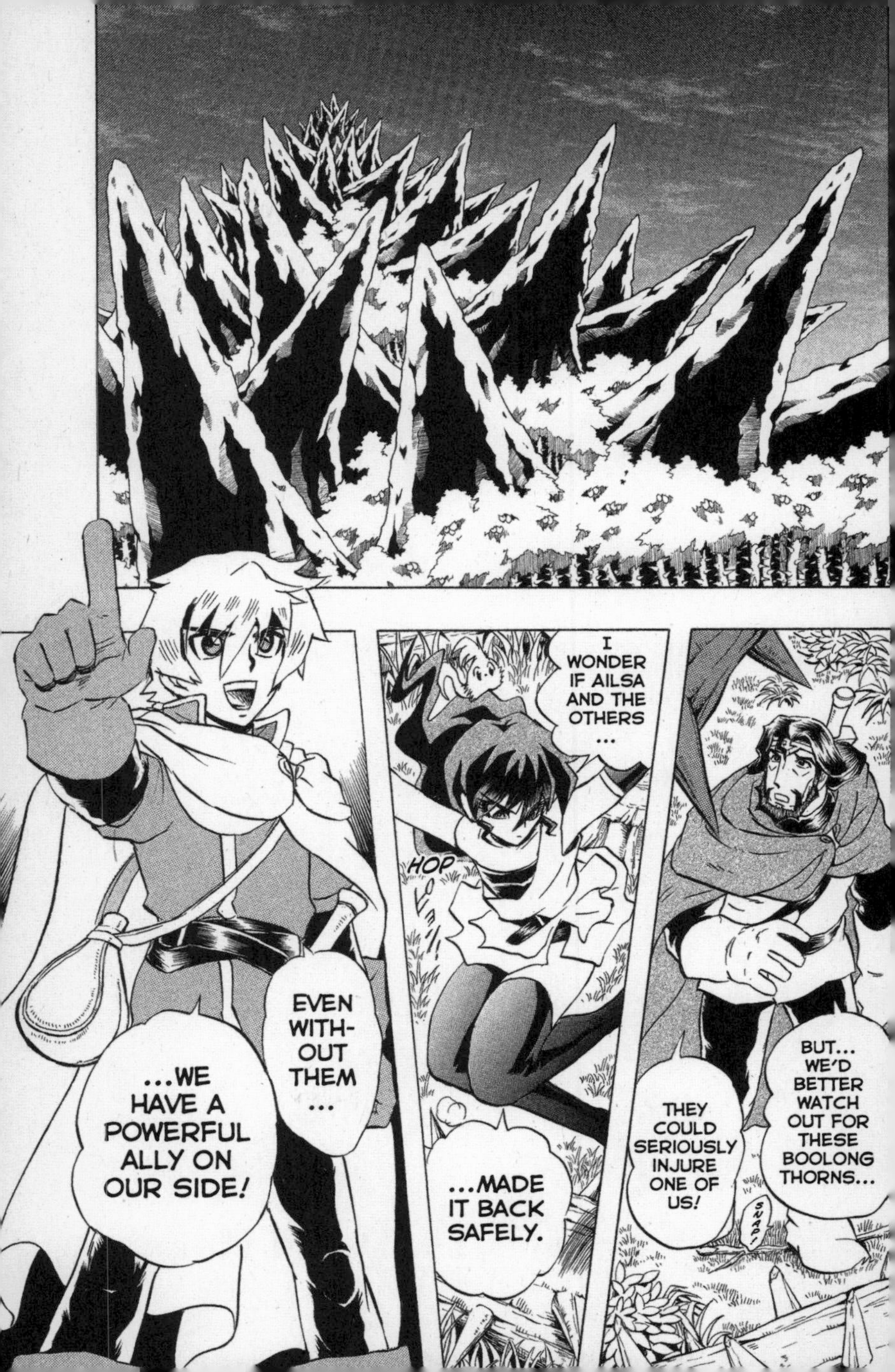
BUT... WE'D BETTER WATCH OUT FOR THESE BOOLONG THORNS...
SNAP!
THEY COULD SERIOUSLY INJURE ONE OF US!
I WONDER IF AILSA AND THE OTHERS ...
HOP
...MADE IT BACK SAFELY.
EVEN WITH-OUT THEM ...
...WE HAVE A POWERFUL ALLY ON OUR SIDE!

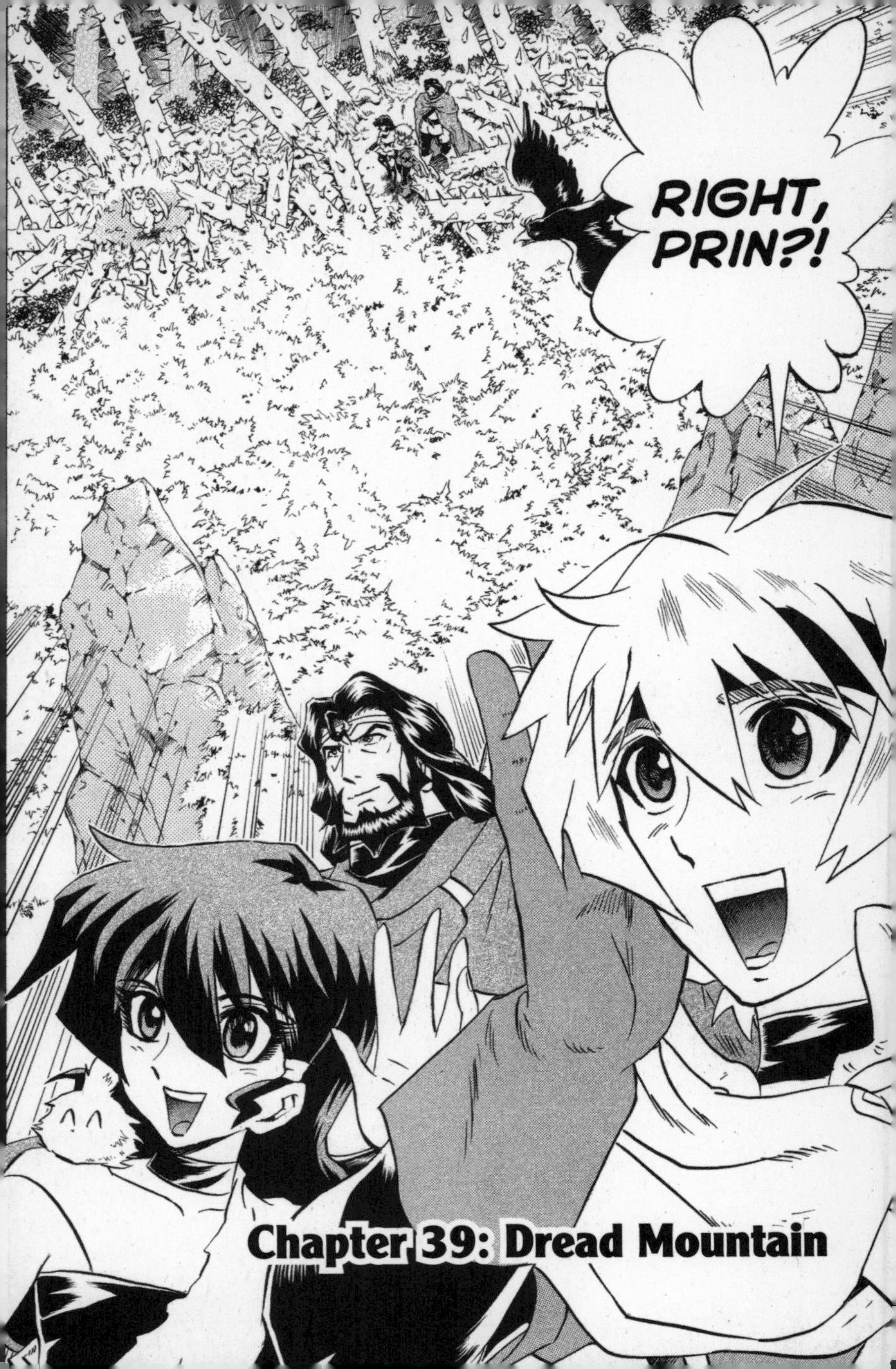
RIGHT, PRIN?!
Chapter 39: Dread Mountain

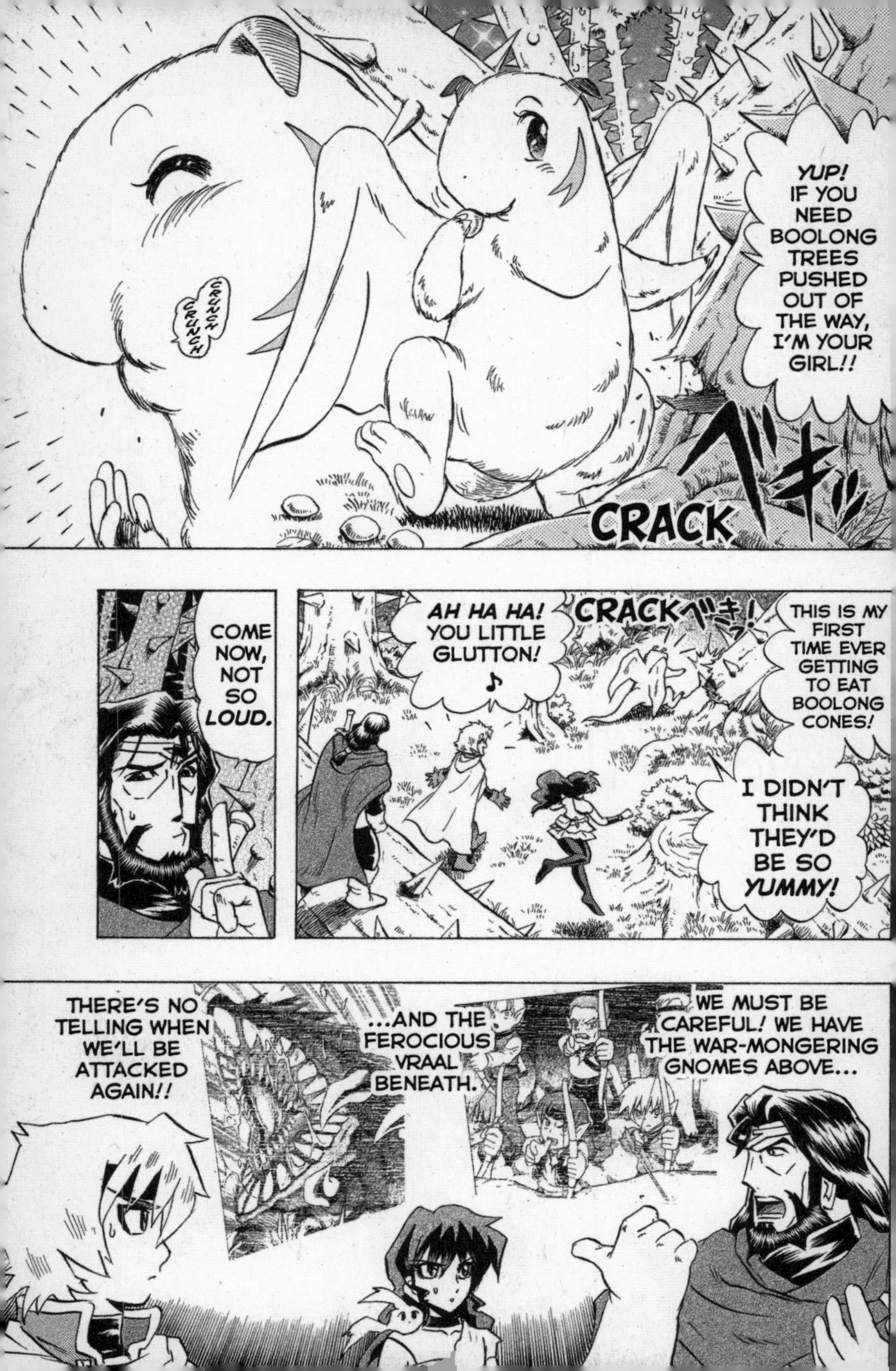
YUP! IF YOU NEED BOOLONG TREES PUSHED OUT OF THE WAY, I'M YOUR GIRL!!
CRUNCH CRUNCH
CRACK
THIS IS MY FIRST TIME EVER GETTING TO EAT BOOLONG CONES!
CRACK
AH HA HA! YOU LITTLE GLUTTON! ♪
I DIDN'T THINK THEY'D BE SO YUMMY!
COME NOW, NOT SO LOUD.
WE MUST BE CAREFUL! WE HAVE THE WAR-MONGERING GNOMES ABOVE...
...AND THE FEROCIOUS VRAAL BENEATH.
THERE'S NO TELLING WHEN WE'LL BE ATTACKED AGAIN!!

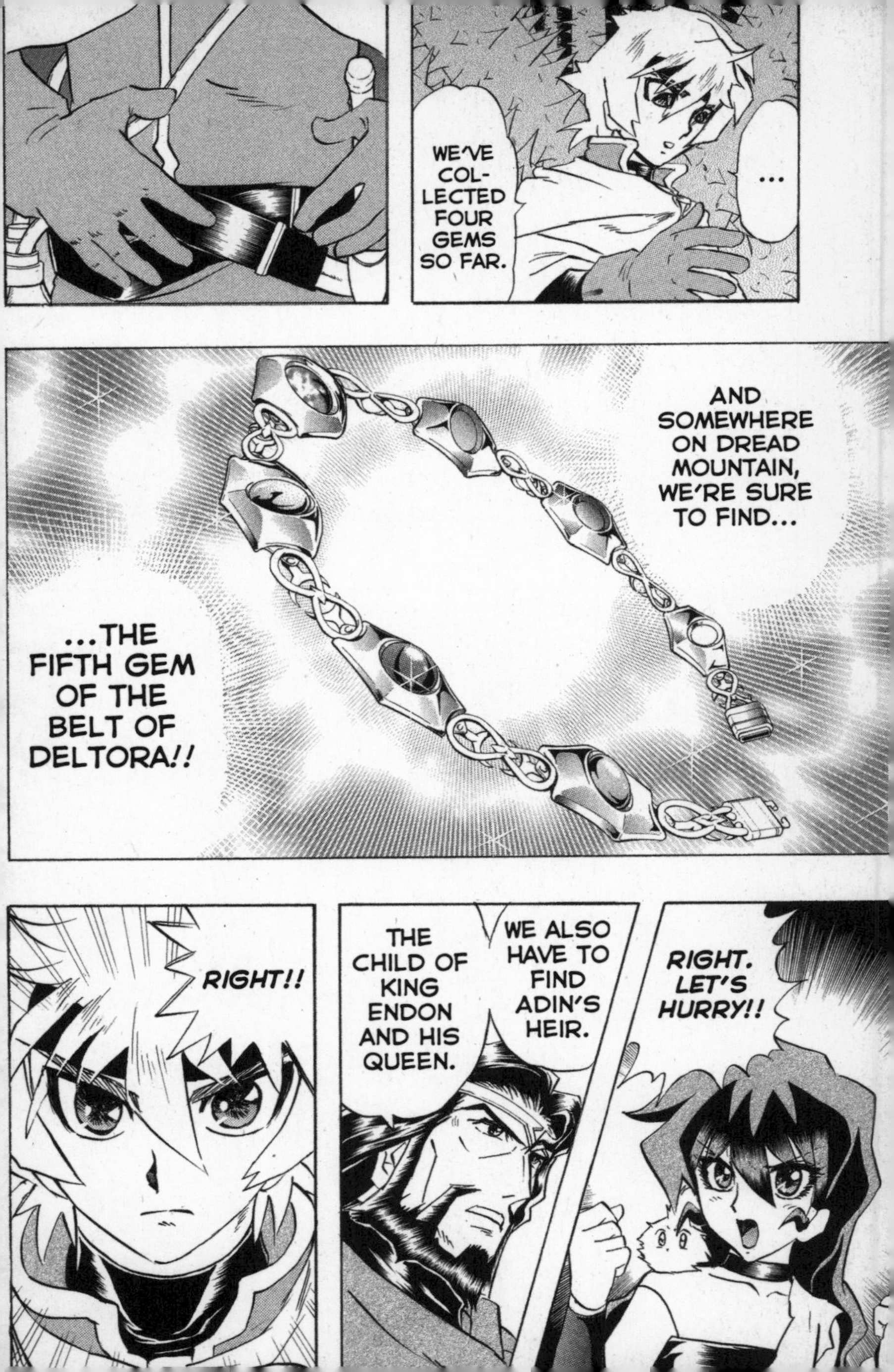
...
WE'VE COL-LECTED FOUR GEMS SO FAR.
AND SOMEWHERE ON DREAD MOUNTAIN, WE'RE SURE TO FIND...
...THE FIFTH GEM OF THE BELT OF DELTORA!!
RIGHT. LET'S HURRY!!
WE ALSO HAVE TO FIND ADIN'S HEIR.
THE CHILD OF KING ENDON AND HIS QUEEN.
RIGHT!!

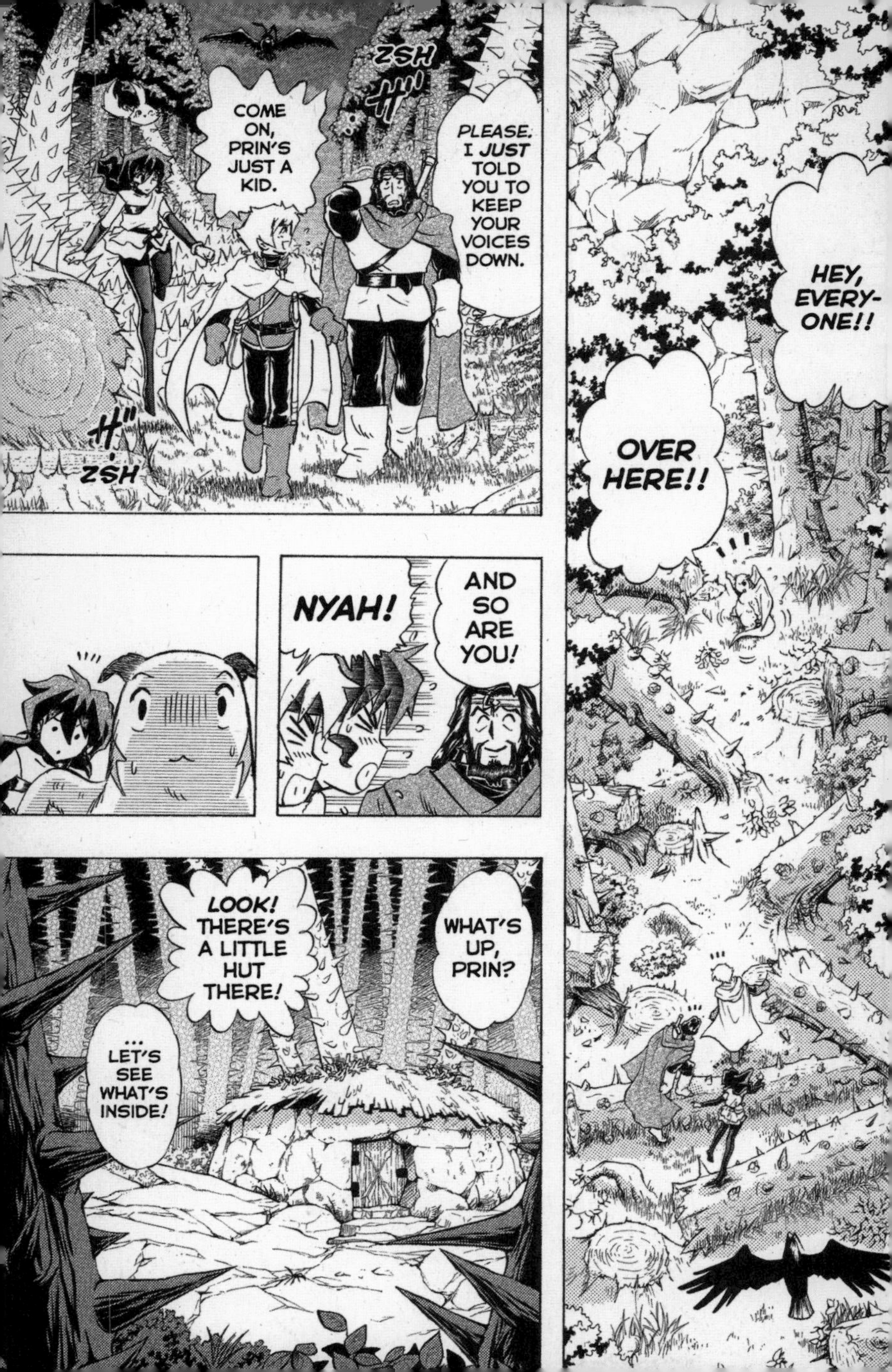
HEY, EVERY-ONE!!
OVER HERE!!
ZSH
PLEASE. I JUST TOLD YOU TO KEEP YOUR VOICES DOWN.
COME ON, PRIN'S JUST A KID.
ZSH
AND SO ARE YOU!
NYAH!
WHAT'S UP, PRIN?
LOOK! THERE'S A LITTLE HUT THERE!
... LET'S SEE WHAT'S INSIDE!

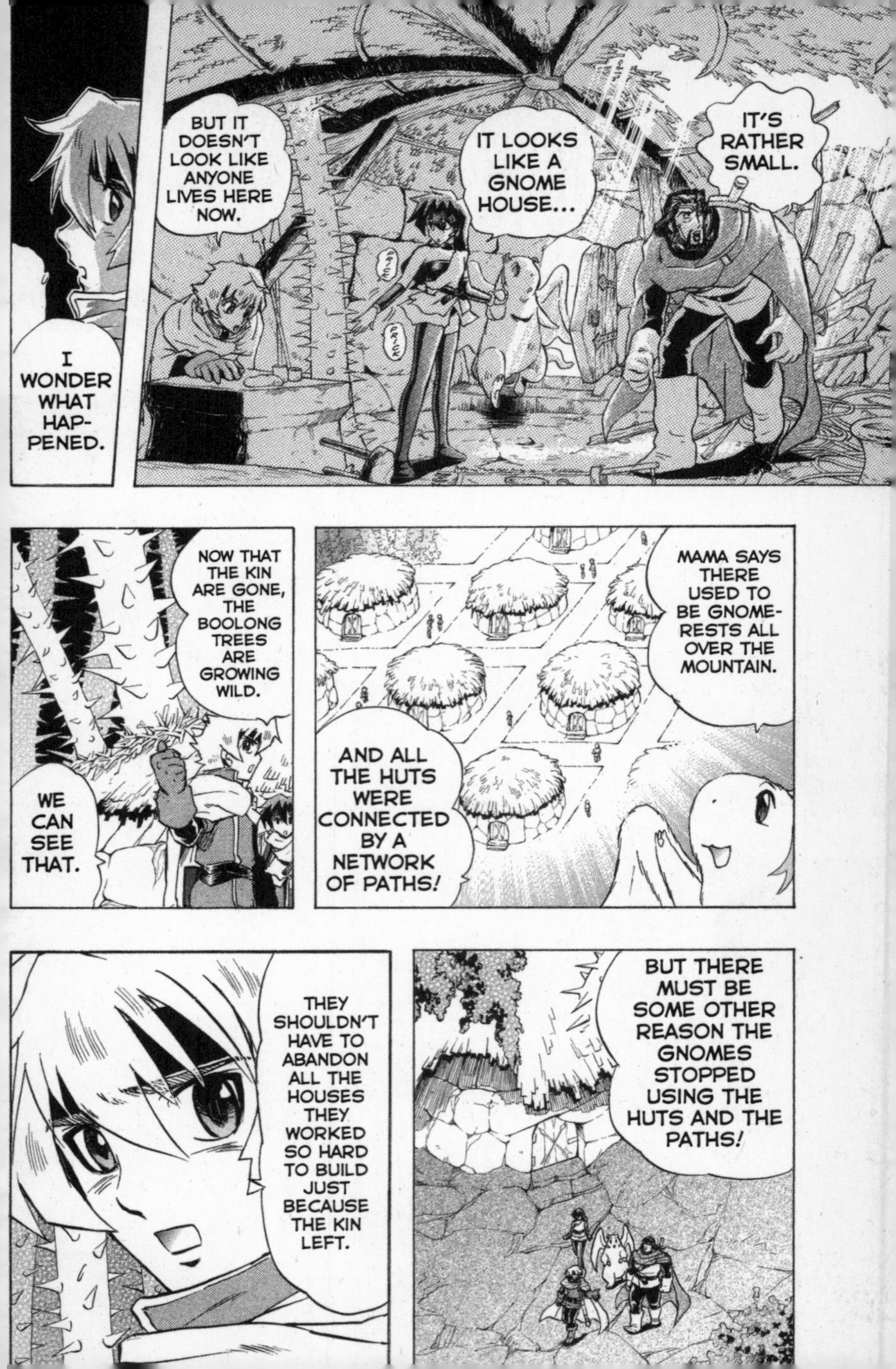
IT'S RATHER SMALL.
IT LOOKS LIKE A GNOME HOUSE...
BUT IT DOESN'T LOOK LIKE ANYONE LIVES HERE NOW.
I WONDER WHAT HAP-PENED.
MAMA SAYS THERE USED TO BE GNOME-RESTS ALL OVER THE MOUNTAIN.
AND ALL THE HUTS WERE CONNECTED BY A NETWORK OF PATHS!
NOW THAT THE KIN ARE GONE, THE BOOLONG TREES ARE GROWING WILD.
WE CAN SEE THAT.
BUT THERE MUST BE SOME OTHER REASON THE GNOMES STOPPED USING THE HUTS AND THE PATHS!
THEY SHOULDN'T HAVE TO ABANDON ALL THE HOUSES THEY WORKED SO HARD TO BUILD JUST BECAUSE THE KIN LEFT.

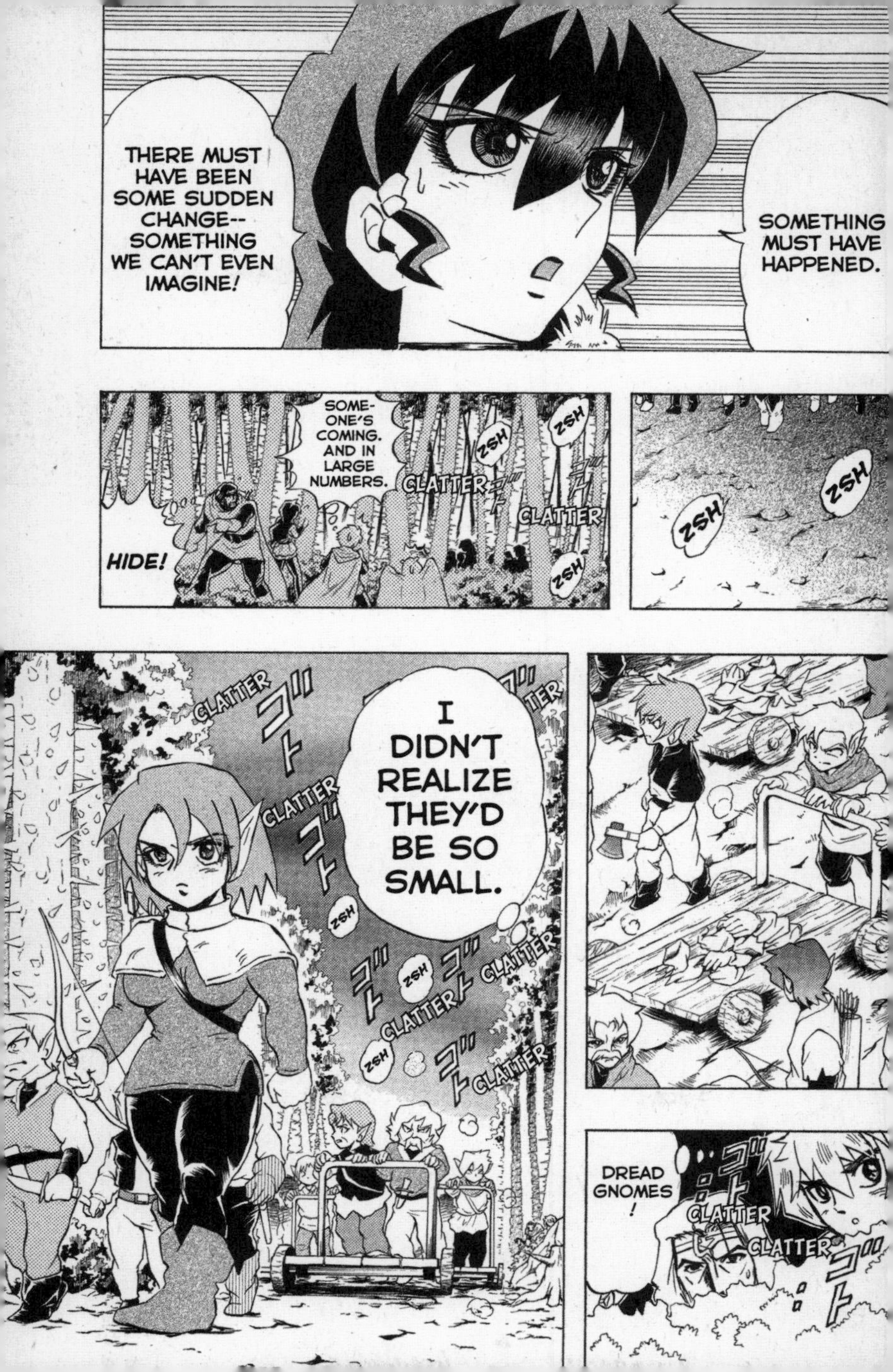
SOMETHING MUST HAVE HAPPENED.
THERE MUST HAVE BEEN SOME SUDDEN CHANGE-- SOMETHING WE CAN'T EVEN IMAGINE!
ZSH
ZSH
SOME-ONE'S COMING. AND IN LARGE NUMBERS.
ZSH
ZSH
CLATTER
CLATTER
HIDE!
ZSH
DREAD GNOMES!
CLATTER
CLATTER
CLATTER
TER
I DIDN'T REALIZE THEY'D BE SO SMALL.
CLATTER
ZSH
ZSH
CLATTER
CLATTER
ZSH
CLATTER

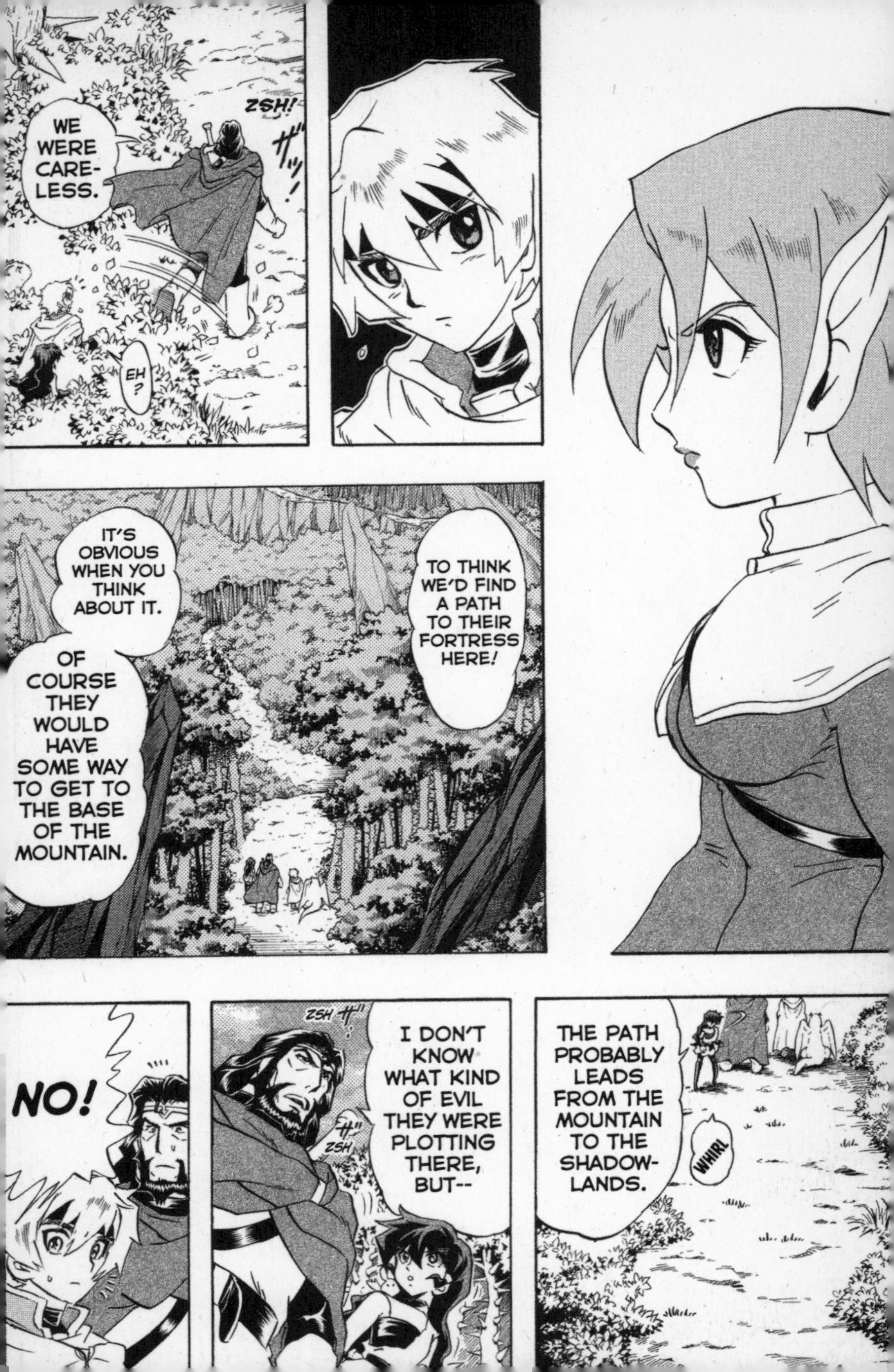
ZSH!
WE WERE CARE-LESS.
EH?
TO THINK WE'D FIND A PATH TO THEIR FORTRESS HERE!
IT'S OBVIOUS WHEN YOU THINK ABOUT IT.
OF COURSE THEY WOULD HAVE SOME WAY TO GET TO THE BASE OF THE MOUNTAIN.
THE PATH PROBABLY LEADS FROM THE MOUNTAIN TO THE SHADOW-LANDS.
WHIRL
ZSH
I DON'T KNOW WHAT KIND OF EVIL THEY WERE PLOTTING THERE, BUT--
ZSH
NO!

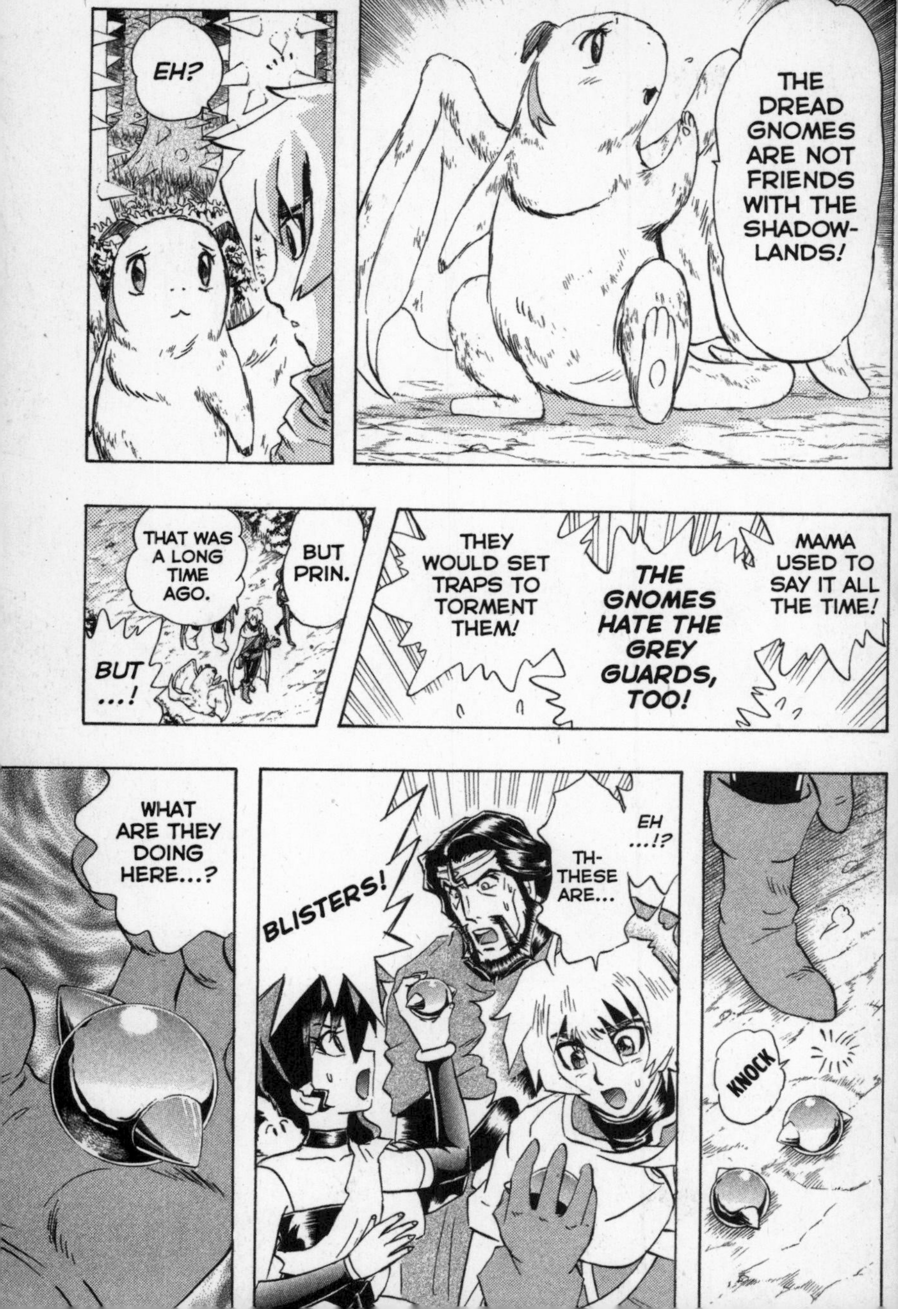

THE DREAD GNOMES ARE NOT FRIENDS WITH THE SHADOW-LANDS!
EH?
MAMA USED TO SAY IT ALL THE TIME!
THE GNOMES HATE THE GREY GUARDS, TOO!
THEY WOULD SET TRAPS TO TORMENT THEM!
BUT PRIN.
THAT WAS A LONG TIME AGO.
BUT ...!
KNOCK
EH ...!?
TH- THESE ARE...
BLISTERS!
WHAT ARE THEY DOING HERE...?

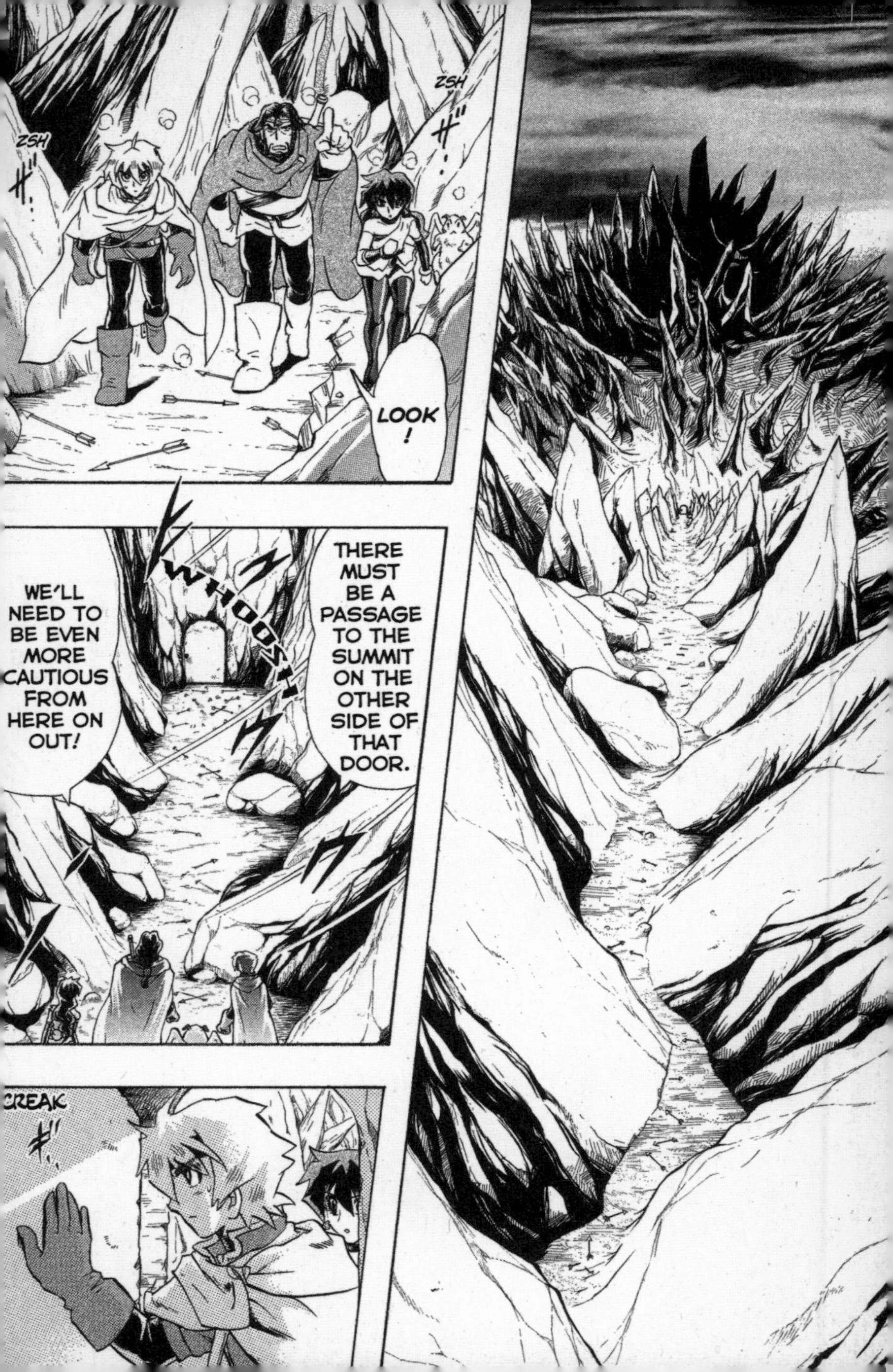
ZSH
LOOK!
ZSH
THERE MUST BE A PASSAGE TO THE SUMMIT ON THE OTHER SIDE OF THAT DOOR.
WHOOSH
WE'LL NEED TO BE EVEN MORE CAUTIOUS FROM HERE ON OUT!
CREAK

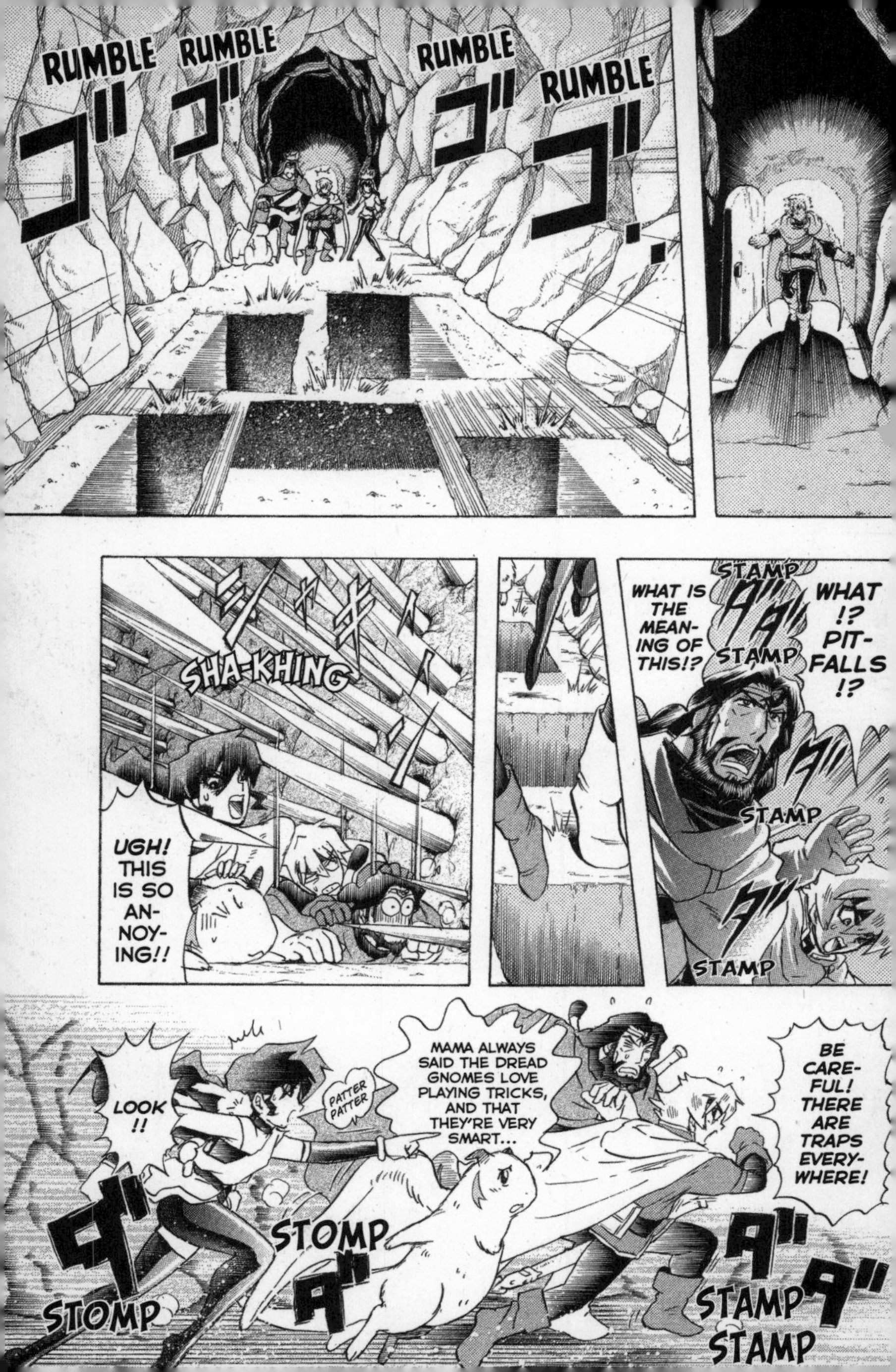
RUMBLE
RUMBLE
ゴゴ!
RUMBLE
RUMBLE
ゴゴ
STAMP
WHAT!? PIT-FALLS!?
STAMP
WHAT IS THE MEANING OF THIS!?
STAMP
STAMP
SHA-KHING
UGH! THIS IS SO AN-NOY-ING!!
BE CARE-FUL! THERE ARE TRAPS EVERY-WHERE!
STAMP
STAMP
MAMA ALWAYS SAID THE DREAD GNOMES LOVE PLAYING TRICKS, AND THAT THEY'RE VERY SMART...
PATTER PATTER
STOMP
LOOK!!
STOMP

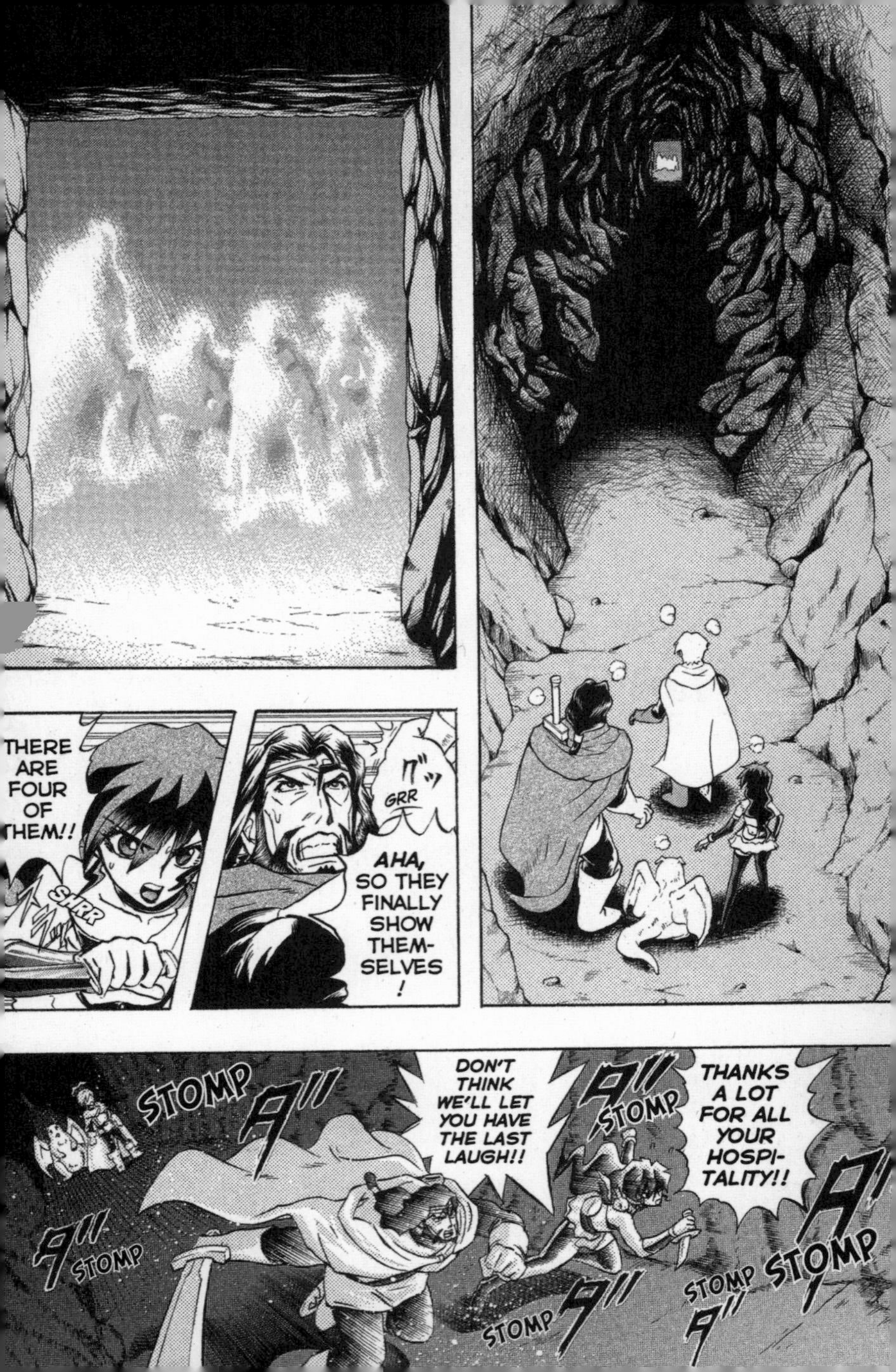
AHA, SO THEY FINALLY SHOW THEMSELVES!
GRR
THERE ARE FOUR OF THEM!!
SHRR
THANKS A LOT FOR ALL YOUR HOSPITALITY!!
DON'T THINK WE'LL LET YOU HAVE THE LAST LAUGH!!
STOMP
STOMP
STOMP
STOMP
STOMP
STOMP

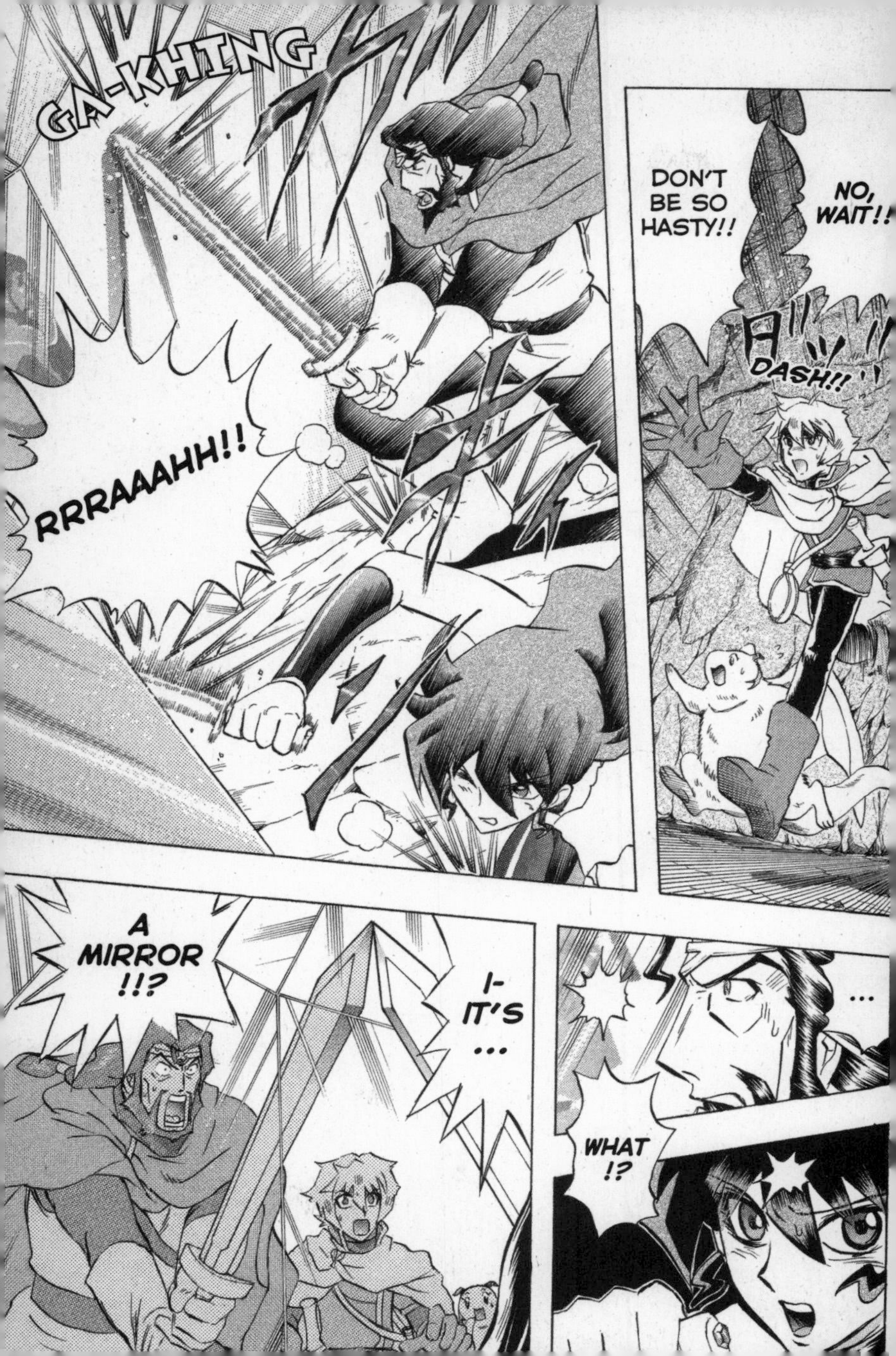
NO, WAIT!!
DON'T BE SO HASTY!!
A!!
DASH!!
GA-KHING
RRRAAAHH!!
...
WHAT!?
I- IT'S ...
A MIRROR!!?

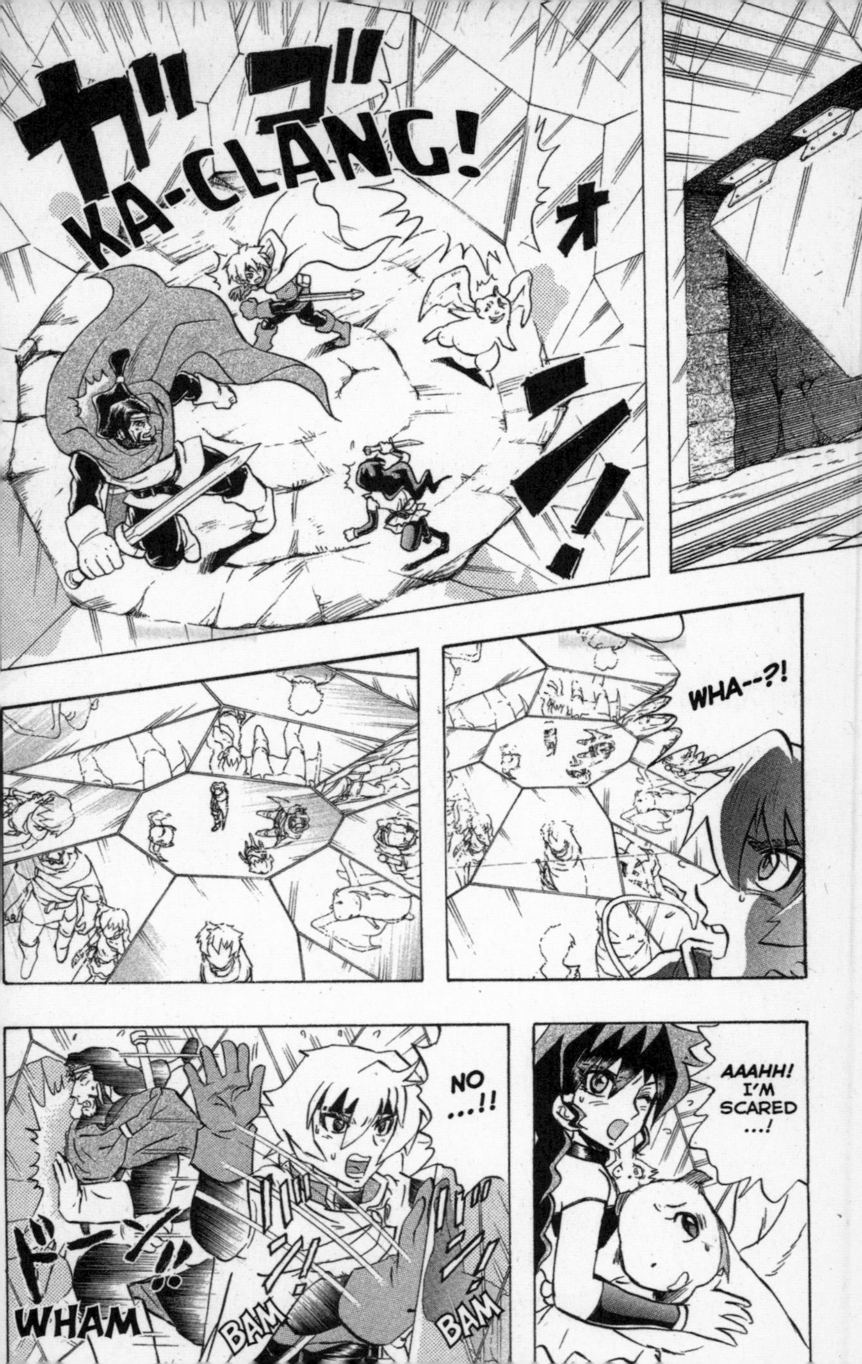
ガゴ
KA-CLANG!
オ
ーン!!
WHA--?!
AAAHH! I'M SCARED ...!
NO ...!!
ドーン!!
WHAM
BAM
BAM

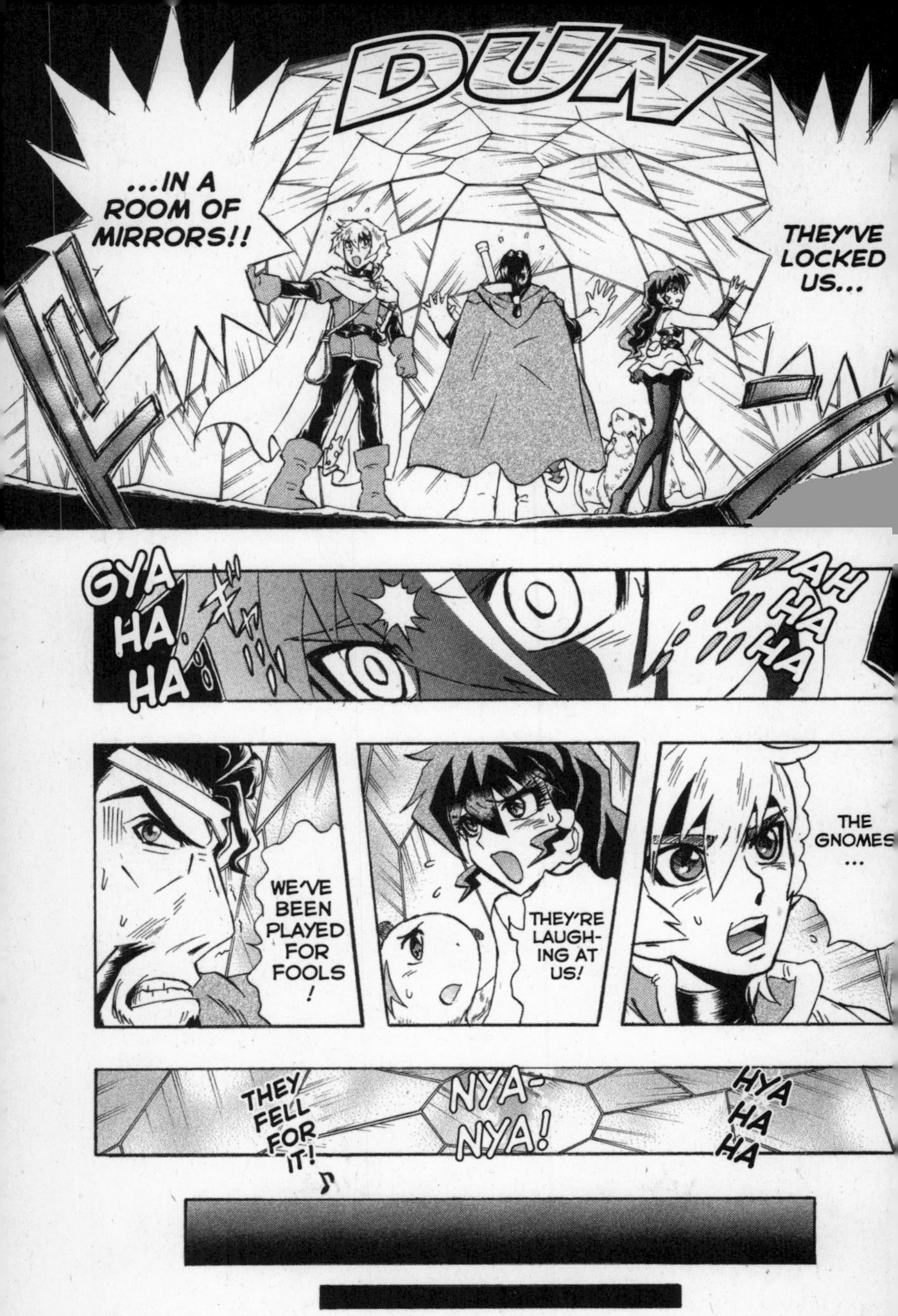
DUN
THEY'VE LOCKED US...
...IN A ROOM OF MIRRORS!!
AH HA HA
GYA HA HA
THE GNOMES...
THEY'RE LAUGHING AT US!
WE'VE BEEN PLAYED FOR FOOLS!
HYA HA HA
NYA-NYA!
THEY FELL FOR IT!

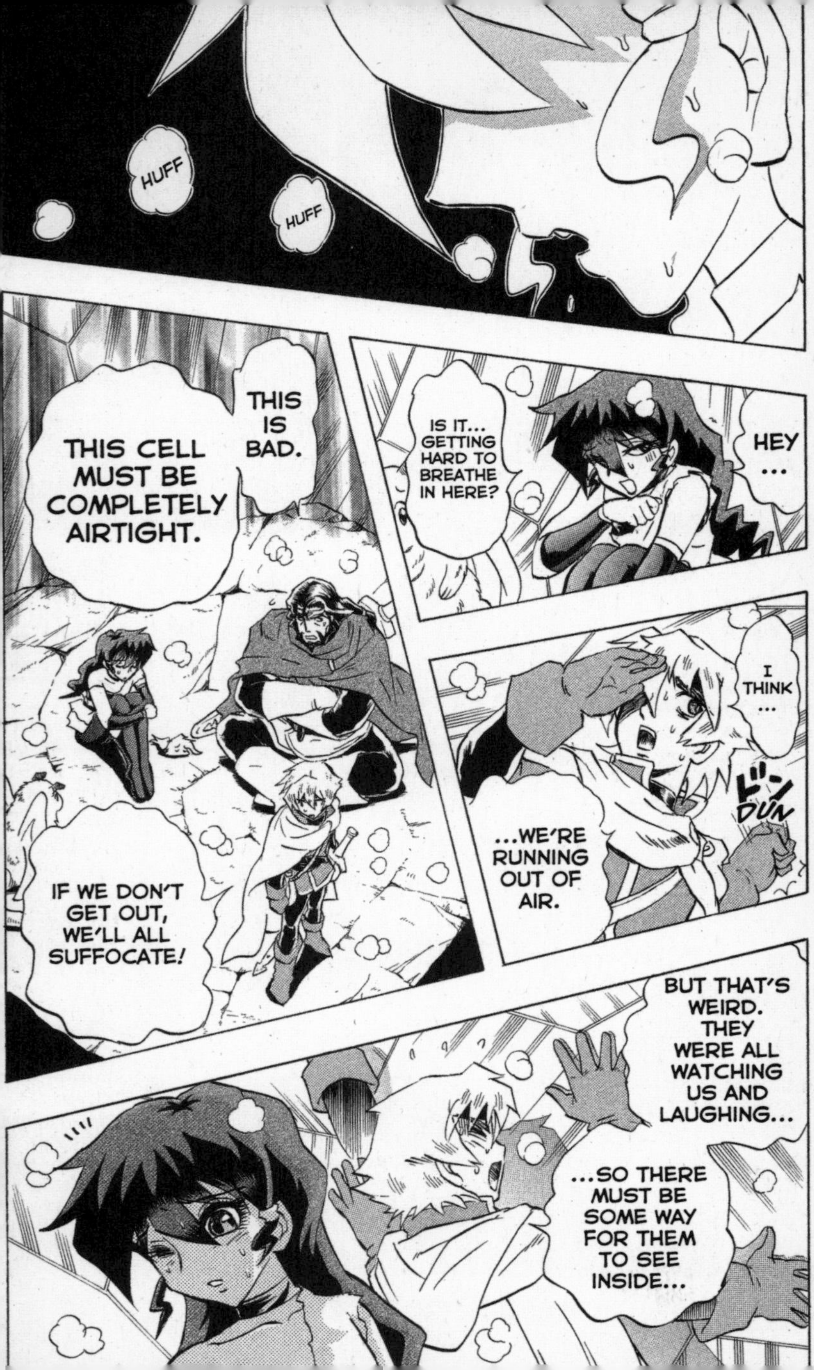

HUFF
HUFF
HEY...
IS IT... GETTING HARD TO BREATHE IN HERE?
I THINK...
...WE'RE RUNNING OUT OF AIR.
ドン
DUN
THIS IS BAD.
THIS CELL MUST BE COMPLETELY AIRTIGHT.
IF WE DON'T GET OUT, WE'LL ALL SUFFOCATE!
BUT THAT'S WEIRD. THEY WERE ALL WATCHING US AND LAUGHING...
...SO THERE MUST BE SOME WAY FOR THEM TO SEE INSIDE...

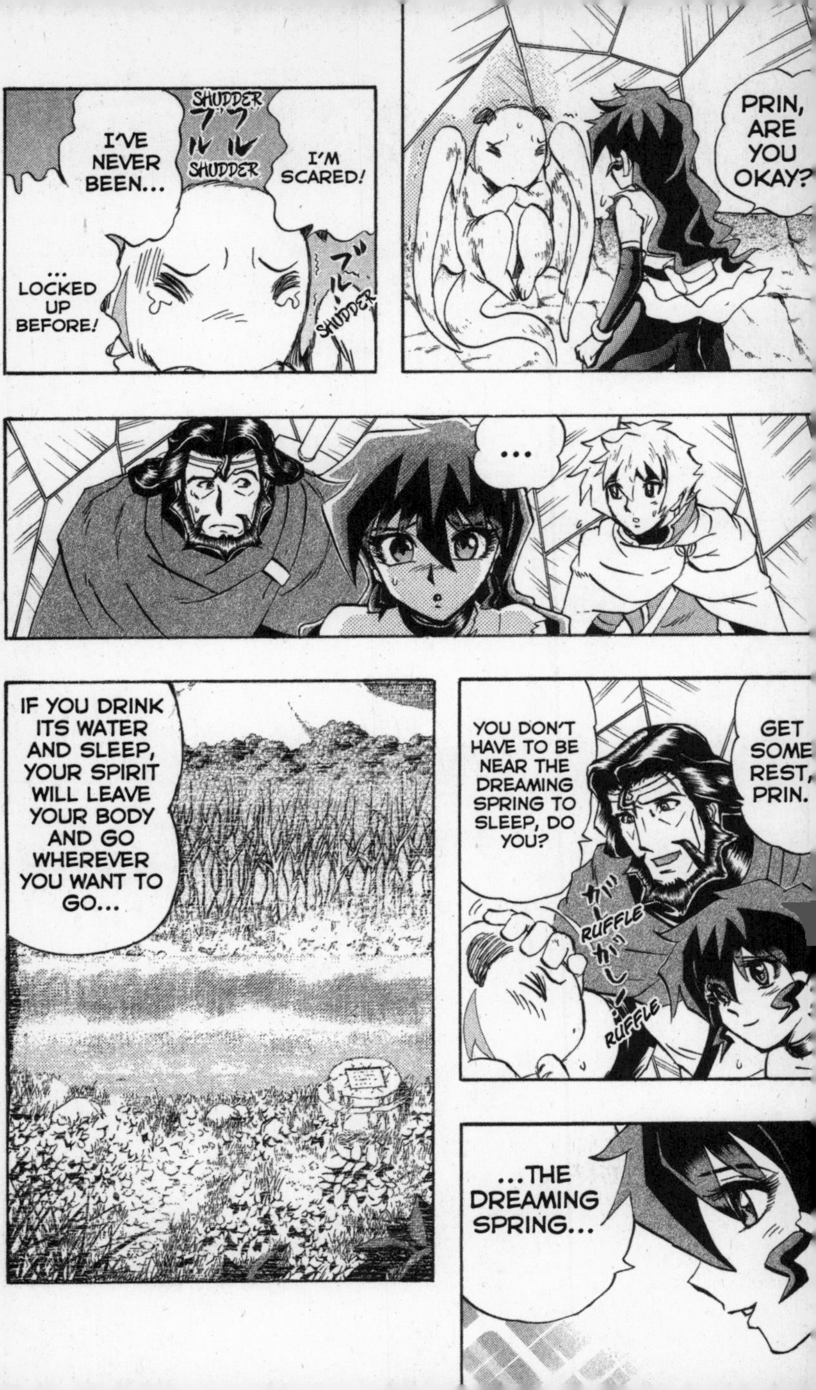
PRIN, ARE YOU OKAY?
I'M SCARED!
SHUDDER ブルブル SHUDDER
I'VE NEVER BEEN...
...LOCKED UP BEFORE!
ブル SHUDDER
...
GET SOME REST, PRIN.
YOU DON'T HAVE TO BE NEAR THE DREAMING SPRING TO SLEEP, DO YOU?
RUFFLE
RUFFLE
...THE DREAMING SPRING...
IF YOU DRINK ITS WATER AND SLEEP, YOUR SPIRIT WILL LEAVE YOUR BODY AND GO WHEREVER YOU WANT TO GO...

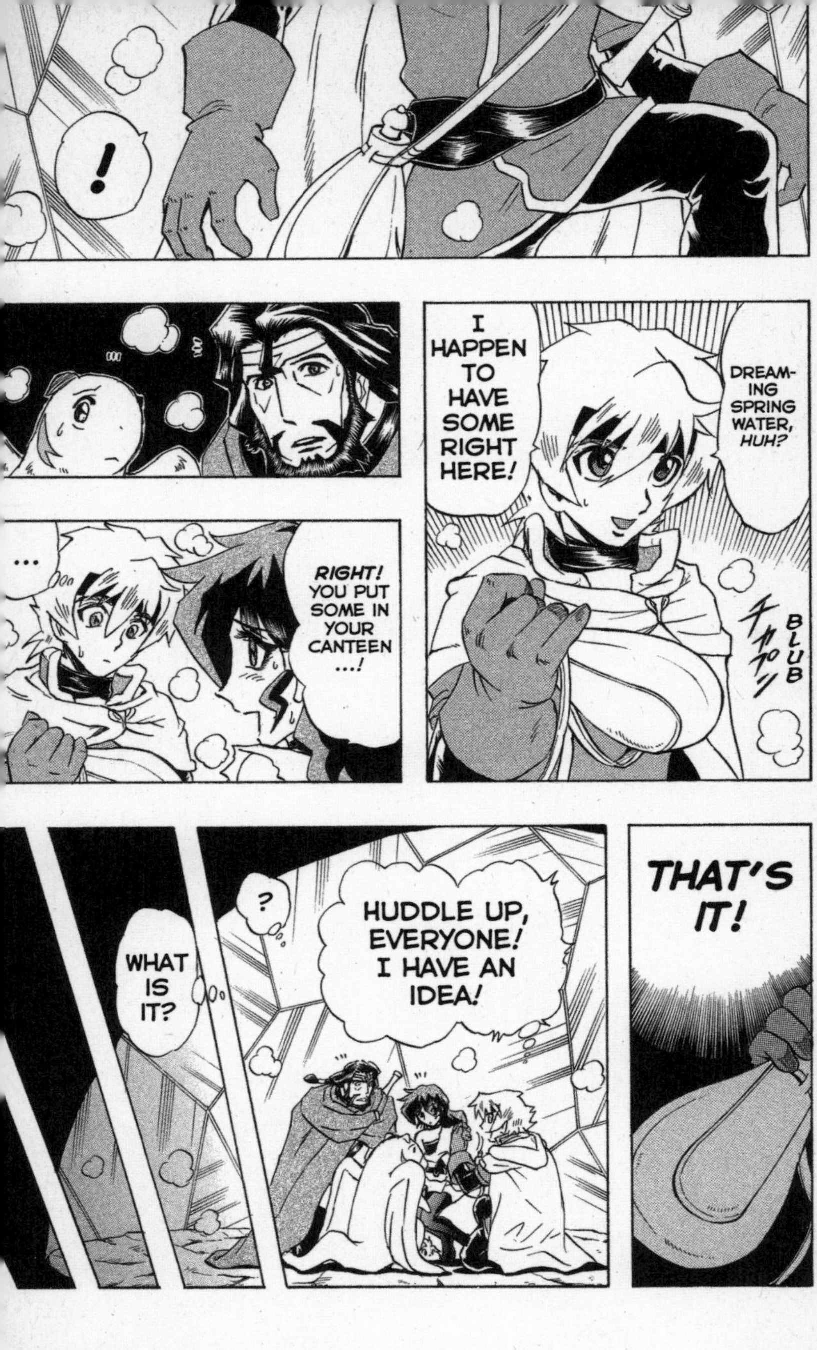
!
DREAMING SPRING WATER, HUH?
I HAPPEN TO HAVE SOME RIGHT HERE!
BLUB
RIGHT! YOU PUT SOME IN YOUR CANTEEN ...!
...
THAT'S IT!
HUDDLE UP, EVERYONE! I HAVE AN IDEA!
?
WHAT IS IT?

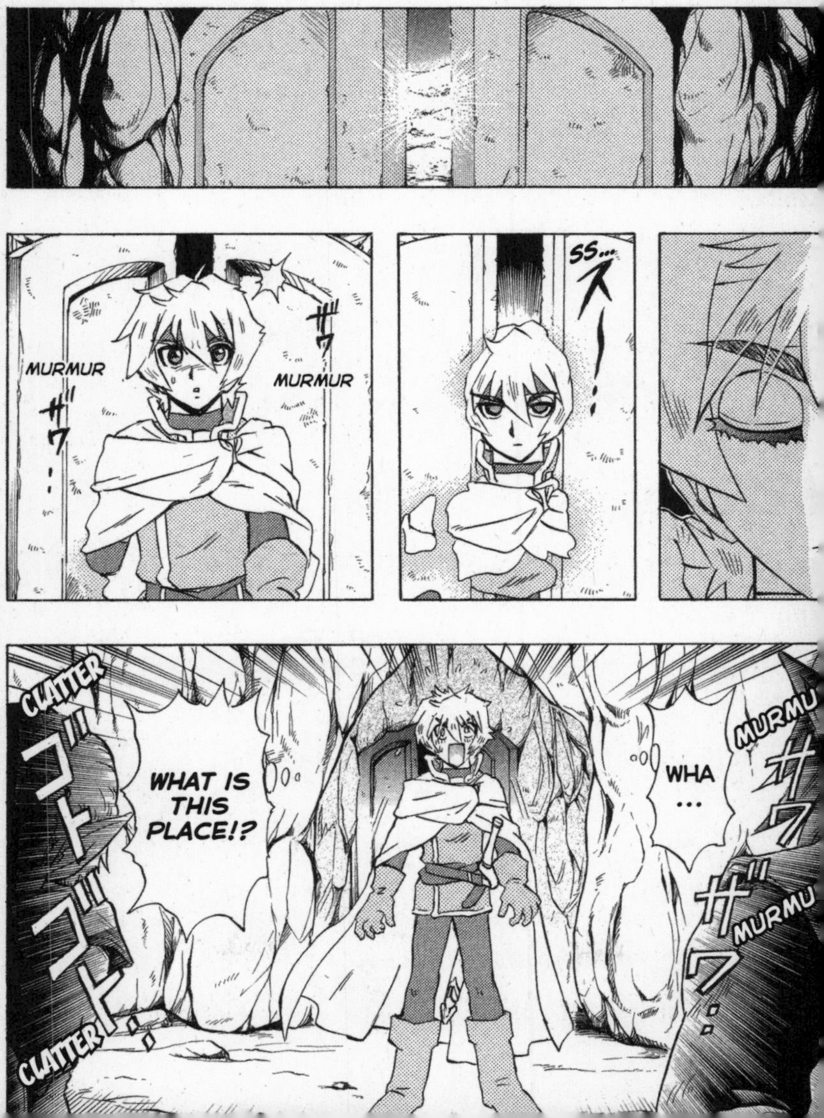

SS...
スー!!
MURMUR
ザワ
MURMUR
ザワ
MURMU
ザワ
MURMU
ザワ
WHA
...
WHAT IS THIS PLACE!?
CLATTER
ゴト
ゴト
CLATTER

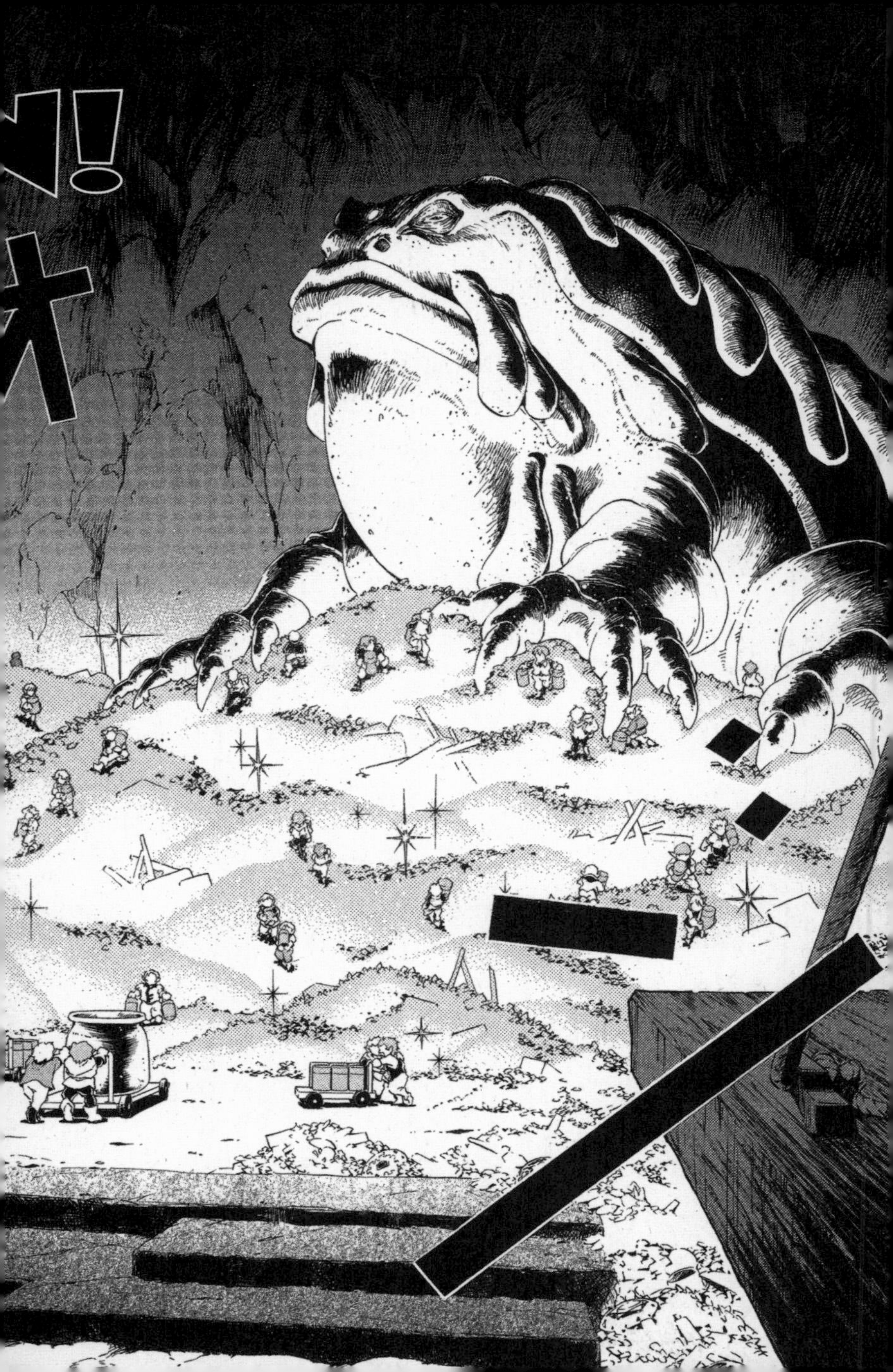

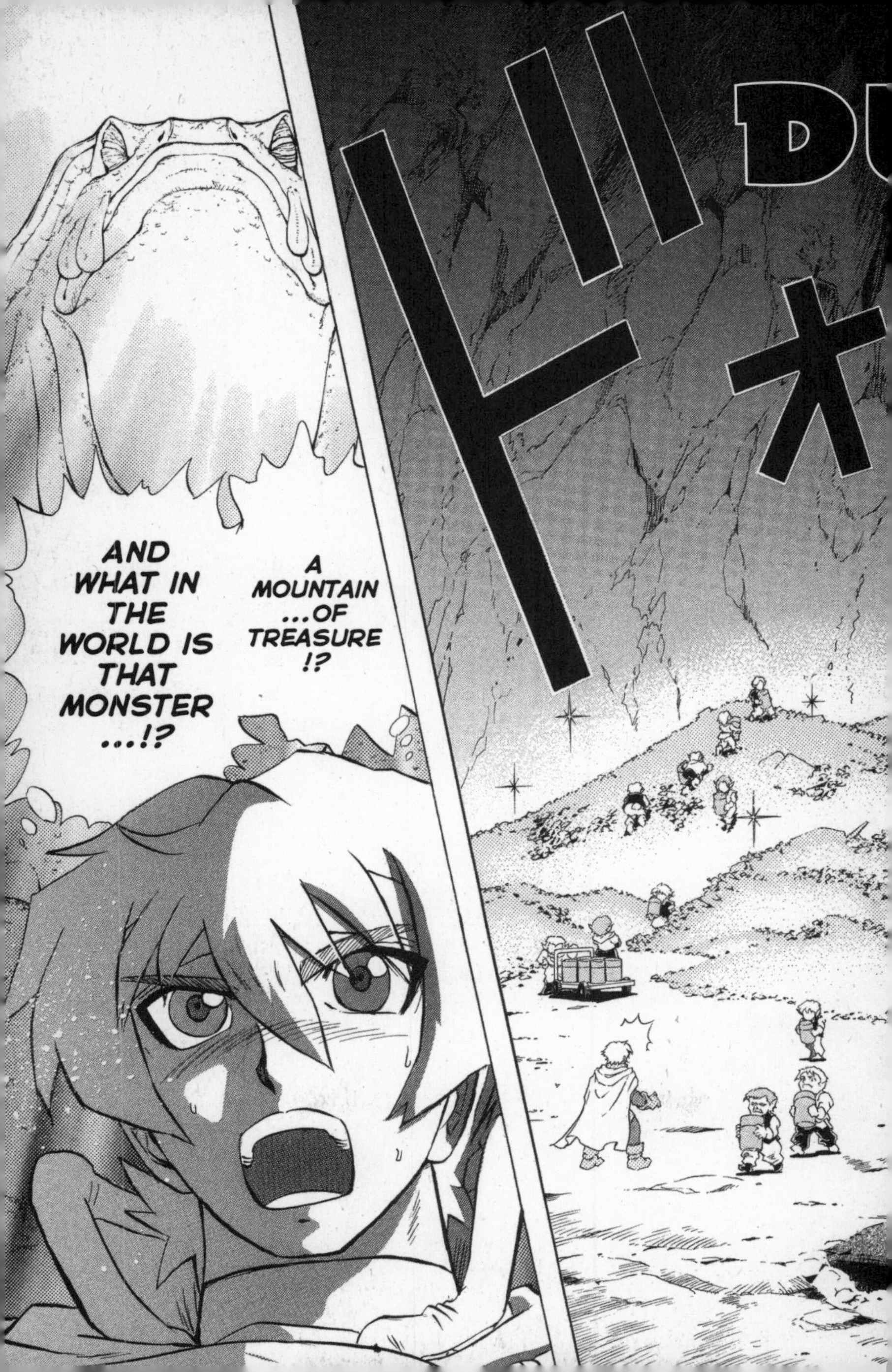
ドォ
DU
A MOUNTAIN ...OF TREASURE !?
AND WHAT IN THE WORLD IS THAT MONSTER ...!?

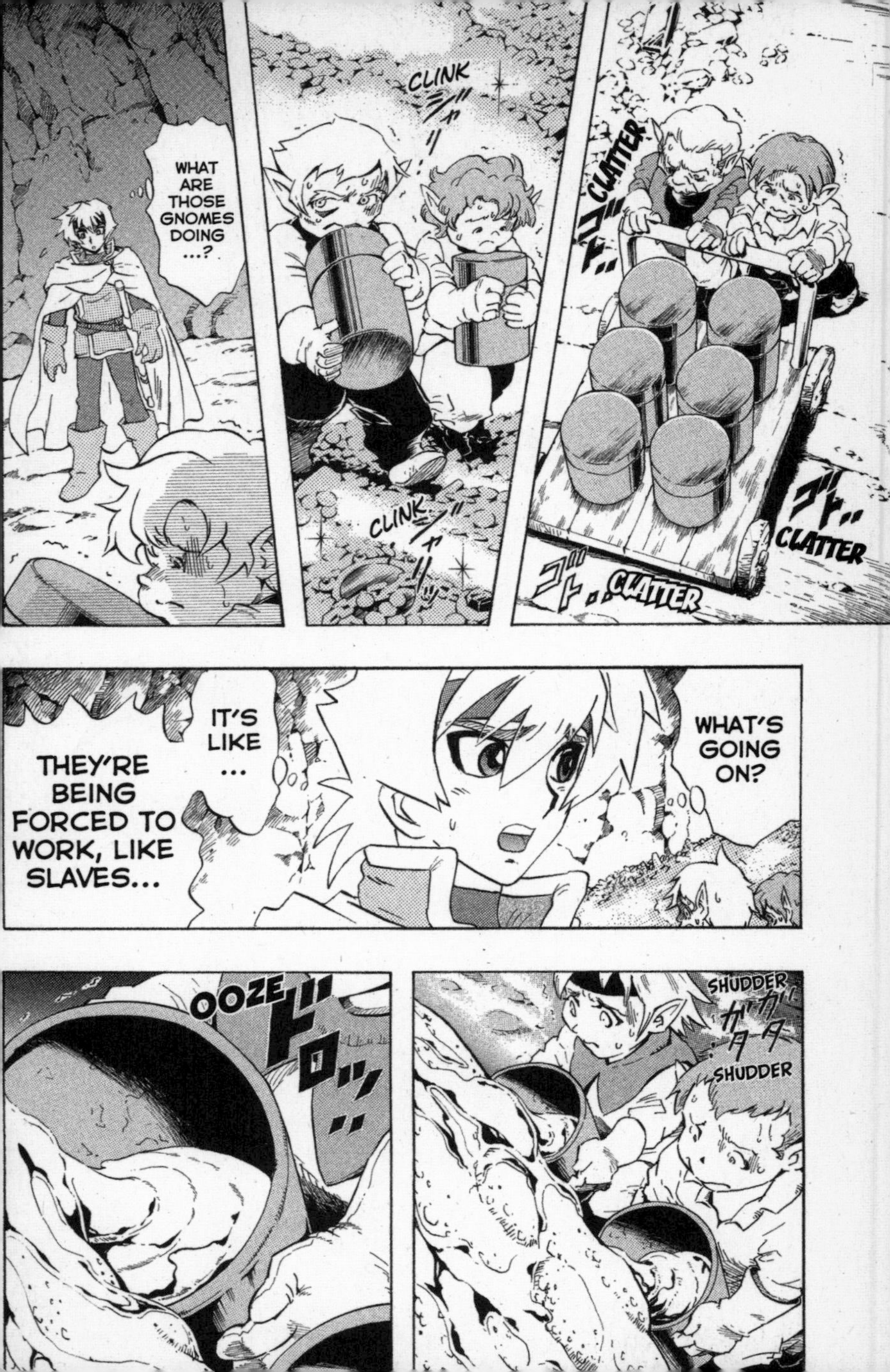
CLATTER
CLATTER
CLATTER
CLINK
CLINK
WHAT ARE THOSE GNOMES DOING ...?
WHAT'S GOING ON?
IT'S LIKE ...
THEY'RE BEING FORCED TO WORK, LIKE SLAVES...
SHUDDER
SHUDDER
OOZE

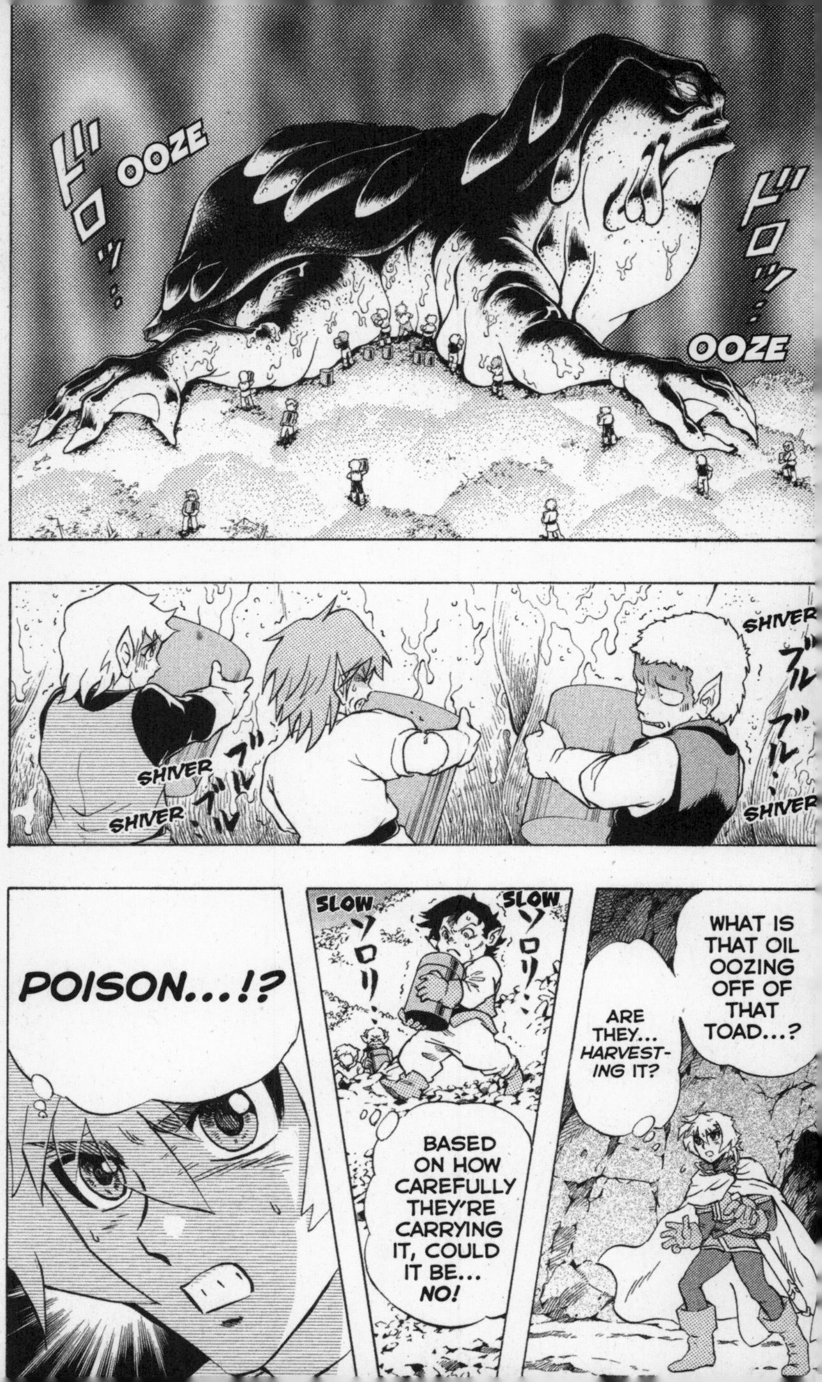
ドロッ…
OOZE
ドロッ…
OOZE
SHIVER
ブルブル
SHIVER
SHIVER
ブル
SHIVER
ブル
WHAT IS THAT OIL OOZING OFF OF THAT TOAD...?
ARE THEY... HARVESTING IT?
SLOW
ソロリ
SLOW
ソロリ
BASED ON HOW CAREFULLY THEY'RE CARRYING IT, COULD IT BE... NO!
POISON...!?

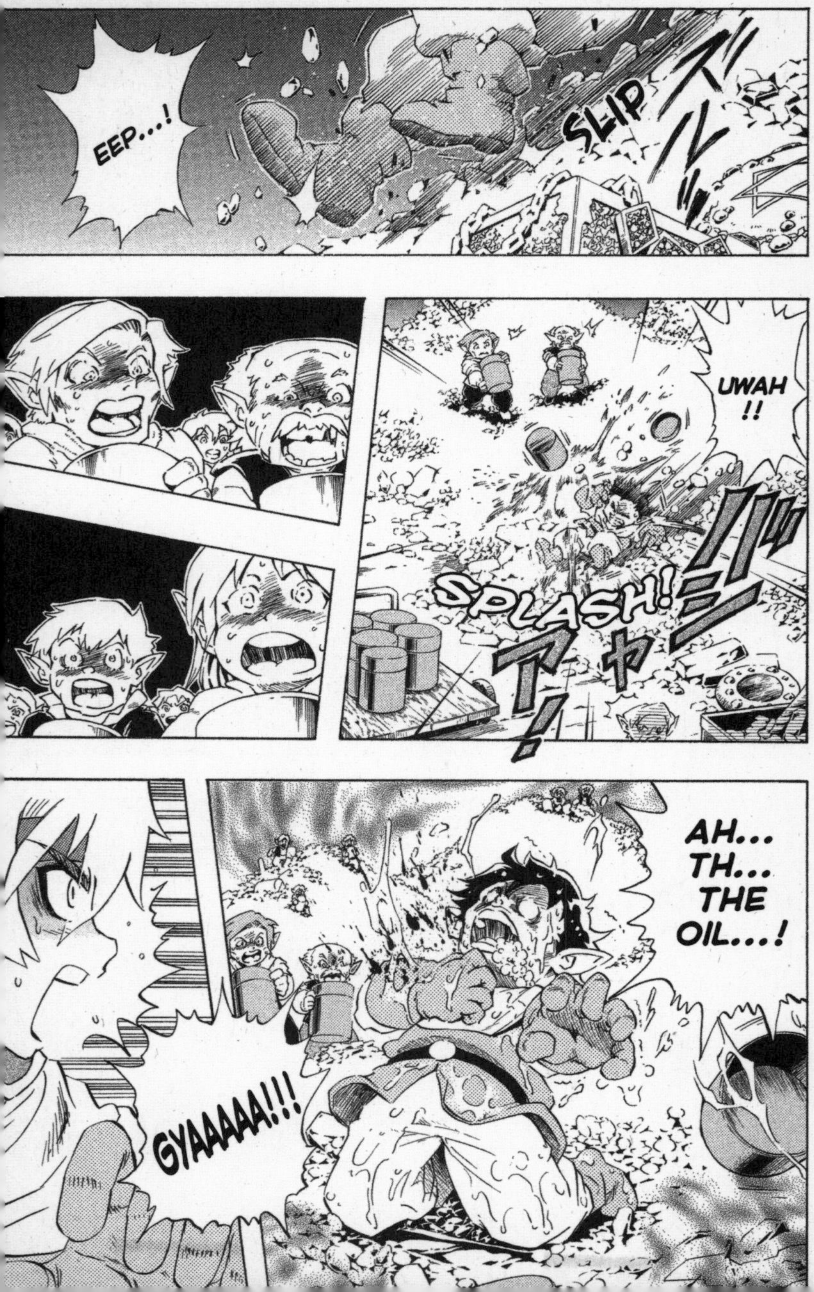
SLIP
EEP...!
UWAH!!
SPLASH!
AH... TH... THE OIL...!
GYAAAAA!!!

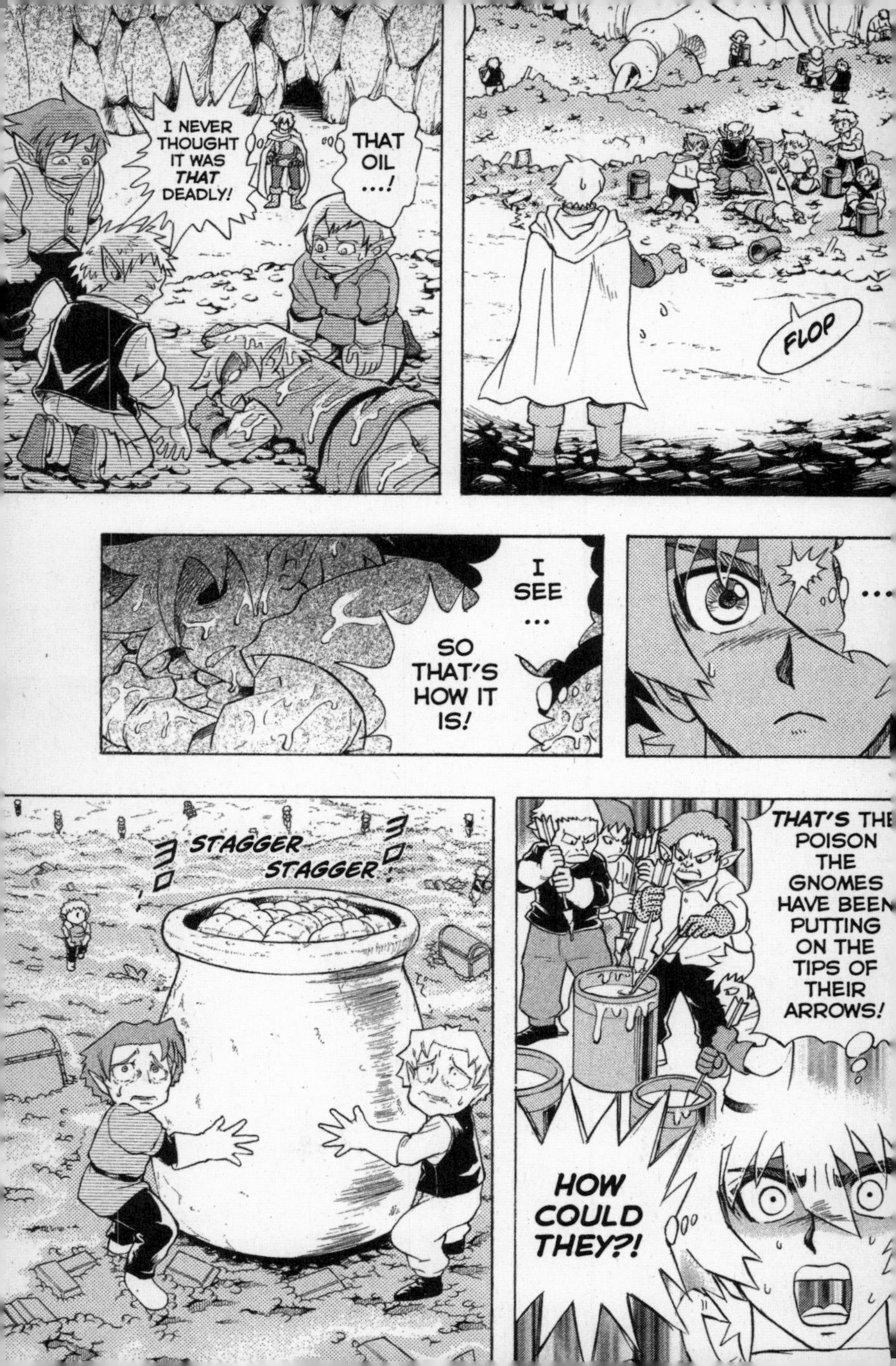
FLOP
THAT OIL ...!
I NEVER THOUGHT IT WAS THAT DEADLY!
...
I SEE ...
SO THAT'S HOW IT IS!
THAT'S THE POISON THE GNOMES HAVE BEEN PUTTING ON THE TIPS OF THEIR ARROWS!
HOW COULD THEY?!
STAGGER
STAGGER

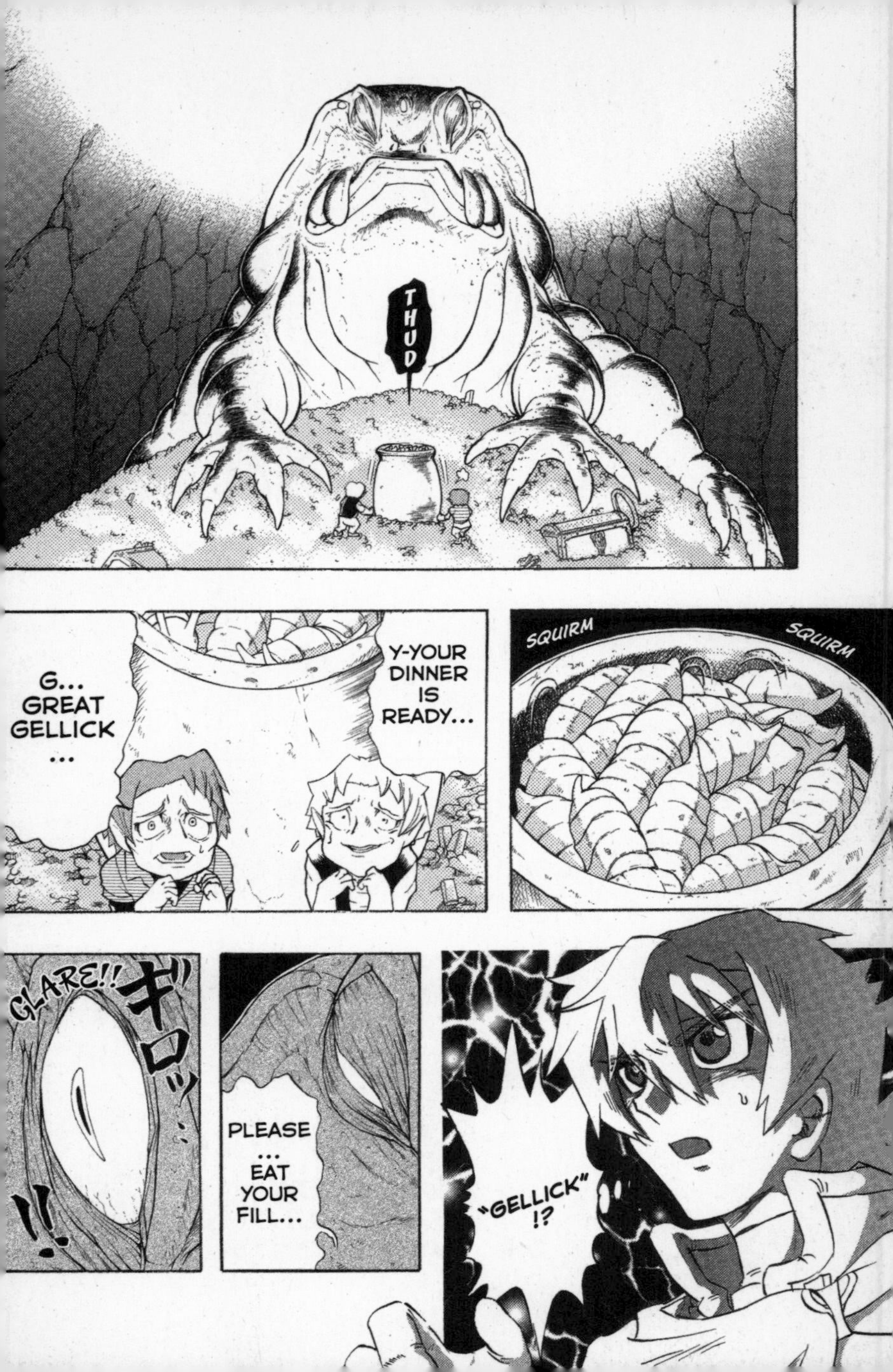
THUD
SQUIRM
SQUIRM
Y-YOUR DINNER IS READY...
G... GREAT GELLICK ...
"GELLICK" !?
PLEASE ... EAT YOUR FILL...
GLARE!!
ギロッ…
!!

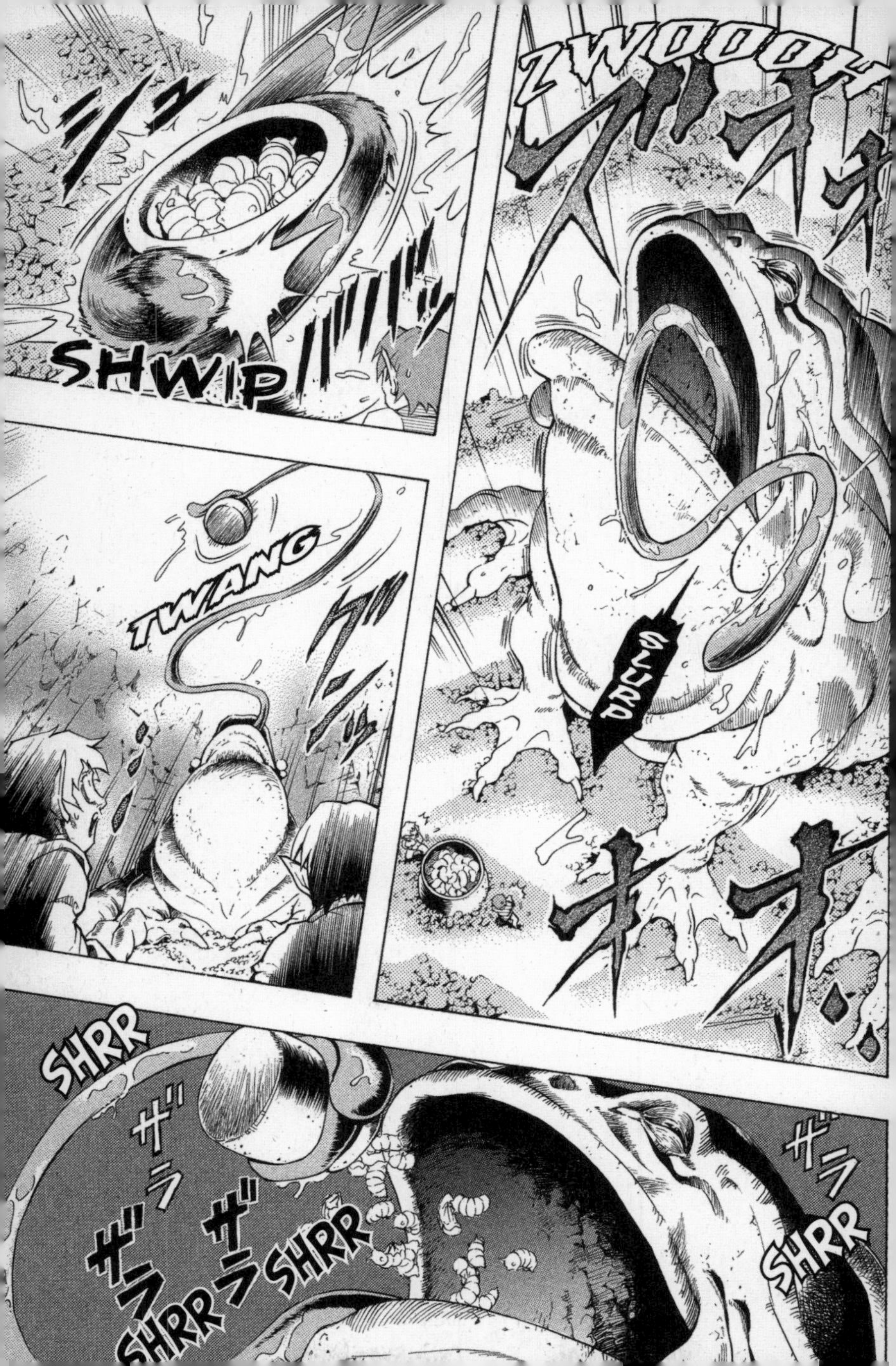
ZWOOOOH
SLURP
SHWIP
TWANG
SHRR
ザラ
SHRR
ザラ
SHRR
ザラ
SHRR

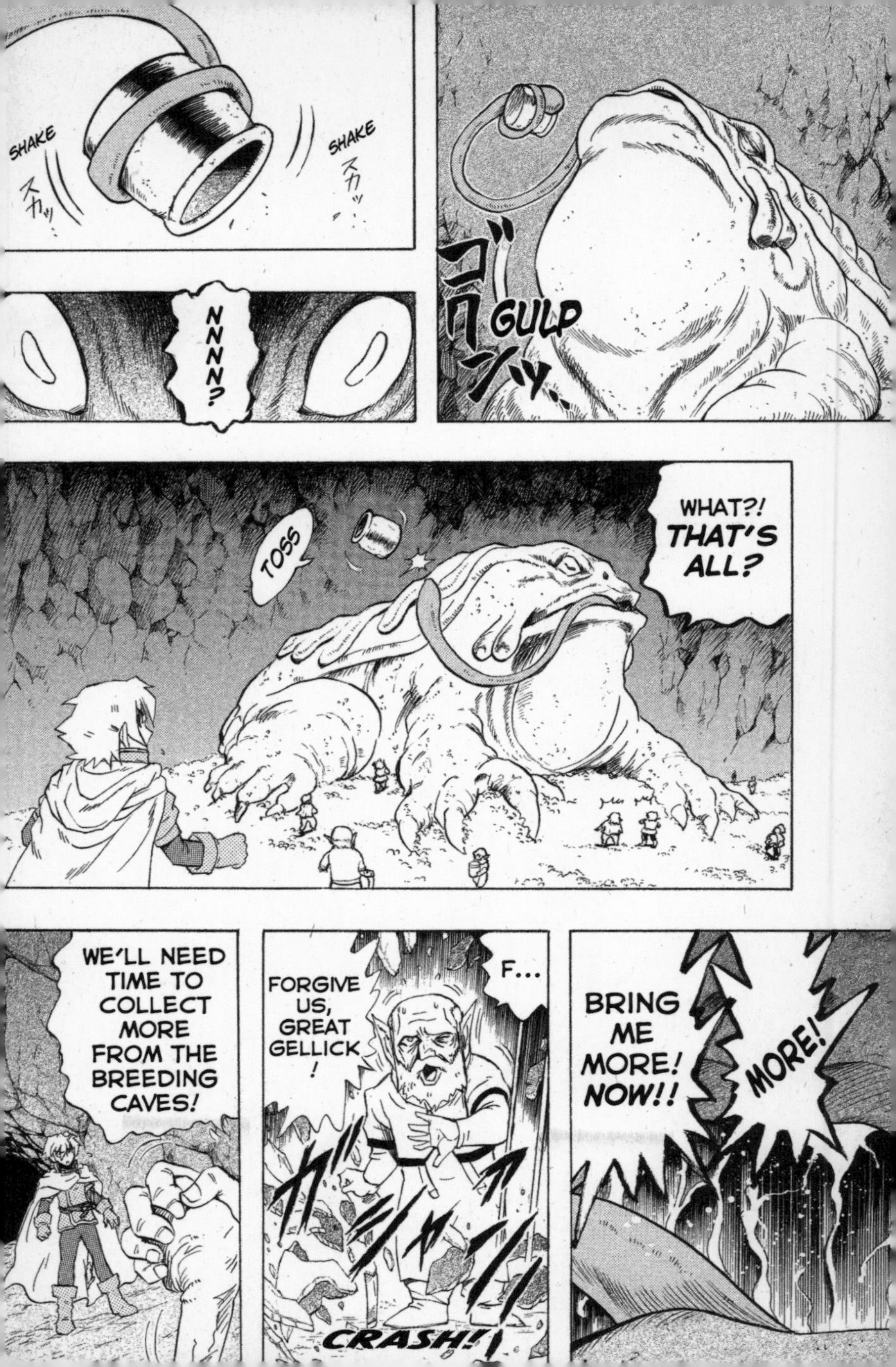

ゴクンッ..
GULP
SHAKE
スカッ
SHAKE
スカッ
NNNN?
WHAT?! THAT'S ALL?
TOSS
MORE!
BRING ME MORE! NOW!!
F...
FORGIVE US, GREAT GELLICK!
CRASH!
WE'LL NEED TIME TO COLLECT MORE FROM THE BREEDING CAVES!

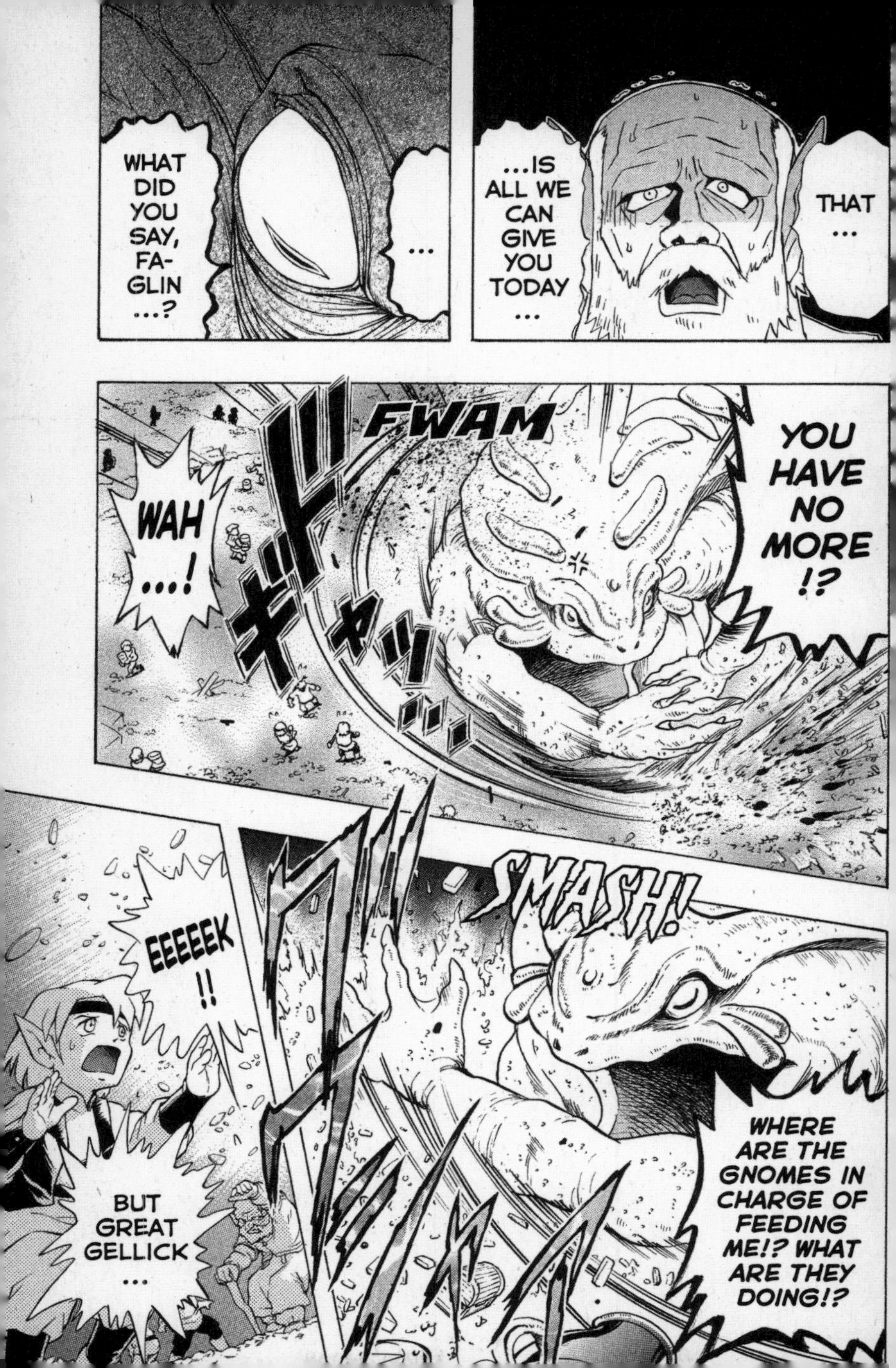
THAT ...
...IS ALL WE CAN GIVE YOU TODAY ...
...
WHAT DID YOU SAY, FA-GLIN ...?
YOU HAVE NO MORE !?
FWAM
WAH ...!
SMASH!
WHERE ARE THE GNOMES IN CHARGE OF FEEDING ME!? WHAT ARE THEY DOING!?
EEEEEK !!
BUT GREAT GELLICK ...

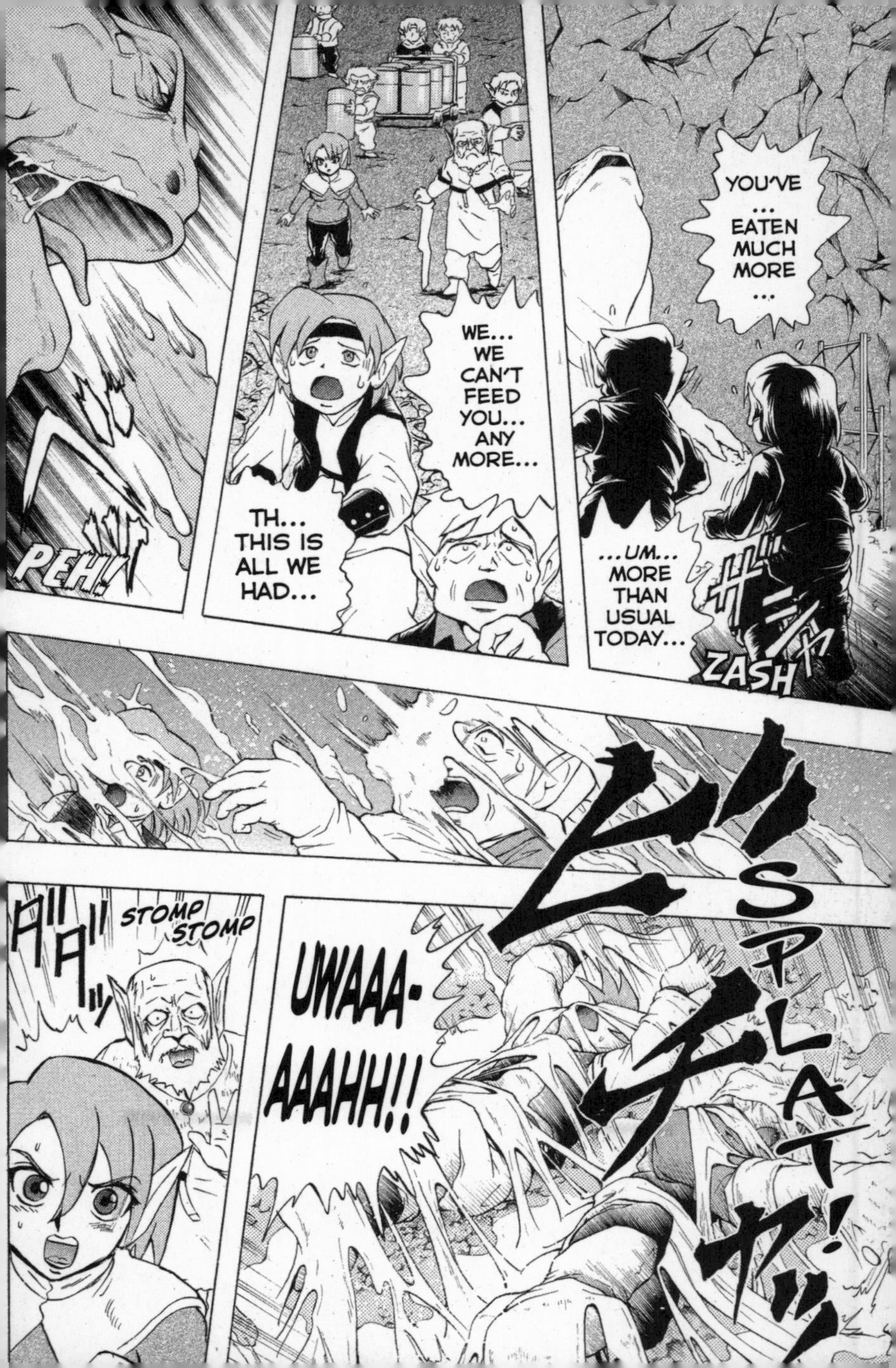

YOU'VE ... EATEN MUCH MORE ...
...UM... MORE THAN USUAL TODAY...
ZASH
WE... WE CAN'T FEED YOU... ANY MORE...
TH... THIS IS ALL WE HAD...
PEH!
SPLAT!
UWAAA-AAAAH!!
STOMP STOMP

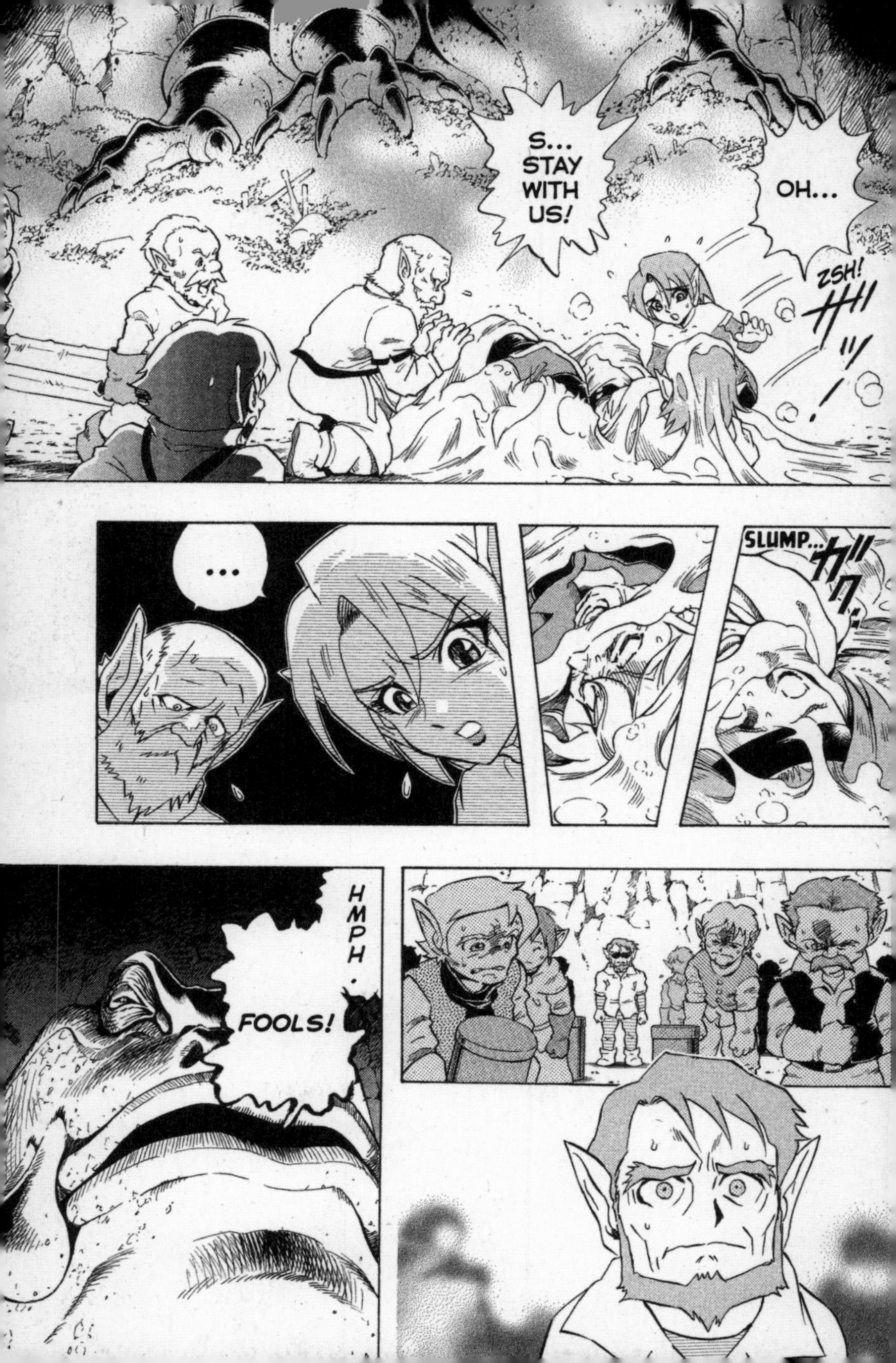
OH...
ZSH!
S... STAY WITH US!
SLUMP...
...
HMPH.
FOOLS!

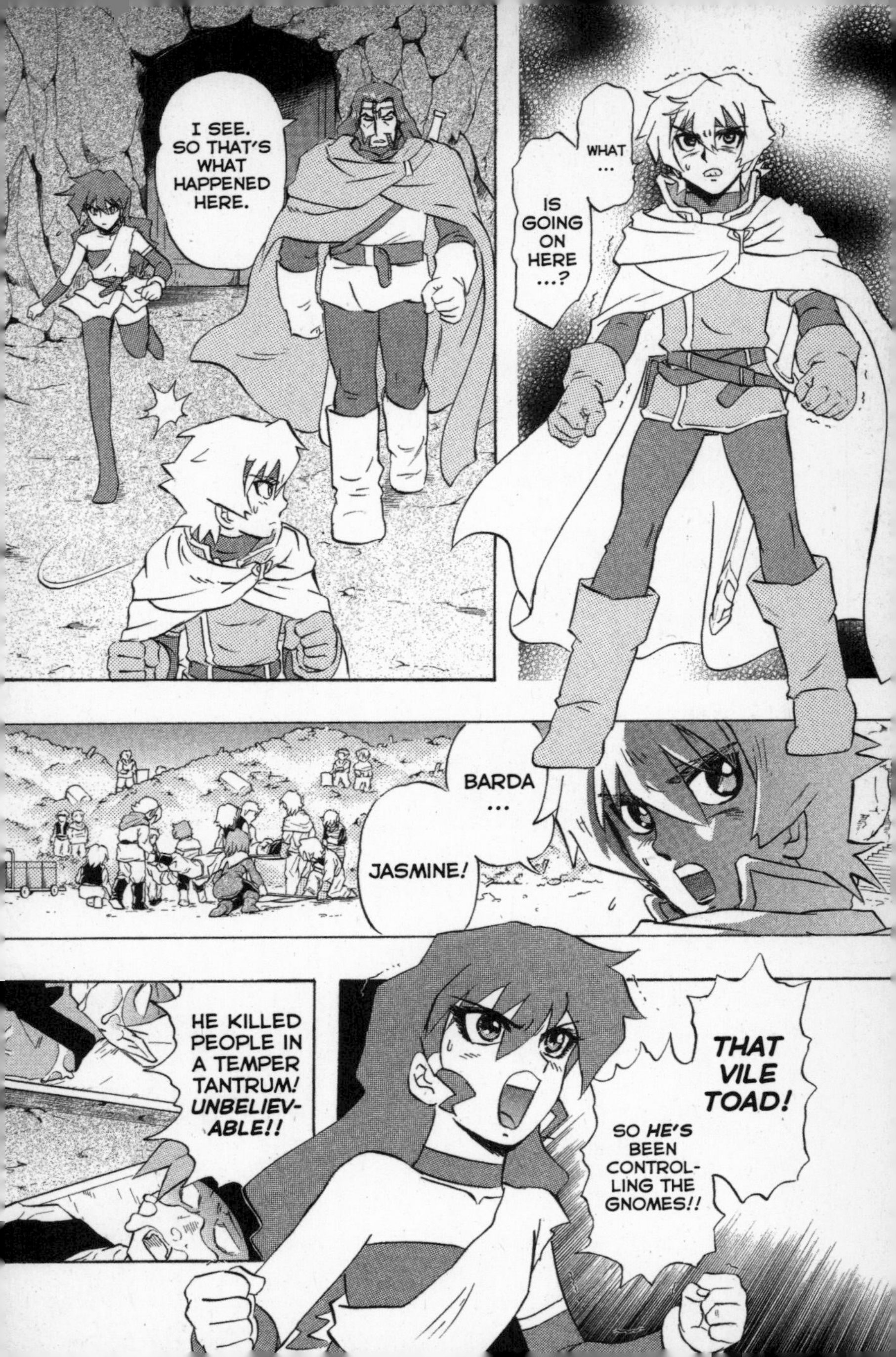
WHAT ... IS GOING ON HERE ...?
I SEE. SO THAT'S WHAT HAPPENED HERE.
BARDA ... JASMINE!
THAT VILE TOAD!
SO HE'S BEEN CONTROL-LING THE GNOMES!!
HE KILLED PEOPLE IN A TEMPER TANTRUM! UNBELIEV-ABLE!!

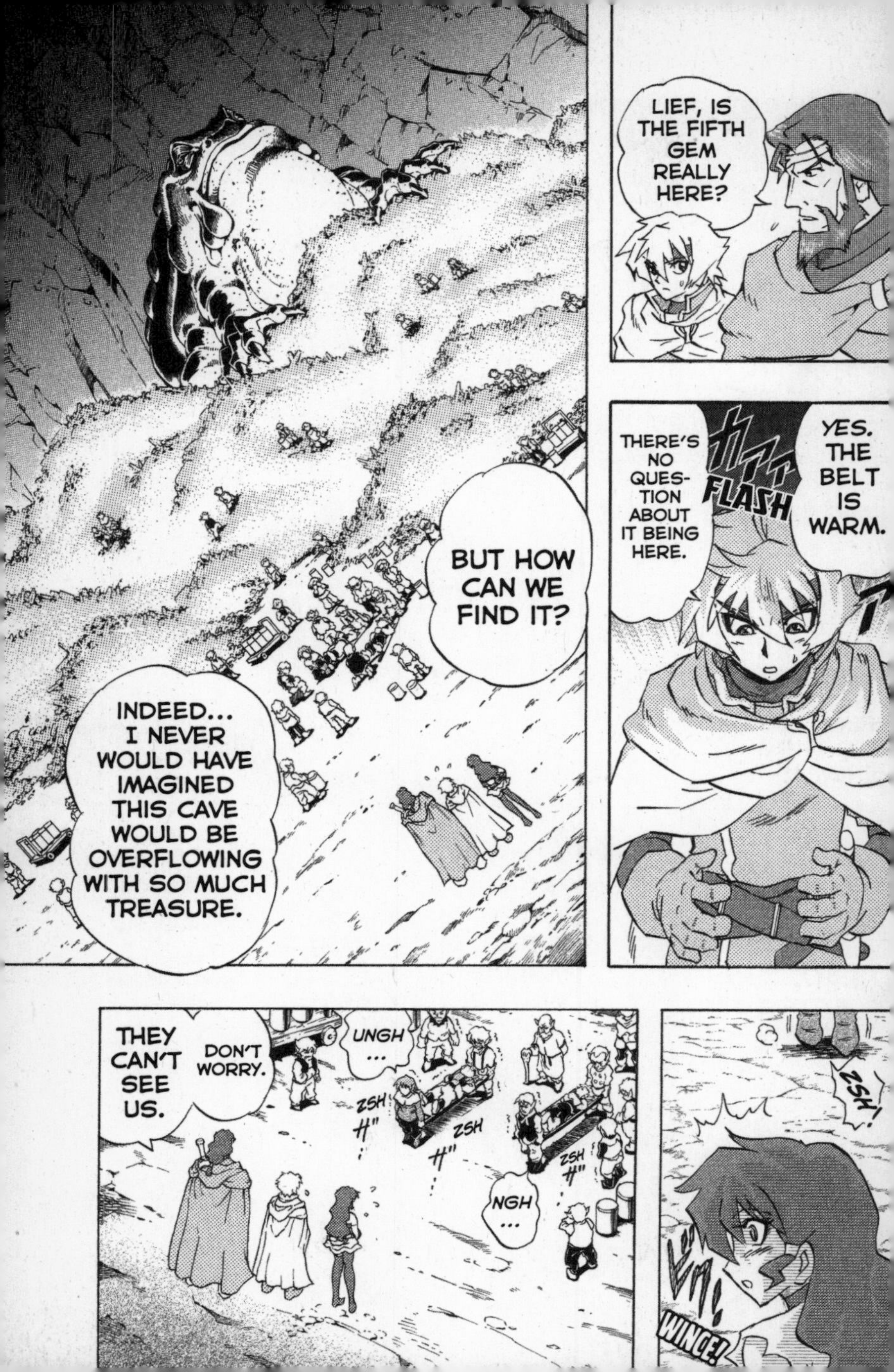
LIEF, IS THE FIFTH GEM REALLY HERE?
YES. THE BELT IS WARM.
FLASH
THERE'S NO QUES- TION ABOUT IT BEING HERE.
BUT HOW CAN WE FIND IT?
INDEED... I NEVER WOULD HAVE IMAGINED THIS CAVE WOULD BE OVERFLOWING WITH SO MUCH TREASURE.
ZSH!
WINCE!
UNGH ...
DON'T WORRY.
THEY CAN'T SEE US.
ZSH
ZSH
ZSH
NGH ...

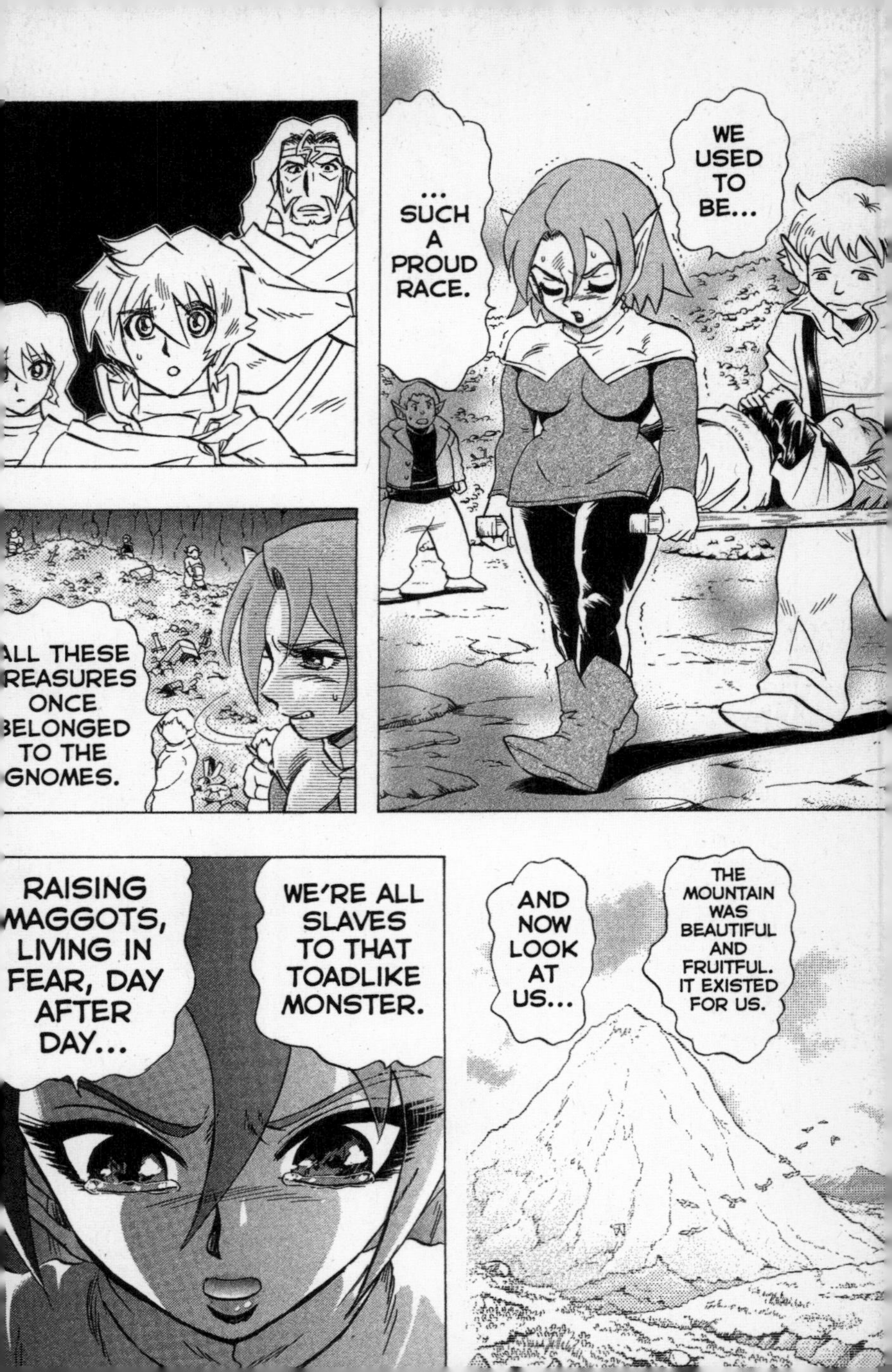
WE USED TO BE...
...SUCH A PROUD RACE.
ALL THESE TREASURES ONCE BELONGED TO THE GNOMES.
THE MOUNTAIN WAS BEAUTIFUL AND FRUITFUL. IT EXISTED FOR US.
AND NOW LOOK AT US...
WE'RE ALL SLAVES TO THAT TOADLIKE MONSTER.
RAISING MAGGOTS, LIVING IN FEAR, DAY AFTER DAY...

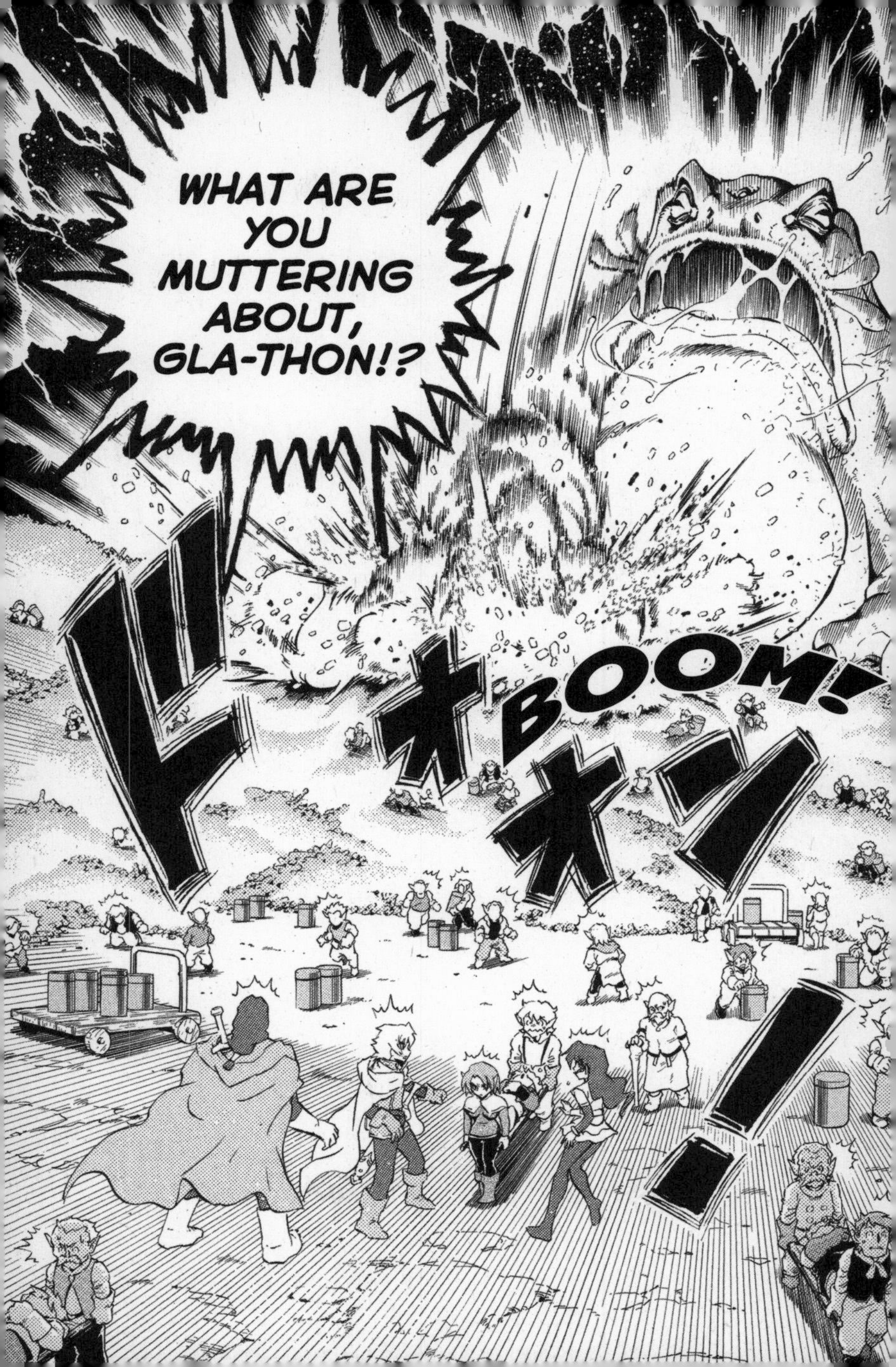
WHAT ARE YOU MUTTERING ABOUT, GLA-THON!?
ドオオン!!
BOOM!

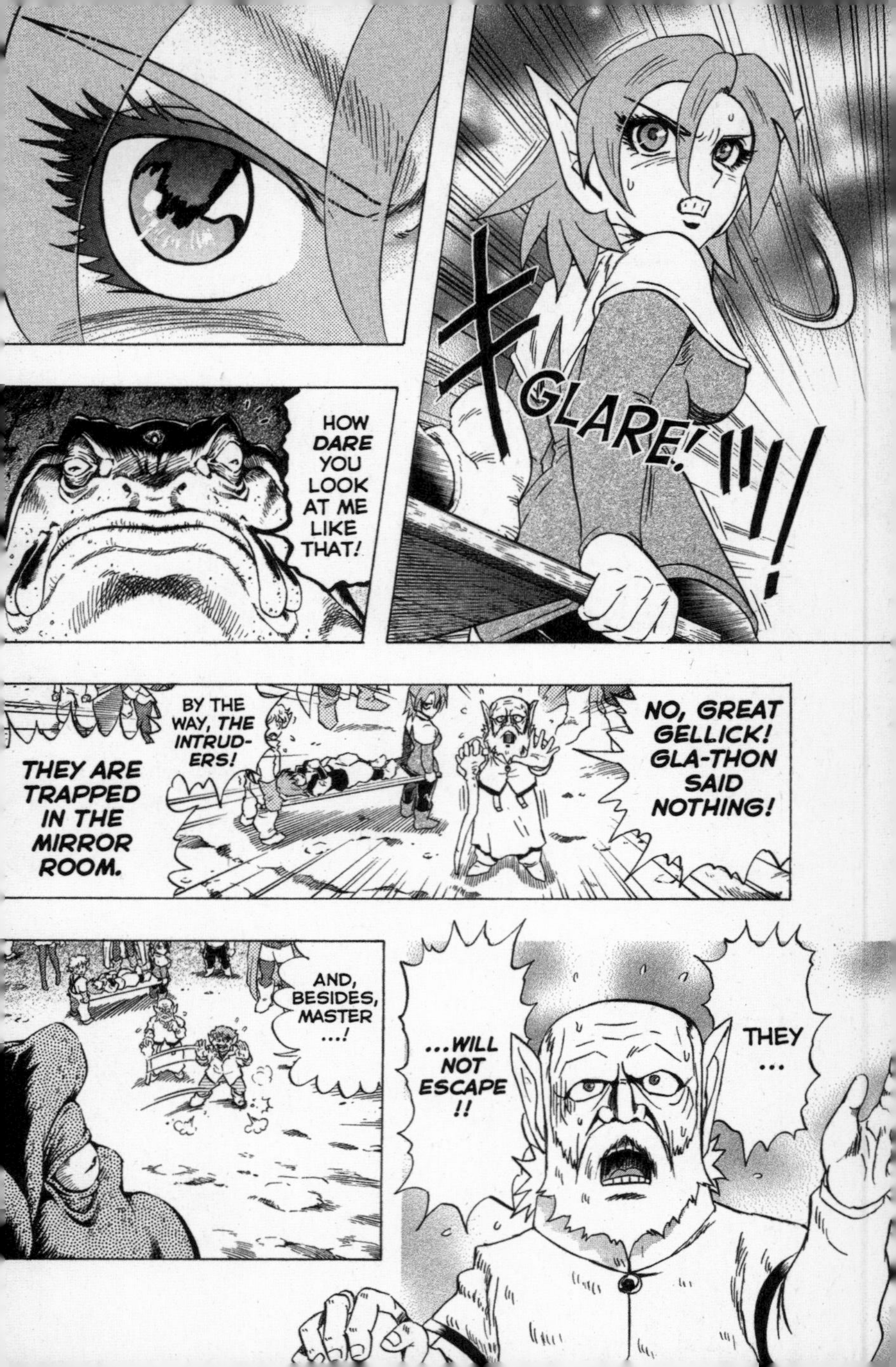
GLARE!
HOW DARE YOU LOOK AT ME LIKE THAT!
NO, GREAT GELLICK! GLA-THON SAID NOTHING!
BY THE WAY, THE INTRUD-ERS!
THEY ARE TRAPPED IN THE MIRROR ROOM.
THEY ...
...WILL NOT ESCAPE !!
AND, BESIDES, MASTER ...!

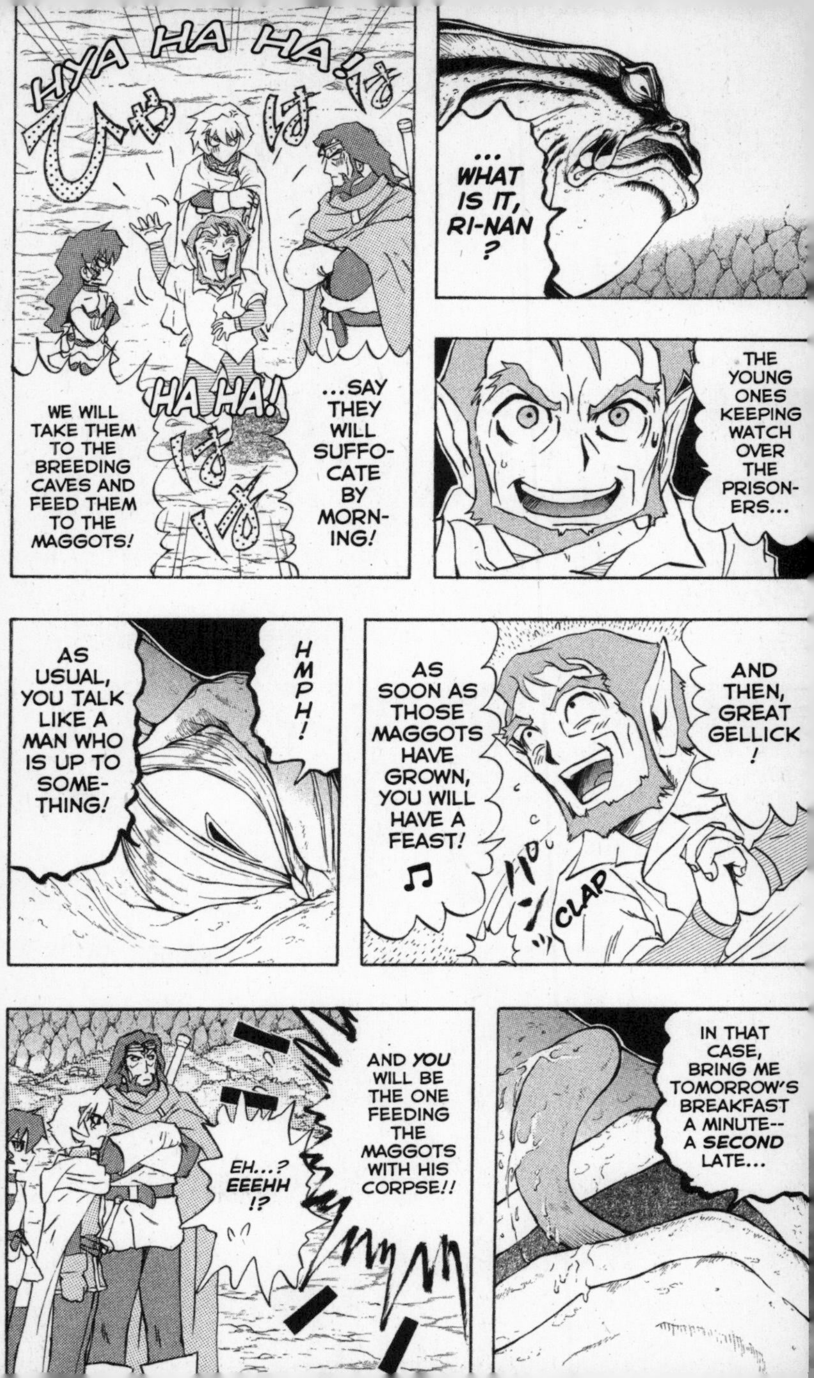

... WHAT IS IT, RI-NAN?
THE YOUNG ONES KEEPING WATCH OVER THE PRISONERS...
HYA HA HA!
...SAY THEY WILL SUFFOCATE BY MORNING!
WE WILL TAKE THEM TO THE BREEDING CAVES AND FEED THEM TO THE MAGGOTS!
HA HA!
AND THEN, GREAT GELLICK!
AS SOON AS THOSE MAGGOTS HAVE GROWN, YOU WILL HAVE A FEAST! ♫
CLAP
HMPH!
AS USUAL, YOU TALK LIKE A MAN WHO IS UP TO SOMETHING!
IN THAT CASE, BRING ME TOMORROW'S BREAKFAST A MINUTE-- A *SECOND* LATE...
AND *YOU* WILL BE THE ONE FEEDING THE MAGGOTS WITH HIS CORPSE!!
EH...? EEEHH!?

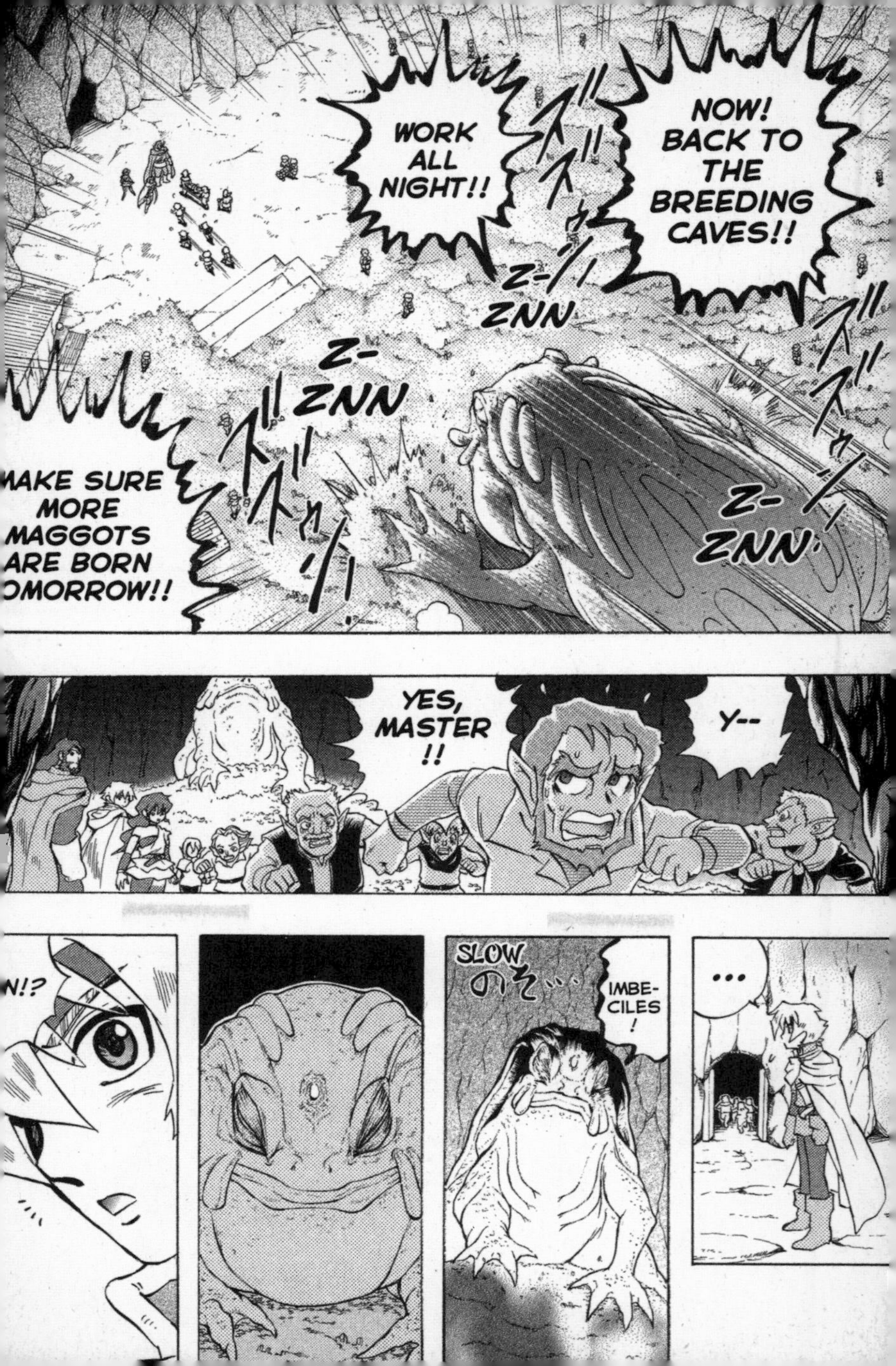

NOW! BACK TO THE BREEDING CAVES!!
Z-ZNN
WORK ALL NIGHT!!
Z-ZNN
Z-ZNN
AKE SURE MORE MAGGOTS ARE BORN OMORROW!!
Y--
YES, MASTER!!
...
IMBE-CILES!
SLOW
N!?

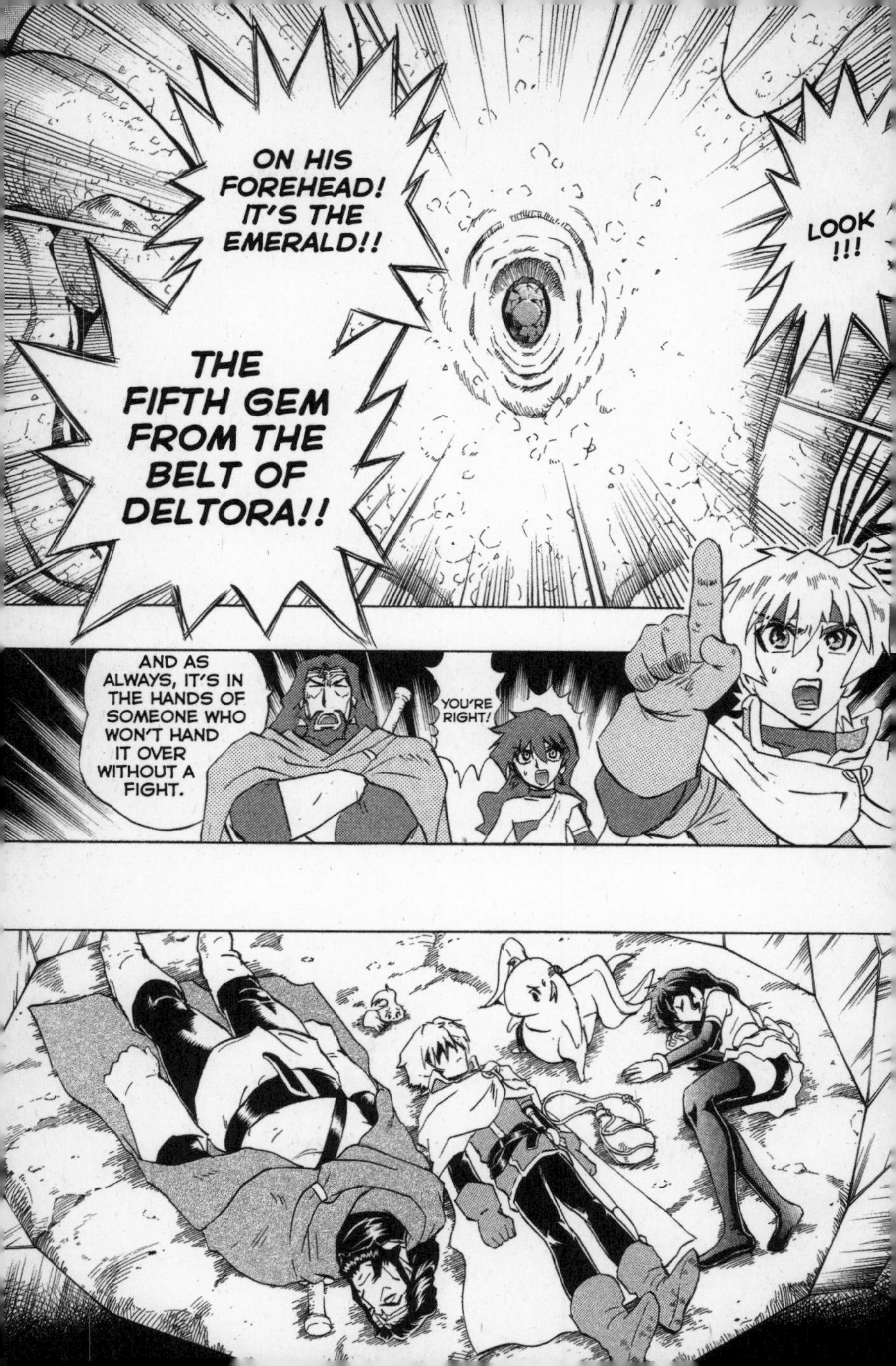
LOOK !!!
ON HIS FOREHEAD! IT'S THE EMERALD!!
THE FIFTH GEM FROM THE BELT OF DELTORA!!
YOU'RE RIGHT!
AND AS ALWAYS, IT'S IN THE HANDS OF SOMEONE WHO WON'T HAND IT OVER WITHOUT A FIGHT.

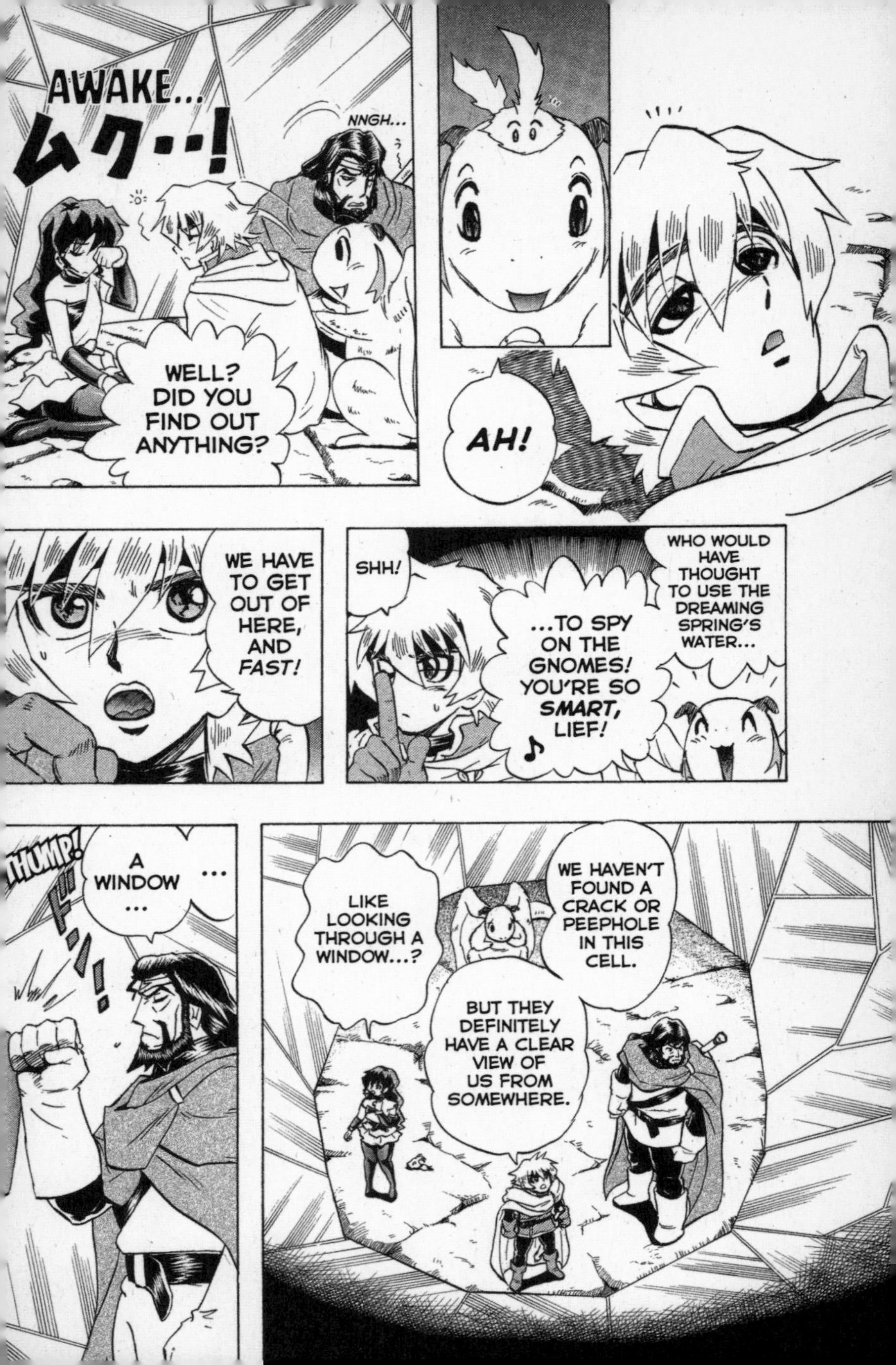

AH!
AWAKE...
ムク・・!
NNGH...
WELL? DID YOU FIND OUT ANYTHING?
WHO WOULD HAVE THOUGHT TO USE THE DREAMING SPRING'S WATER...
SHH!
...TO SPY ON THE GNOMES! YOU'RE SO SMART, LIEF! ♪
WE HAVE TO GET OUT OF HERE, AND FAST!
WE HAVEN'T FOUND A CRACK OR PEEPHOLE IN THIS CELL.
LIKE LOOKING THROUGH A WINDOW...?
BUT THEY DEFINITELY HAVE A CLEAR VIEW OF US FROM SOMEWHERE.
THUMP!
A WINDOW ... ...

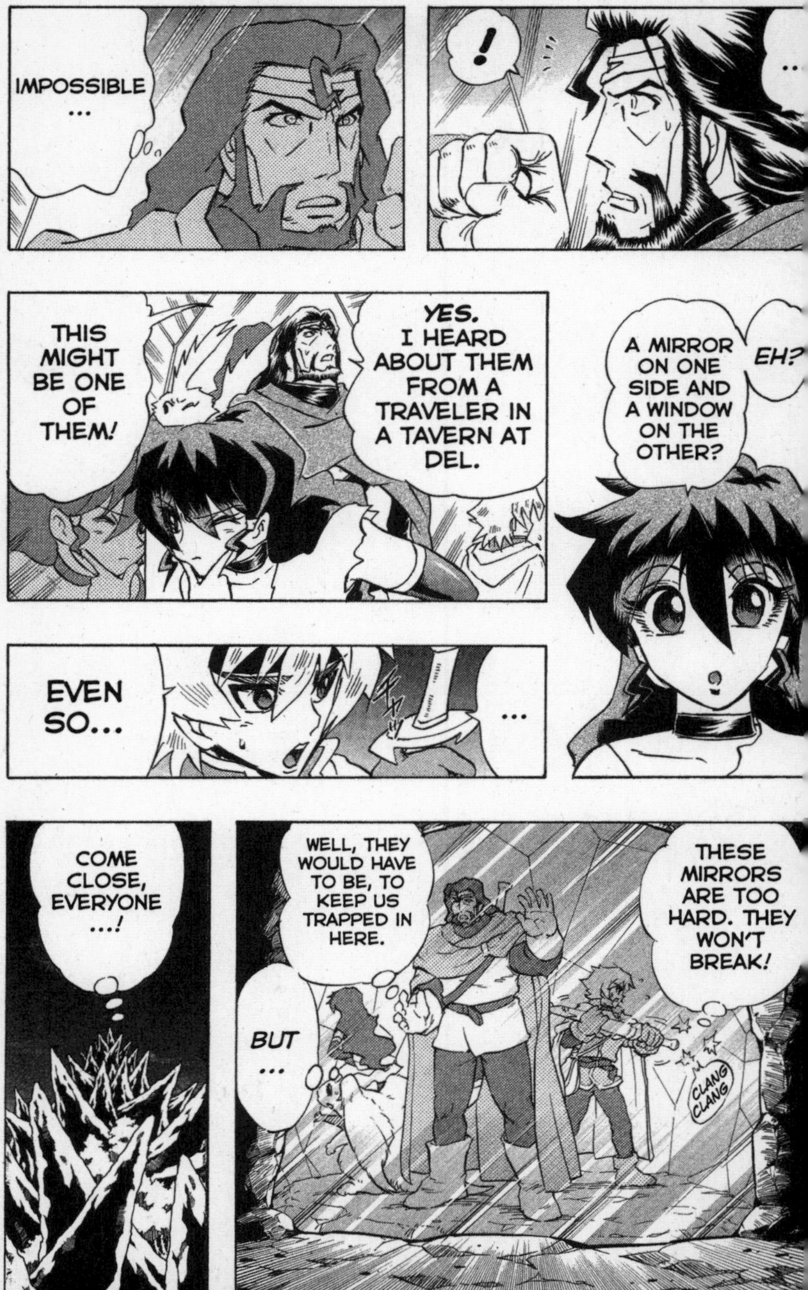

!
..
IMPOSSIBLE ...
EH?
A MIRROR ON ONE SIDE AND A WINDOW ON THE OTHER?
YES. I HEARD ABOUT THEM FROM A TRAVELER IN A TAVERN AT DEL.
THIS MIGHT BE ONE OF THEM!
...
EVEN SO...
THESE MIRRORS ARE TOO HARD. THEY WON'T BREAK!
CLANG CLANG
WELL, THEY WOULD HAVE TO BE, TO KEEP US TRAPPED IN HERE.
BUT ...
COME CLOSE, EVERYONE ...!

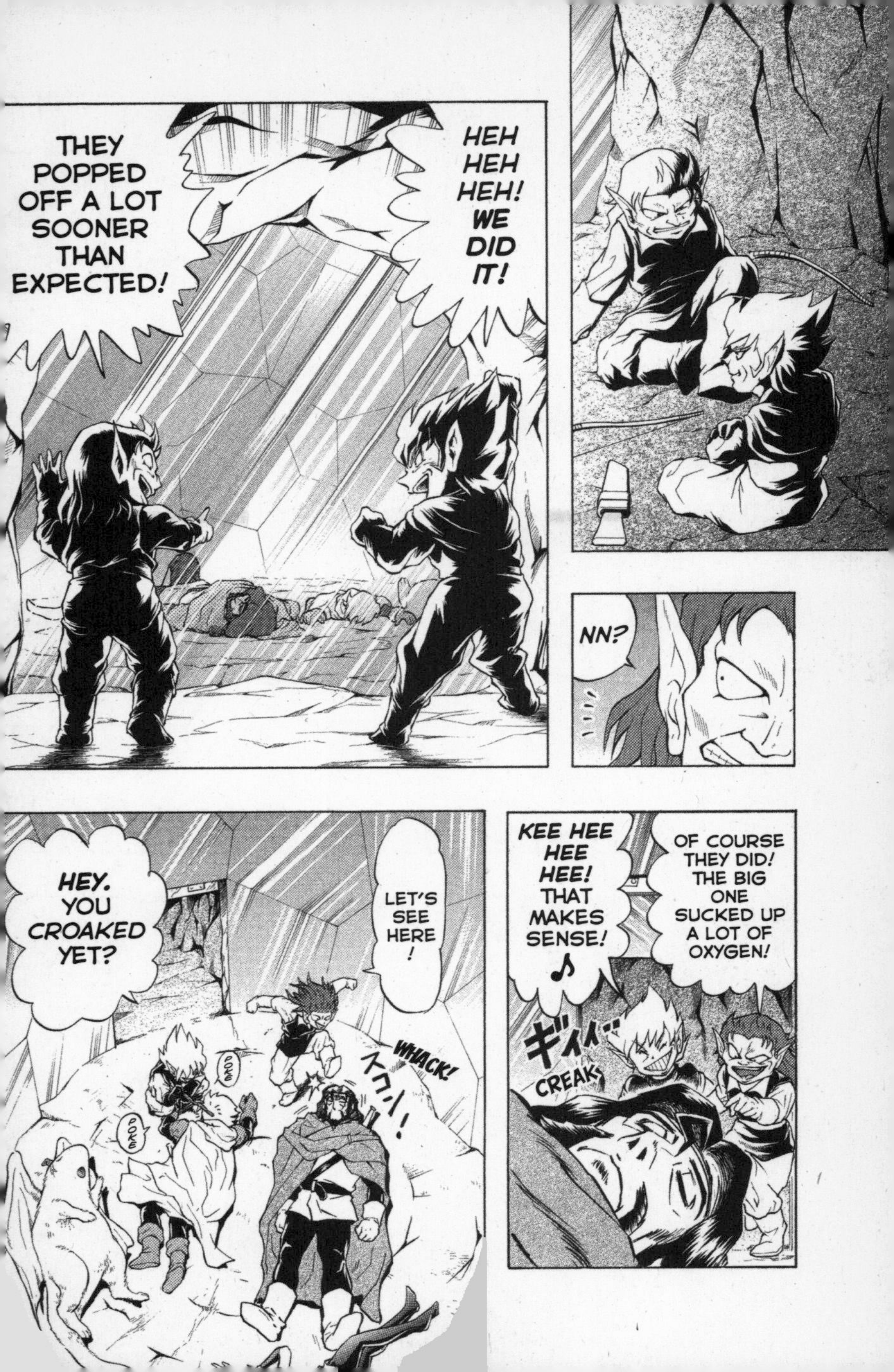
HEH HEH HEH! WE DID IT!
THEY POPPED OFF A LOT SOONER THAN EXPECTED!
NN?
OF COURSE THEY DID! THE BIG ONE SUCKED UP A LOT OF OXYGEN!
KEE HEE HEE HEE! THAT MAKES SENSE! ♪
ギィィ
CREAK
LET'S SEE HERE!
HEY. YOU CROAKED YET?
WHACK!
POKE
POKE

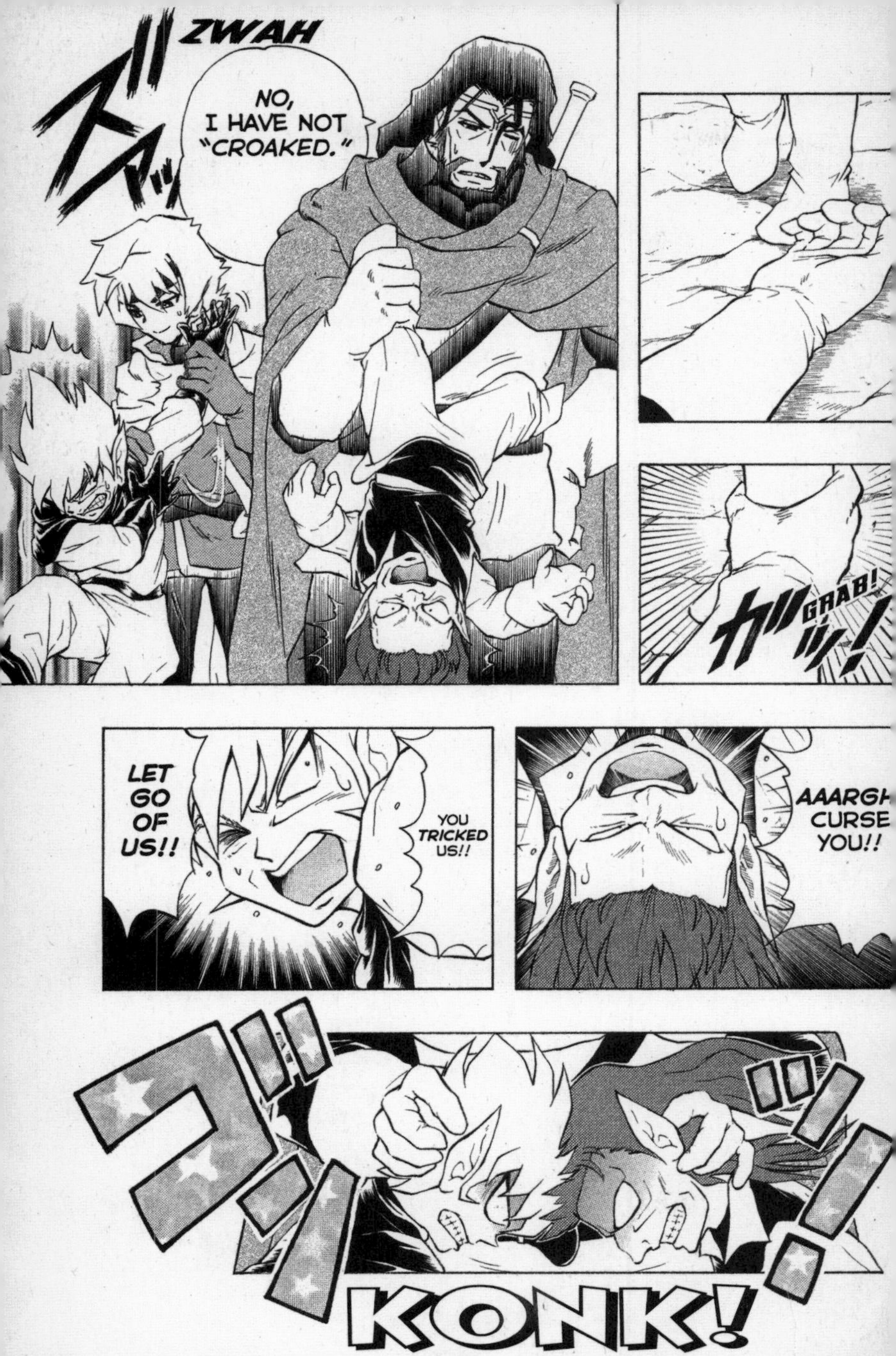
GRAB!
ZWAH
NO, I HAVE NOT "CROAKED."
AAARGH CURSE YOU!!
YOU TRICKED US!!
LET GO OF US!!
KONK!

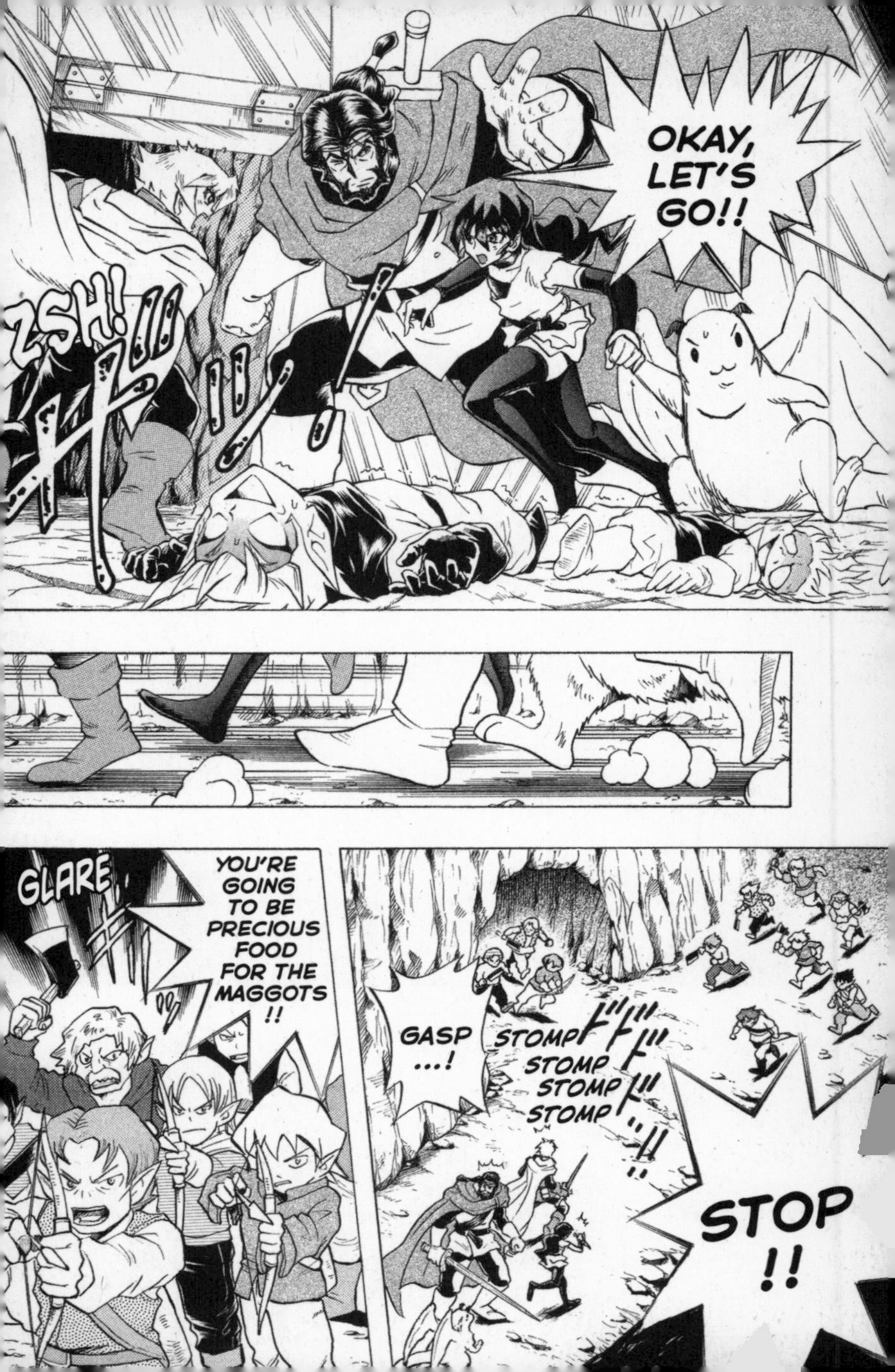
OKAY, LET'S GO!!
ZSH!
STOMP STOMP STOMP STOMP
GASP ...!
STOP !!
GLARE
YOU'RE GOING TO BE PRECIOUS FOOD FOR THE MAGGOTS !!

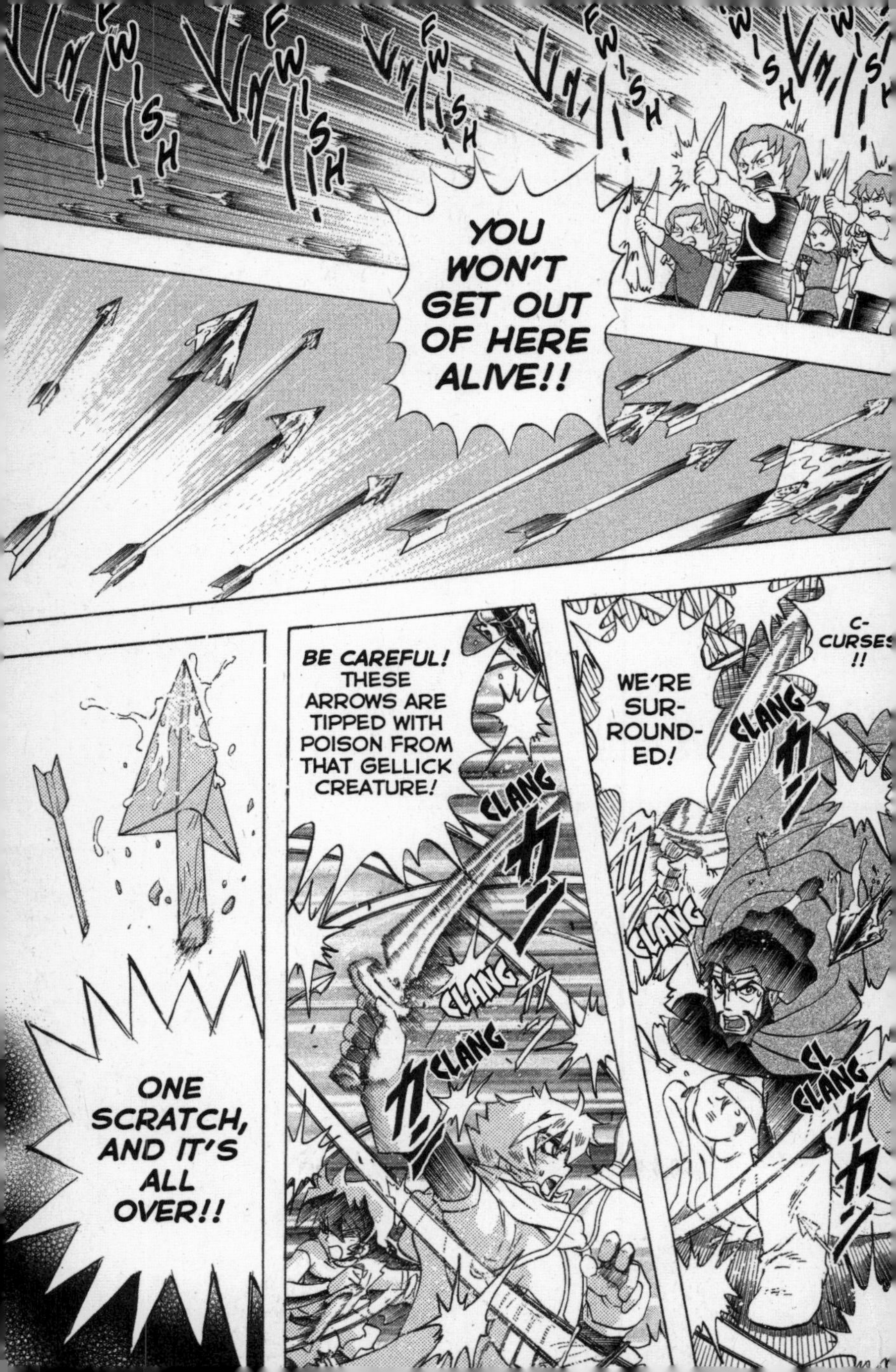

FWISH
FWISH
FWISH
FWISH
FWISH
FWISH
YOU WON'T GET OUT OF HERE ALIVE!!
C-CURSES!!
WE'RE SURROUNDED!
CLANG
CLANG
CL CLANG
BE CAREFUL! THESE ARROWS ARE TIPPED WITH POISON FROM THAT GELLICK CREATURE!
CLANG
CLANG
CLANG
CLANG
ONE SCRATCH, AND IT'S ALL OVER!!

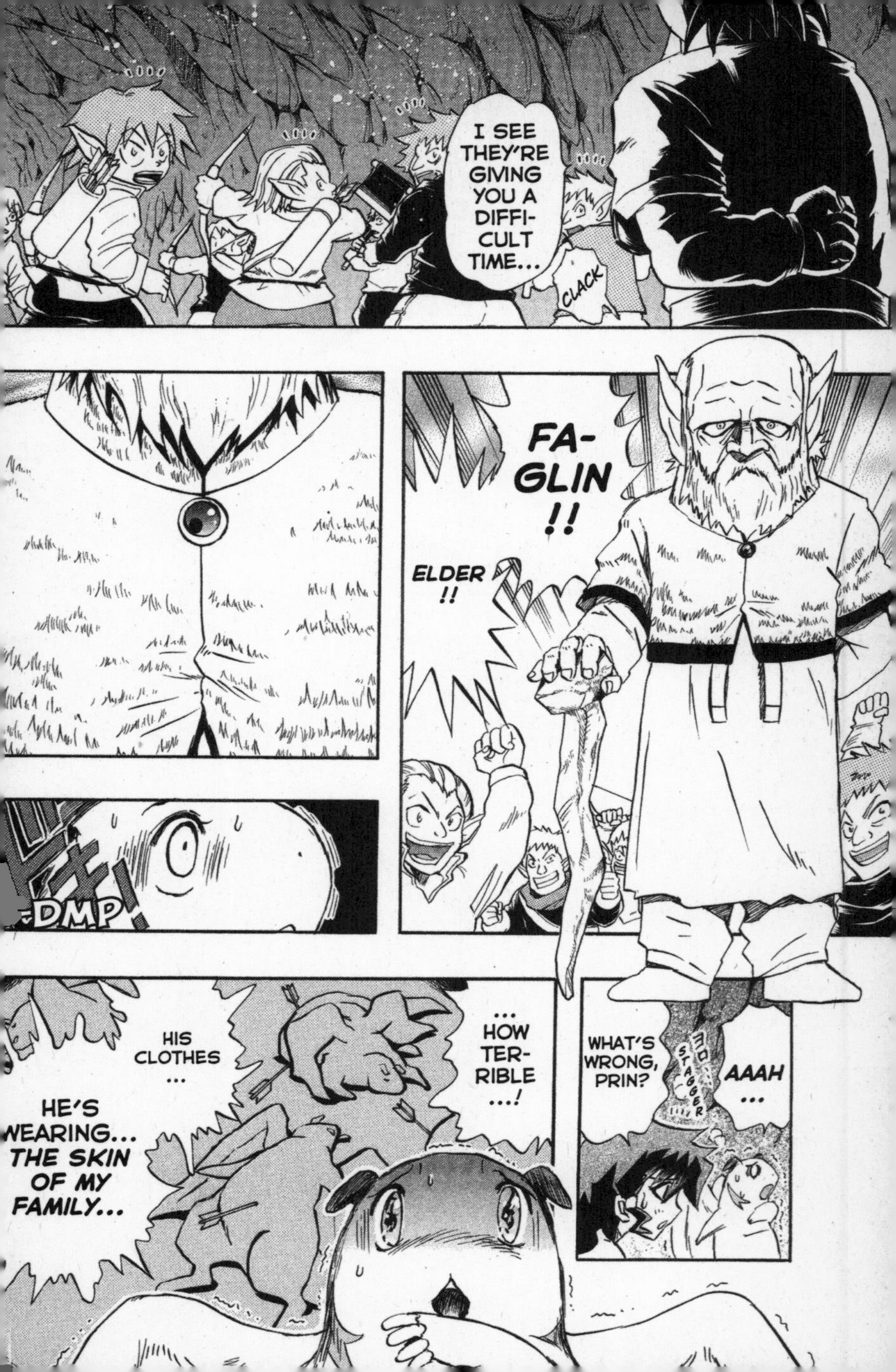
I SEE THEY'RE GIVING YOU A DIFFI-CULT TIME...
CLACK
FA-GLIN!!
ELDER!!
DMP
WHAT'S WRONG, PRIN?
STAGGER
AAAH...
...HOW TER-RIBLE...!
HIS CLOTHES...
HE'S WEARING... THE SKIN OF MY FAMILY...

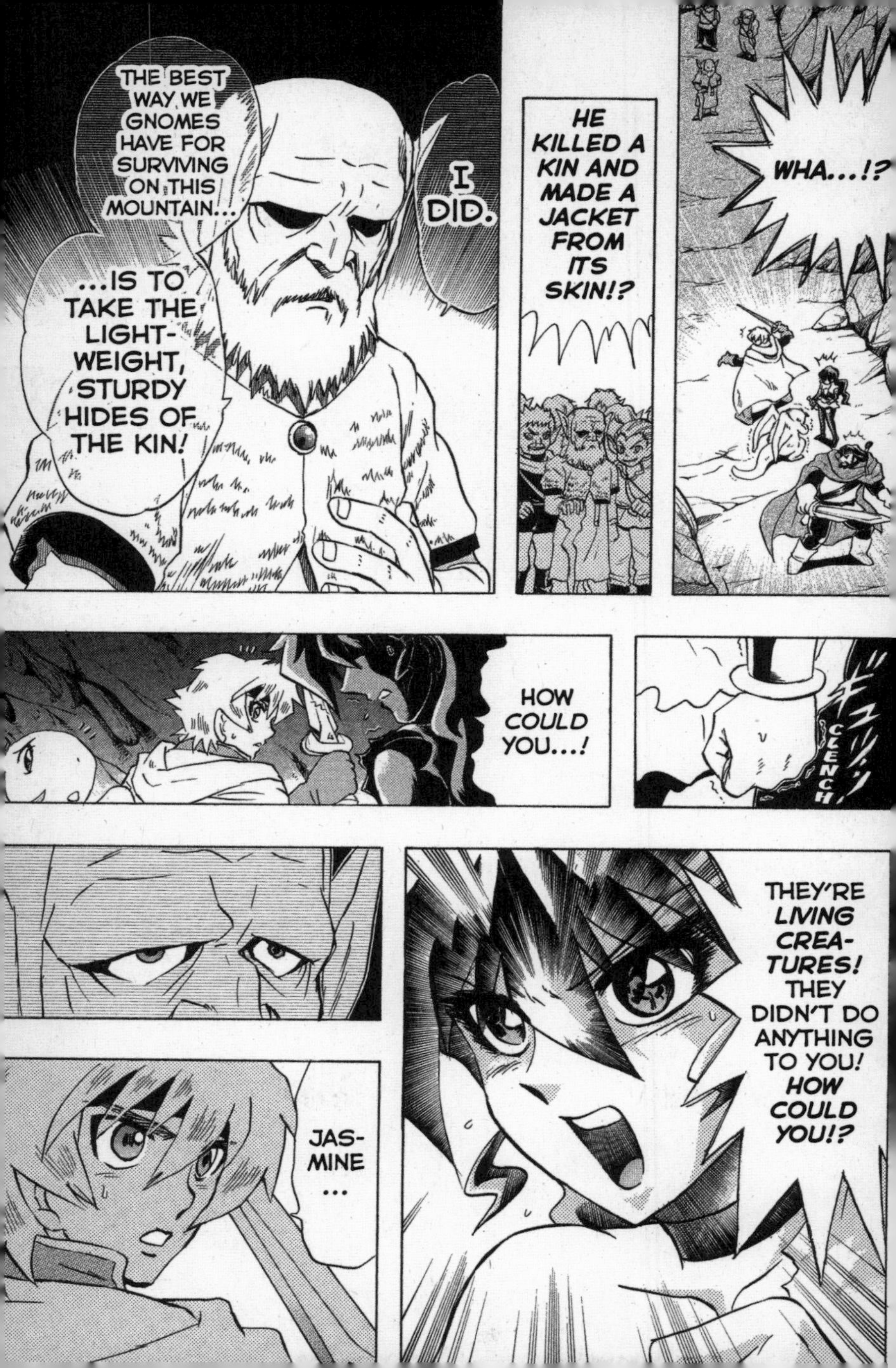
WHA...!?
HE KILLED A KIN AND MADE A JACKET FROM ITS SKIN!?
I DID.
THE BEST WAY WE GNOMES HAVE FOR SURVIVING ON THIS MOUNTAIN...
...IS TO TAKE THE LIGHT-WEIGHT, STURDY HIDES OF THE KIN!
CLENCH
HOW COULD YOU...!
THEY'RE LIVING CREA-TURES! THEY DIDN'T DO ANYTHING TO YOU! HOW COULD YOU!?
JAS-MINE ...

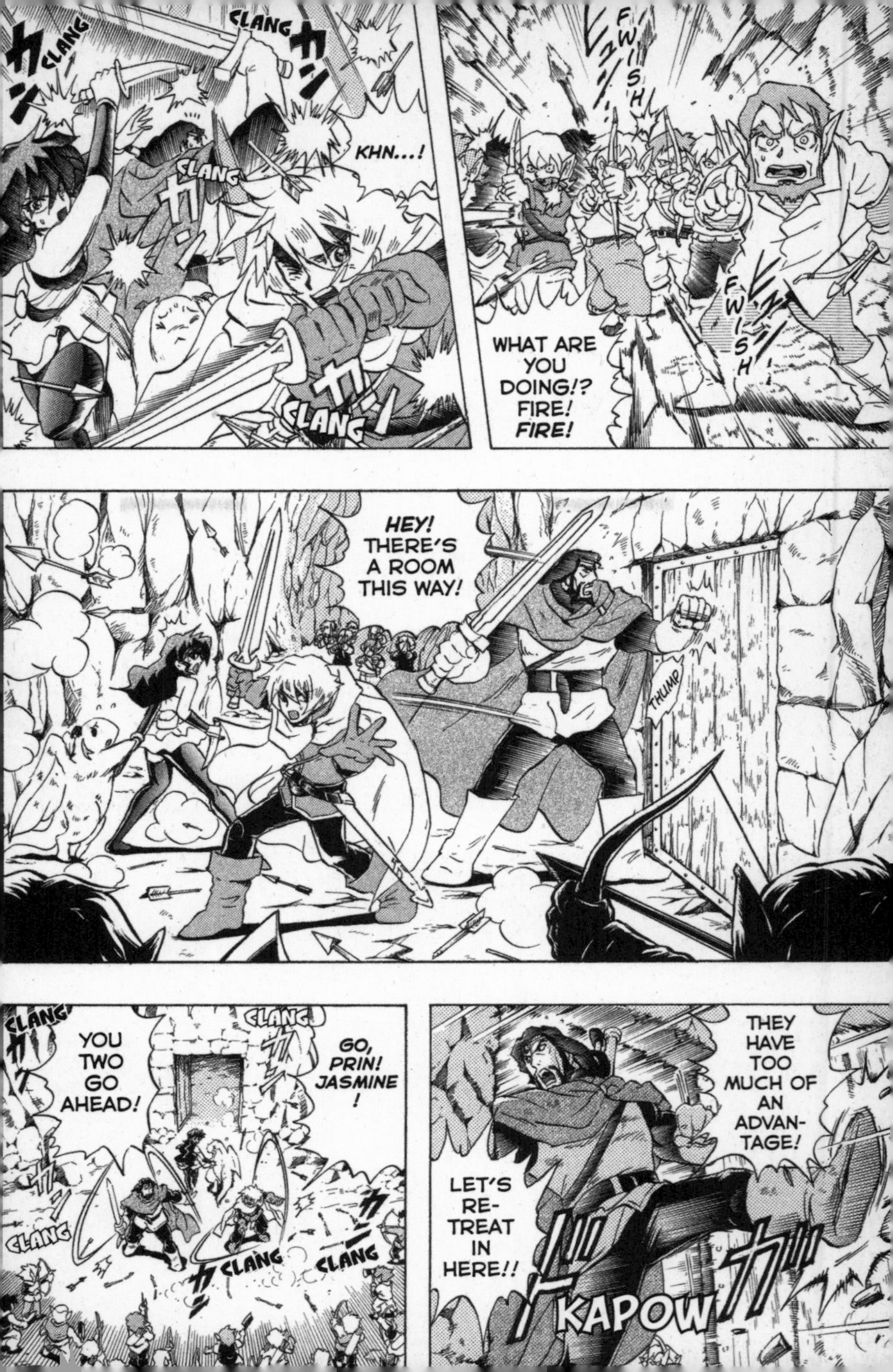
FWISH
WHAT ARE YOU DOING!? FIRE! FIRE!
FWISH
CLANG
CLANG
CLANG
KHN...!
CLANG
CLANG
HEY! THERE'S A ROOM THIS WAY!
THUMP
THEY HAVE TOO MUCH OF AN ADVANTAGE!
LET'S RETREAT IN HERE!!
KAPOW
CLANG
GO, PRIN! JASMINE!
CLANG
YOU TWO GO AHEAD!
CLANG
CLANG
CLANG

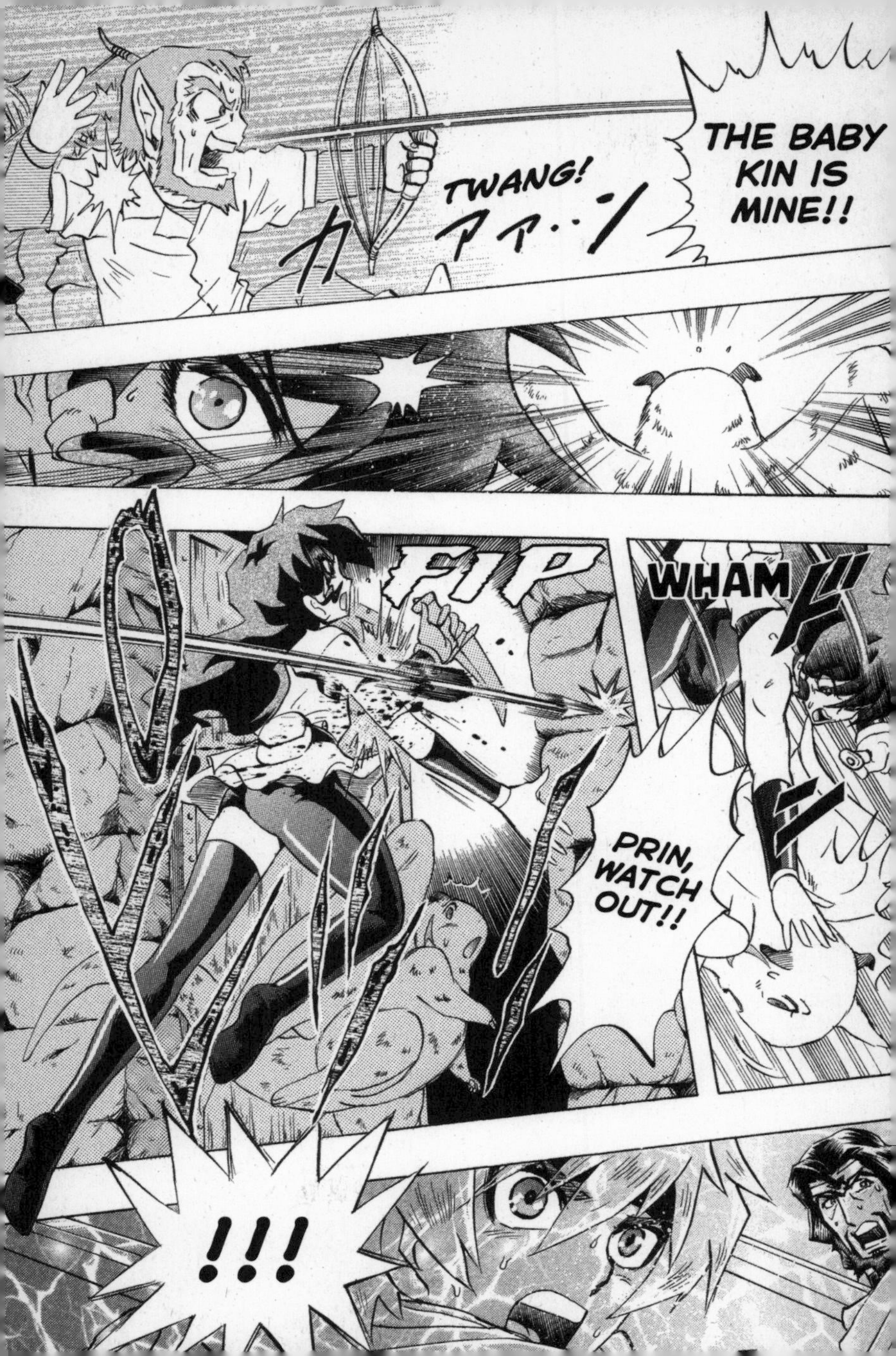
THE BABY KIN IS MINE!!
TWANG!
WHAM
PRIN, WATCH OUT!!
FIP
!!!

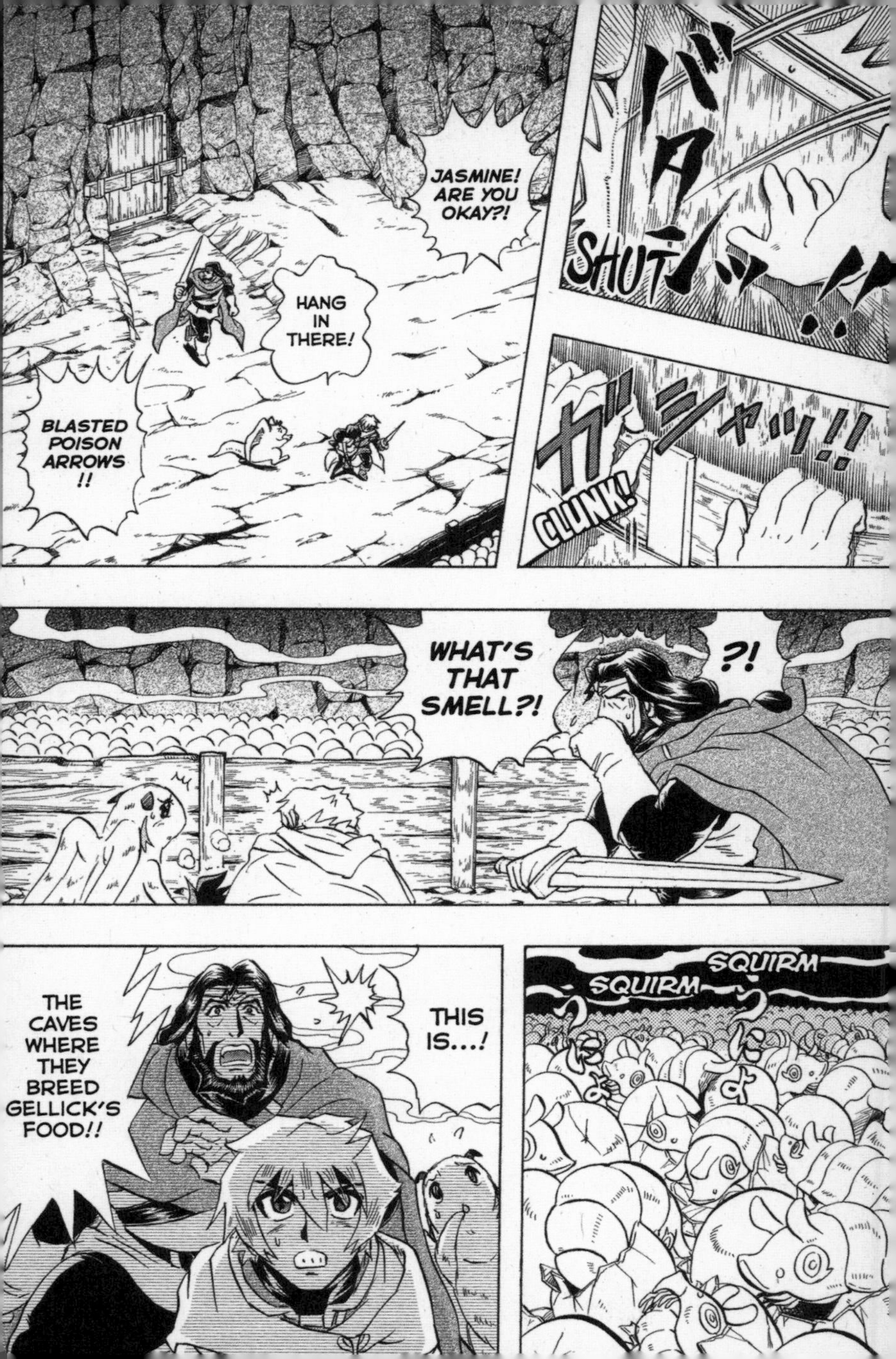
SHUT
バタッ!!
CLUNK!
ガシャッ!!
JASMINE! ARE YOU OKAY?!
HANG IN THERE!
BLASTED POISON ARROWS !!
?!
WHAT'S THAT SMELL?!
SQUIRM
SQUIRM
THIS IS...!
THE CAVES WHERE THEY BREED GELLICK'S FOOD!!

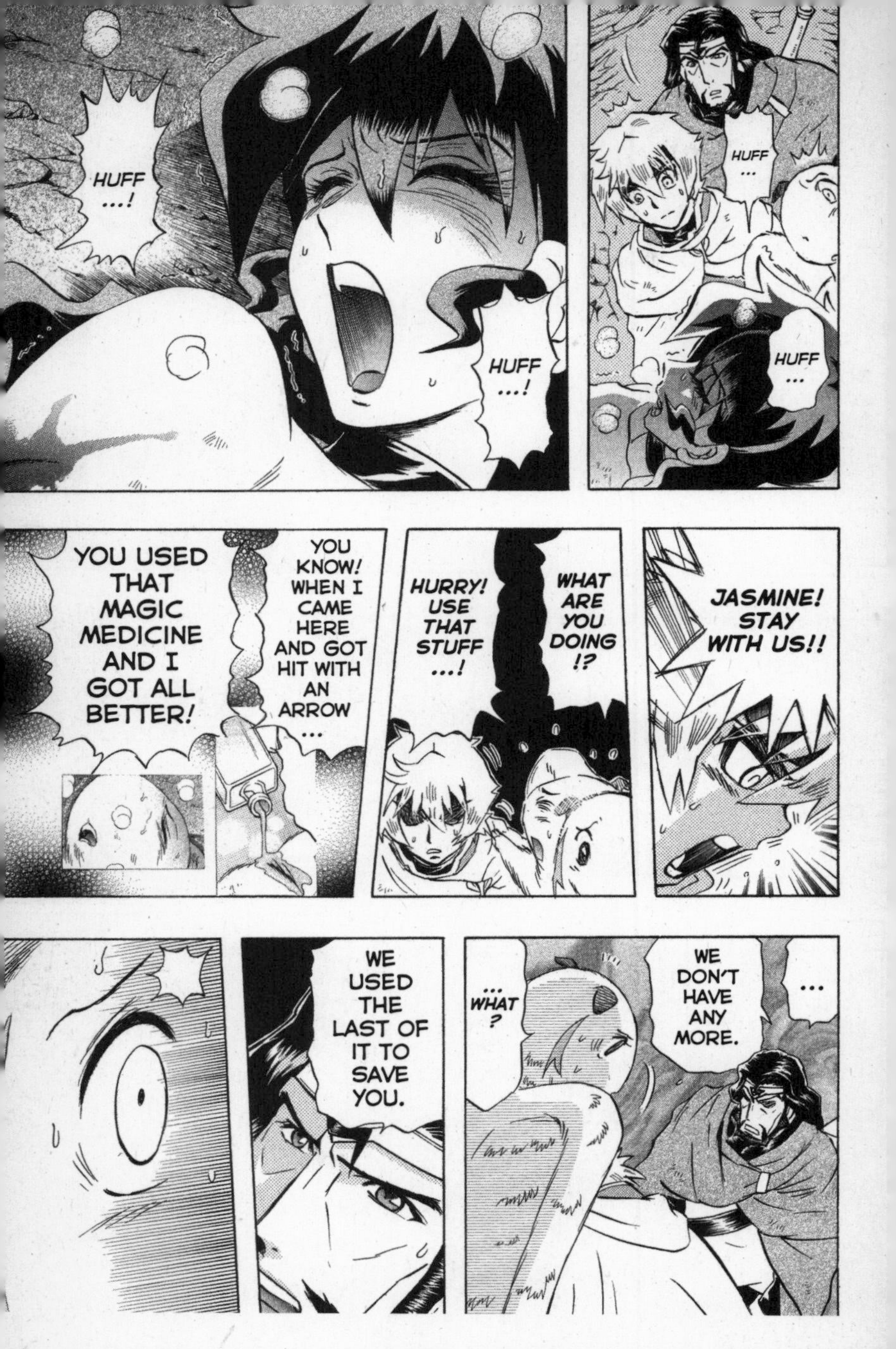
HUFF ...
HUFF ...
HUFF ...!
HUFF ...!
JASMINE! STAY WITH US!!
WHAT ARE YOU DOING !?
HURRY! USE THAT STUFF ...!
YOU KNOW! WHEN I CAME HERE AND GOT HIT WITH AN ARROW ...
YOU USED THAT MAGIC MEDICINE AND I GOT ALL BETTER!
...
WE DON'T HAVE ANY MORE.
... WHAT ?
WE USED THE LAST OF IT TO SAVE YOU.

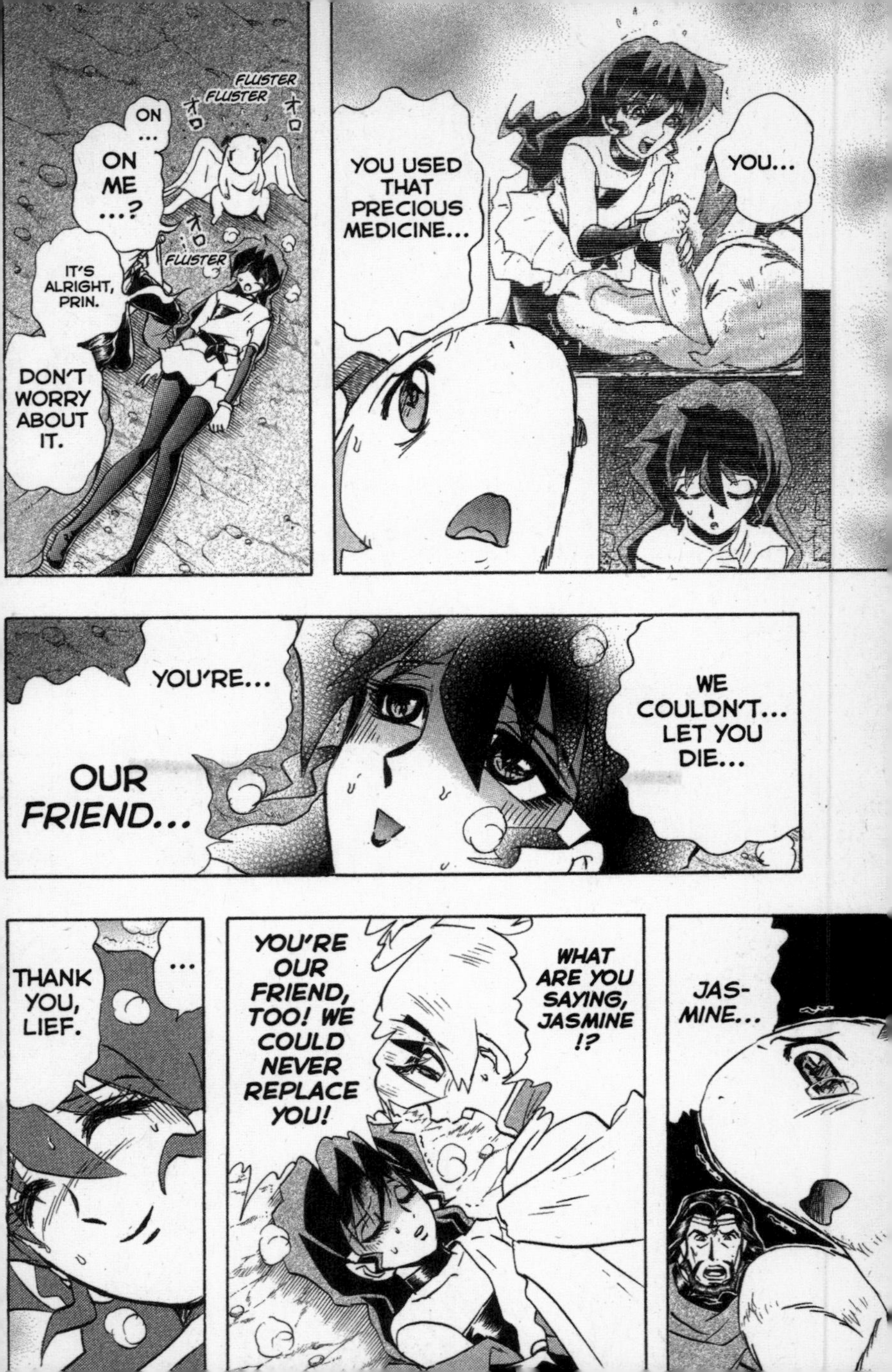
YOU...
YOU USED THAT PRECIOUS MEDICINE...
FLUSTER FLUSTER
オロ
オロ
ON... ON ME...?
オロ
FLUSTER
IT'S ALRIGHT, PRIN.
DON'T WORRY ABOUT IT.
WE COULDN'T... LET YOU DIE...
YOU'RE...
OUR FRIEND...
JAS-MINE...
WHAT ARE YOU SAYING, JASMINE!?
YOU'RE OUR FRIEND, TOO! WE COULD NEVER REPLACE YOU!
...
THANK YOU, LIEF.

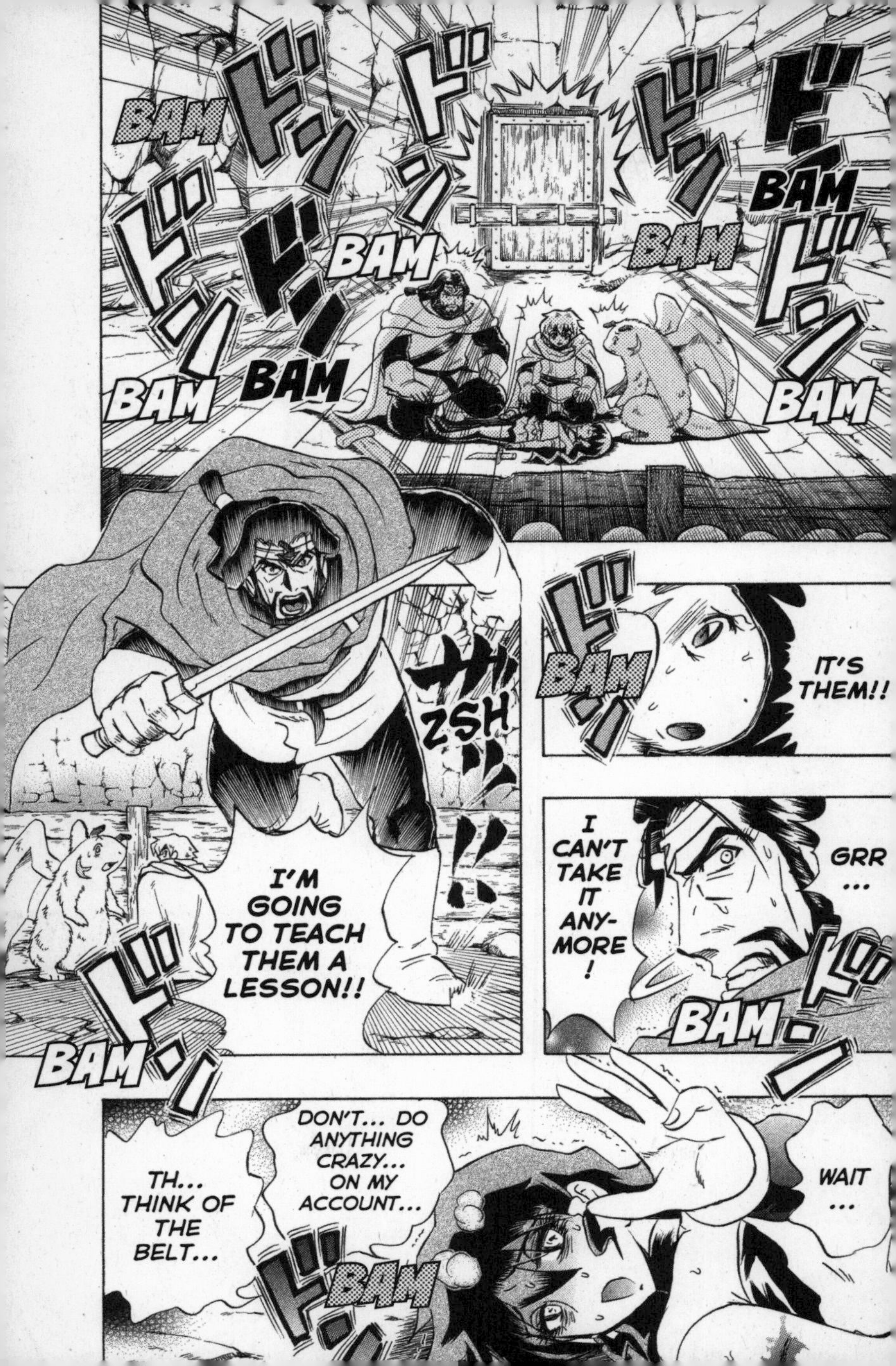
BAM
BAM
BAM
BAM
BAM
BAM
BAM
BAM
IT'S THEM!!
BAM
GRR ...
I CAN'T TAKE IT ANY-MORE!
BAM
ZSH
I'M GOING TO TEACH THEM A LESSON!!
BAM
WAIT ...
DON'T... DO ANYTHING CRAZY... ON MY ACCOUNT...
TH... THINK OF THE BELT...
BAM

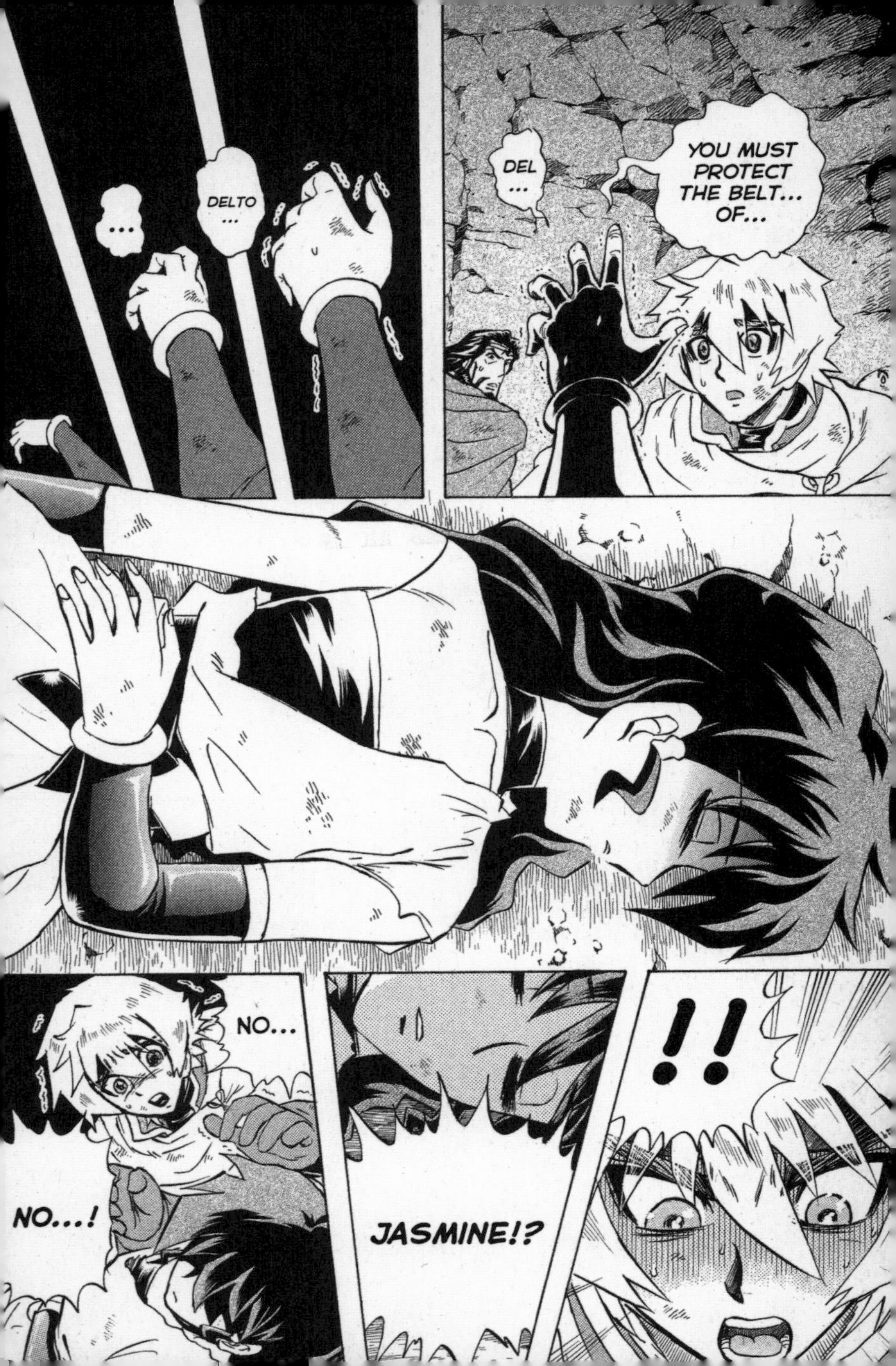
YOU MUST PROTECT THE BELT... OF...
DEL ...
DELTO ...
...
!!
JASMINE!?
NO...
NO...!

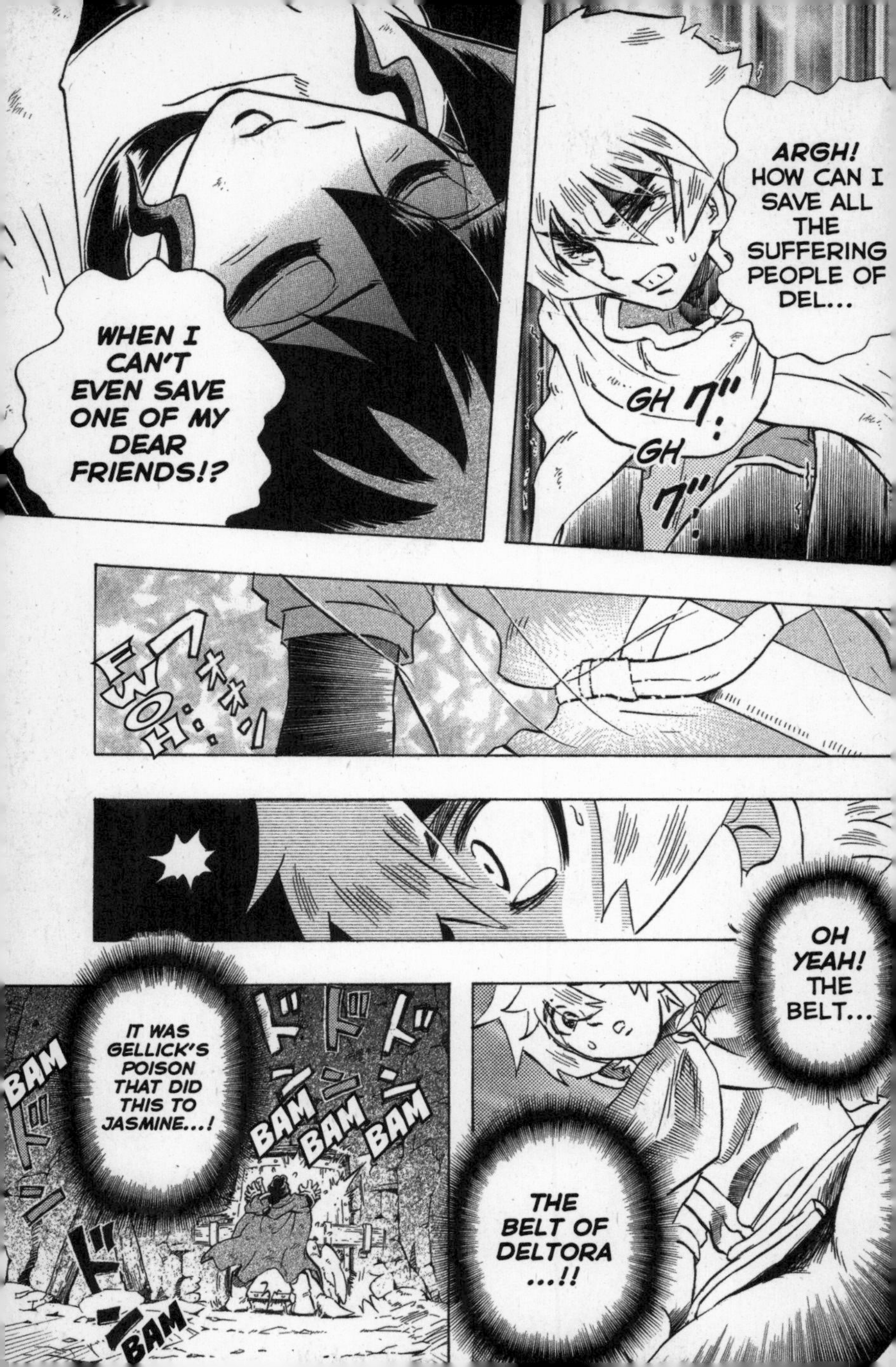
ARGH! HOW CAN I SAVE ALL THE SUFFERING PEOPLE OF DEL...
GH
GH
WHEN I CAN'T EVEN SAVE ONE OF MY DEAR FRIENDS!?
OH YEAH! THE BELT...
THE BELT OF DELTORA ...!!
IT WAS GELLICK'S POISON THAT DID THIS TO JASMINE...!
BAM
BAM
BAM
BAM
BAM

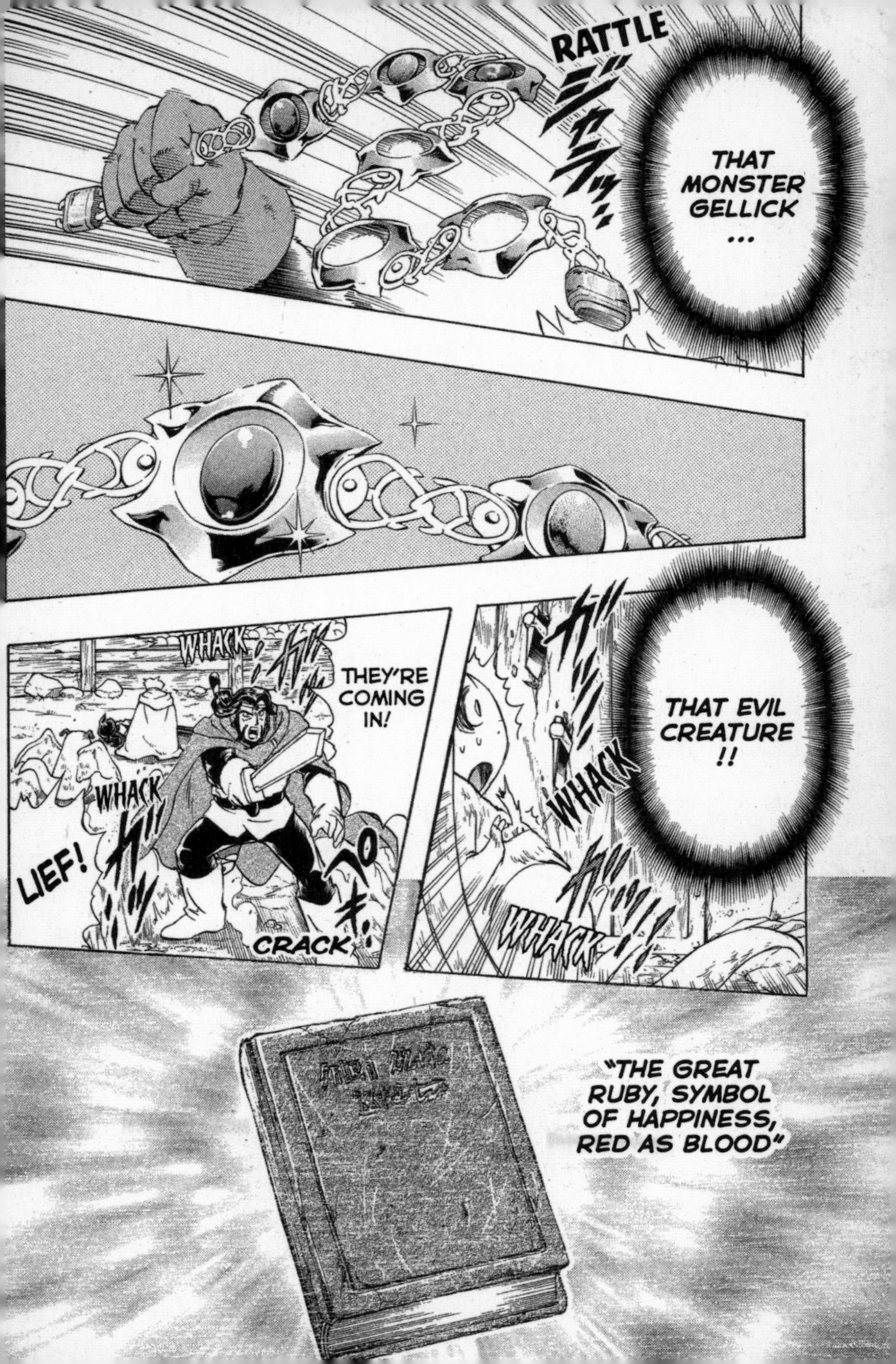
RATTLE
THAT MONSTER GELLICK ...
THAT EVIL CREATURE !!
WHACK
WHACK
WHACK
THEY'RE COMING IN!
WHACK
LIEF!
CRACK
"THE GREAT RUBY, SYMBOL OF HAPPINESS, RED AS BLOOD"

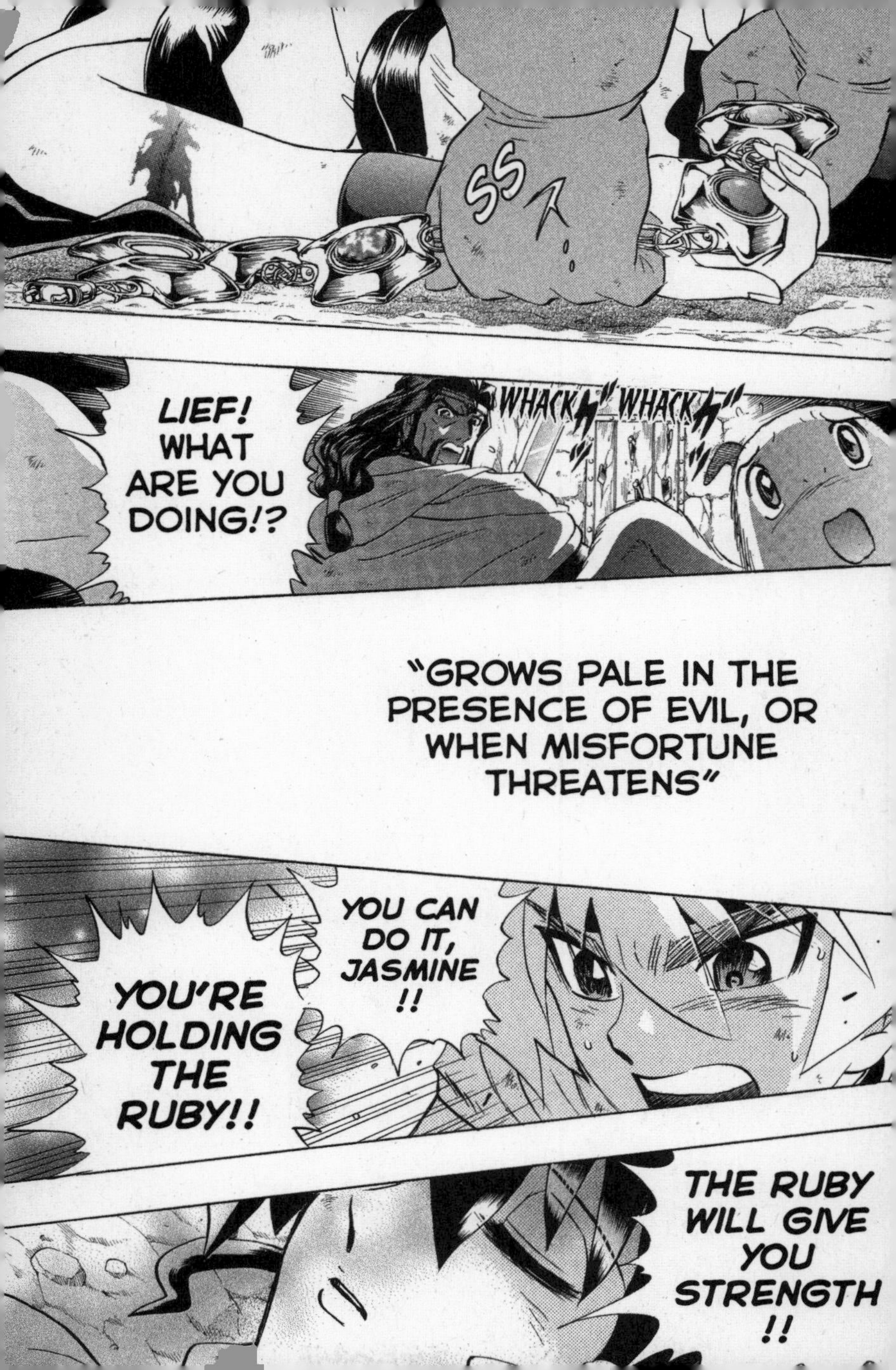
SS
WHACK WHACK
LIEF! WHAT ARE YOU DOING!?
"GROWS PALE IN THE PRESENCE OF EVIL, OR WHEN MISFORTUNE THREATENS"
YOU CAN DO IT, JASMINE!!
YOU'RE HOLDING THE RUBY!!
THE RUBY WILL GIVE YOU STRENGTH!!

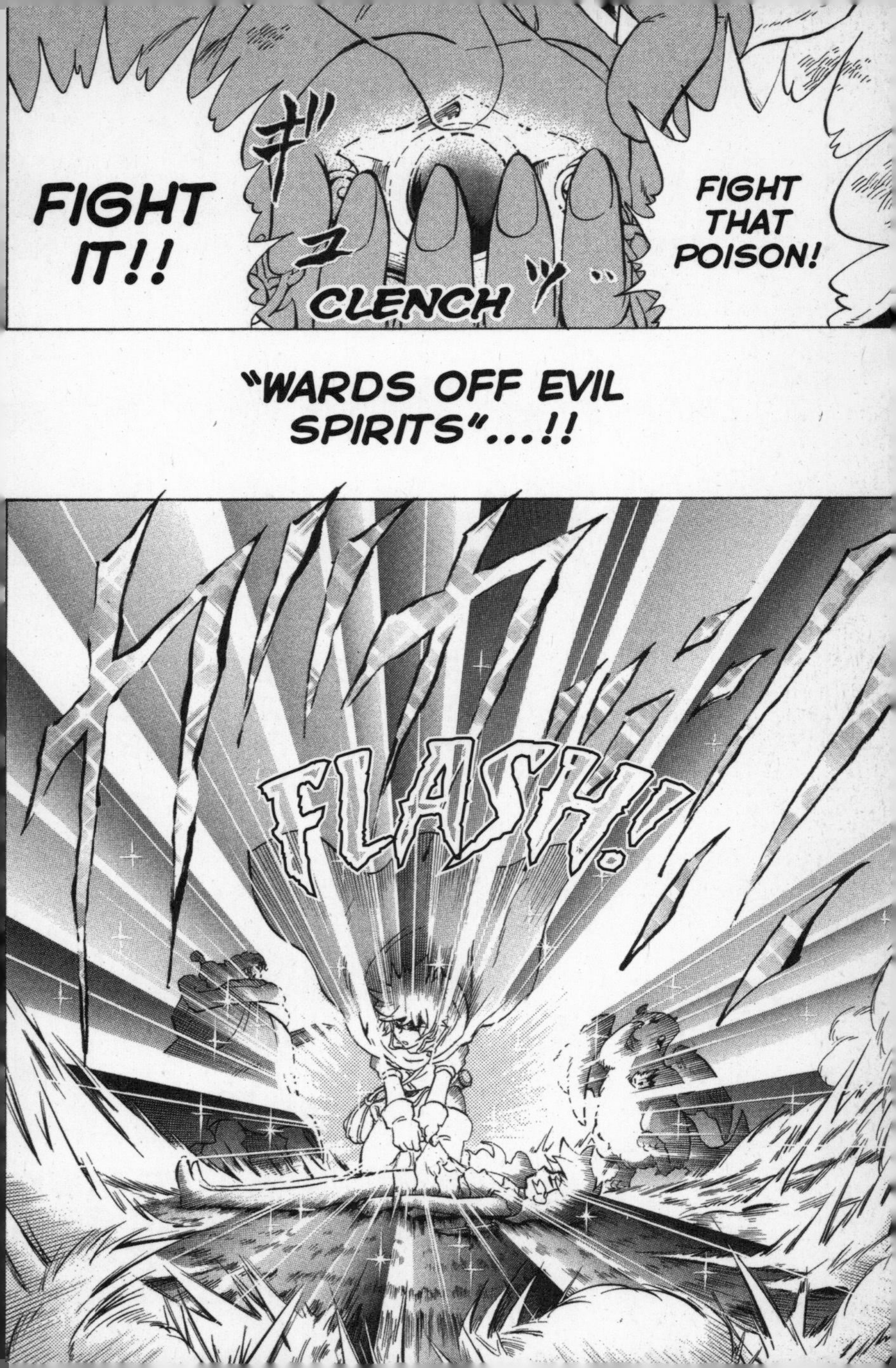
FIGHT THAT POISON!
CLENCH
FIGHT IT!!
"WARDS OFF EVIL SPIRITS"...!!
FLASH!

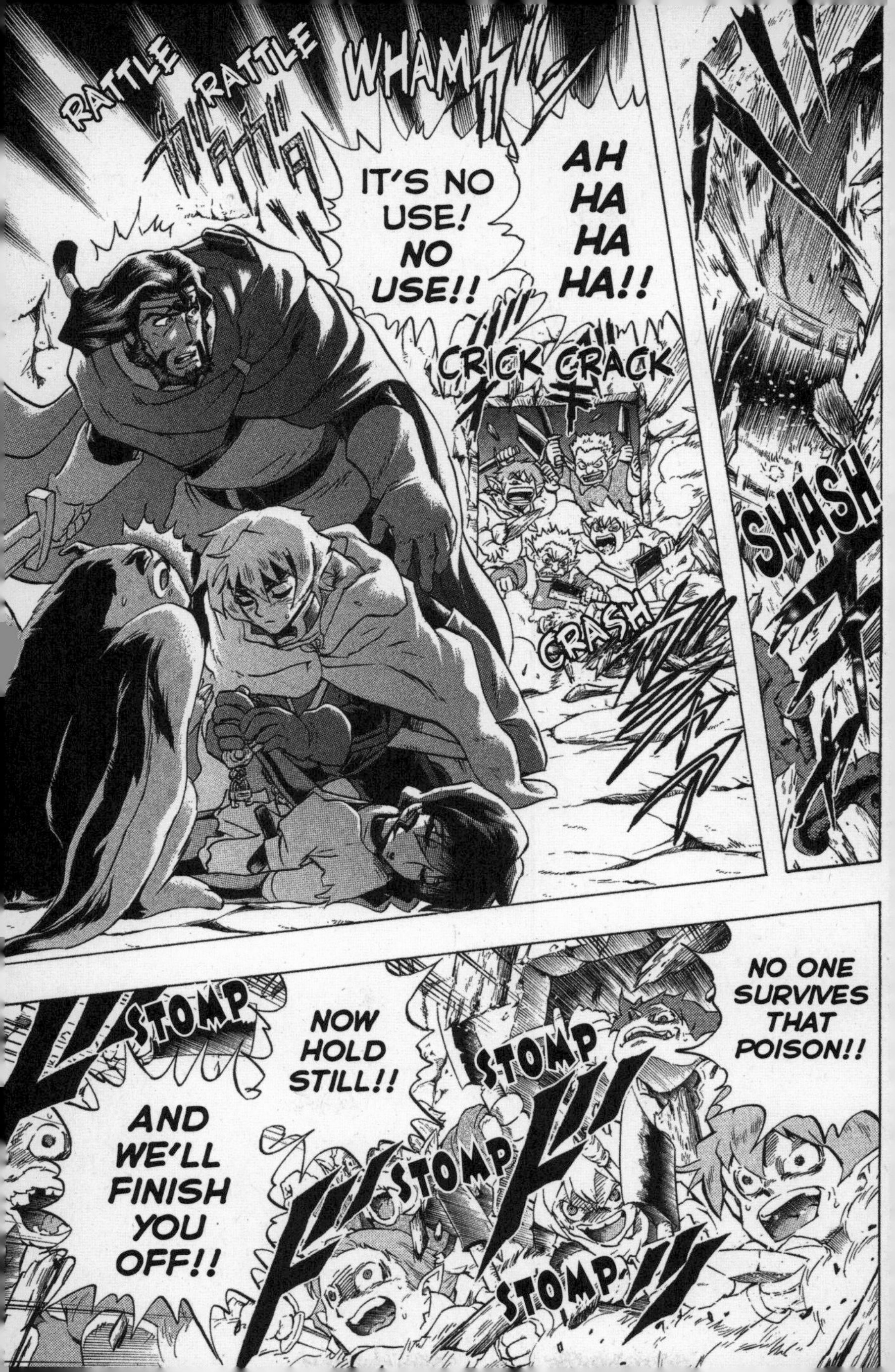

SHASH
AH HA HA HA!!
IT'S NO USE! NO USE!!
CRICK CRACK
CRASH
WHAM
RATTLE RATTLE
NO ONE SURVIVES THAT POISON!!
STOMP
NOW HOLD STILL!!
STOMP
AND WE'LL FINISH YOU OFF!!
STOMP
STOMP!!

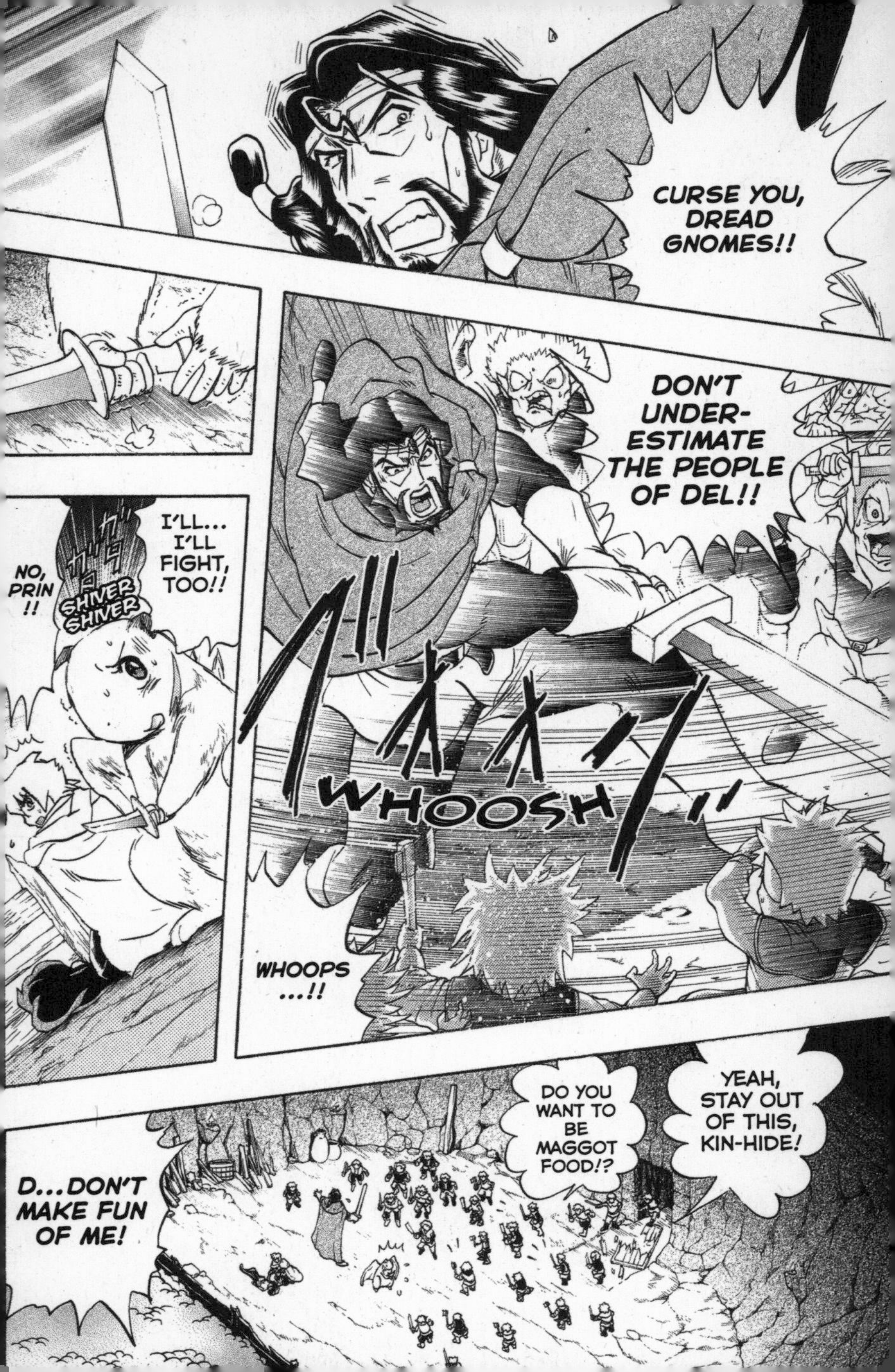

CURSE YOU, DREAD GNOMES!!
DON'T UNDER-ESTIMATE THE PEOPLE OF DEL!!
WHOOSH
WHOOPS ...!!
I'LL... I'LL FIGHT, TOO!!
SHIVER SHIVER
NO, PRIN !!
YEAH, STAY OUT OF THIS, KIN-HIDE!
DO YOU WANT TO BE MAGGOT FOOD!?
D...DON'T MAKE FUN OF ME!

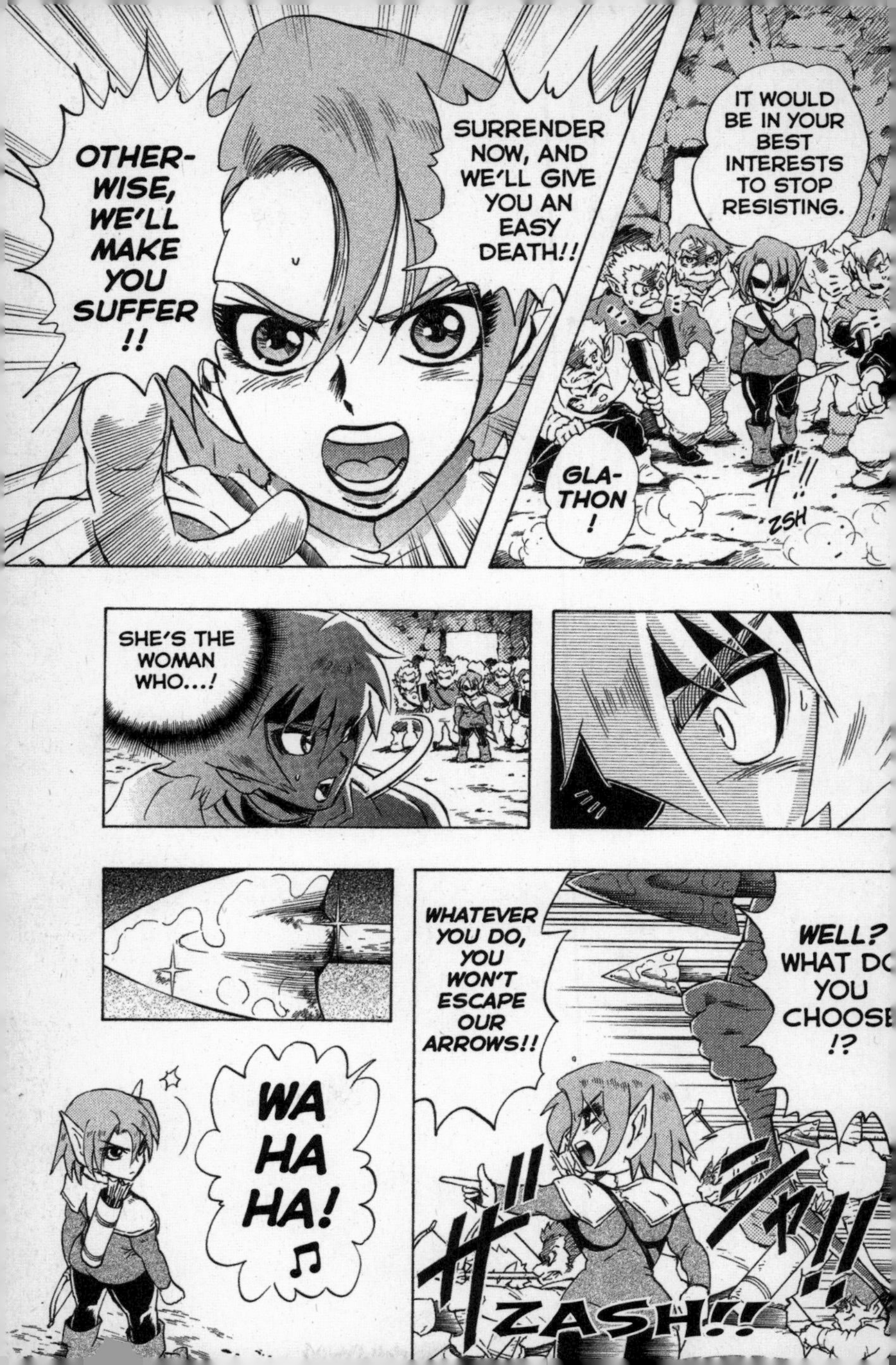
IT WOULD BE IN YOUR BEST INTERESTS TO STOP RESISTING.
GLA-THON!
ZSH
SURRENDER NOW, AND WE'LL GIVE YOU AN EASY DEATH!!
OTHER-WISE, WE'LL MAKE YOU SUFFER!!
SHE'S THE WOMAN WHO...!
WELL? WHAT DO YOU CHOOSE!?
WHATEVER YOU DO, YOU WON'T ESCAPE OUR ARROWS!!
ZASH!!
WA HA HA! ♫

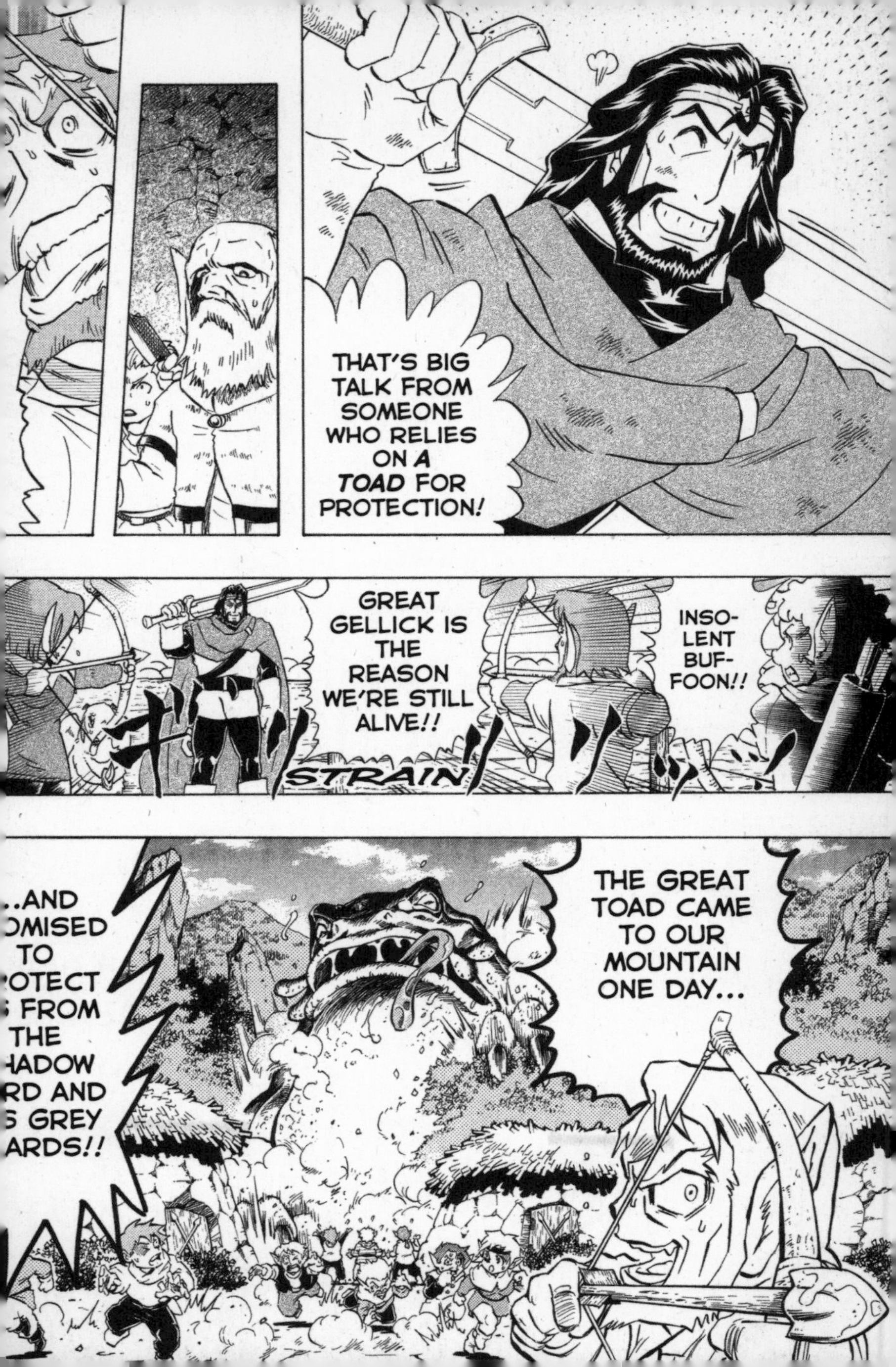
THAT'S BIG TALK FROM SOMEONE WHO RELIES ON *A* *TOAD* FOR PROTECTION!
INSO-LENT BUF-FOON!!
GREAT GELLICK IS THE REASON WE'RE STILL ALIVE!!
STRAIN
THE GREAT TOAD CAME TO OUR MOUNTAIN ONE DAY...
..AND OMISED TO OTECT FROM THE HADOW RD AND GREY ARDS!!

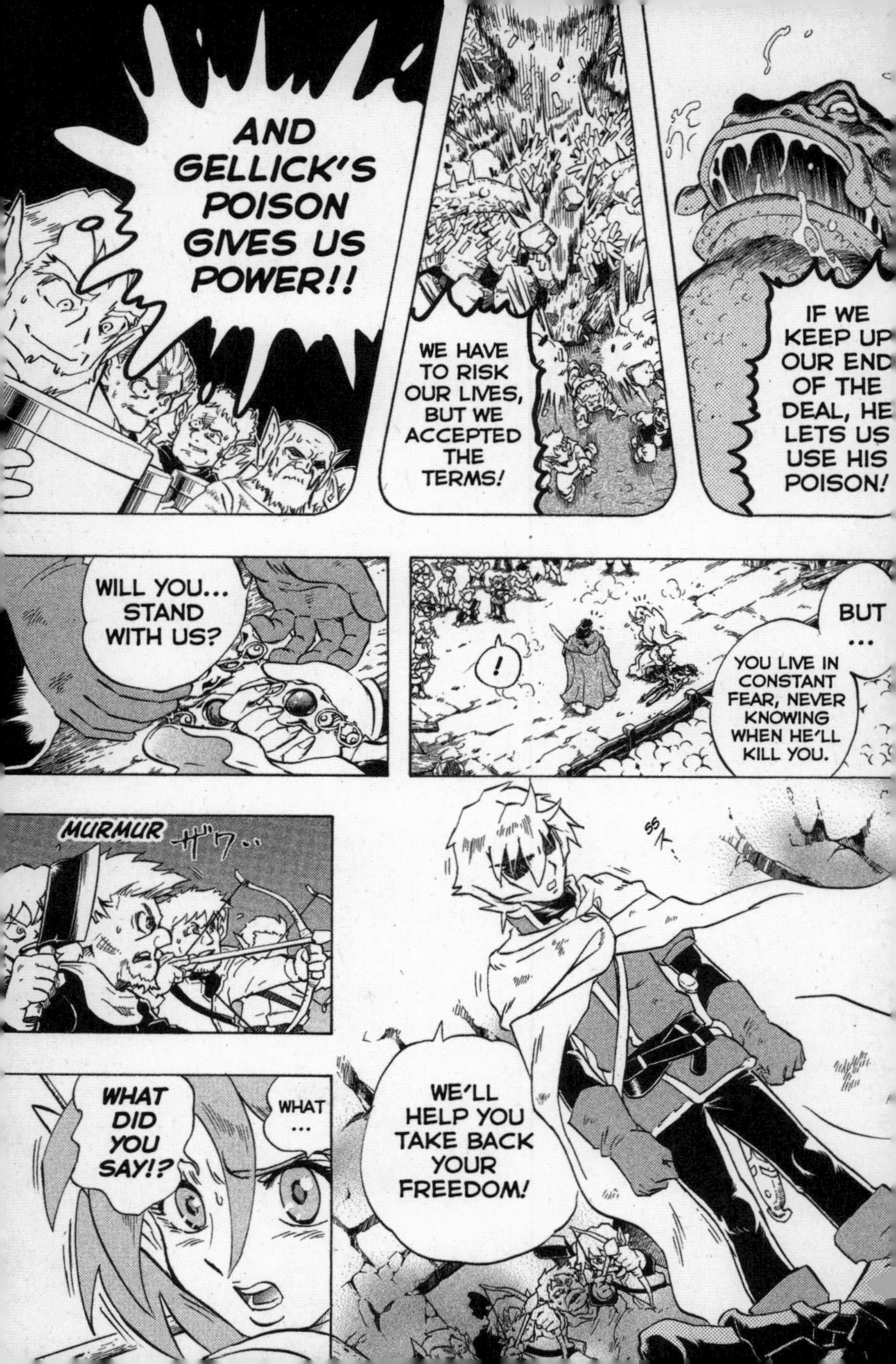
IF WE KEEP UP OUR END OF THE DEAL, HE LETS US USE HIS POISON!
WE HAVE TO RISK OUR LIVES, BUT WE ACCEPTED THE TERMS!
AND GELLICK'S POISON GIVES US POWER!!
BUT ...
YOU LIVE IN CONSTANT FEAR, NEVER KNOWING WHEN HE'LL KILL YOU.
!
WILL YOU... STAND WITH US?
SS
WE'LL HELP YOU TAKE BACK YOUR FREEDOM!
MURMUR
ザワ…
WHAT ...
WHAT DID YOU SAY!?

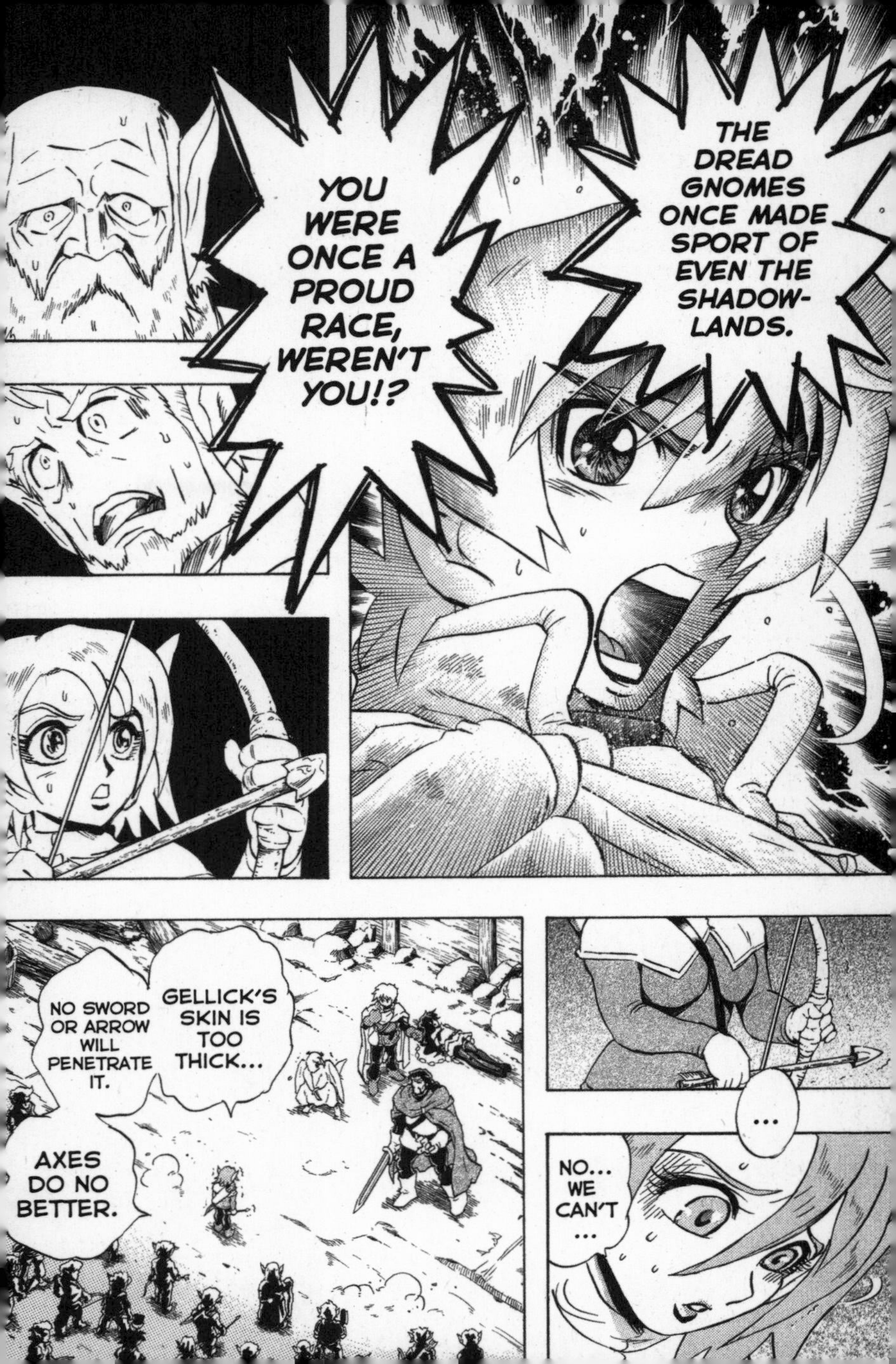
THE DREAD GNOMES ONCE MADE SPORT OF EVEN THE SHADOW-LANDS.
YOU WERE ONCE A PROUD RACE, WEREN'T YOU!?
...
NO... WE CAN'T ...
GELLICK'S SKIN IS TOO THICK...
NO SWORD OR ARROW WILL PENETRATE IT.
AXES DO NO BETTER.

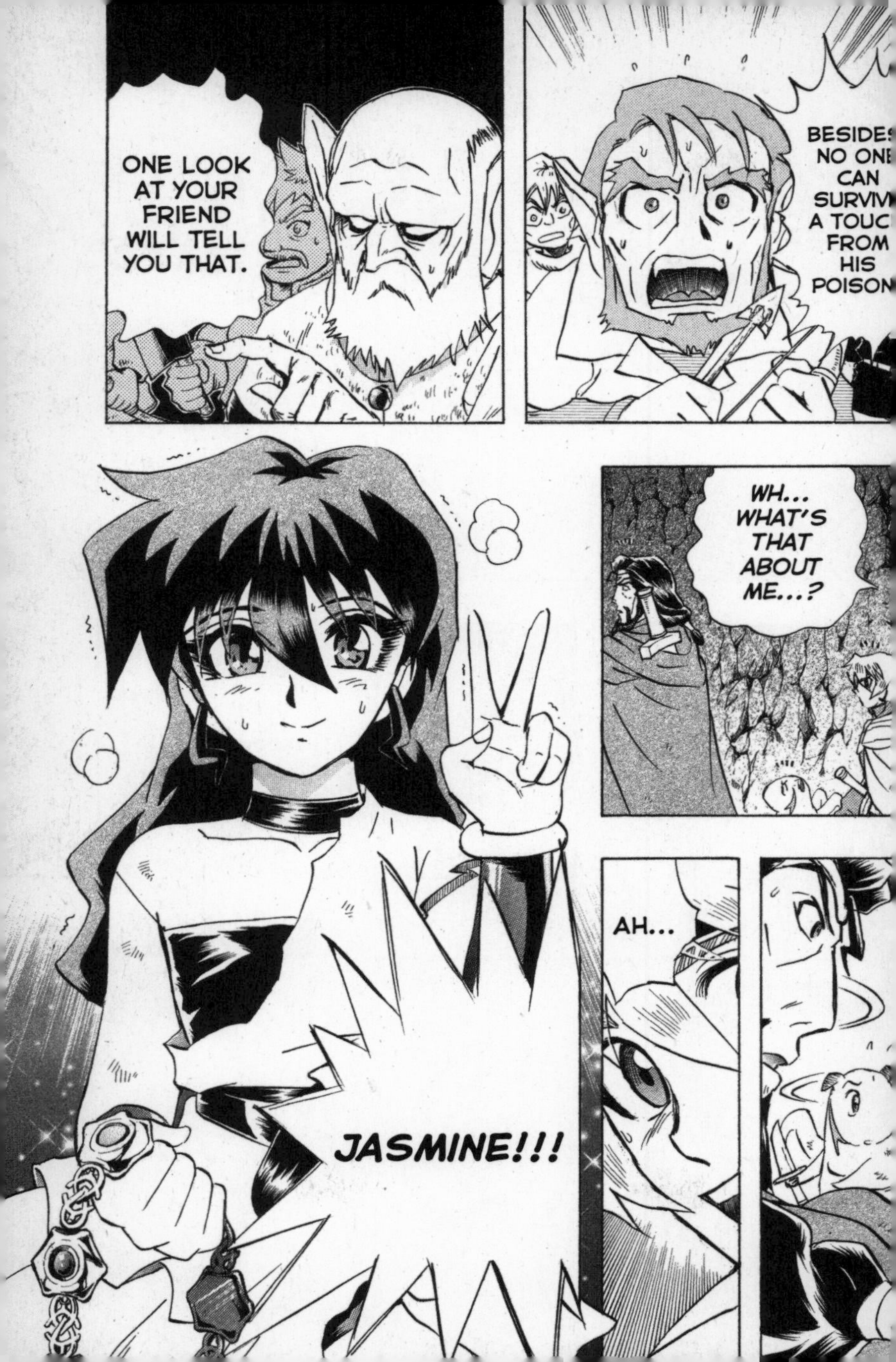
BESIDES NO ONE CAN SURVIV A TOUC FROM HIS POISON
ONE LOOK AT YOUR FRIEND WILL TELL YOU THAT.
WH... WHAT'S THAT ABOUT ME...?
AH...
JASMINE!!!

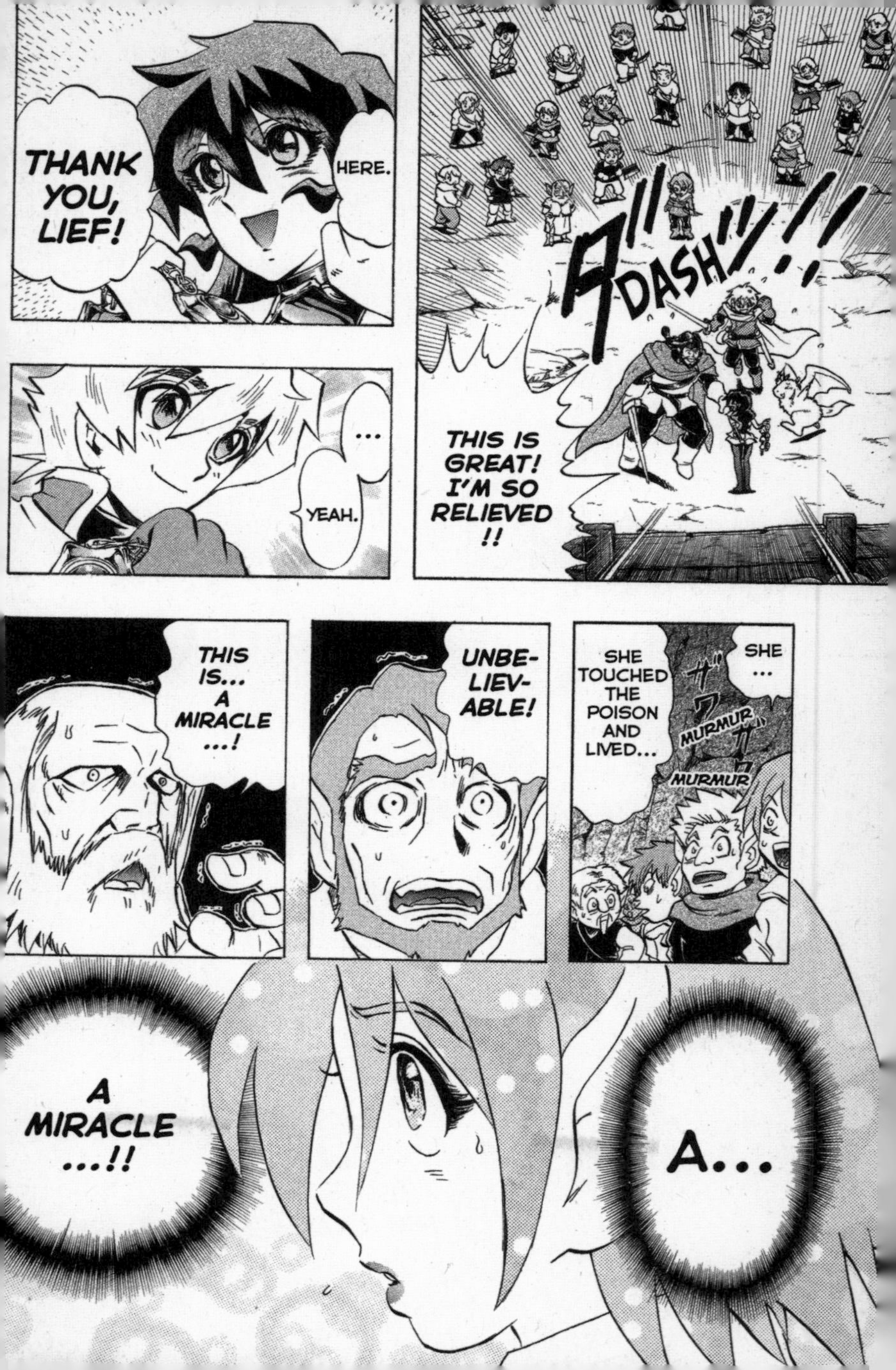
DASH!!
THIS IS GREAT! I'M SO RELIEVED!!
HERE.
THANK YOU, LIEF!
...
YEAH.
SHE...
SHE TOUCHED THE POISON AND LIVED...
MURMUR
MURMUR
UNBE-LIEV-ABLE!
THIS IS... A MIRACLE...!
A...
A MIRACLE...!!

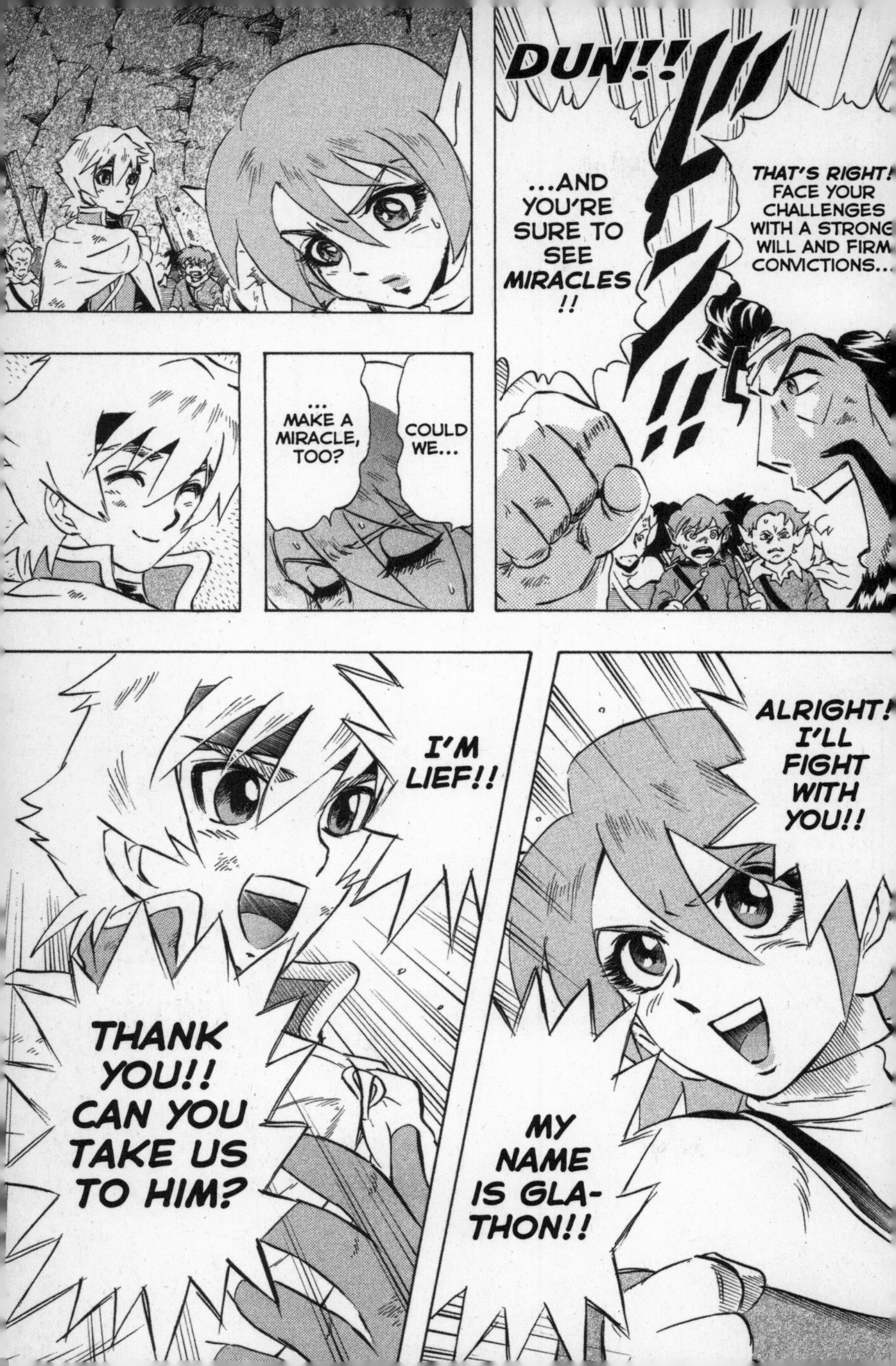

DUN!!
THAT'S RIGHT! FACE YOUR CHALLENGES WITH A STRONG WILL AND FIRM CONVICTIONS...
...AND YOU'RE SURE TO SEE MIRACLES!!
COULD WE...
...MAKE A MIRACLE, TOO?
ALRIGHT! I'LL FIGHT WITH YOU!!
MY NAME IS GLA-THON!!
I'M LIEF!!
THANK YOU!! CAN YOU TAKE US TO HIM?

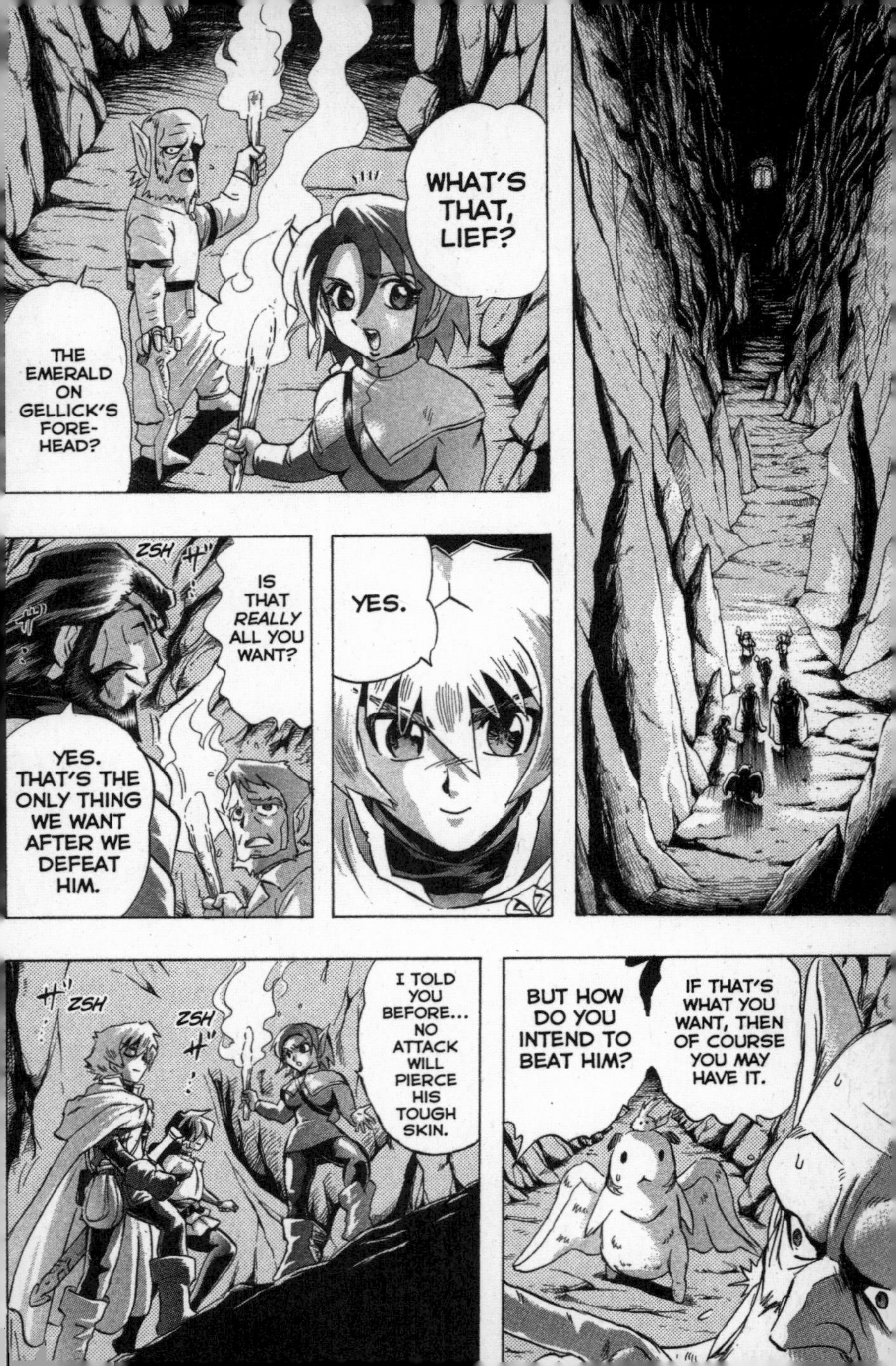
WHAT'S THAT, LIEF?
THE EMERALD ON GELLICK'S FORE-HEAD?
ZSH
IS THAT *REALLY* ALL YOU WANT?
YES. THAT'S THE ONLY THING WE WANT AFTER WE DEFEAT HIM.
YES.
ZSH
ZSH
I TOLD YOU BEFORE... NO ATTACK WILL PIERCE HIS TOUGH SKIN.
BUT HOW DO YOU INTEND TO BEAT HIM?
IF THAT'S WHAT YOU WANT, THEN OF COURSE YOU MAY HAVE IT.

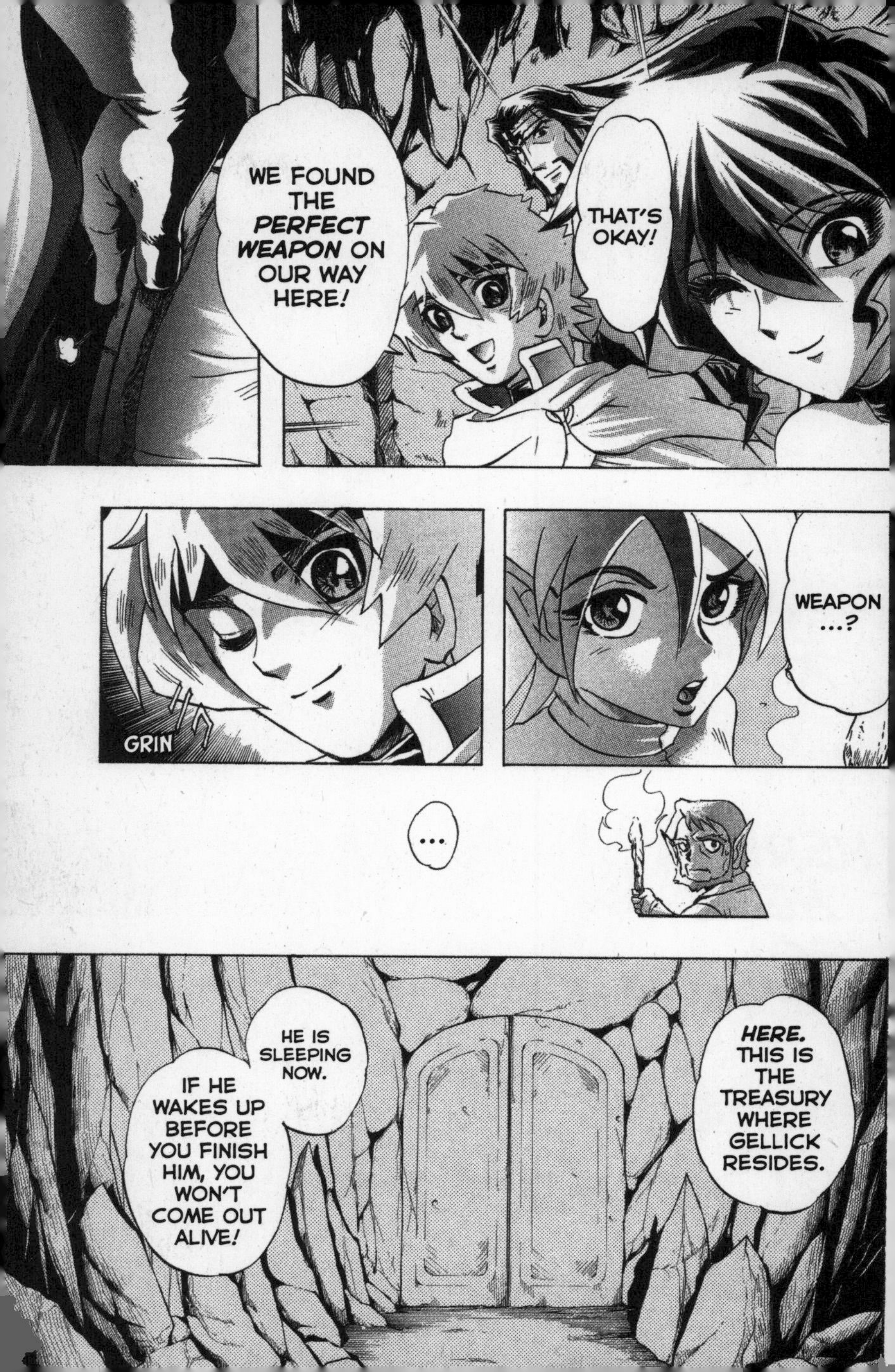
THAT'S OKAY!
WE FOUND THE PERFECT WEAPON ON OUR WAY HERE!
WEAPON ...?
GRIN
...
HERE. THIS IS THE TREASURY WHERE GELLICK RESIDES.
HE IS SLEEPING NOW.
IF HE WAKES UP BEFORE YOU FINISH HIM, YOU WON'T COME OUT ALIVE!

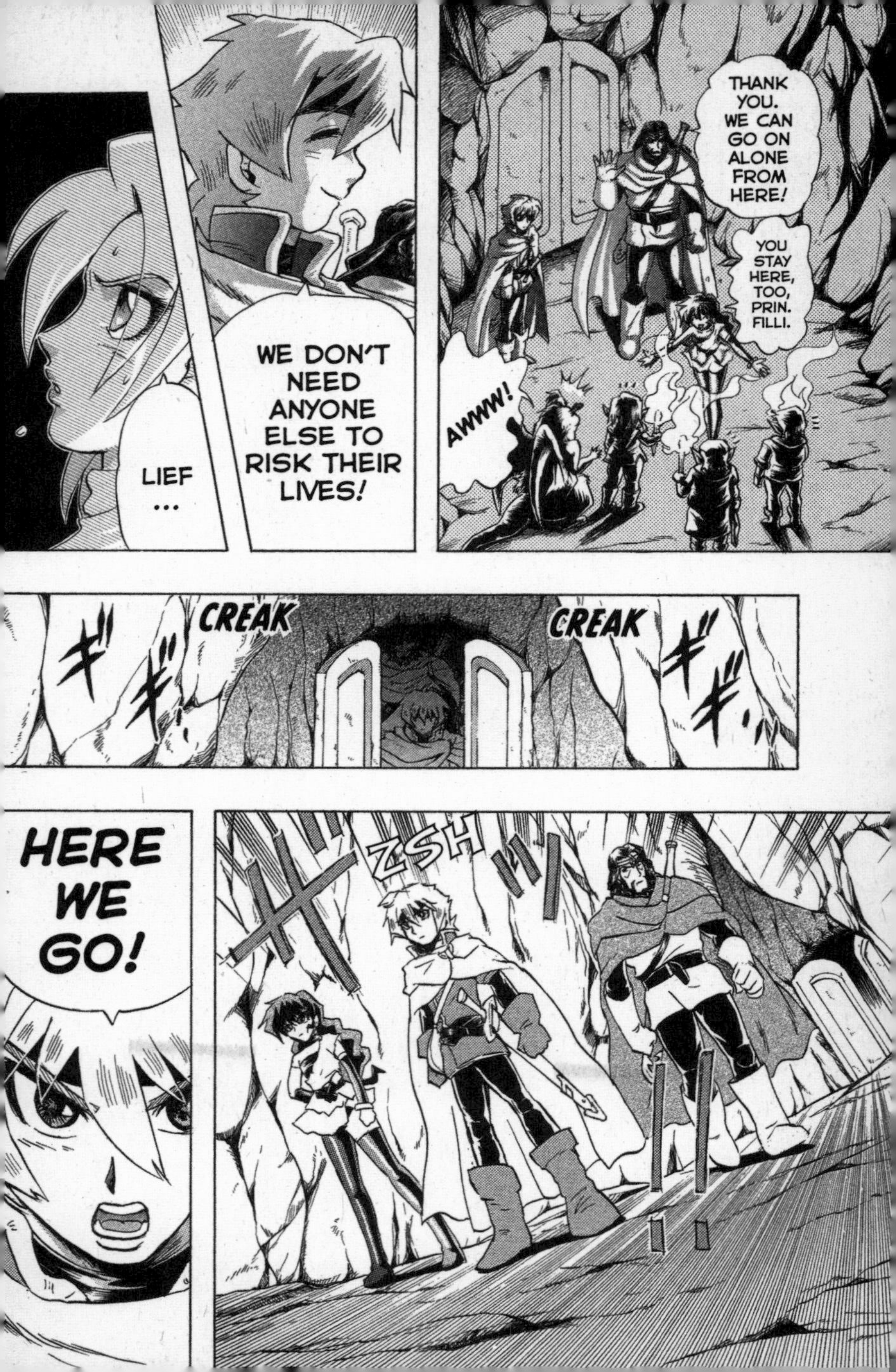
THANK YOU. WE CAN GO ON ALONE FROM HERE!
YOU STAY HERE, TOO, PRIN. FILLI.
AWWW!
WE DON'T NEED ANYONE ELSE TO RISK THEIR LIVES!
LIEF ...
CREAK
ギギ
CREAK
ギギ
ZSH
HERE WE GO!

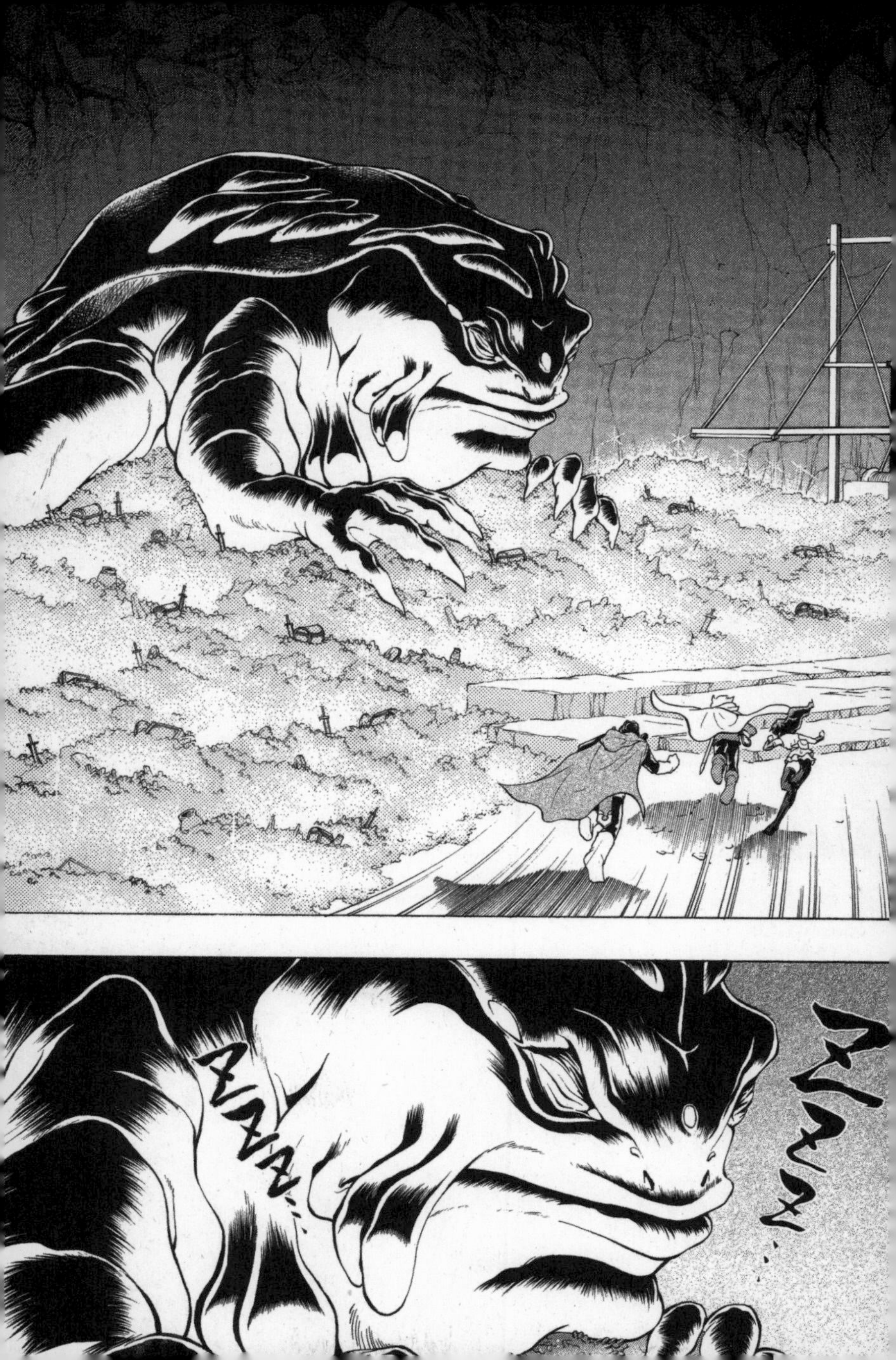
ZZZZ...
ZZZZ...

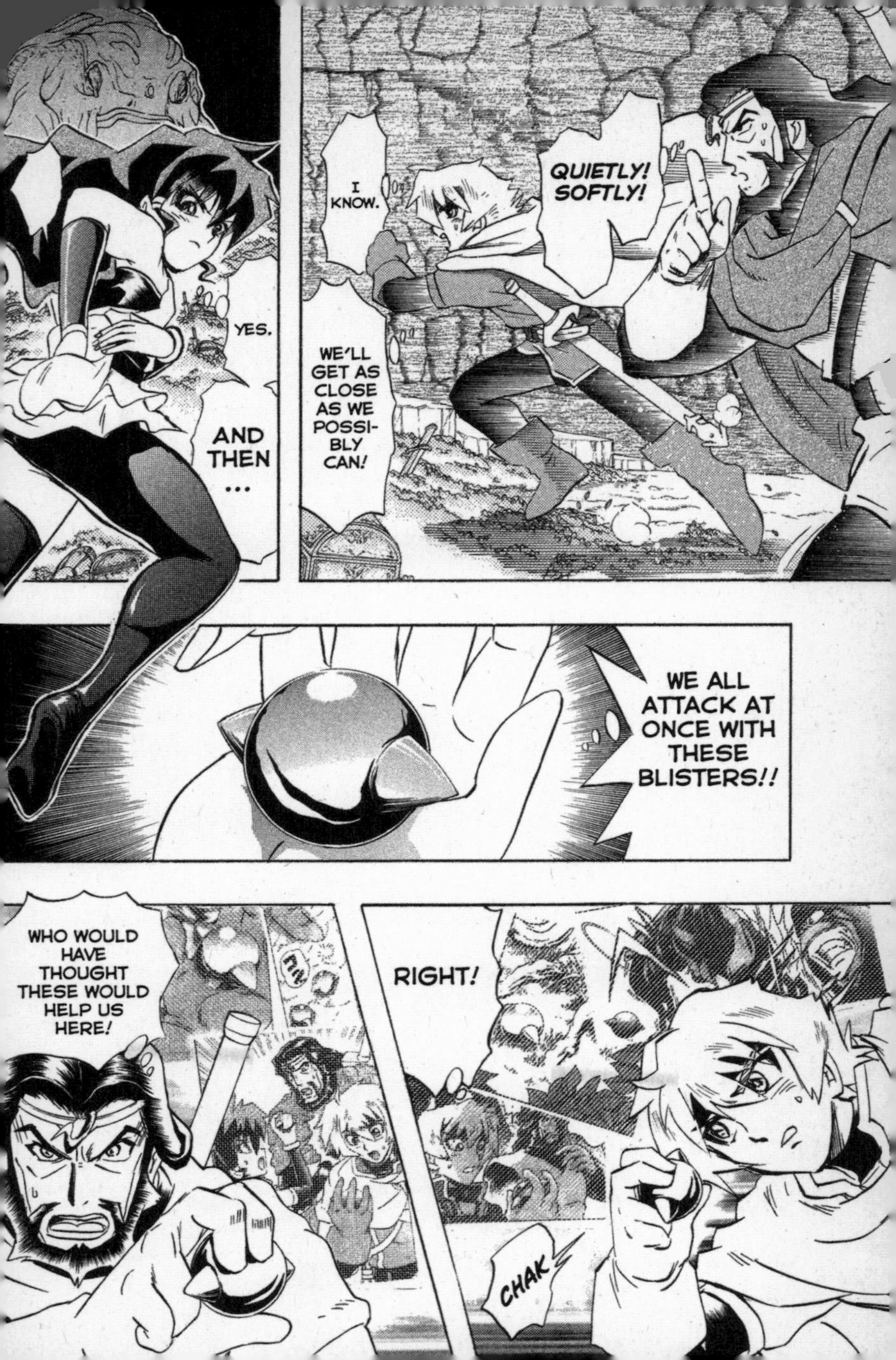
QUIETLY! SOFTLY!
I KNOW.
WE'LL GET AS CLOSE AS WE POSSIBLY CAN!
YES.
AND THEN ...
WE ALL ATTACK AT ONCE WITH THESE BLISTERS!!
RIGHT!
CHAK
WHO WOULD HAVE THOUGHT THESE WOULD HELP US HERE!

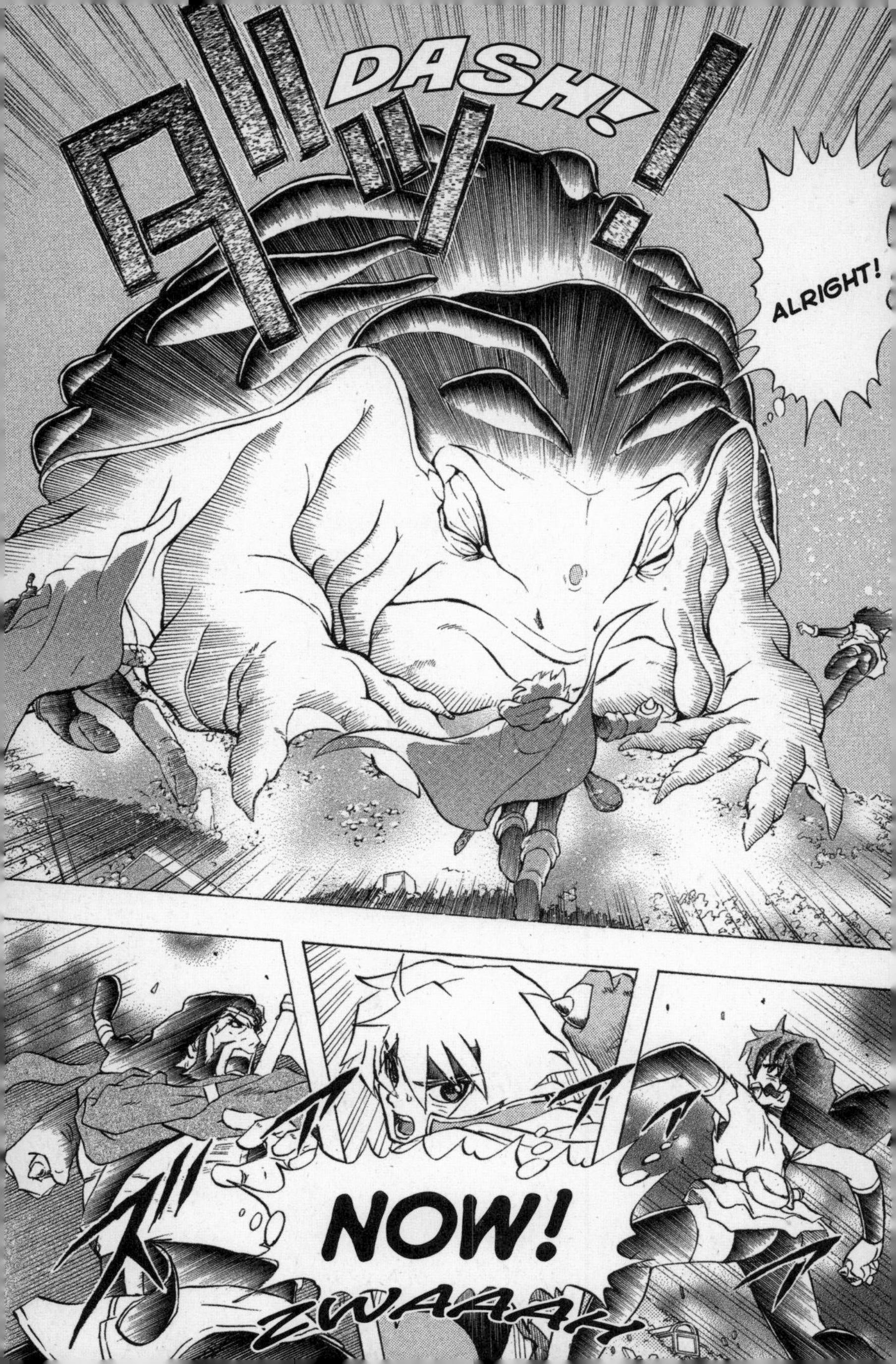

DASH!
ALRIGHT!
NOW!
ZWAAAH

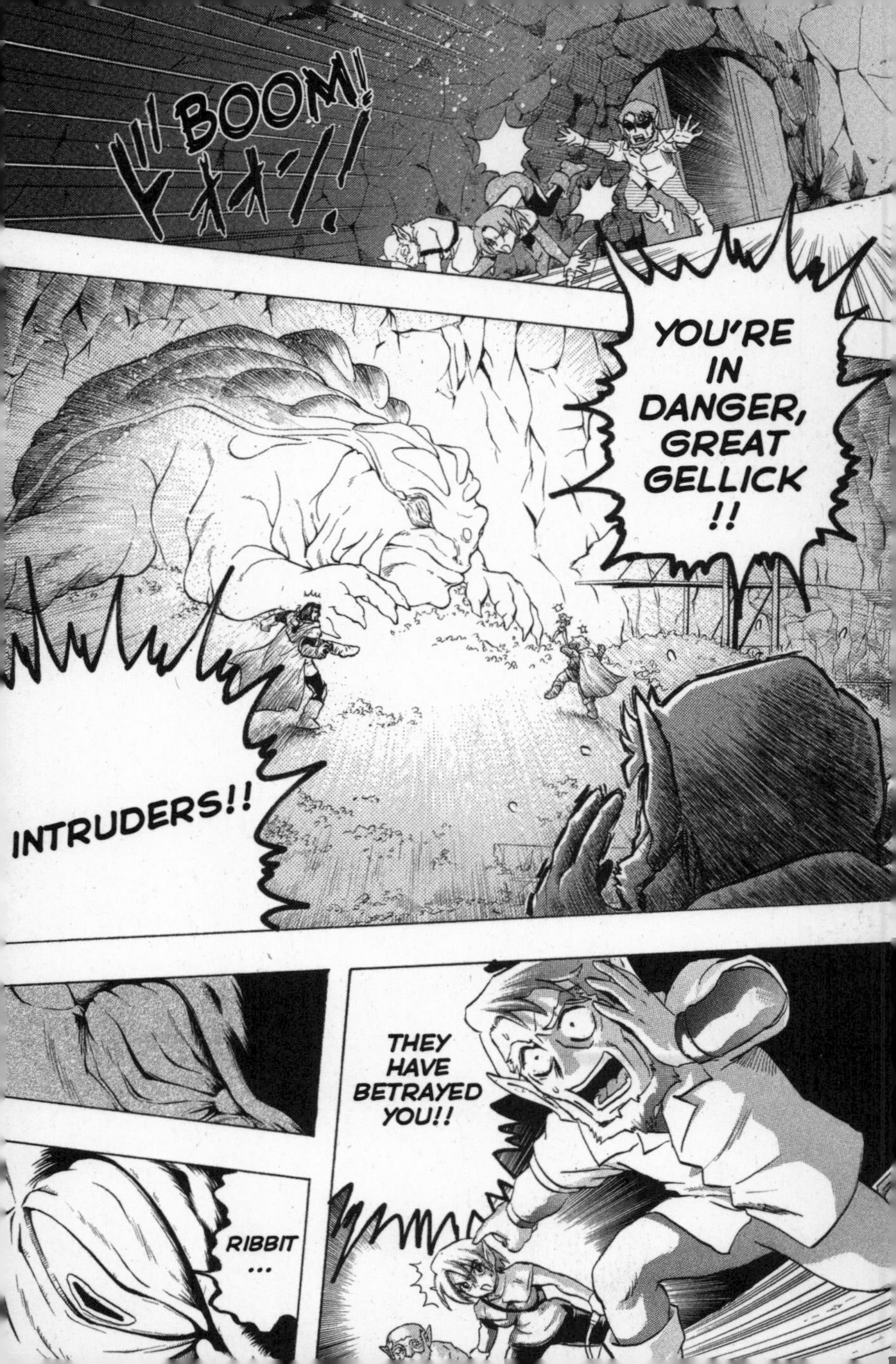
BOOM!!
YOU'RE IN DANGER, GREAT GELLICK!!
INTRUDERS!!
THEY HAVE BETRAYED YOU!!
RIBBIT...

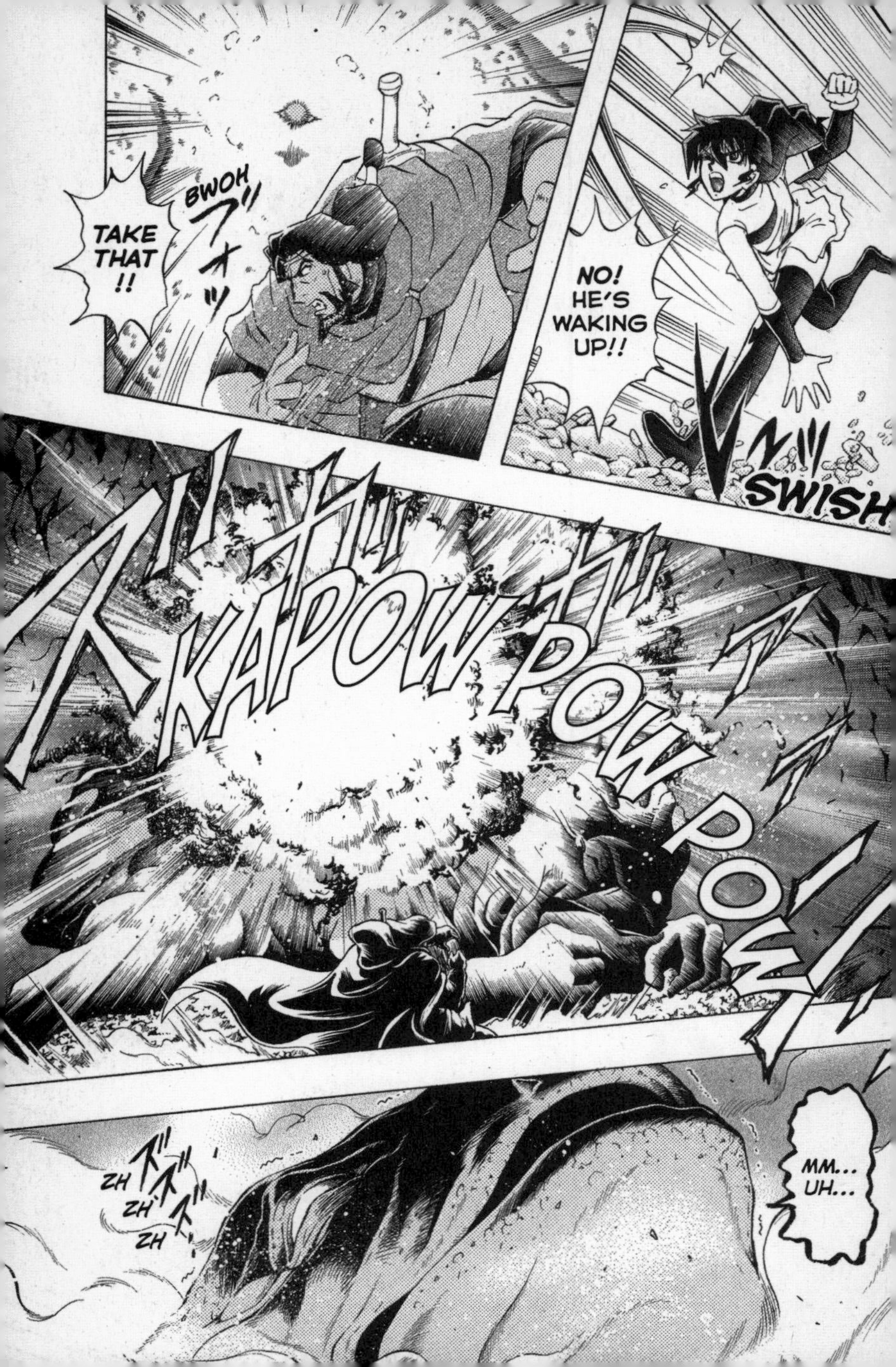
NO! HE'S WAKING UP!!
SWISH
BWOH
TAKE THAT !!
KAPOW POW POW POW!
MM... UH...
ZH ZH ZH

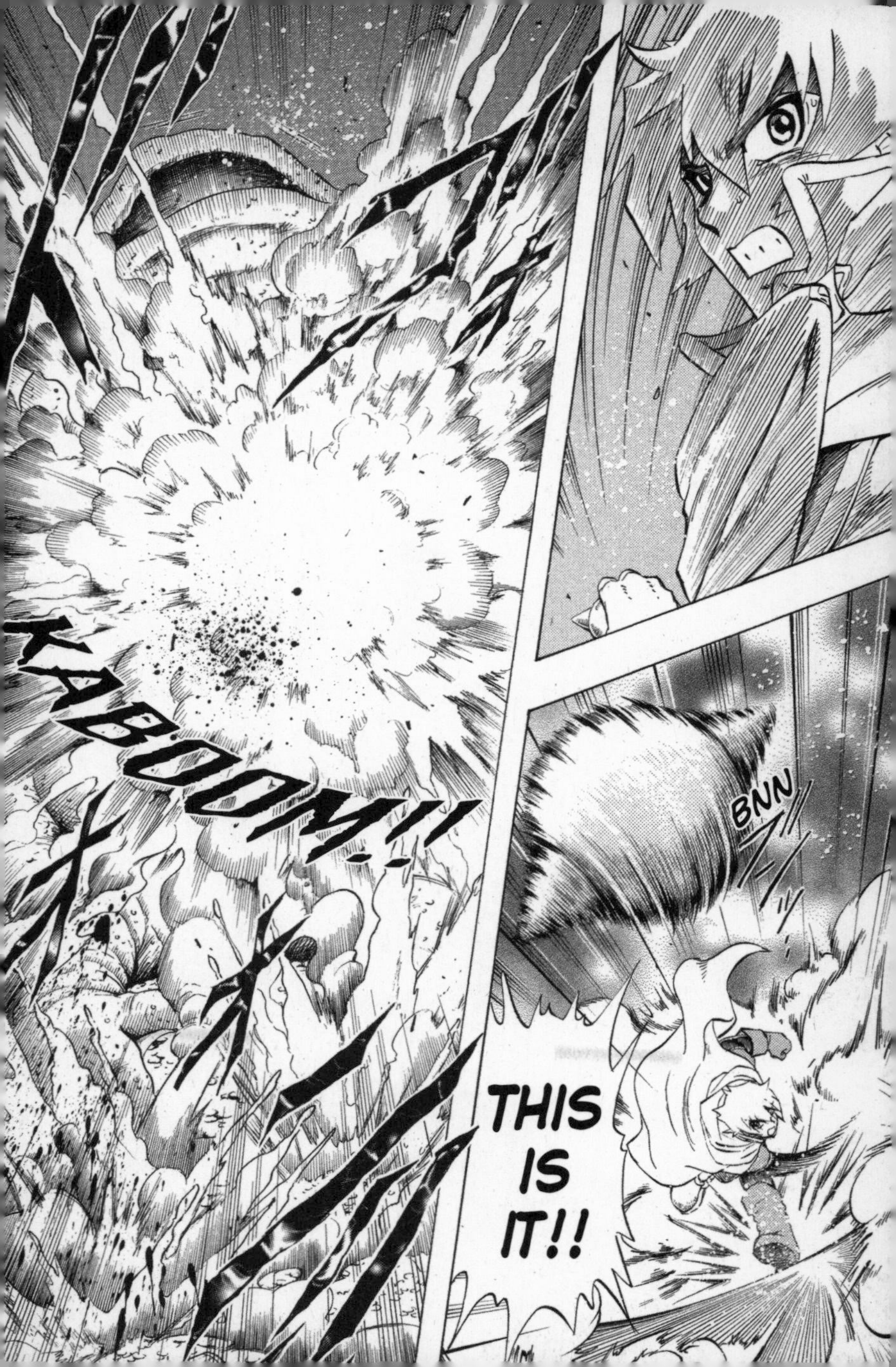
BNN
THIS IS IT!!
KABOOM!!

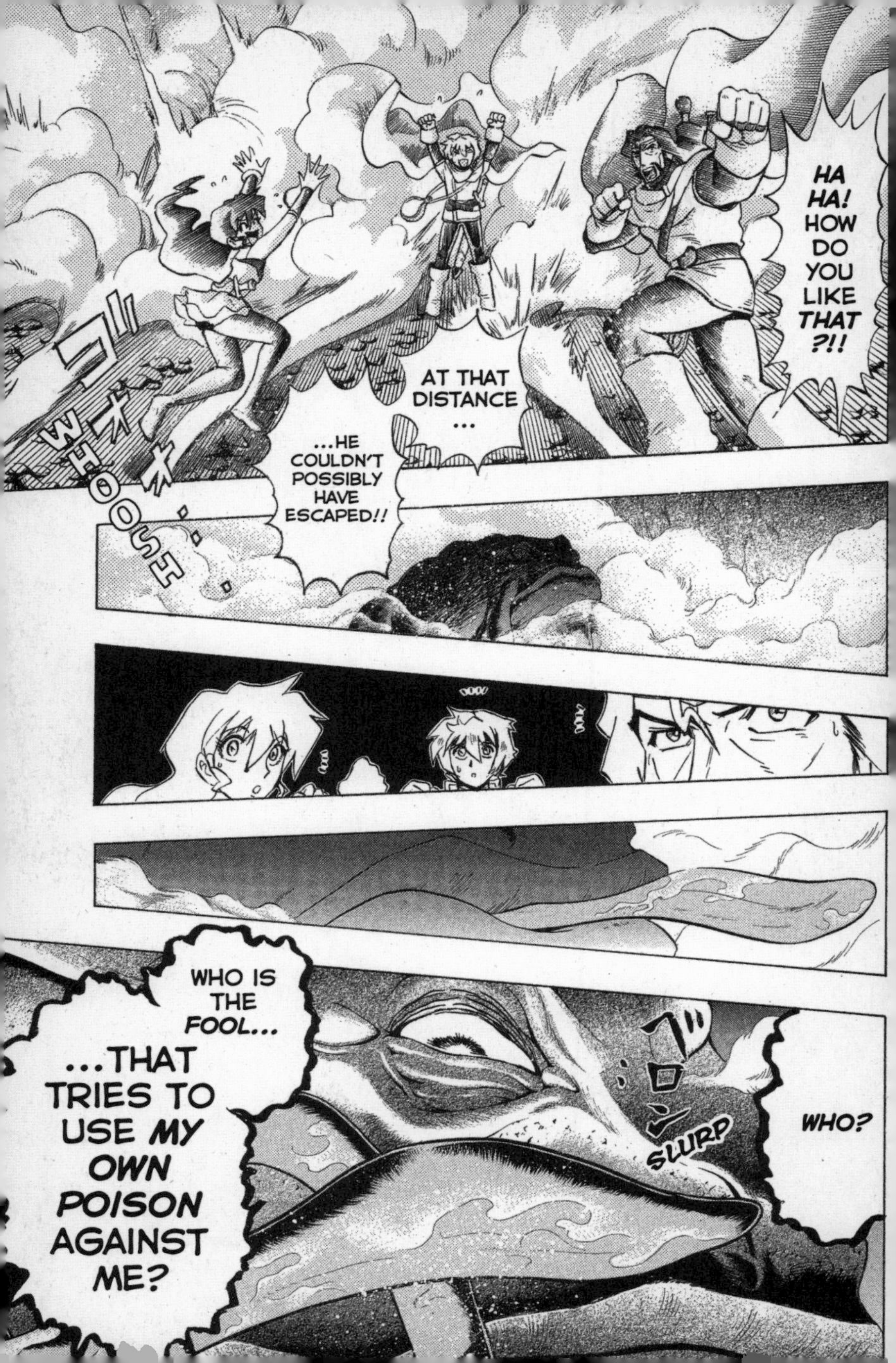
HA HA! HOW DO YOU LIKE THAT?!!
AT THAT DISTANCE...
...HE COULDN'T POSSIBLY HAVE ESCAPED!!
WHOOSH
WHO?
SLURP
WHO IS THE FOOL...
...THAT TRIES TO USE MY OWN POISON AGAINST ME?

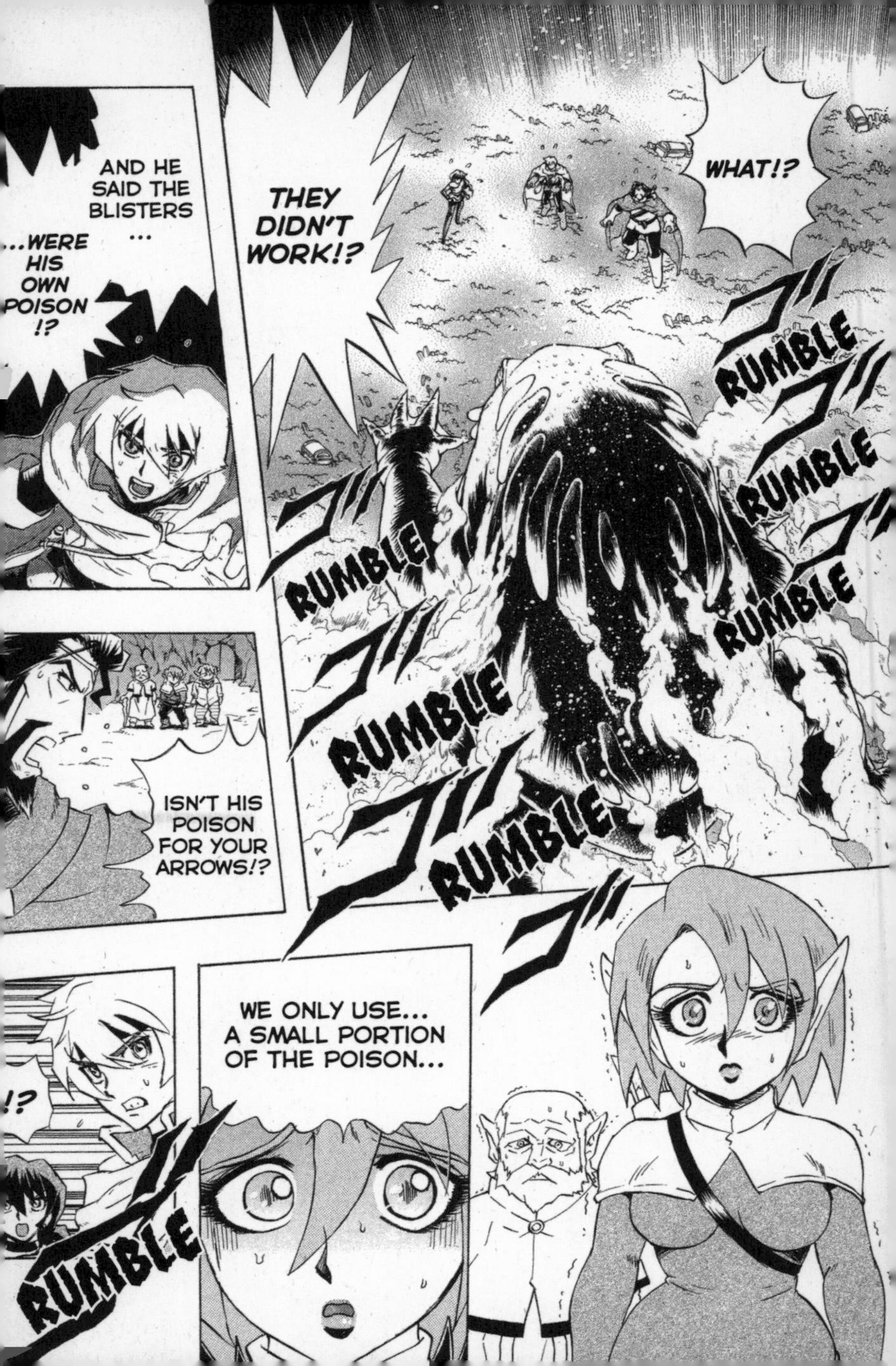

WHAT!?
THEY DIDN'T WORK!?
RUMBLE
RUMBLE
RUMBLE
RUMBLE
RUMBLE
RUMBLE
RUMBLE
AND HE SAID THE BLISTERS ...
...WERE HIS OWN POISON !?
ISN'T HIS POISON FOR YOUR ARROWS!?
WE ONLY USE... A SMALL PORTION OF THE POISON...
!?
RUMBLE

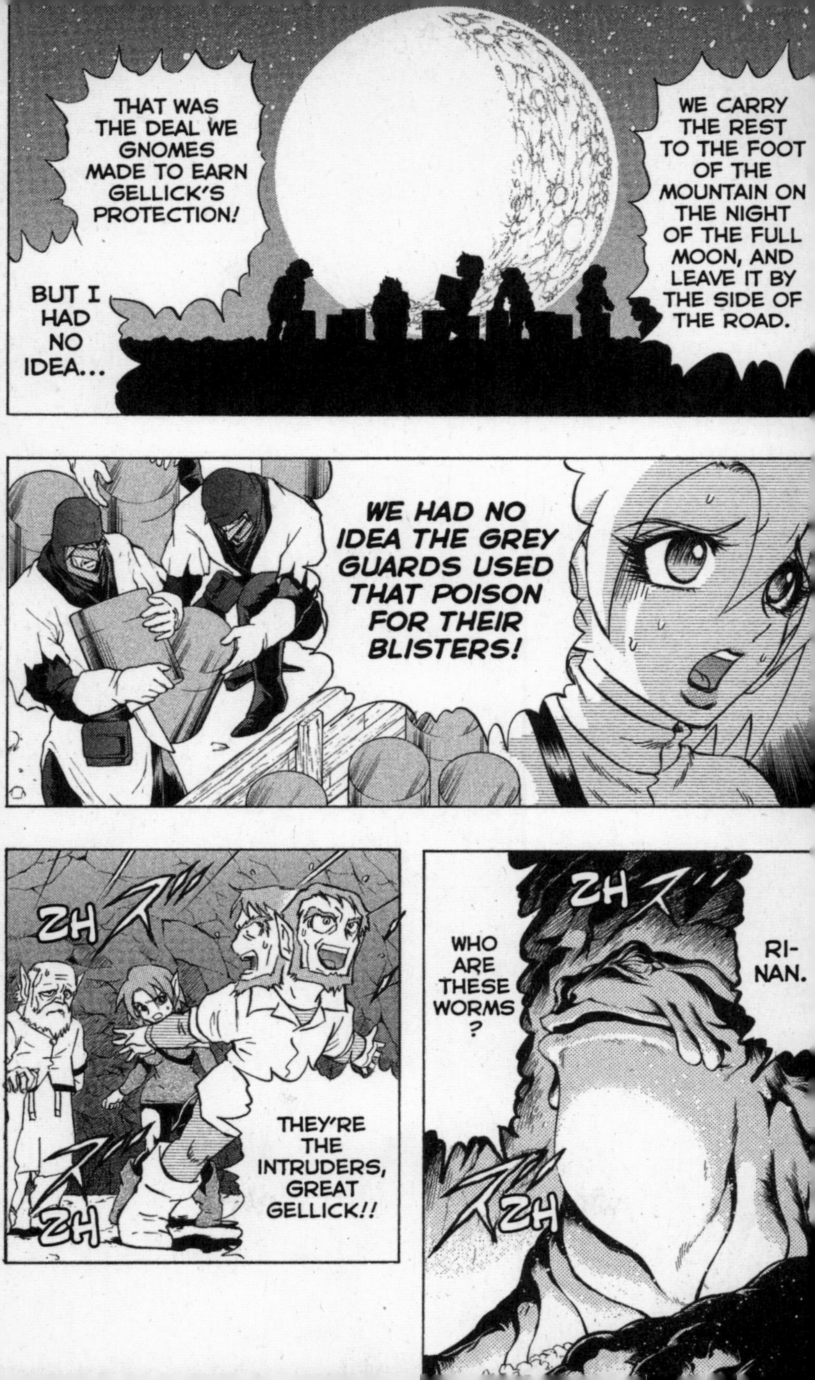

WE CARRY THE REST TO THE FOOT OF THE MOUNTAIN ON THE NIGHT OF THE FULL MOON, AND LEAVE IT BY THE SIDE OF THE ROAD.
THAT WAS THE DEAL WE GNOMES MADE TO EARN GELLICK'S PROTECTION!
BUT I HAD NO IDEA...
WE HAD NO IDEA THE GREY GUARDS USED THAT POISON FOR THEIR BLISTERS!
ZH
RI-NAN.
WHO ARE THESE WORMS?
ZH
ZH
THEY'RE THE INTRUDERS, GREAT GELLICK!!
ZH

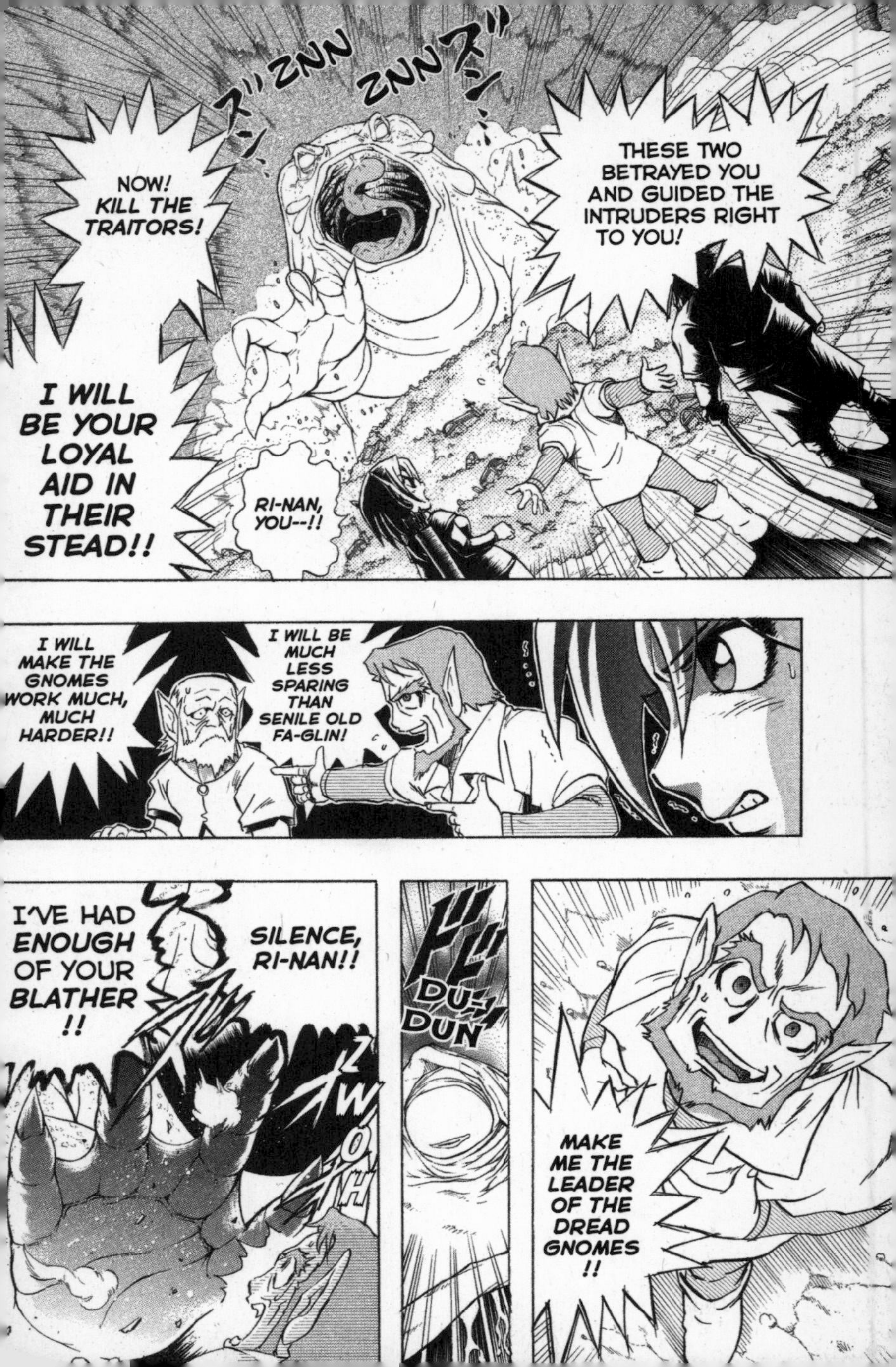
ZNN
ZNN
THESE TWO BETRAYED YOU AND GUIDED THE INTRUDERS RIGHT TO YOU!
NOW! KILL THE TRAITORS!
RI-NAN, YOU--!!
I WILL BE YOUR LOYAL AID IN THEIR STEAD!!
I WILL BE MUCH LESS SPARING THAN SENILE OLD FA-GLIN!
I WILL MAKE THE GNOMES WORK MUCH, MUCH HARDER!!
MAKE ME THE LEADER OF THE DREAD GNOMES!!
DU-DUN
SILENCE, RI-NAN!!
I'VE HAD ENOUGH OF YOUR BLATHER!!
ZWOOH

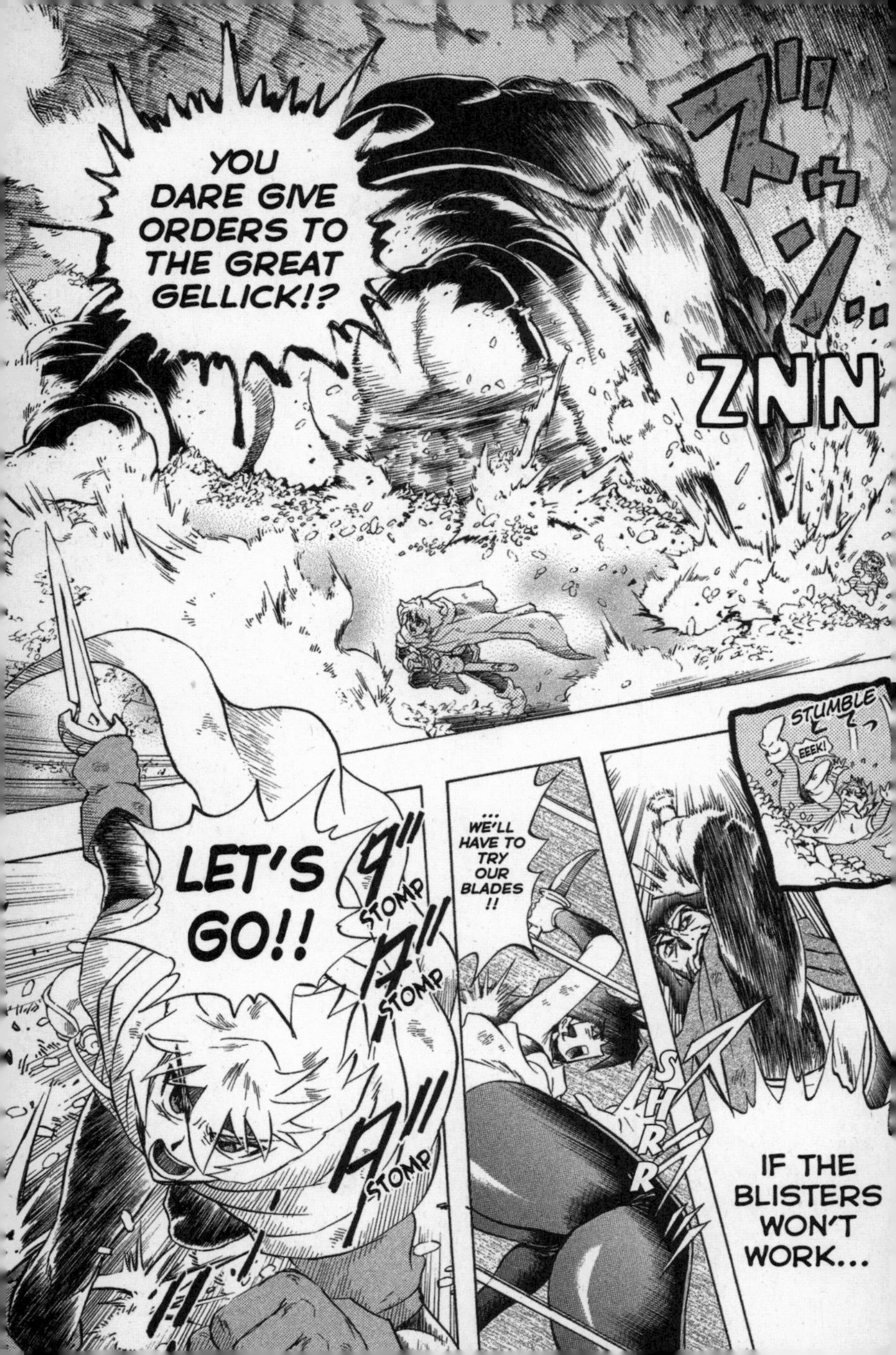

ZNN
YOU DARE GIVE ORDERS TO THE GREAT GELLICK!?
STUMBLE
EEEK!
IF THE BLISTERS WON'T WORK...
SHRR
...WE'LL HAVE TO TRY OUR BLADES!!
LET'S GO!!
STOMP
STOMP
STOMP

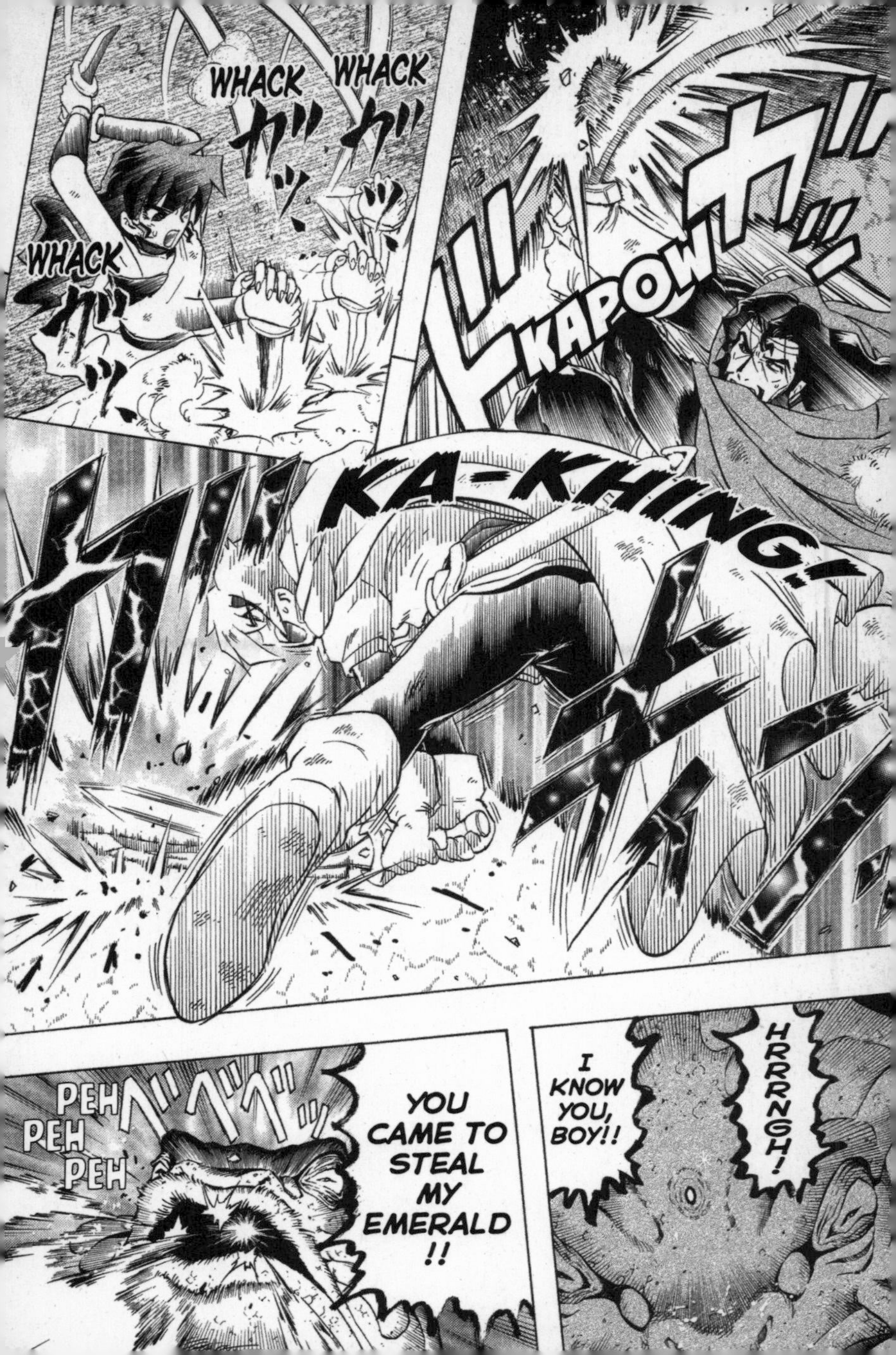
KAPOW!!
WHACK
WHACK
WHACK
KA-KHING!!
HRRRNGH!
I KNOW YOU, BOY!!
YOU CAME TO STEAL MY EMERALD!!
PEH PEH PEH

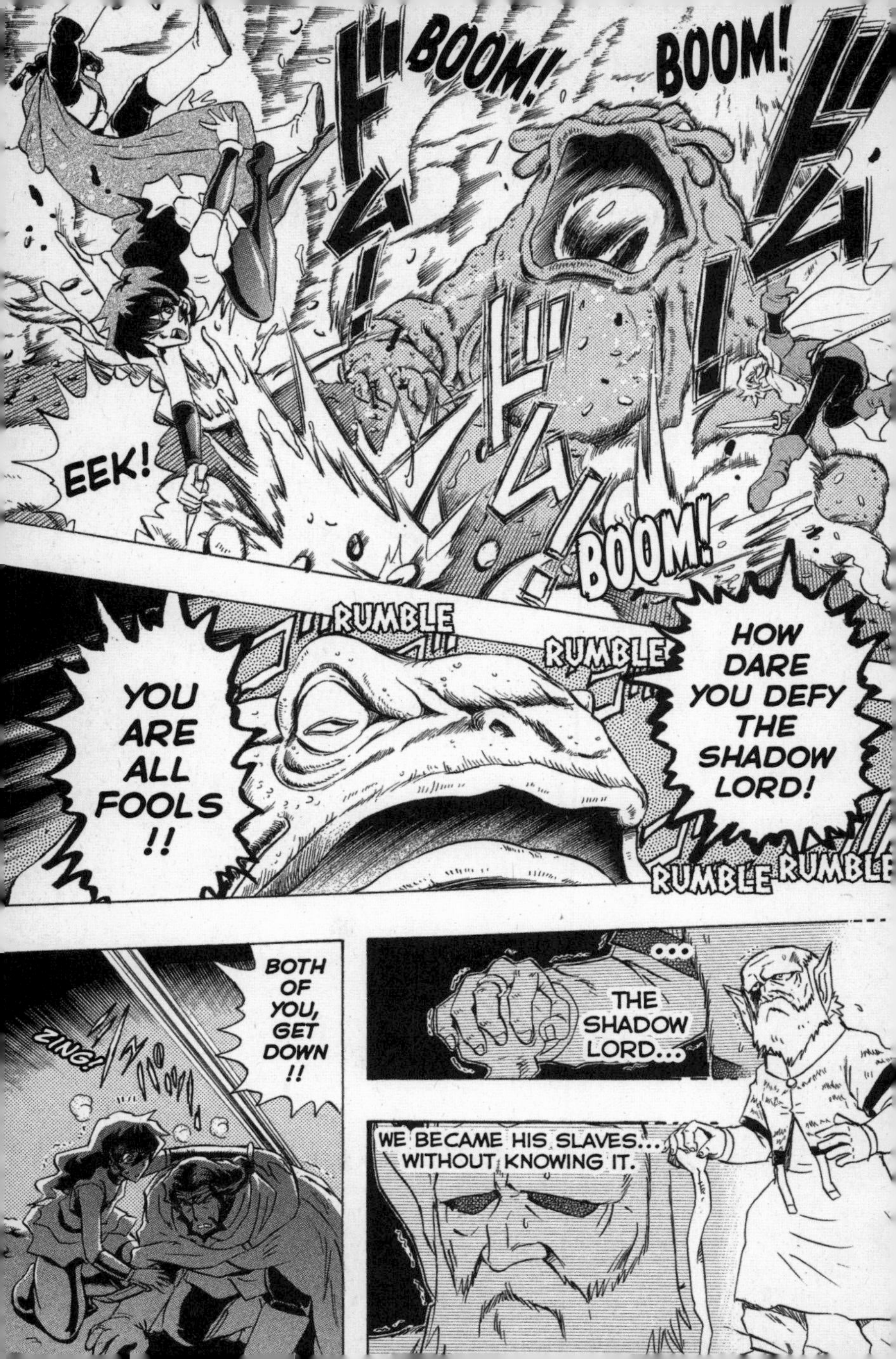
BOOM!
BOOM!
EEK!
BOOM!
RUMBLE
RUMBLE
HOW DARE YOU DEFY THE SHADOW LORD!
YOU ARE ALL FOOLS!!
RUMBLE
RUMBLE
...
THE SHADOW LORD...
WE BECAME HIS SLAVES... WITHOUT KNOWING IT.
BOTH OF YOU, GET DOWN!!
ZING!

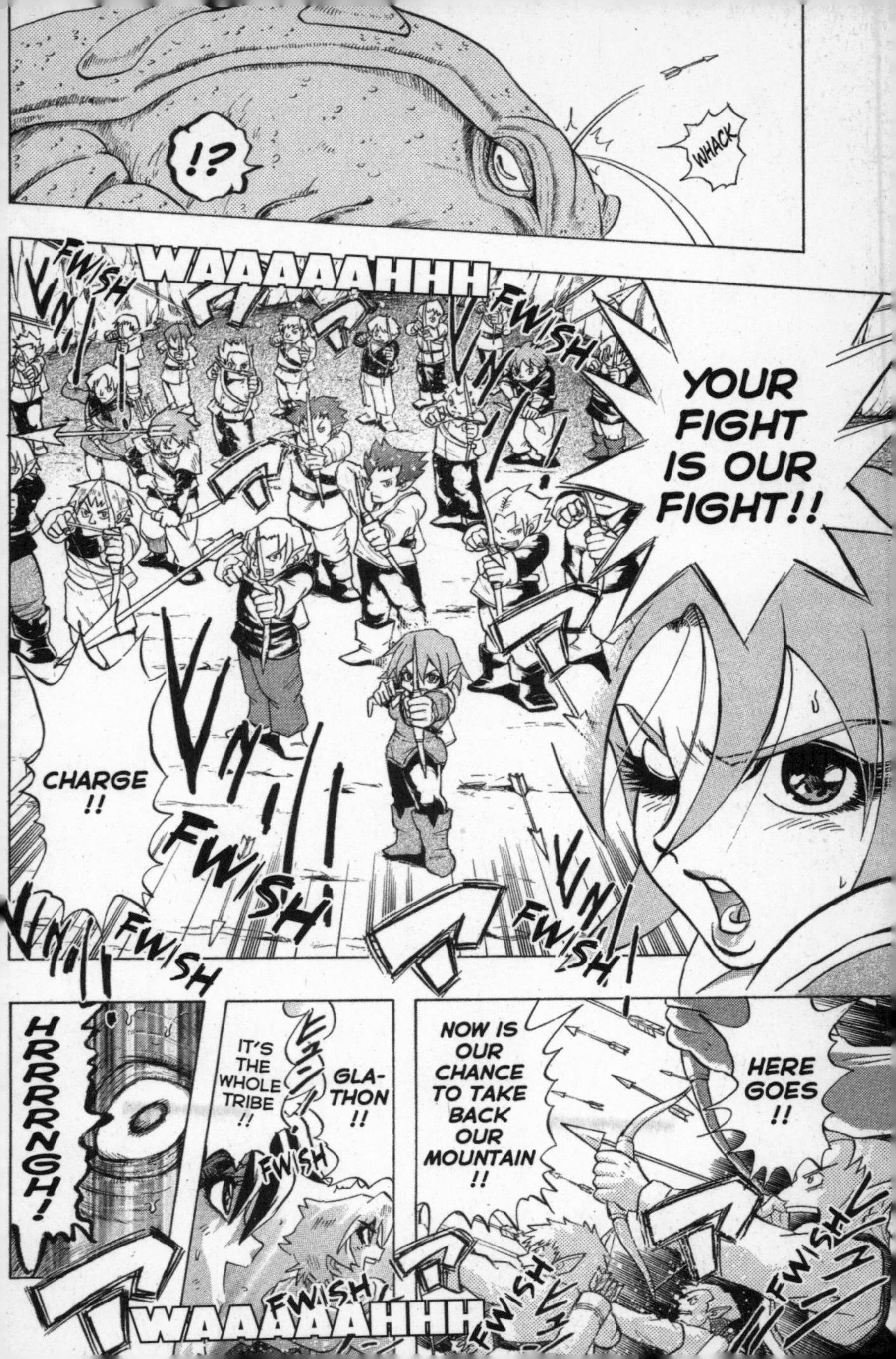
WHACK
!?
YOUR FIGHT IS OUR FIGHT!!
FWISH
WAAAAAAHHH
FWISH
CHARGE!!
FWISH
FWISH
FWISH
HERE GOES!!
NOW IS OUR CHANCE TO TAKE BACK OUR MOUNTAIN!!
FWISH
FWISH
GLA-THON!!
IT'S THE WHOLE TRIBE!!
FWISH
FWISH
HRRRRNGH!
WAAAAAAHHH

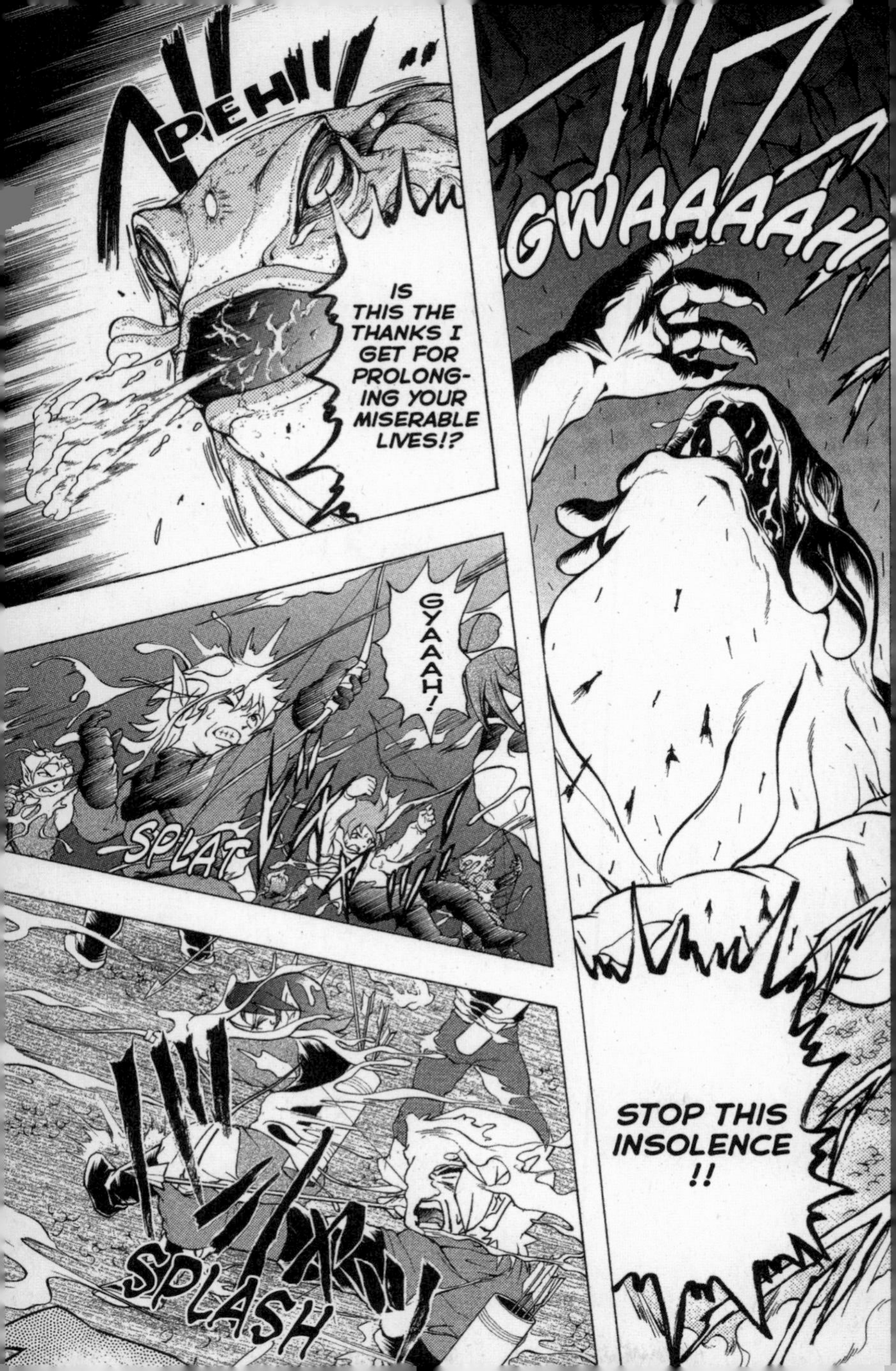
GWAAAAAH
STOP THIS INSOLENCE !!
IS THIS THE THANKS I GET FOR PROLONG-ING YOUR MISERABLE LIVES!?
GYAAAAH!
SPLAT
SPLASH

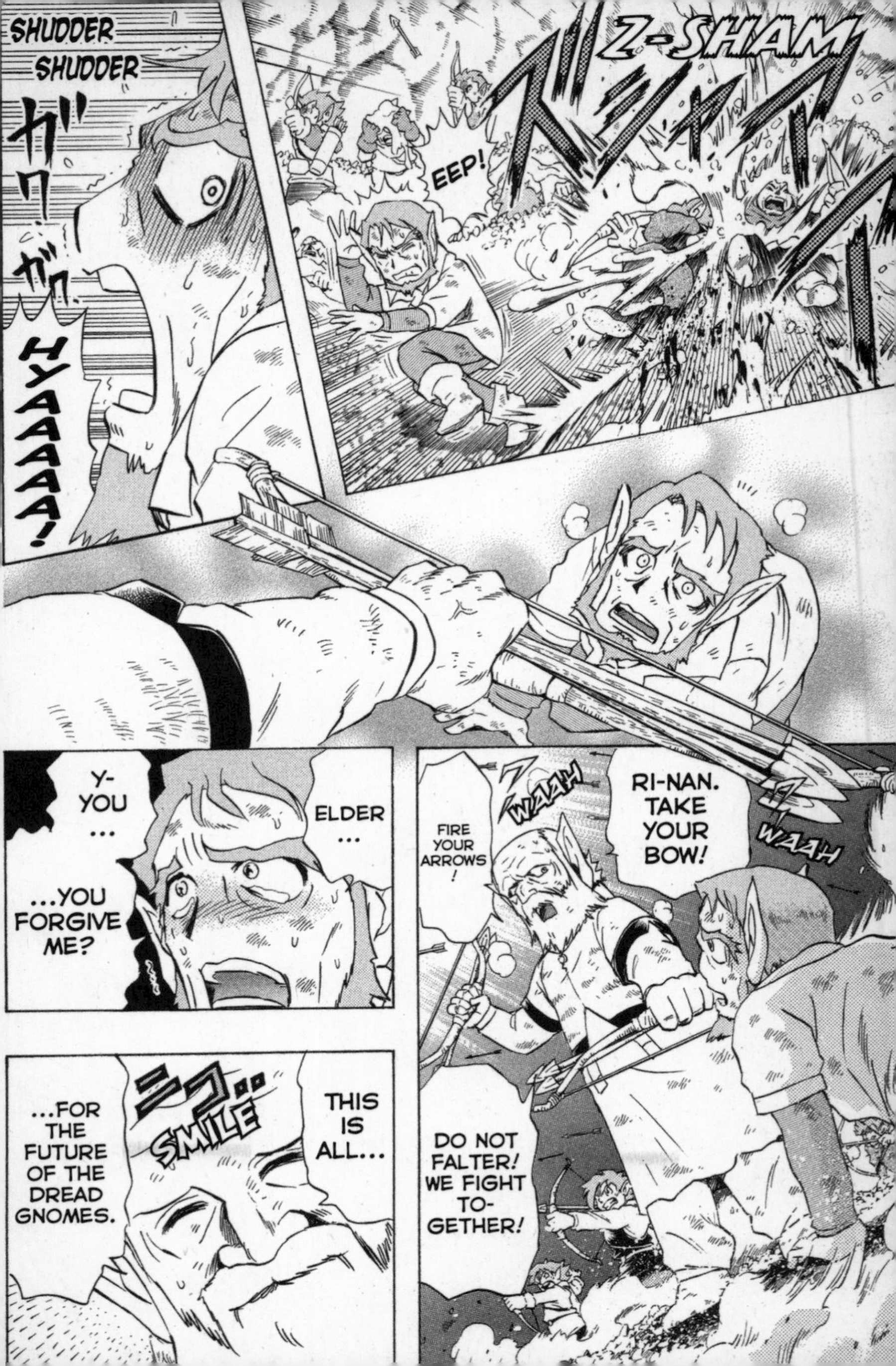

Z-SHAM
ズシャア
EEP!
SHUDDER
SHUDDER
ガク
ガク
HYAAAAAA!
RI-NAN. TAKE YOUR BOW!
WAAH
WAAH
FIRE YOUR ARROWS!
DO NOT FALTER! WE FIGHT TO-GETHER!
ELDER...
Y-YOU...
...YOU FORGIVE ME?
THIS IS ALL...
ニコ
SMILE
...FOR THE FUTURE OF THE DREAD GNOMES.

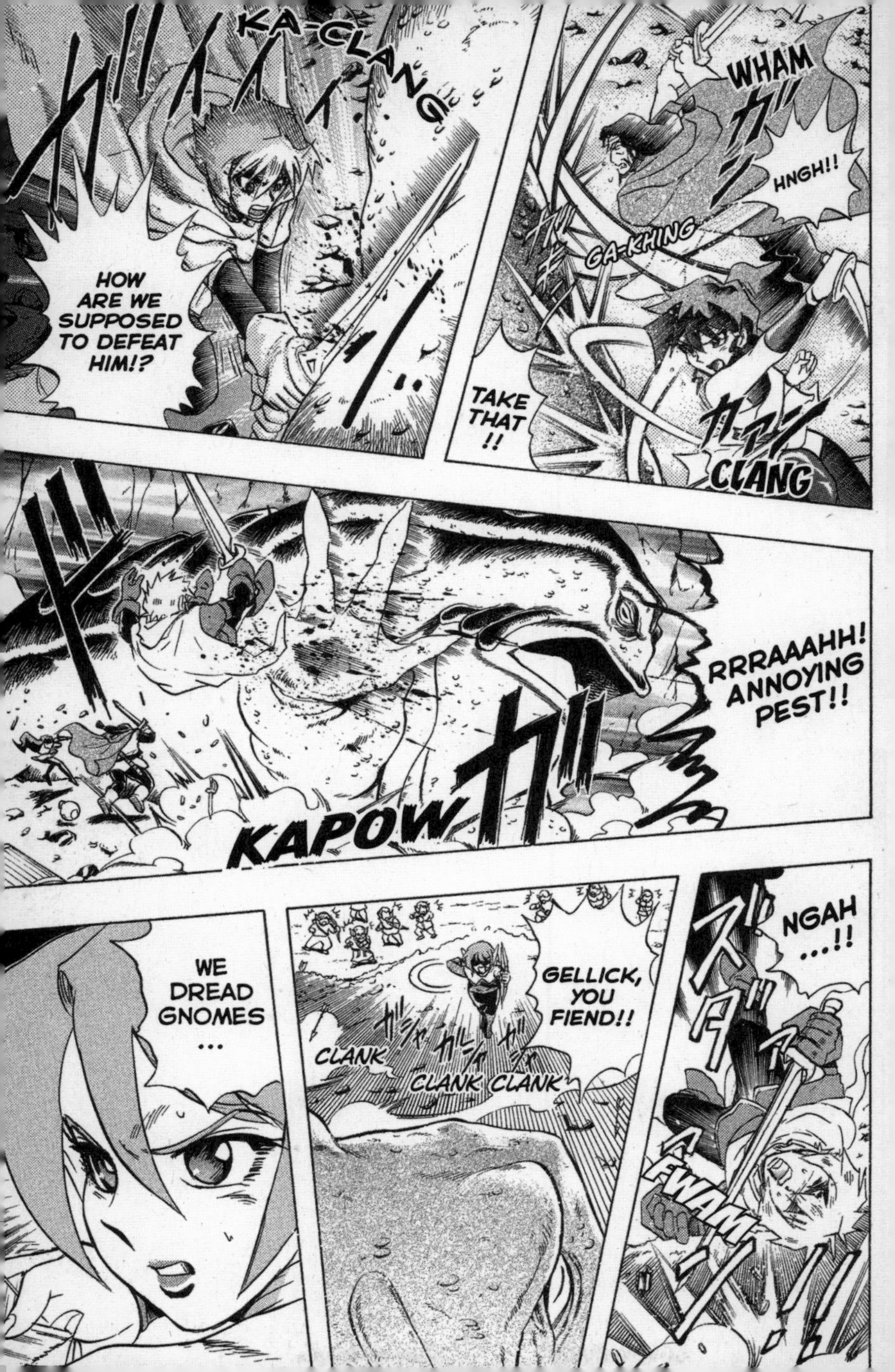

WHAM
HNGH!!
GA-KHING
TAKE THAT!!
CLANG
KA-CLANG
HOW ARE WE SUPPOSED TO DEFEAT HIM!?
RRRAAAHH! ANNOYING PEST!!
KAPOW
NGAH ...!!
FWAM
GELLICK, YOU FIEND!!
CLANK
CLANK CLANK
WE DREAD GNOMES ...

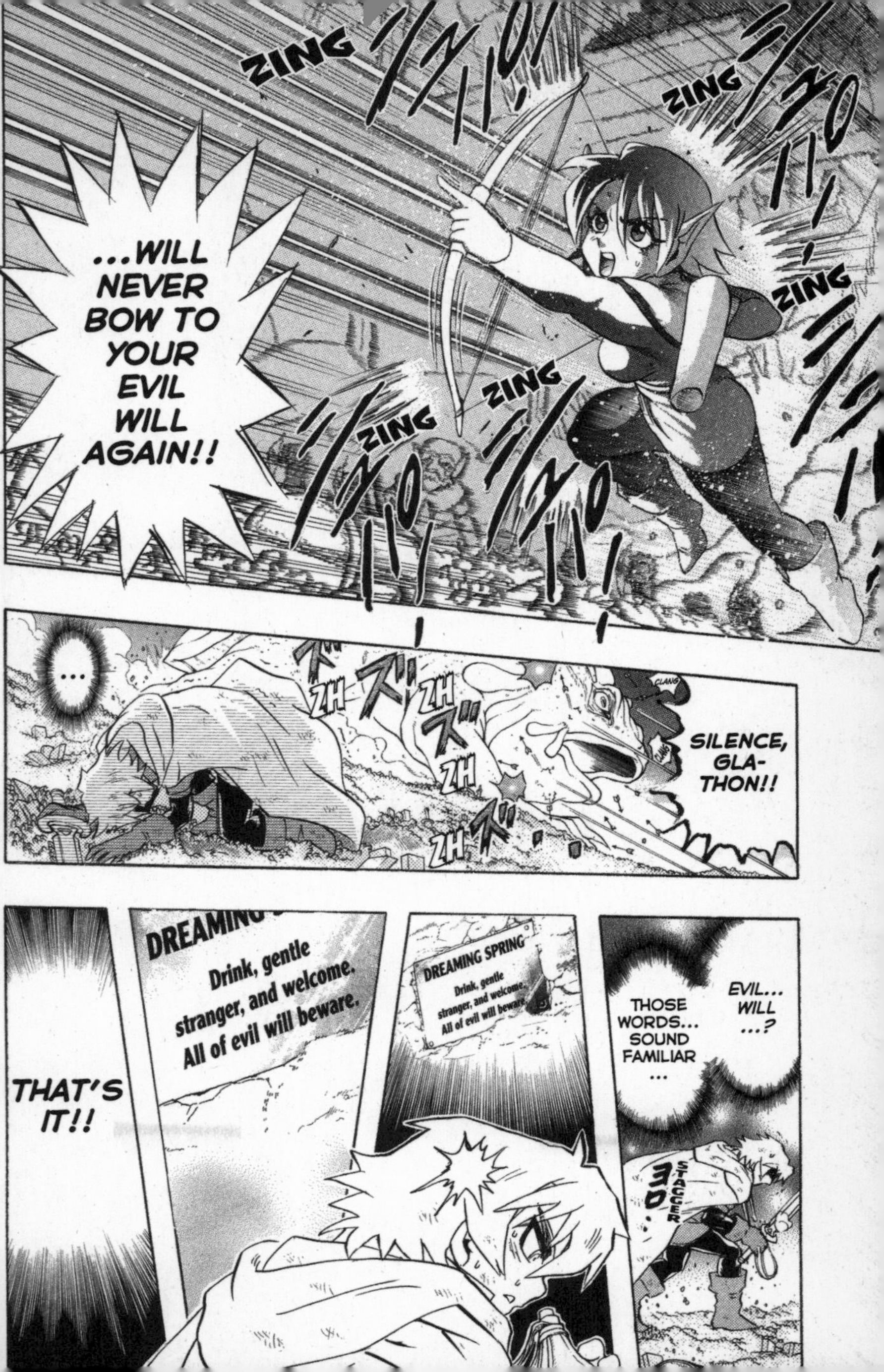
ZING
ZING
ZING
...WILL NEVER BOW TO YOUR EVIL WILL AGAIN!!
ZING
ZING
SILENCE, GLA-THON!!
CLANG
CLANG
ZH
ZH
ZH
ZH
...
EVIL... WILL ...?
THOSE WORDS... SOUND FAMILIAR ...
STAGGER
DREAMING SPRING
Drink, gentle stranger, and welcome. All of evil will beware.
DREAMING
Drink, gentle stranger, and welcome. All of evil will beware.
THAT'S IT!!

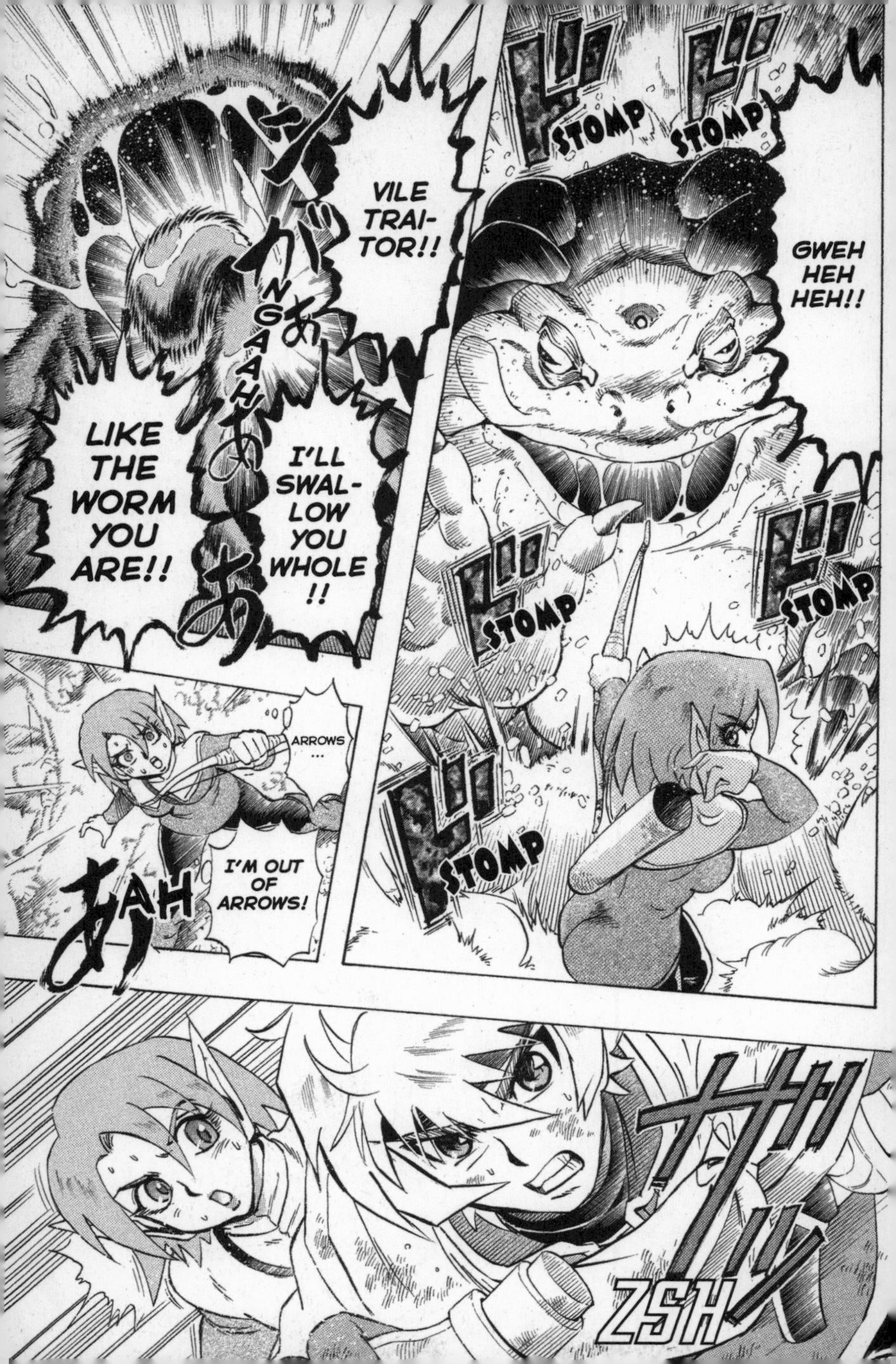
STOMP
STOMP
GWEH HEH HEH!!
STOMP
STOMP
STOMP
VILE TRAI-TOR!!
NGAAH
I'LL SWAL-LOW YOU WHOLE!!
LIKE THE WORM YOU ARE!!
ARROWS ...
I'M OUT OF ARROWS!
AH
ZSH

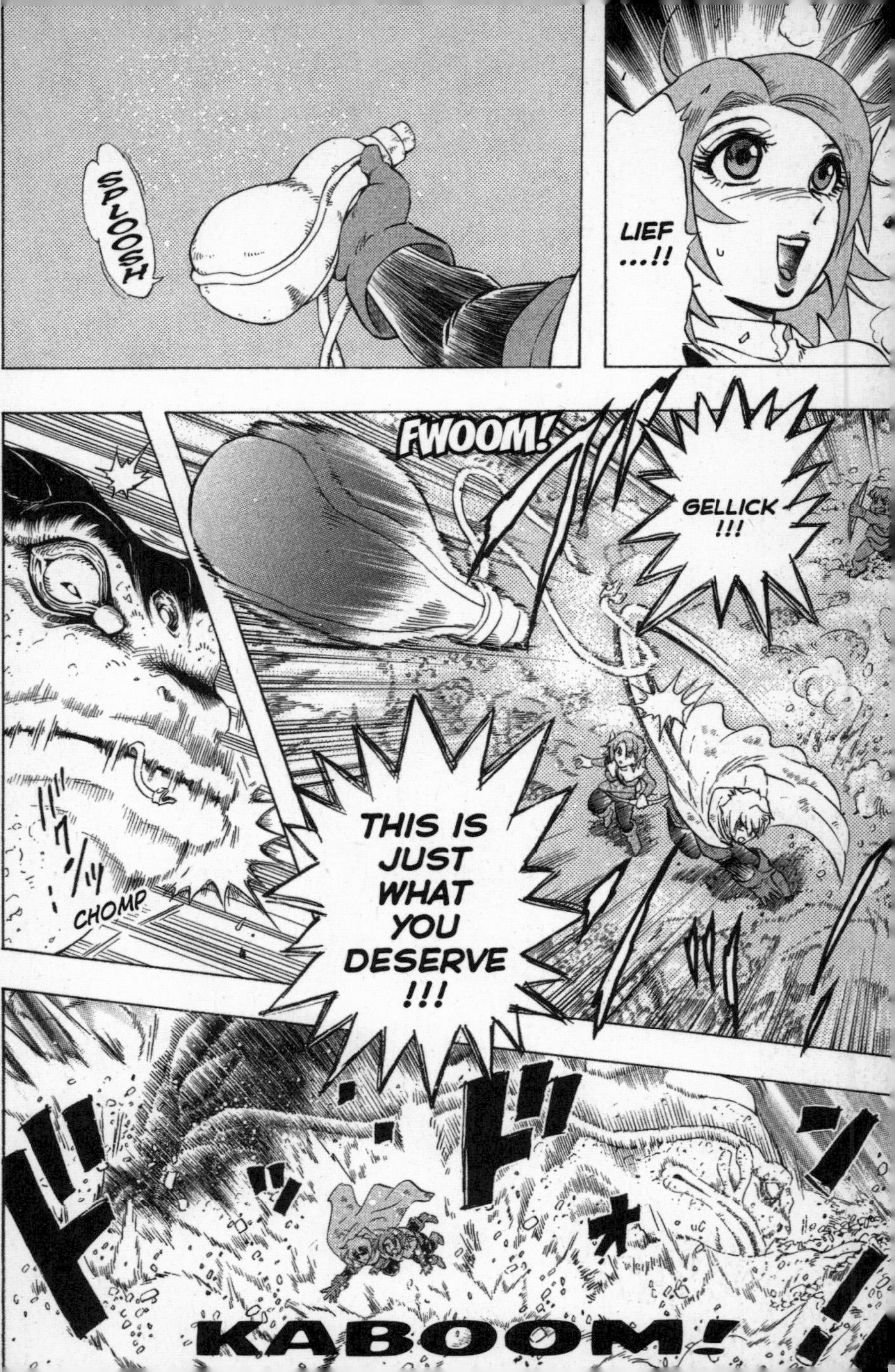
LIEF ...!!
SPLOOSH
FWOOM!
GELLICK !!!
THIS IS JUST WHAT YOU DESERVE !!!
CHOMP
KABOOM!

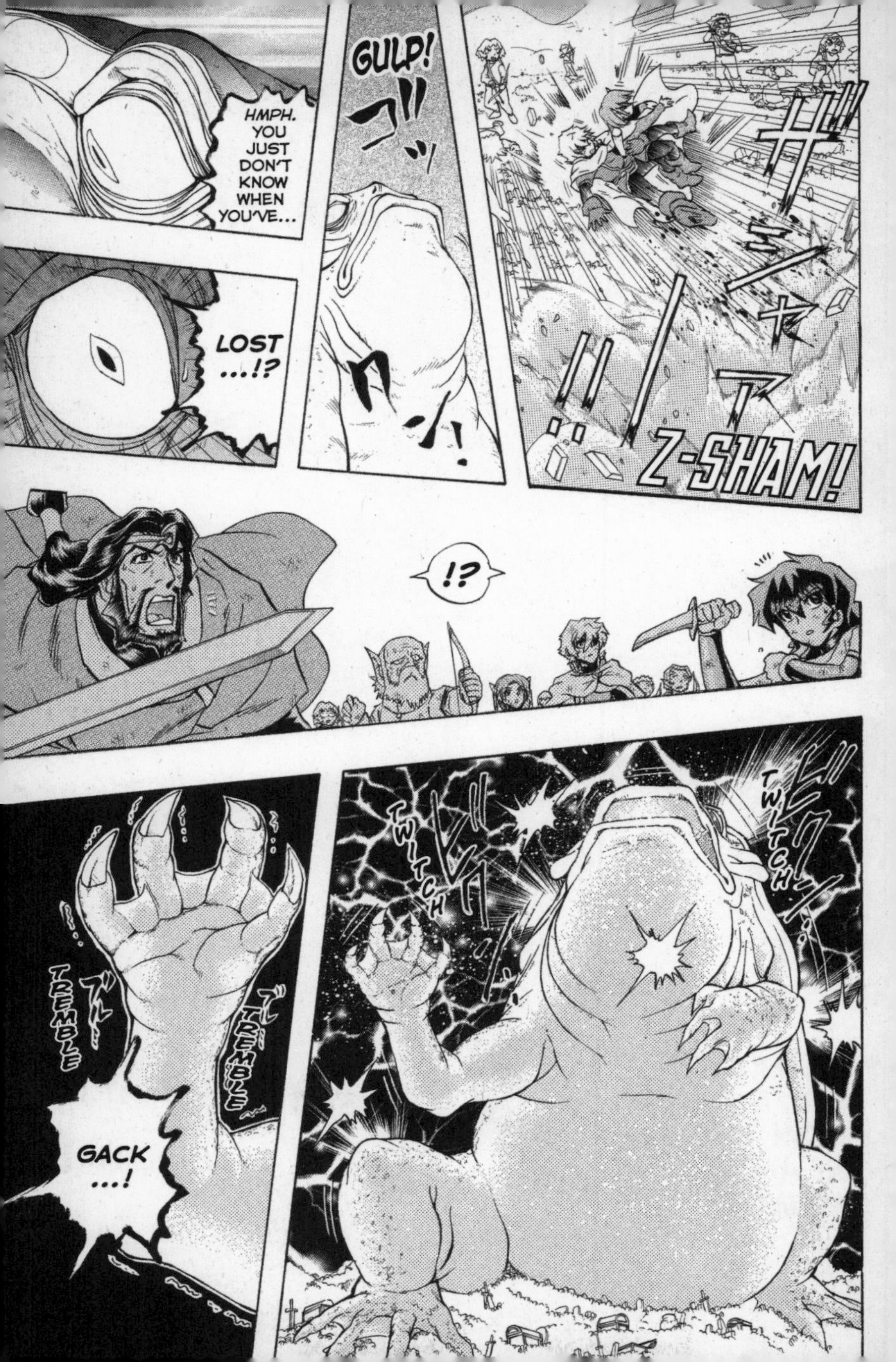

Z-SHAM!
GULP!
HMPH. YOU JUST DON'T KNOW WHEN YOU'VE...
LOST ...!?
!?
TWITCH
TWITCH
TREMBLE
TREMBLE
GACK ...!

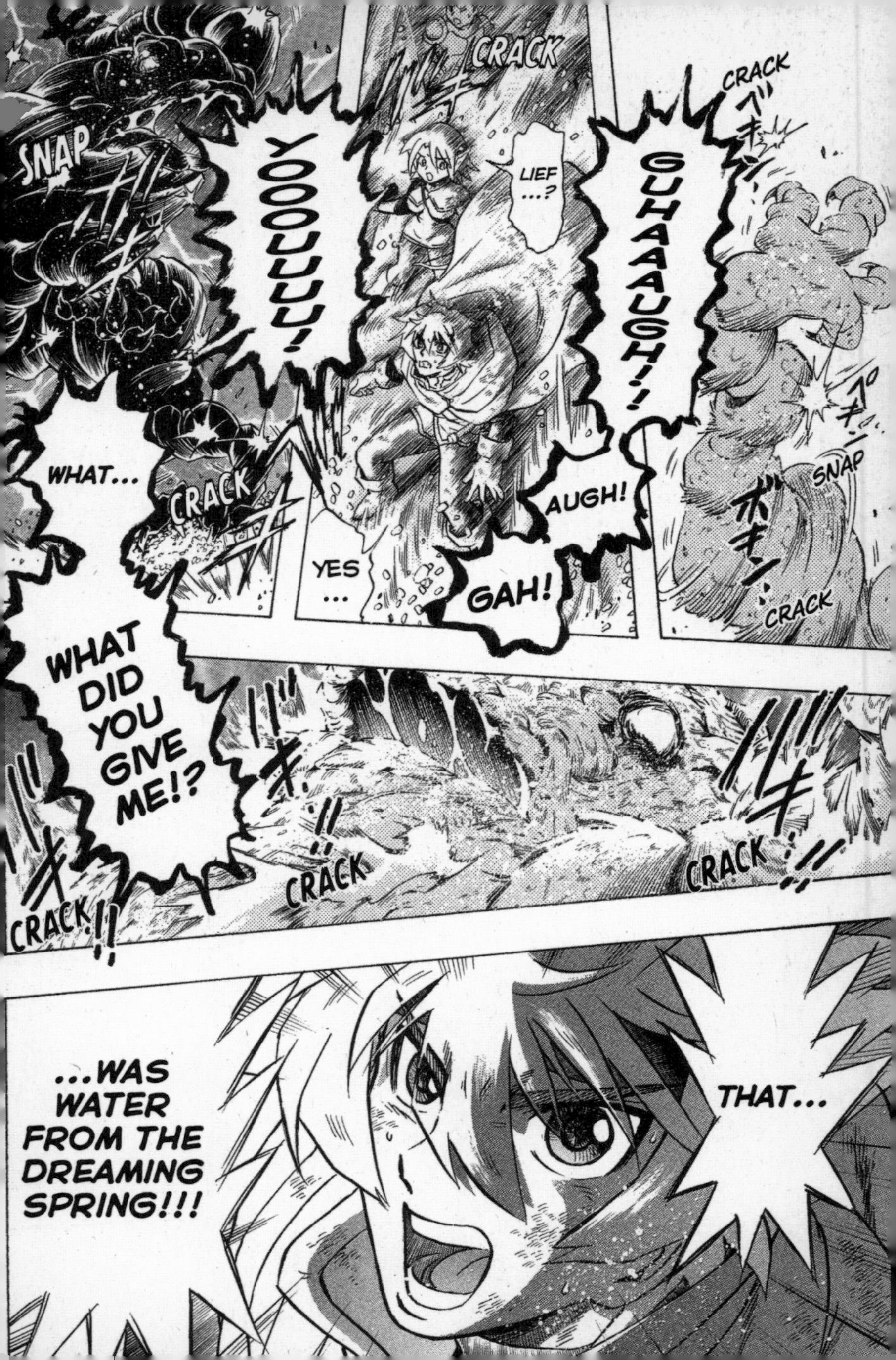
CRACK
GUHAAAAUGH!!
SNAP
CRACK
AUGH!
GAH!
CRACK
LIEF ...?
YES ...
YOOOUUUUU!
SNAP
CRACK
WHAT...
WHAT DID YOU GIVE ME!?
CRACK!!
CRACK!!
CRACK!!
THAT...
...WAS WATER FROM THE DREAMING SPRING!!!

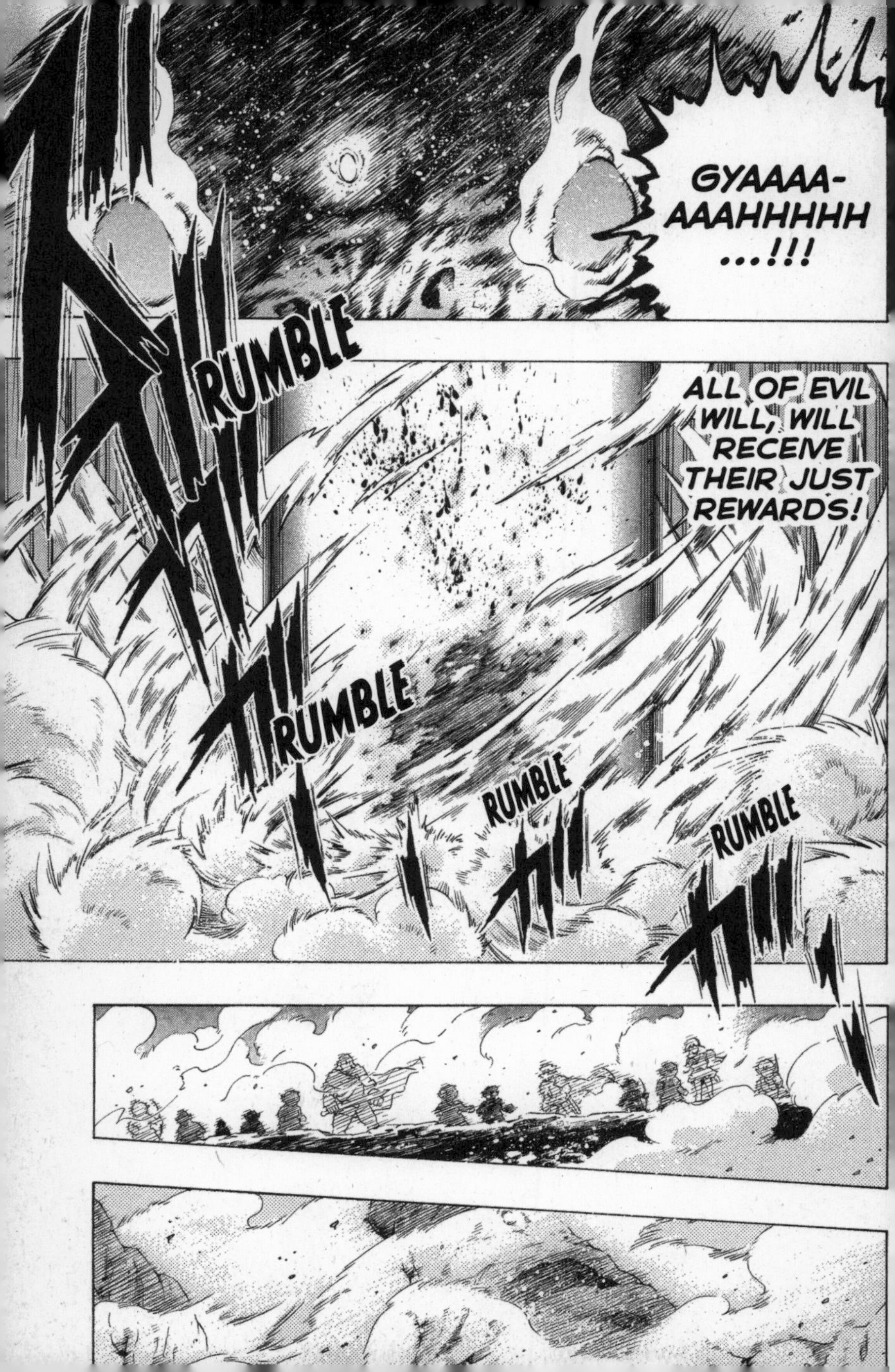
GYAAAA-AAAHHHHH ...!!!
RUMBLE
ALL OF EVIL WILL, WILL RECEIVE THEIR JUST REWARDS!
RUMBLE
RUMBLE
RUMBLE
RUMBLE

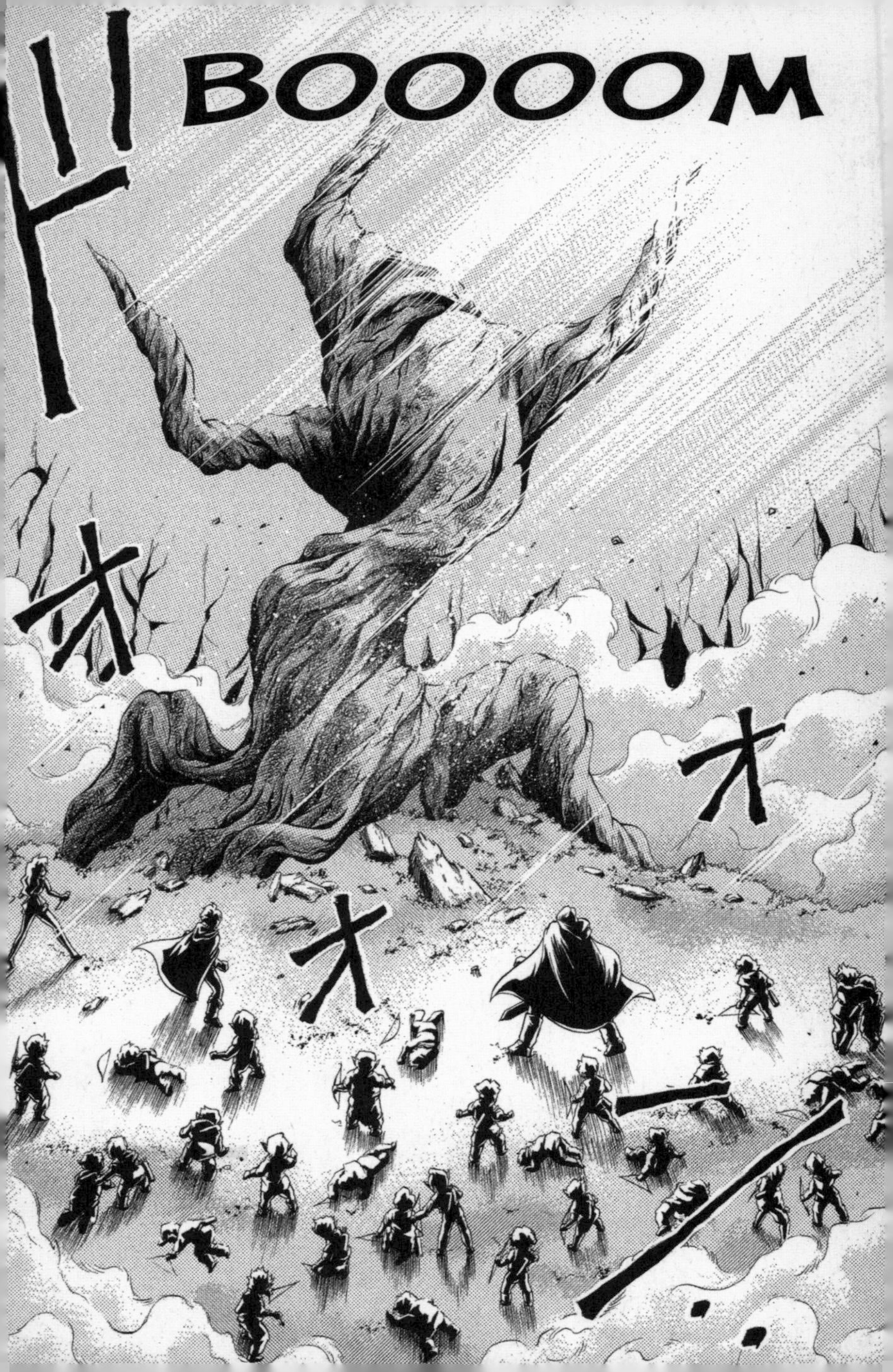
BOOOOM

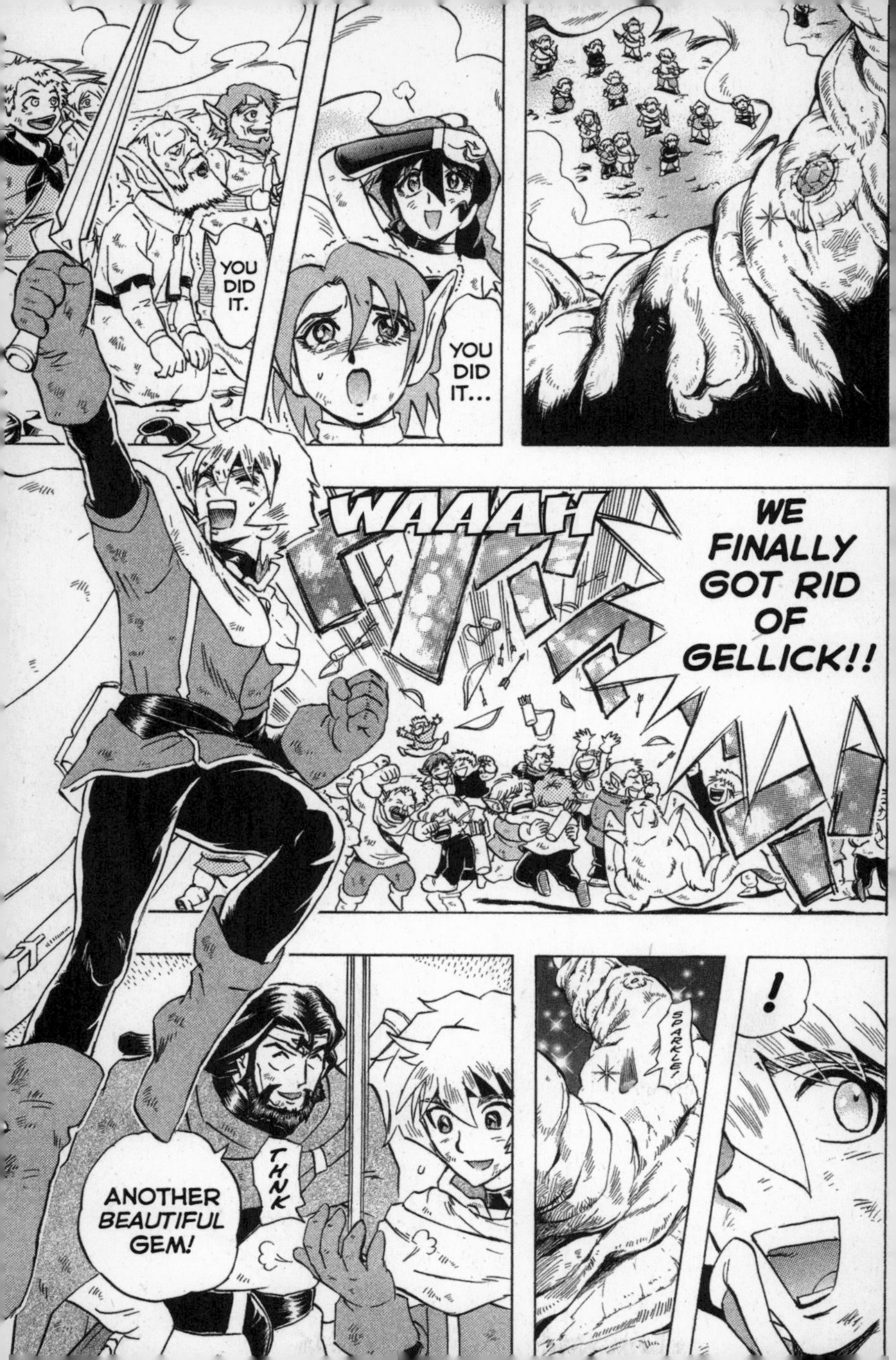
YOU DID IT...
YOU DID IT.
WE FINALLY GOT RID OF GELLICK!!
WAAAH
!
SPARKLE!
THNK
ANOTHER BEAUTIFUL GEM!

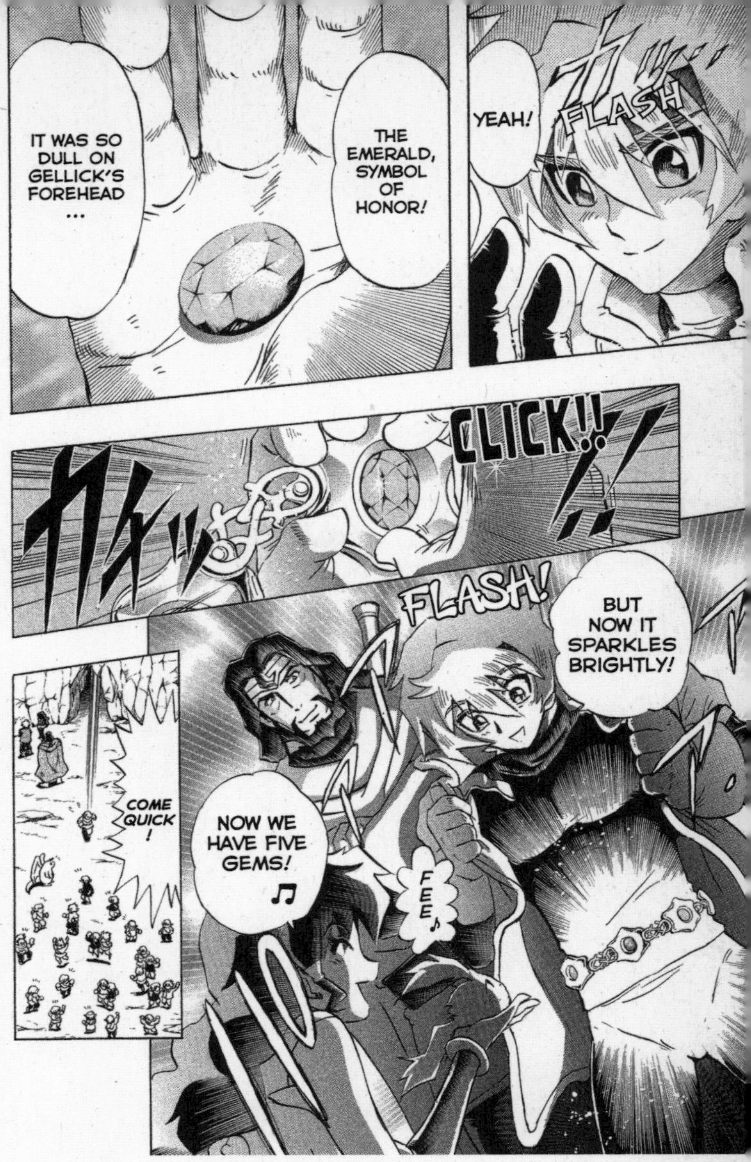
FLASH
YEAH!
THE EMERALD, SYMBOL OF HONOR!
IT WAS SO DULL ON GELLICK'S FOREHEAD ...
CLICK!!
FLASH!
BUT NOW IT SPARKLES BRIGHTLY!
FEE ♪
NOW WE HAVE FIVE GEMS! ♫
COME QUICK!

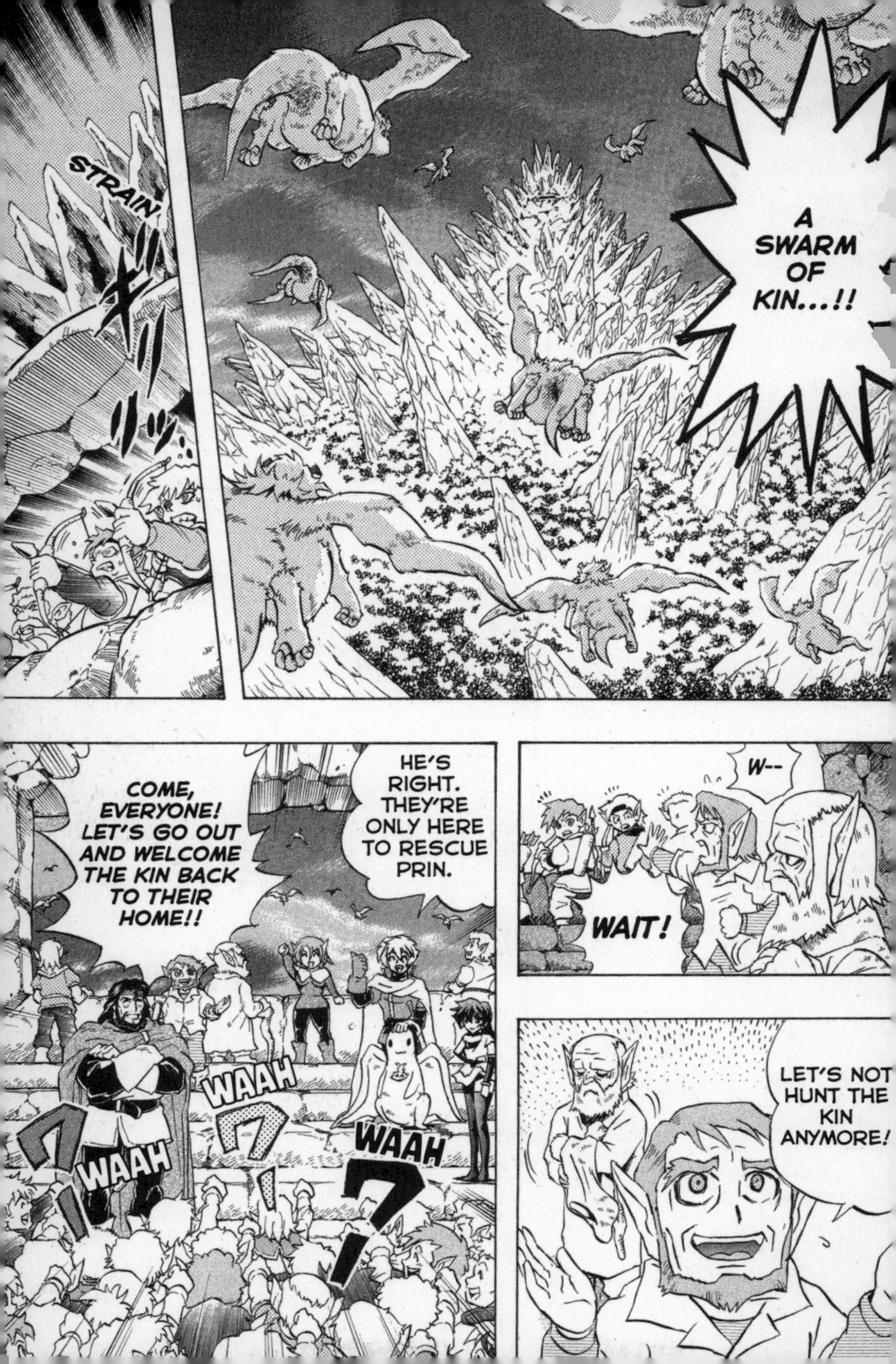
A SWARM OF KIN...!!
STRAIN
W--
WAIT!
LET'S NOT HUNT THE KIN ANYMORE!
HE'S RIGHT. THEY'RE ONLY HERE TO RESCUE PRIN.
COME, EVERYONE! LET'S GO OUT AND WELCOME THE KIN BACK TO THEIR HOME!!
WAAH?!
WAAH?!
WAAH!

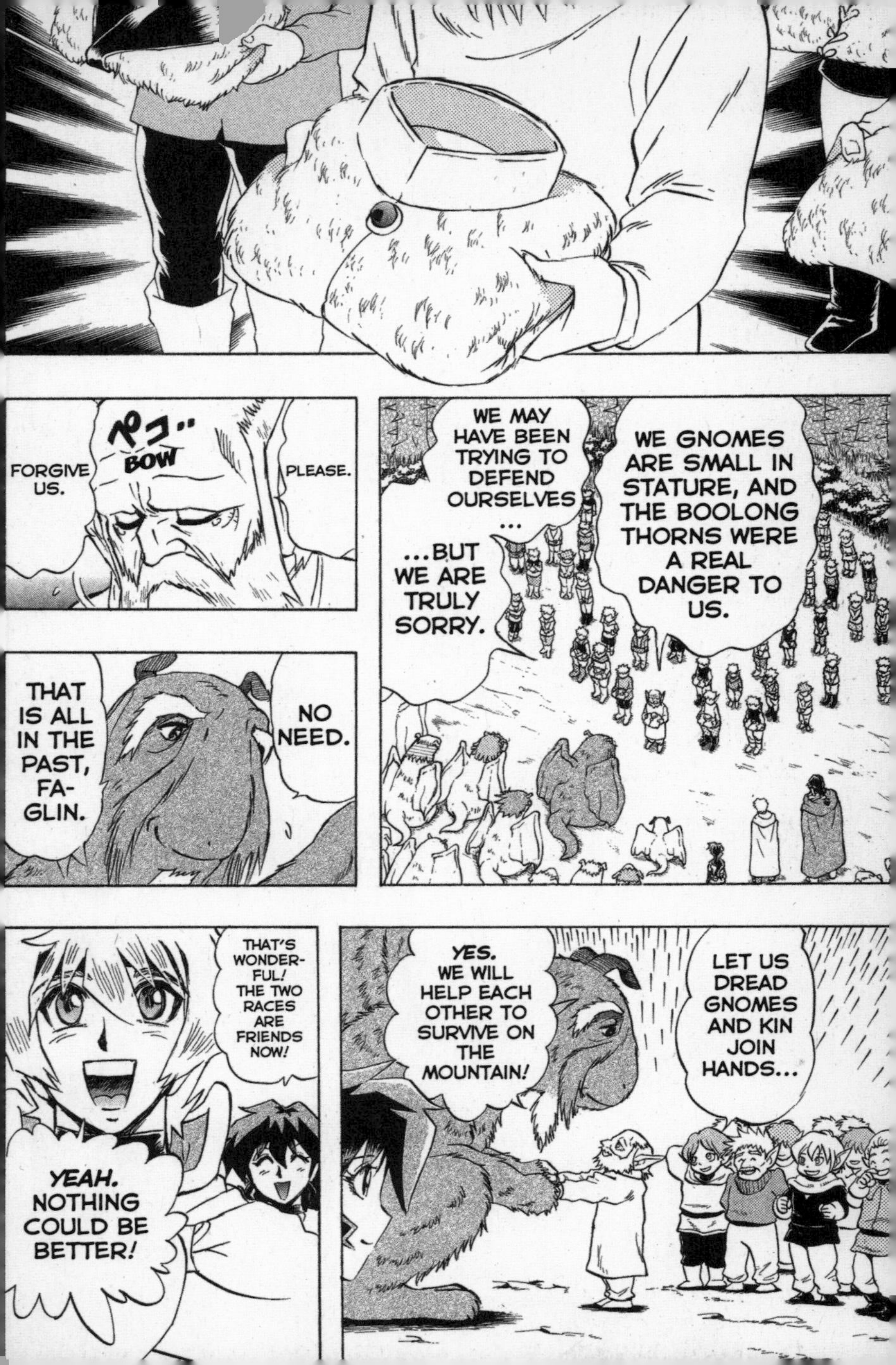
WE GNOMES ARE SMALL IN STATURE, AND THE BOOLONG THORNS WERE A REAL DANGER TO US.
WE MAY HAVE BEEN TRYING TO DEFEND OURSELVES ...
...BUT WE ARE TRULY SORRY.
PLEASE.
ペコ.. BOW
FORGIVE US.
NO NEED.
THAT IS ALL IN THE PAST, FA-GLIN.
LET US DREAD GNOMES AND KIN JOIN HANDS...
YES. WE WILL HELP EACH OTHER TO SURVIVE ON THE MOUNTAIN!
THAT'S WONDERFUL! THE TWO RACES ARE FRIENDS NOW!
YEAH. NOTHING COULD BE BETTER!

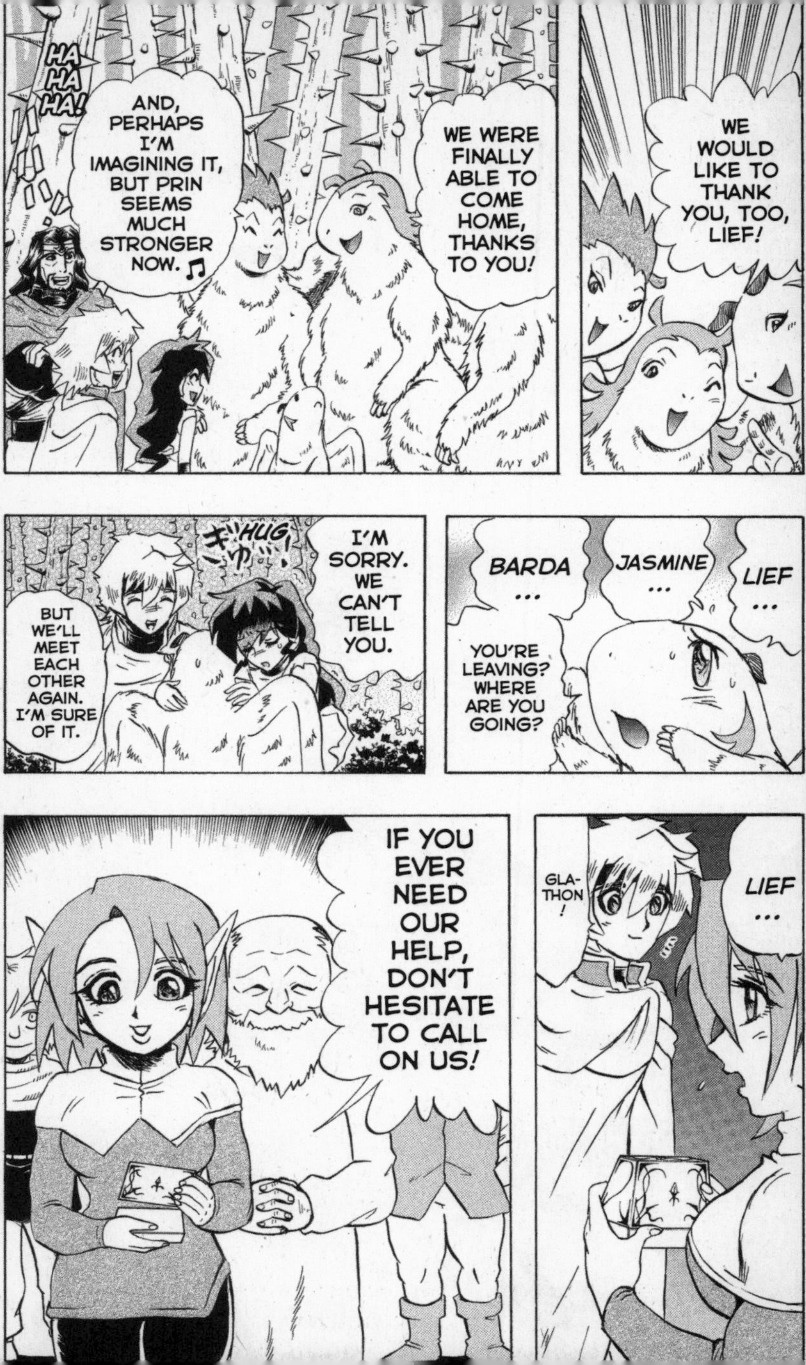
WE WOULD LIKE TO THANK YOU, TOO, LIEF!
WE WERE FINALLY ABLE TO COME HOME, THANKS TO YOU!
HA HA HA!
AND, PERHAPS I'M IMAGINING IT, BUT PRIN SEEMS MUCH STRONGER NOW. ♫
LIEF ...
JASMINE ...
BARDA ...
YOU'RE LEAVING? WHERE ARE YOU GOING?
I'M SORRY. WE CAN'T TELL YOU.
HUG
BUT WE'LL MEET EACH OTHER AGAIN. I'M SURE OF IT.
LIEF ...
GLA-THON!
IF YOU EVER NEED OUR HELP, DON'T HESITATE TO CALL ON US!

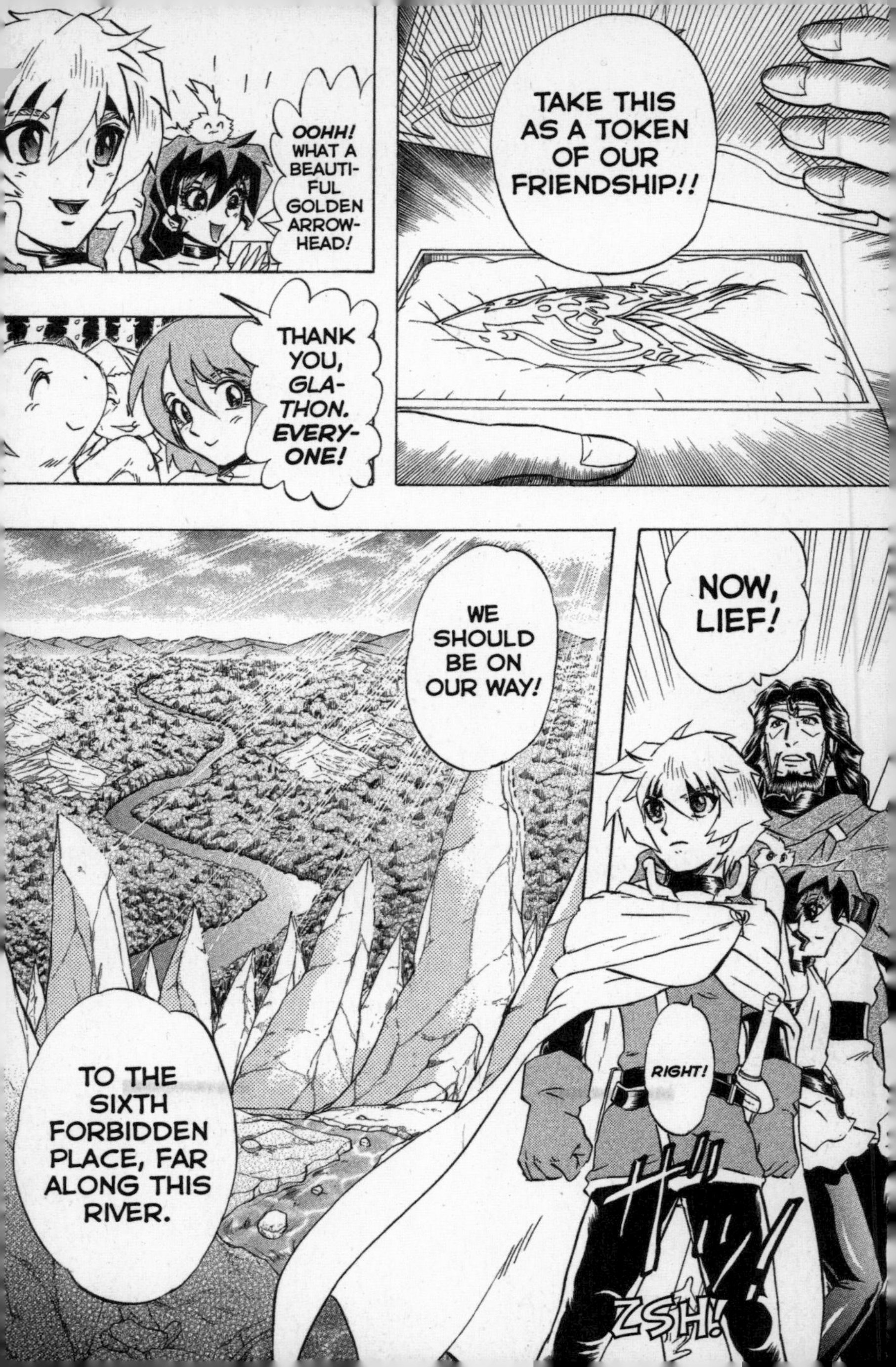
TAKE THIS AS A TOKEN OF OUR FRIENDSHIP!!
OOHH! WHAT A BEAUTIFUL GOLDEN ARROWHEAD!
THANK YOU, GLATHON. EVERYONE!
NOW, LIEF!
RIGHT!
ZSH!
WE SHOULD BE ON OUR WAY!
TO THE SIXTH FORBIDDEN PLACE, FAR ALONG THIS RIVER.

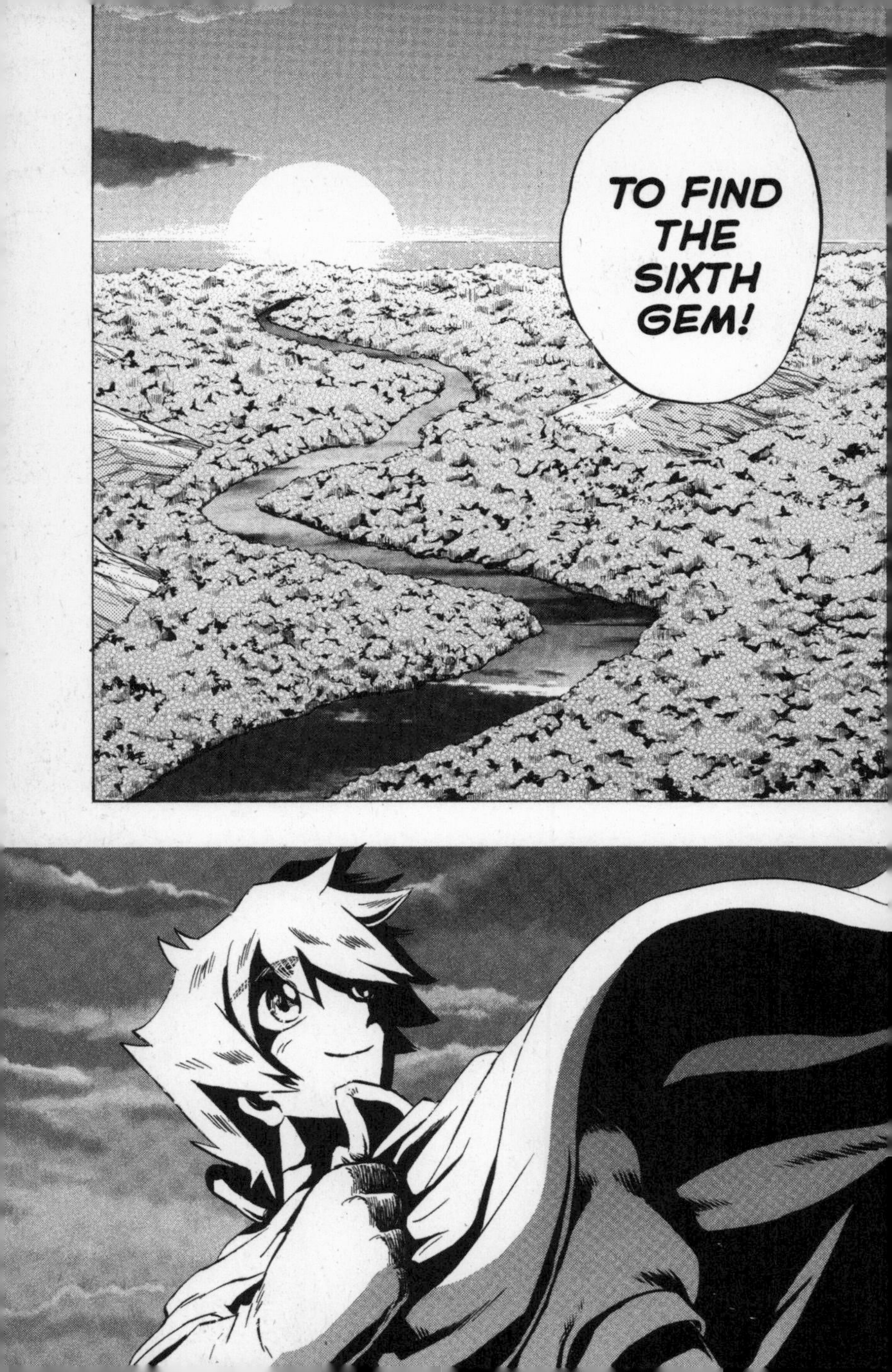
TO FIND THE SIXTH GEM!

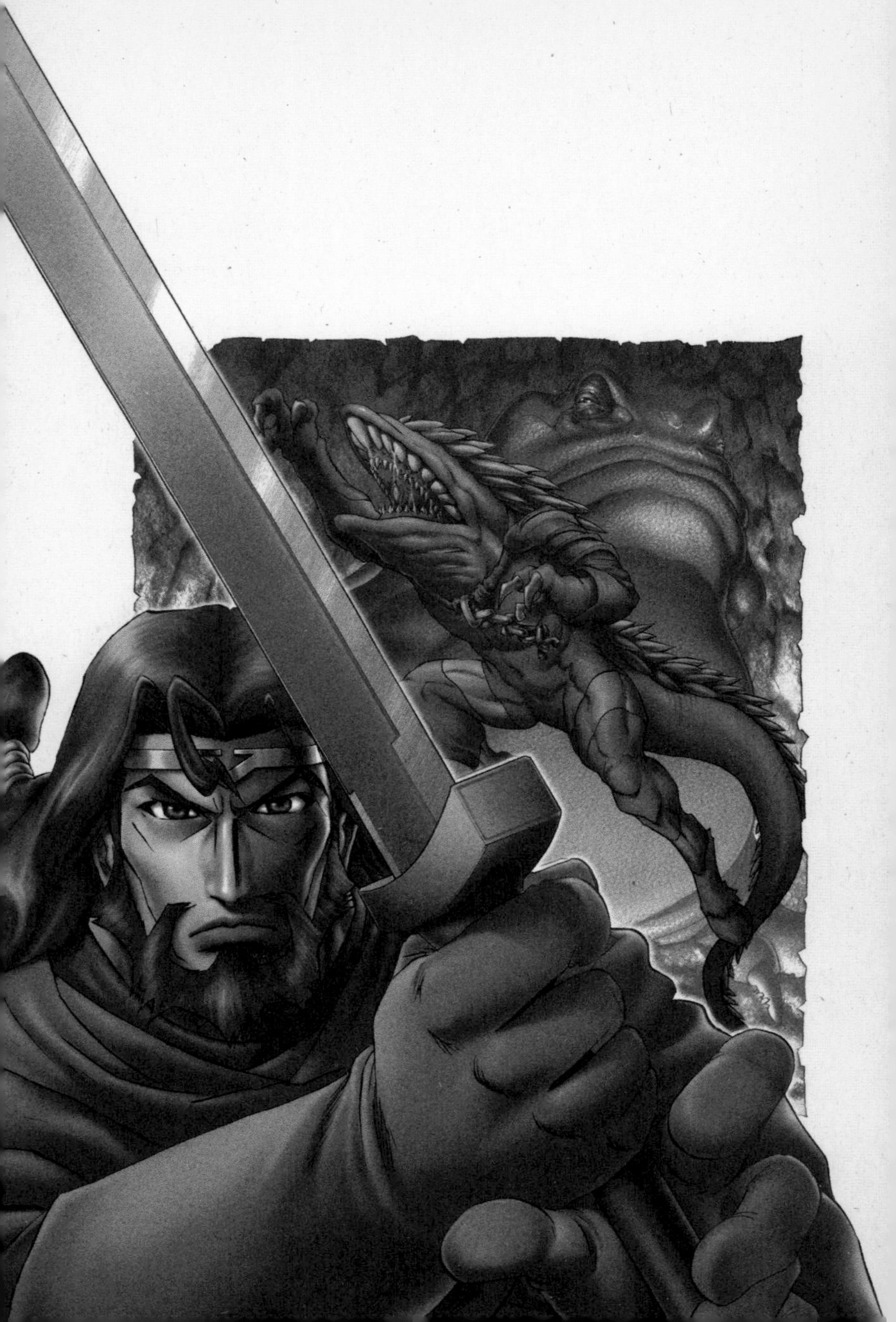

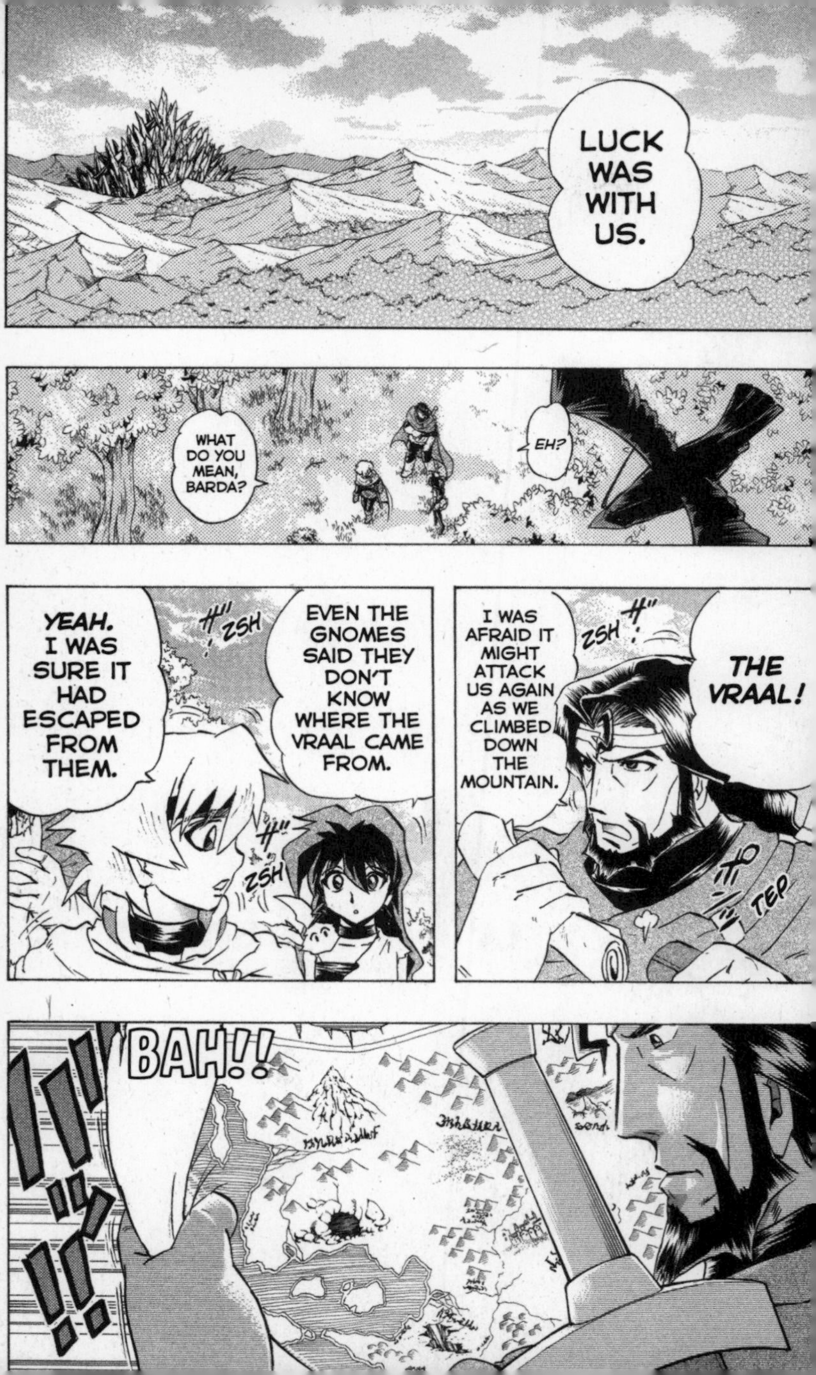
LUCK WAS WITH US.
EH?
WHAT DO YOU MEAN, BARDA?
THE VRAAL!
ZSH
I WAS AFRAID IT MIGHT ATTACK US AGAIN AS WE CLIMBED DOWN THE MOUNTAIN.
TEP
EVEN THE GNOMES SAID THEY DON'T KNOW WHERE THE VRAAL CAME FROM.
ZSH
YEAH. I WAS SURE IT HAD ESCAPED FROM THEM.
ZSH
BAH!!

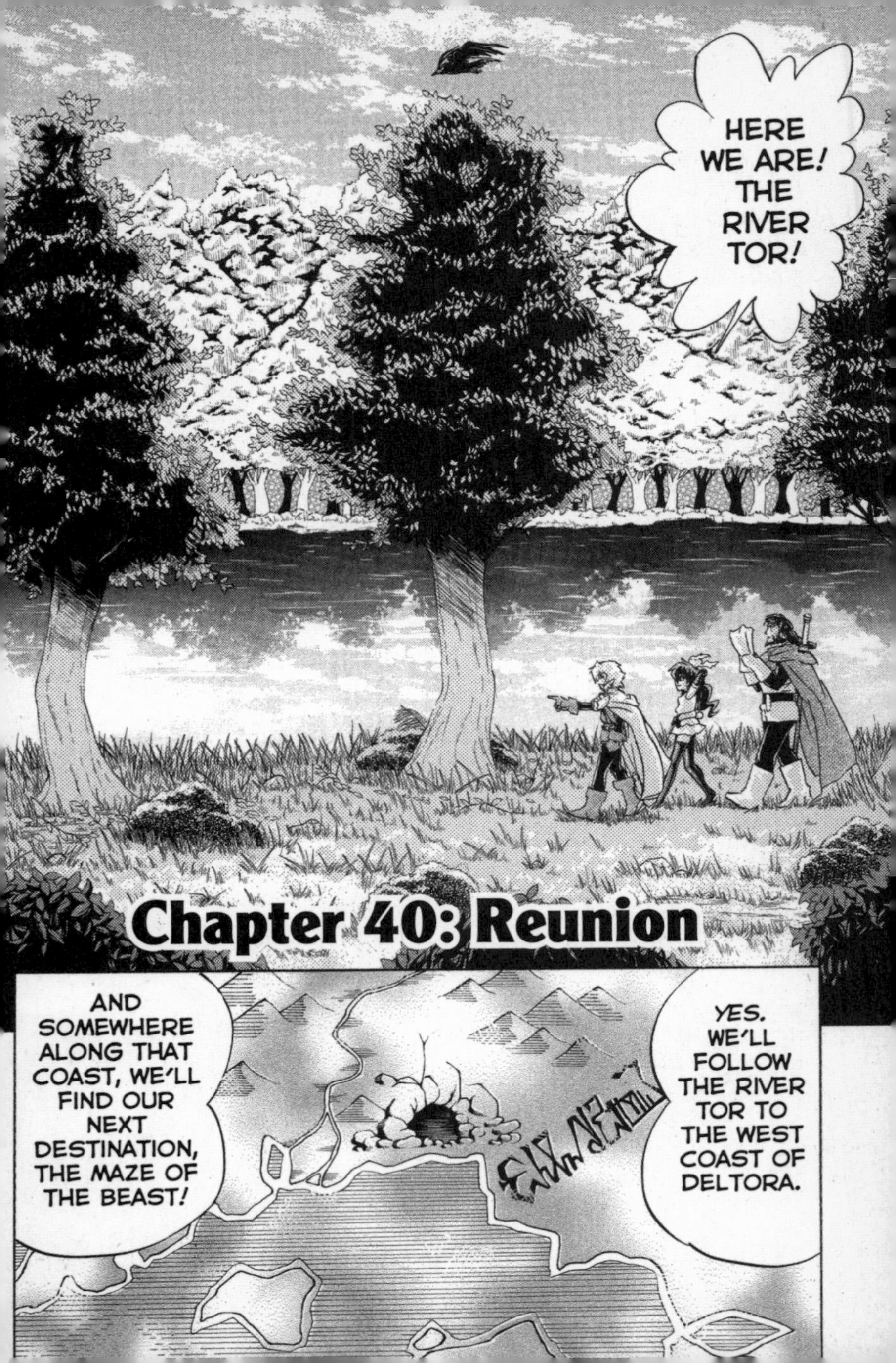
HERE WE ARE! THE RIVER TOR!
Chapter 40: Reunion
YES. WE'LL FOLLOW THE RIVER TOR TO THE WEST COAST OF DELTORA.
AND SOMEWHERE ALONG THAT COAST, WE'LL FIND OUR NEXT DESTINATION, THE MAZE OF THE BEAST!

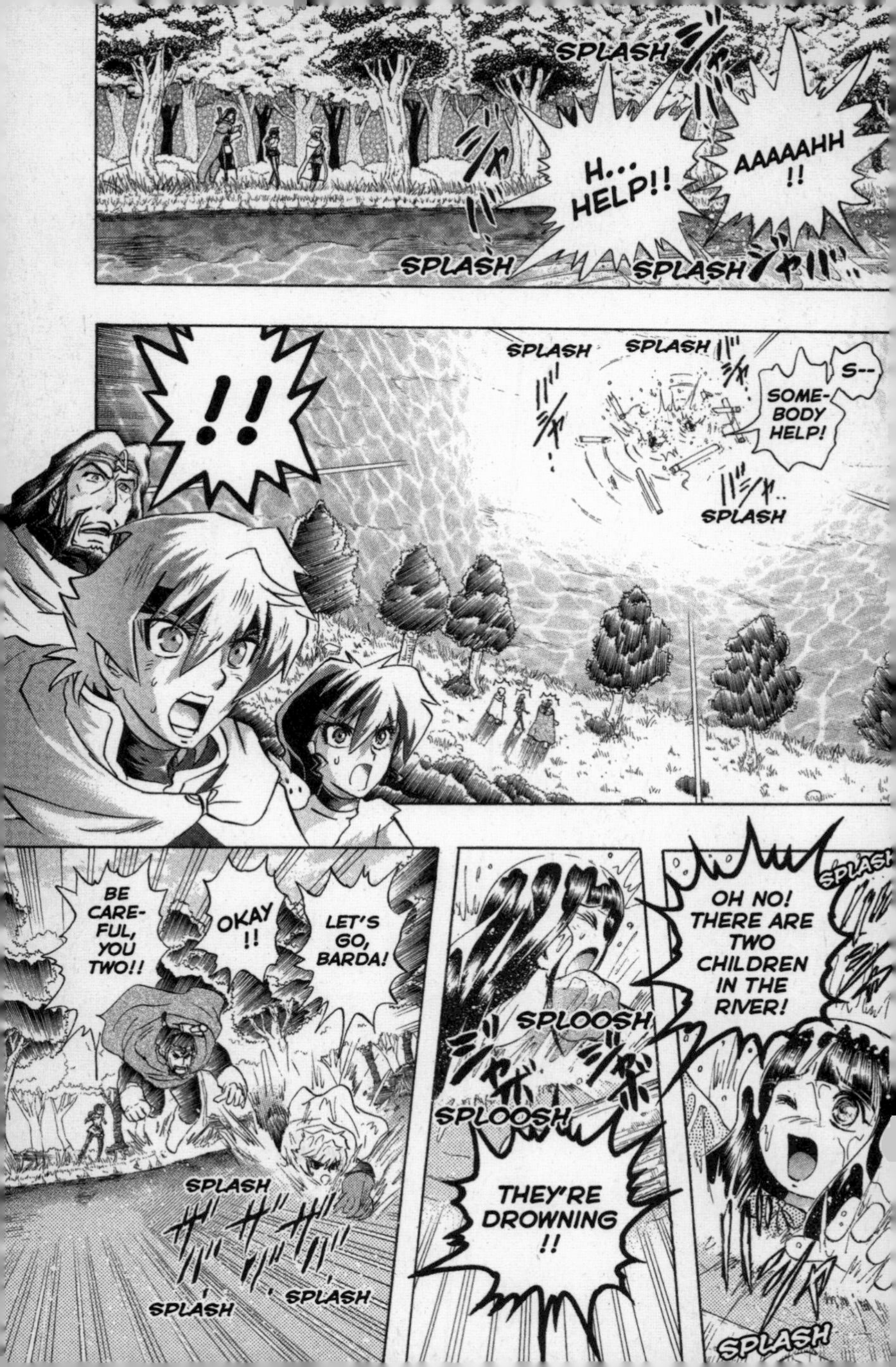
SPLASH
AAAAAHH !!
H... HELP!!
SPLASH
SPLASH
S--
SOME-BODY HELP!
SPLASH
SPLASH
SPLASH
!!
SPLASH
OH NO! THERE ARE TWO CHILDREN IN THE RIVER!
SPLASH
SPLOOSH
SPLOOSH
THEY'RE DROWNING !!
LET'S GO, BARDA!
OKAY !!
BE CARE-FUL, YOU TWO!!
SPLASH
SPLASH
SPLASH

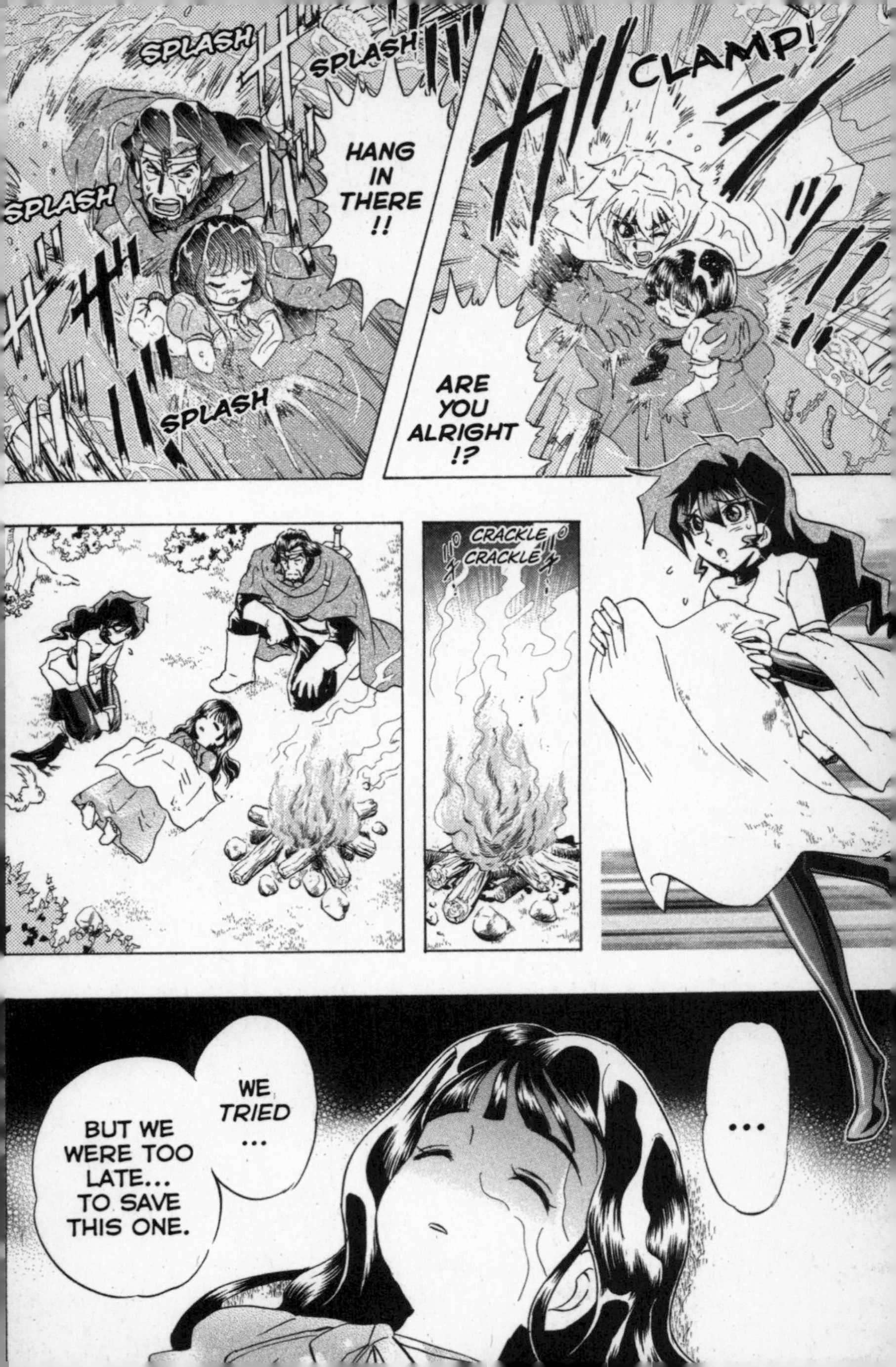

CLAMP!
ARE YOU ALRIGHT !?
SPLASH
SPLASH
SPLASH
HANG IN THERE !!
SPLASH
CRACKLE CRACKLE
...
WE TRIED ...
BUT WE WERE TOO LATE... TO SAVE THIS ONE.

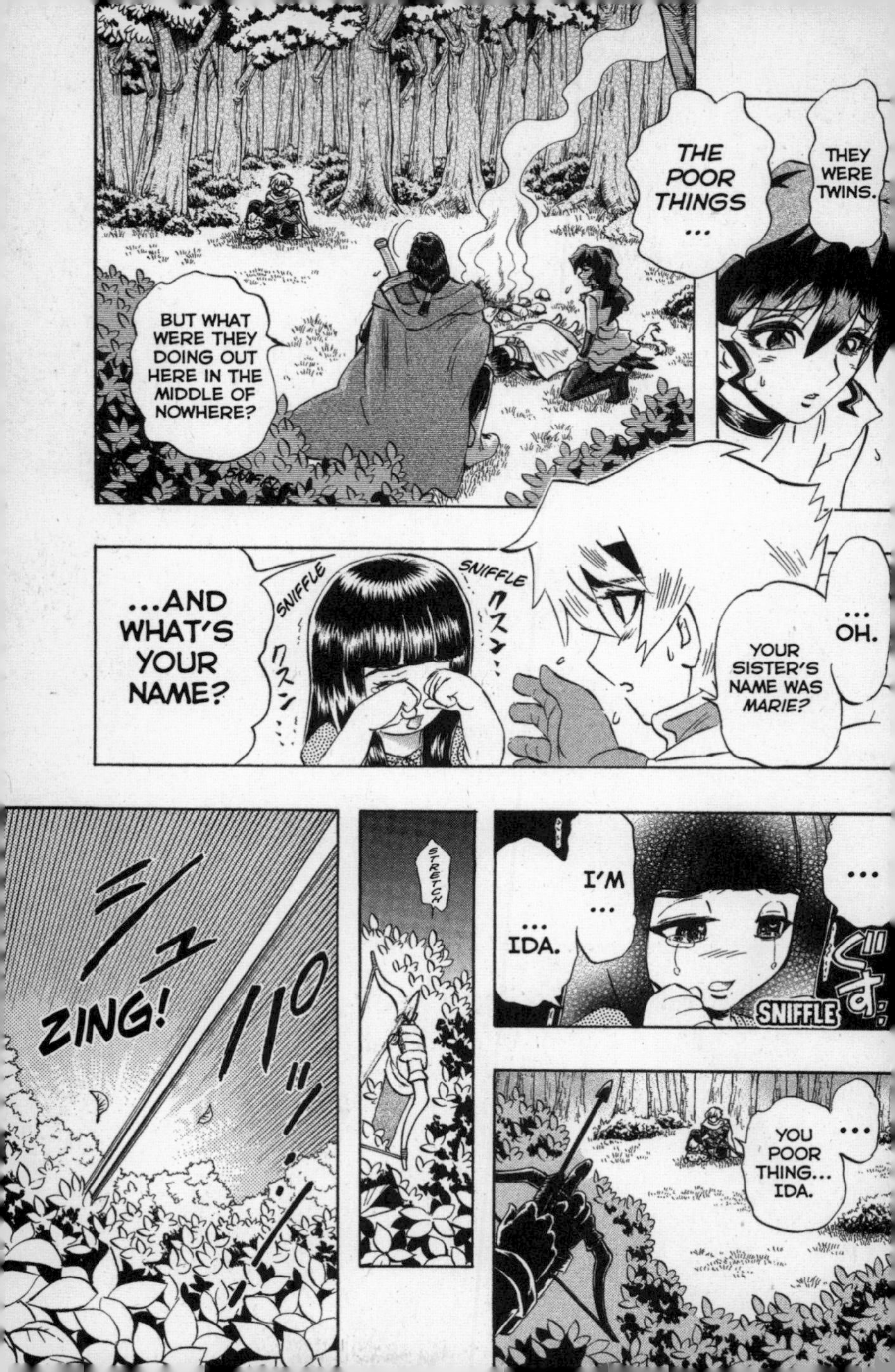
THEY WERE TWINS.
THE POOR THINGS ...
BUT WHAT WERE THEY DOING OUT HERE IN THE MIDDLE OF NOWHERE?
SNIFFLE
... OH.
YOUR SISTER'S NAME WAS MARIE?
SNIFFLE
クスン
SNIFFLE
クスン
...AND WHAT'S YOUR NAME?
...
I'M ... ... IDA.
ぐす
SNIFFLE
... YOU POOR THING... IDA.
STRETCH
ZING!

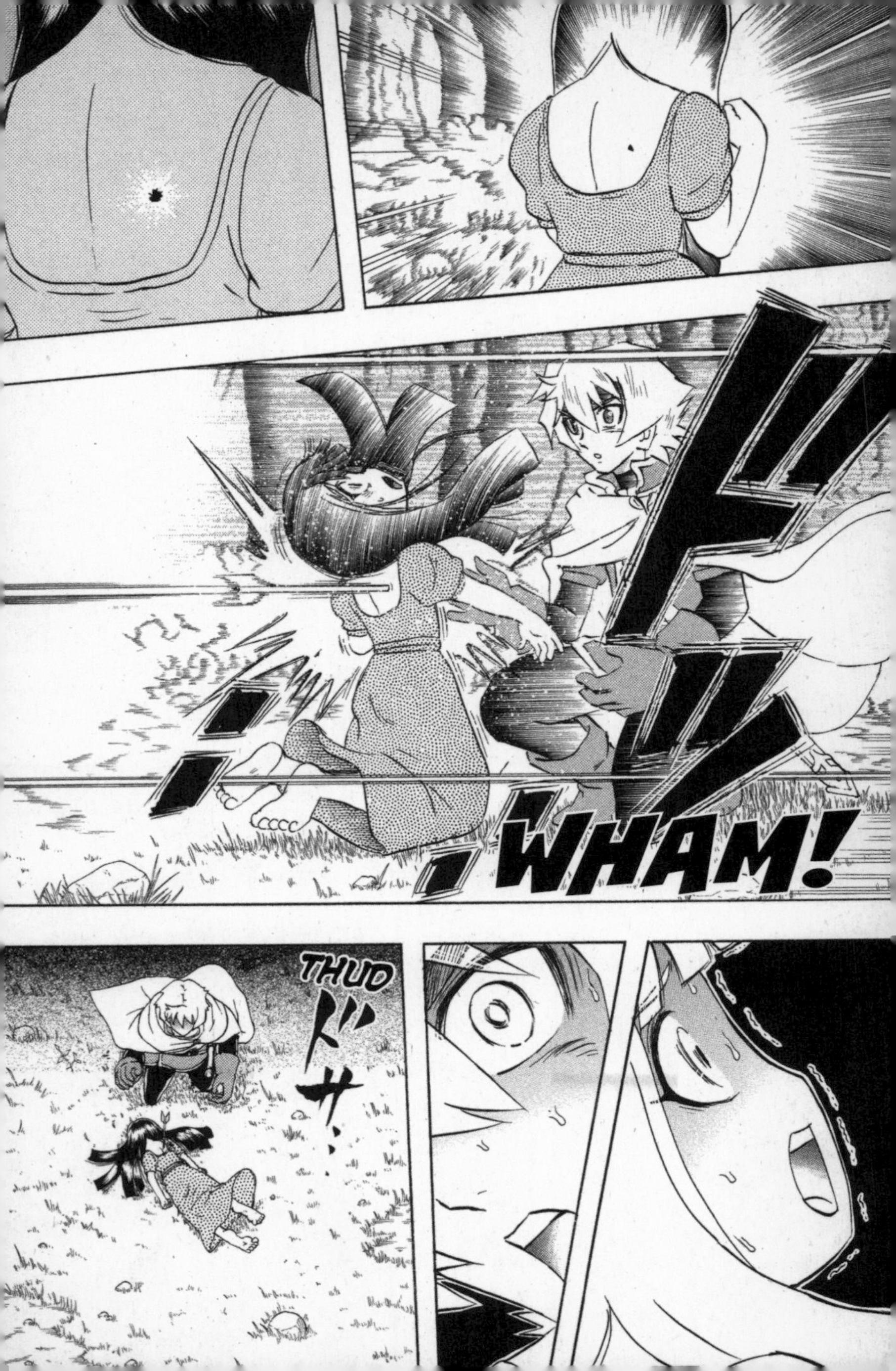
WHAM!
THUD

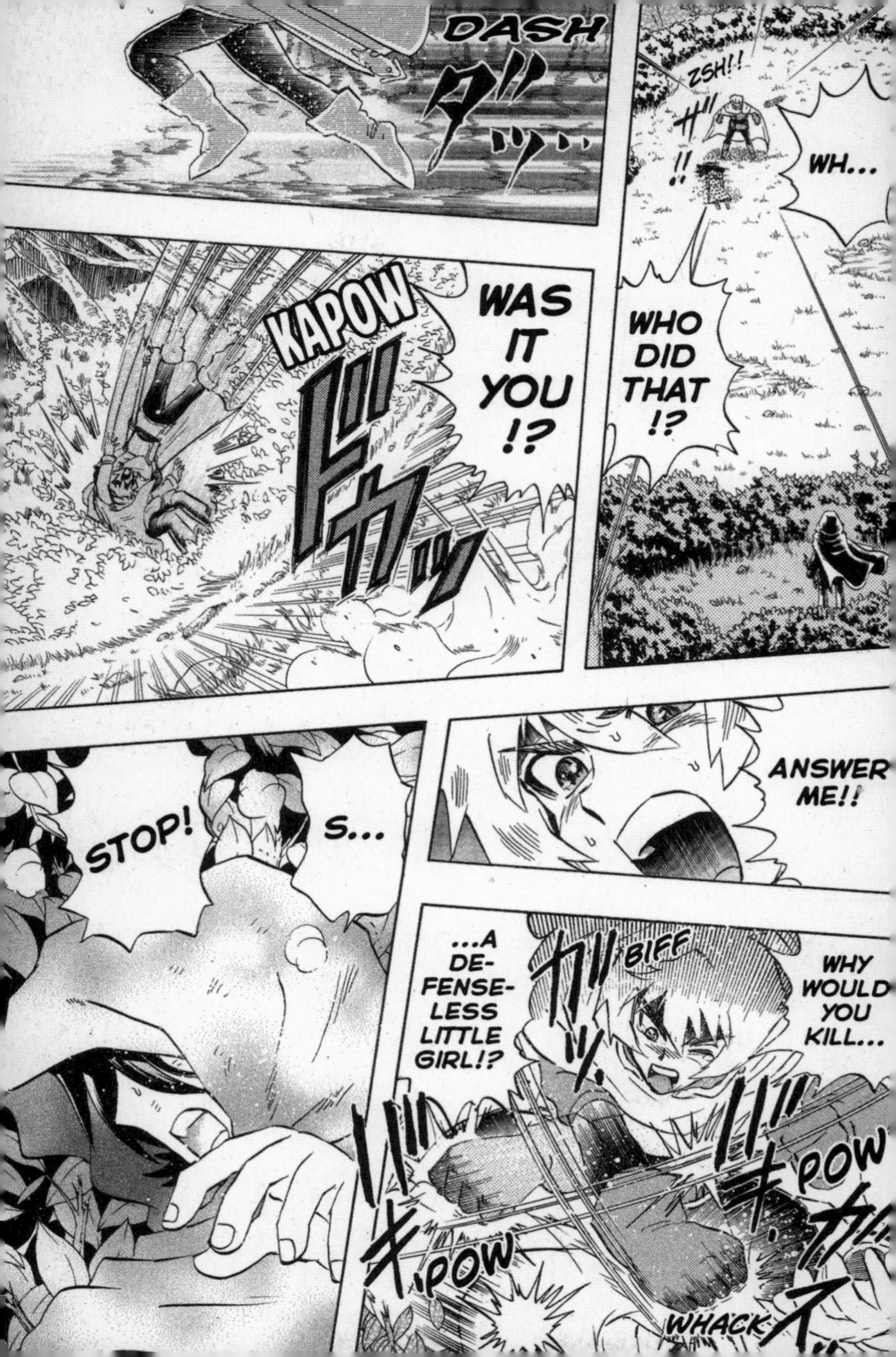
ZSH!!
WH...
WHO DID THAT!?
DASH
KAPOW
WAS IT YOU!?
ANSWER ME!!
WHY WOULD YOU KILL...
BIFF
...A DEFENSE-LESS LITTLE GIRL!?
POW
POW
WHACK
S...
STOP!

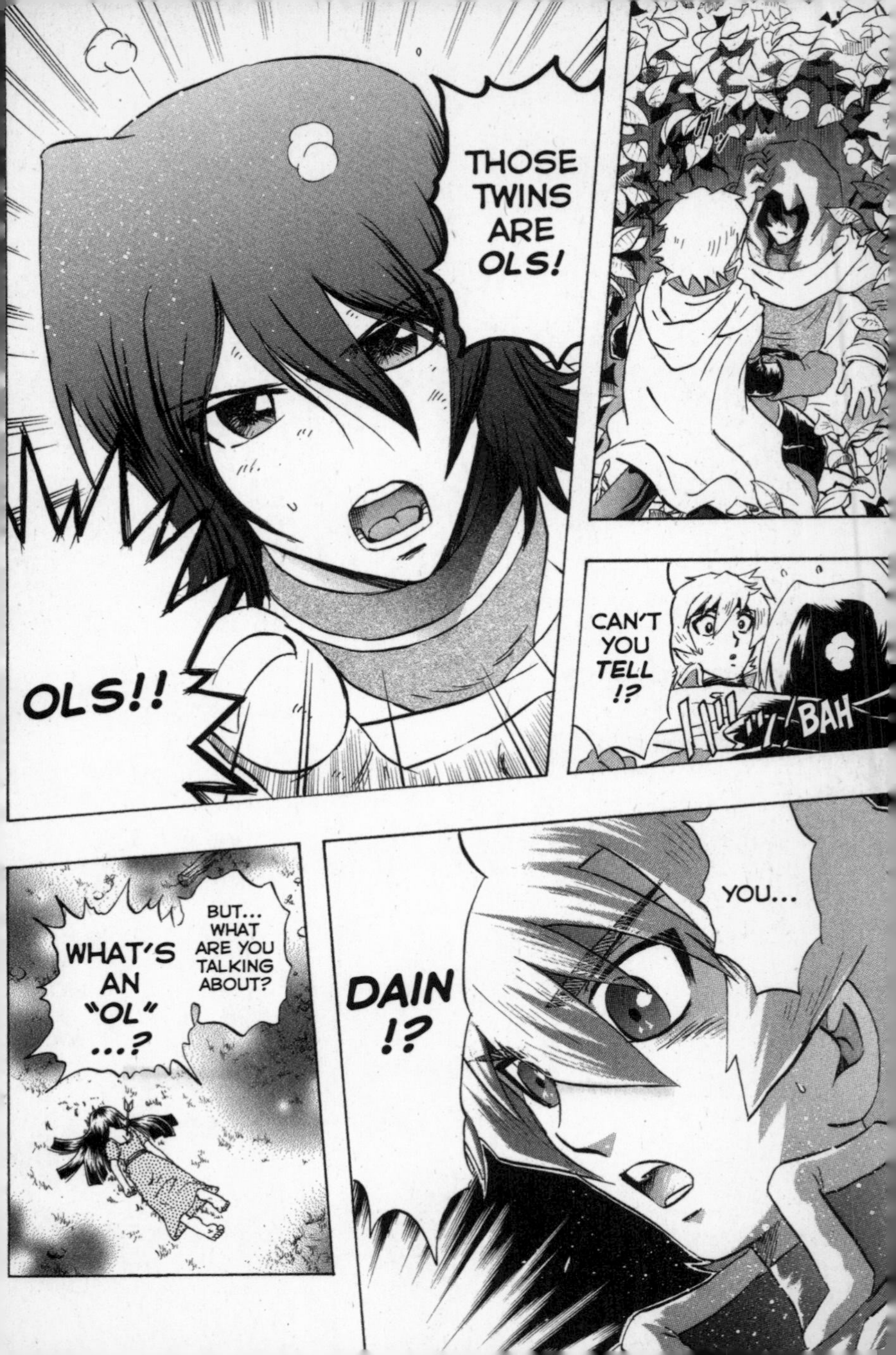
CAN'T YOU TELL !?
BAH
THOSE TWINS ARE OLS!
OLS!!
YOU...
DAIN !?
BUT... WHAT ARE YOU TALKING ABOUT?
WHAT'S AN "OL" ...?

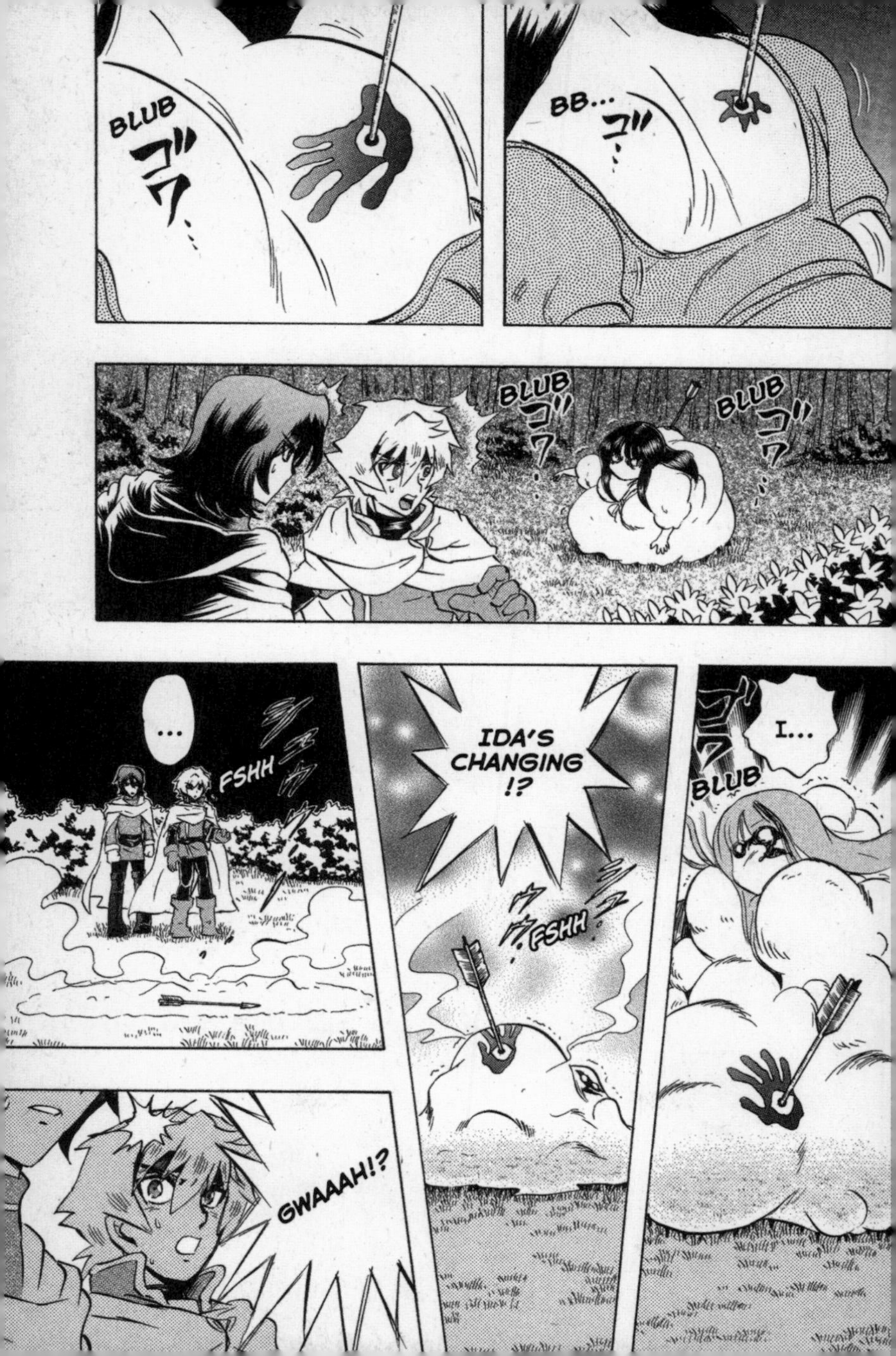
BB...
ゴ"...
BLUB
ゴワ...
BLUB
ゴワ...
BLUB
ゴワ...
I...
ゴワ
BLUB
IDA'S CHANGING !?
FSHH
...
FSHH
GWAAAH!?

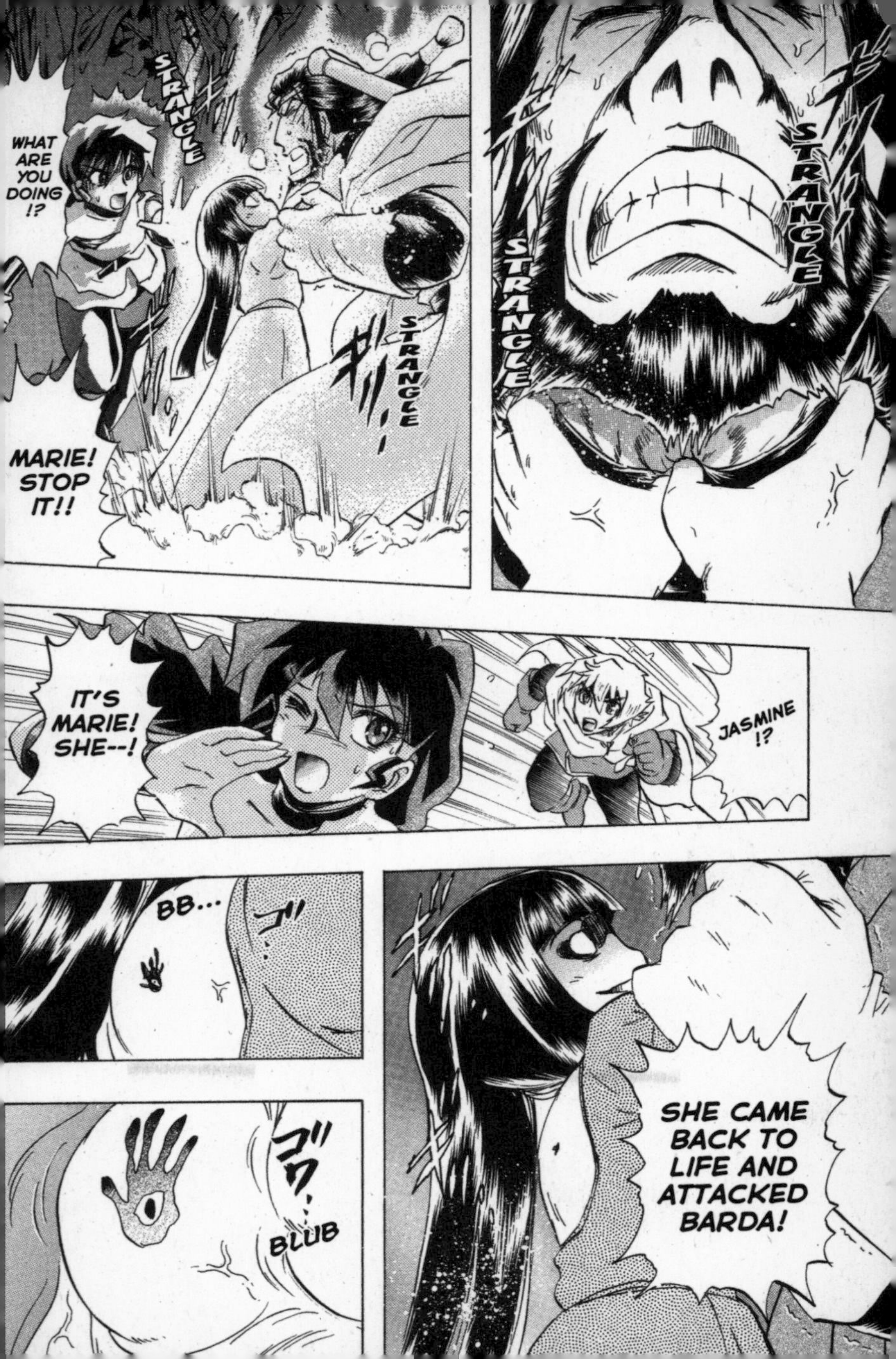
STRANGLE
STRANGLE
STRANGLE
WHAT ARE YOU DOING !?
STRANGLE
MARIE! STOP IT!!
JASMINE !?
IT'S MARIE! SHE--!
SHE CAME BACK TO LIFE AND ATTACKED BARDA!
BB...
BLUB

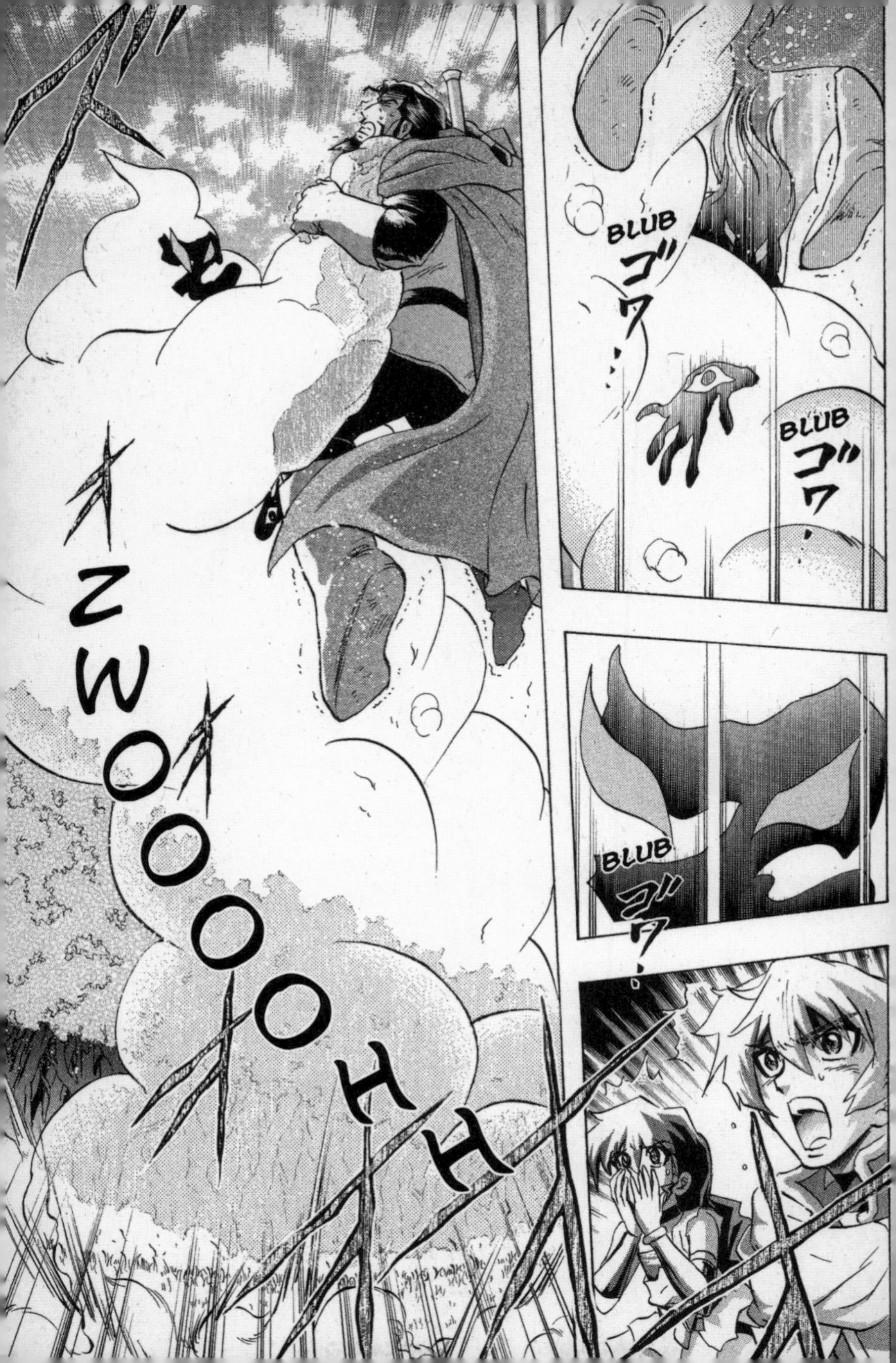
BLUB
ゴワ…
BLUB
ゴワ…
BLUB
ゴワ…
ZWOOOOHH

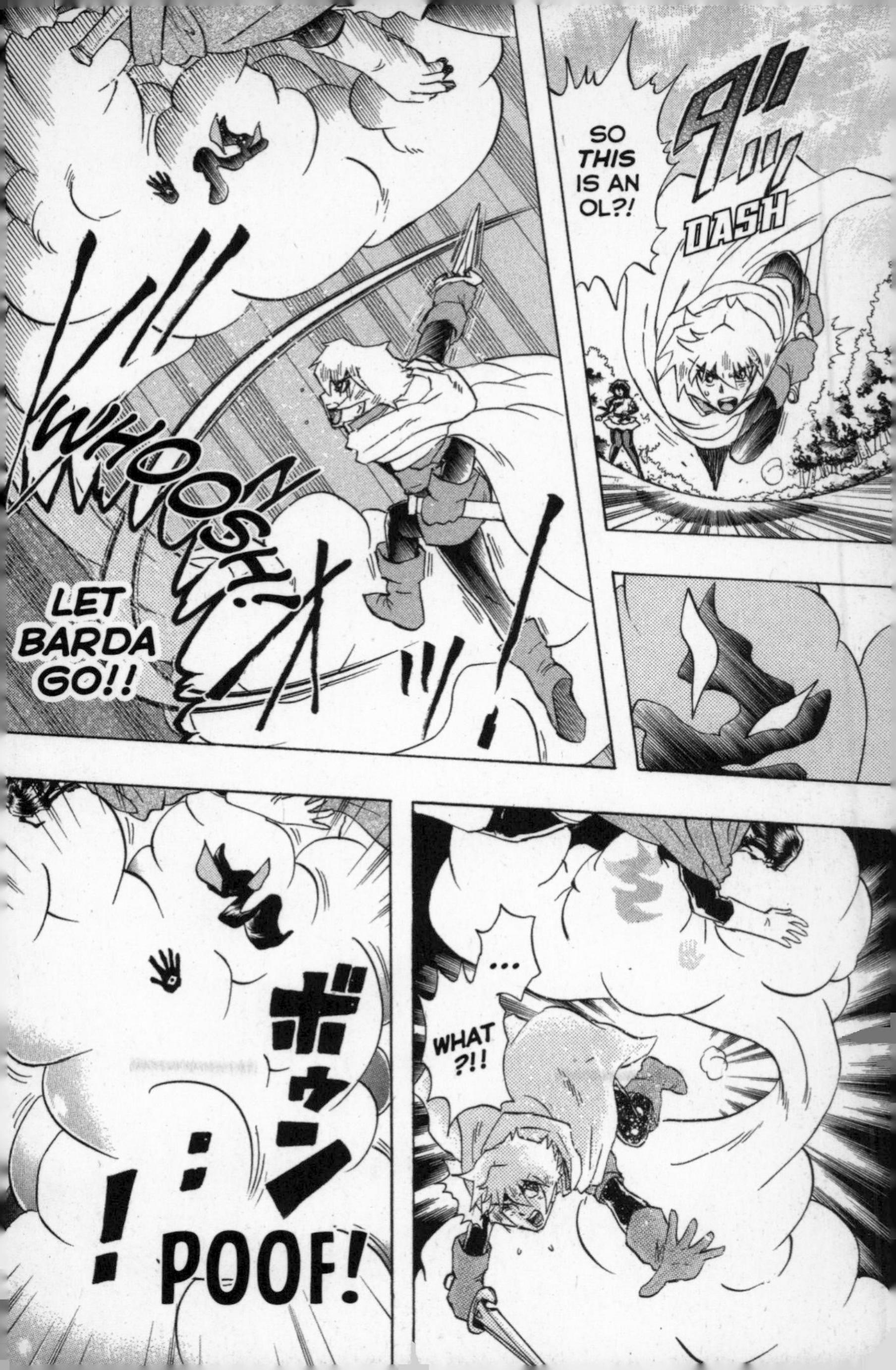

ダッ
DASH
SO THIS IS AN OL?!
WHOOSH!
LET BARDA GO!!
...
WHAT ?!!
ボウン
POOF!
!...

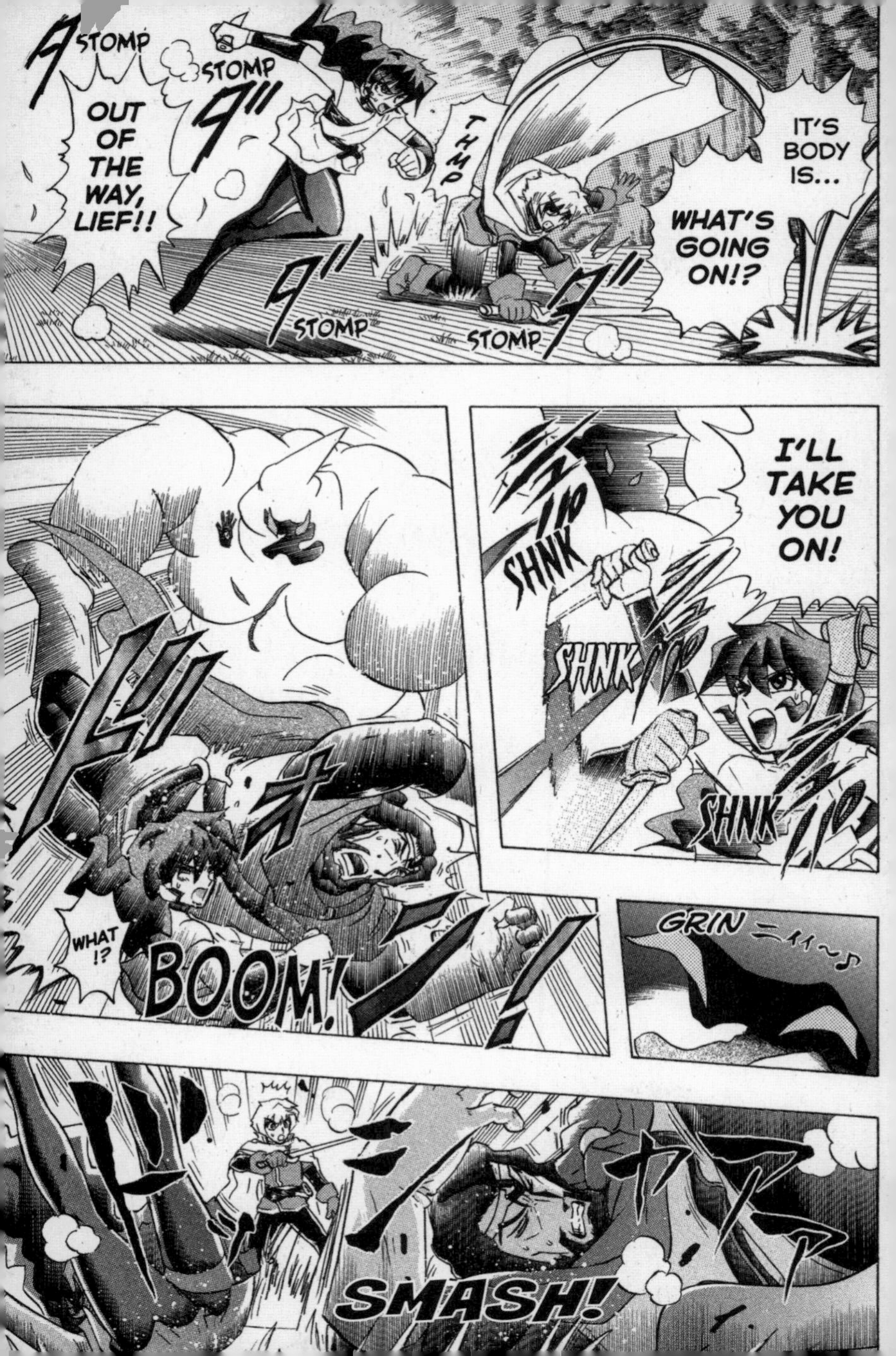
IT'S BODY IS...
WHAT'S GOING ON!?
THMP
STOMP
STOMP
OUT OF THE WAY, LIEF!!
STOMP
STOMP
I'LL TAKE YOU ON!
SHNK
SHNK
SHNK
GRIN
WHAT!?
BOOM!
SMASH!

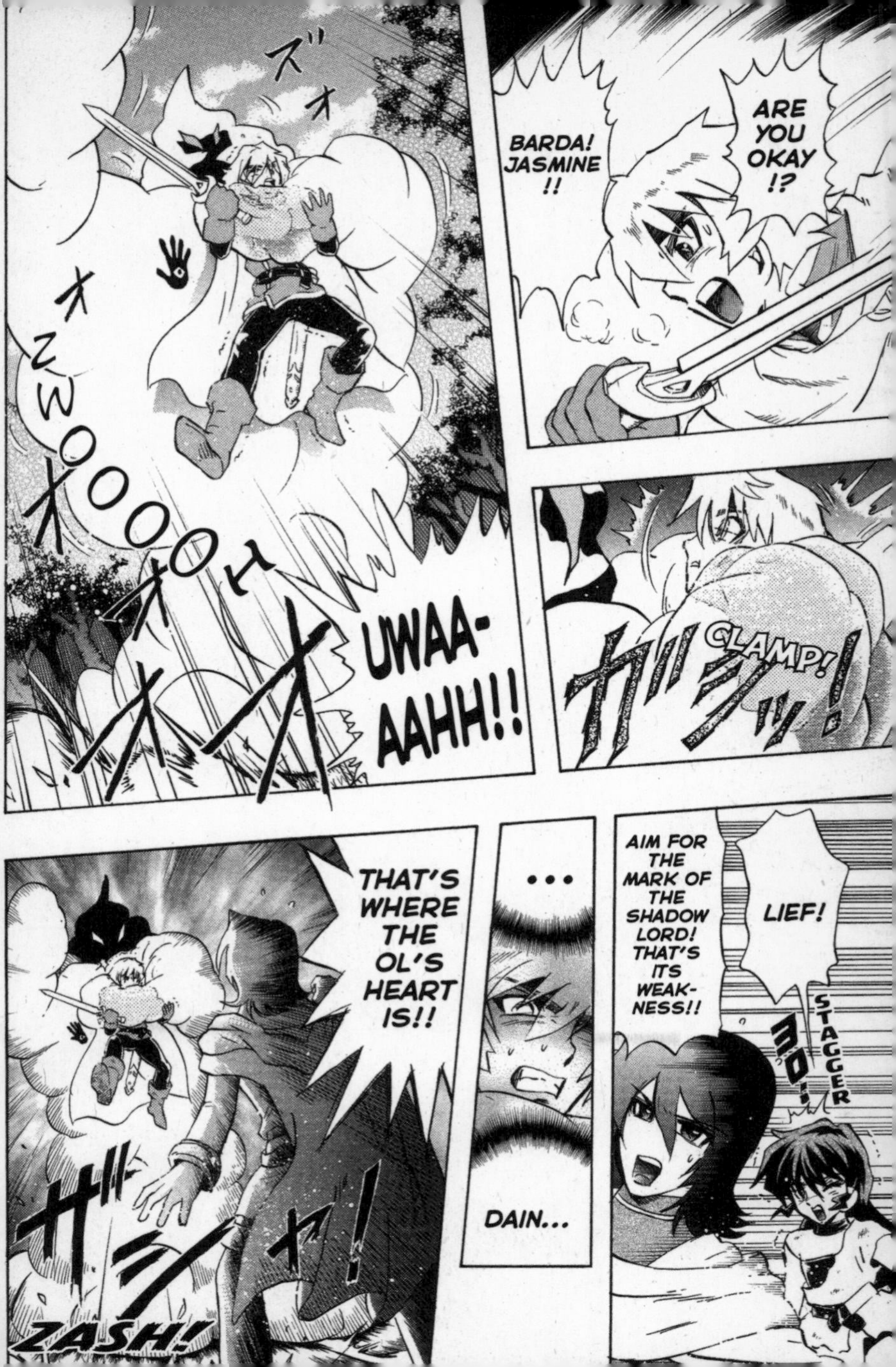
ARE YOU OKAY!?
BARDA! JASMINE!!
CLAMP!
WOOOOH
UWAA-AAHH!!
LIEF!
AIM FOR THE MARK OF THE SHADOW LORD! THAT'S ITS WEAK-NESS!!
STAGGER
...
DAIN...
THAT'S WHERE THE OL'S HEART IS!!
ZASH!

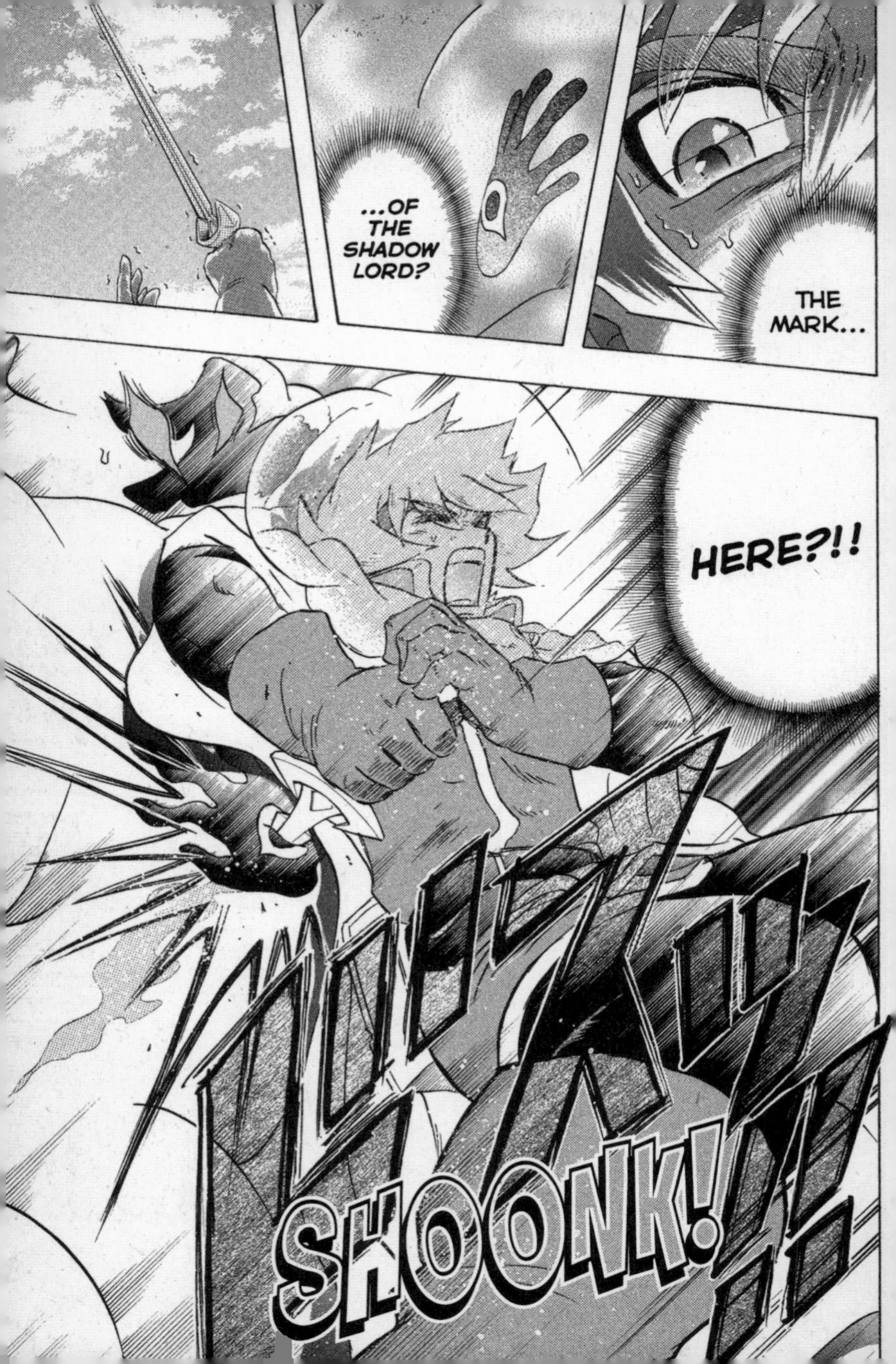
THE MARK...
...OF THE SHADOW LORD?
HERE?!!
SHOONK!!

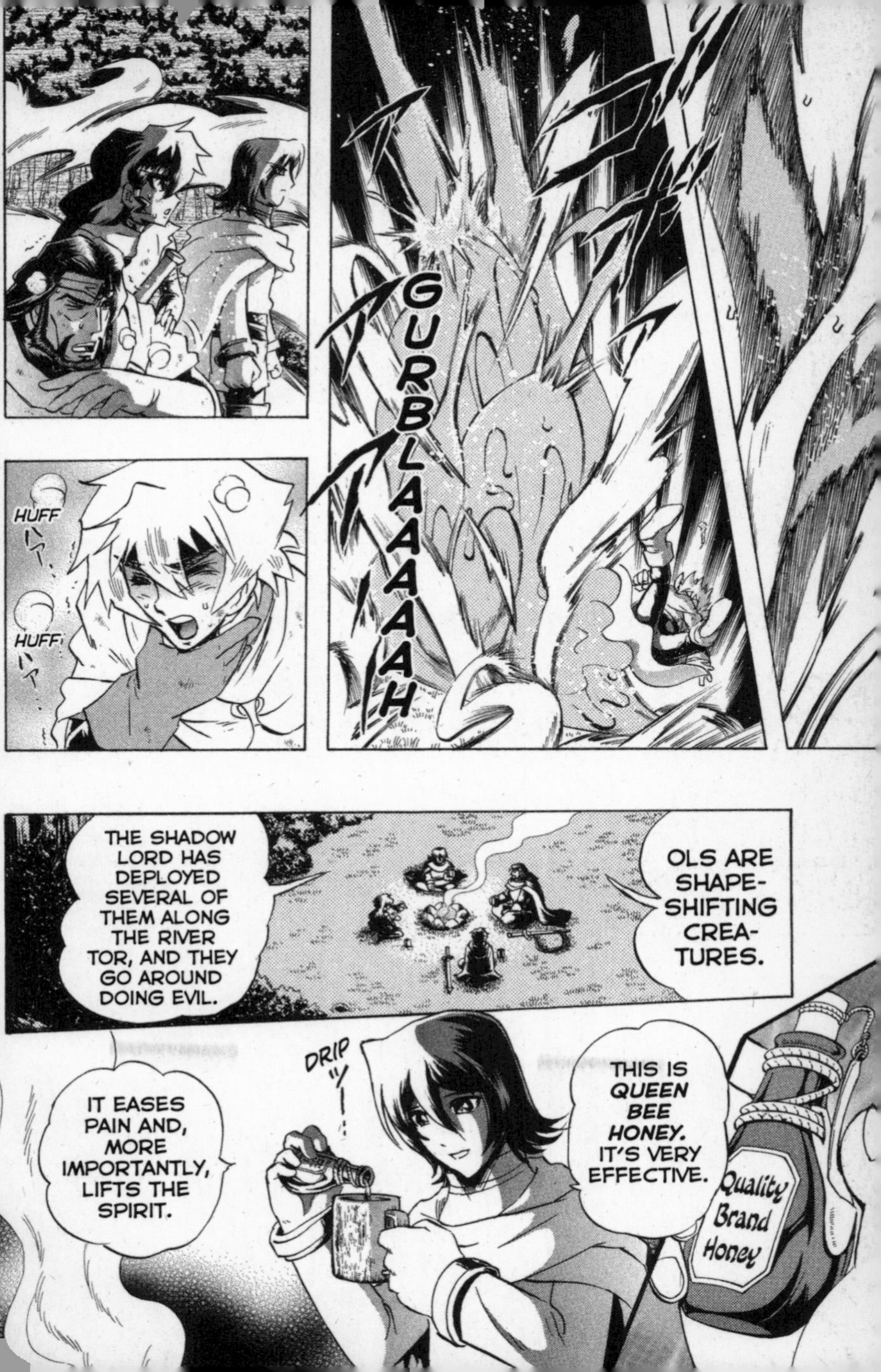
GURBLAAAAAAH
HUFF
HUFF
OLS ARE SHAPE-SHIFTING CREATURES.
THE SHADOW LORD HAS DEPLOYED SEVERAL OF THEM ALONG THE RIVER TOR, AND THEY GO AROUND DOING EVIL.
THIS IS *QUEEN BEE HONEY.* IT'S VERY EFFECTIVE.
DRIP
Quality Brand Honey
IT EASES PAIN AND, MORE IMPORTANTLY, LIFTS THE SPIRIT.

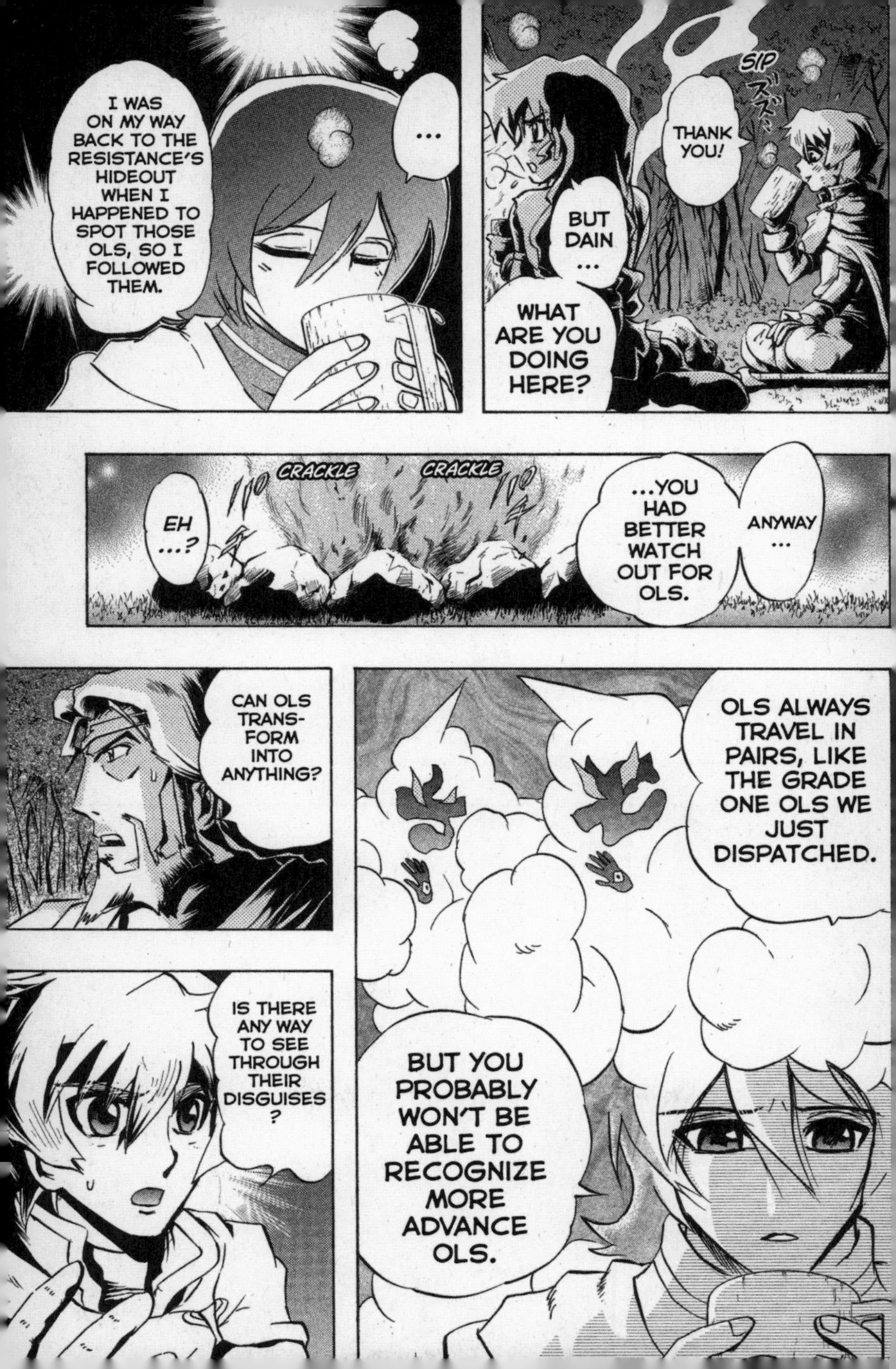
SIP
THANK YOU!
BUT DAIN ...
WHAT ARE YOU DOING HERE?
...
I WAS ON MY WAY BACK TO THE RESISTANCE'S HIDEOUT WHEN I HAPPENED TO SPOT THOSE OLS, SO I FOLLOWED THEM.
ANYWAY ...
...YOU HAD BETTER WATCH OUT FOR OLS.
CRACKLE
CRACKLE
EH ...?
OLS ALWAYS TRAVEL IN PAIRS, LIKE THE GRADE ONE OLS WE JUST DISPATCHED.
BUT YOU PROBABLY WON'T BE ABLE TO RECOGNIZE MORE ADVANCE OLS.
CAN OLS TRANS-FORM INTO ANYTHING?
IS THERE ANY WAY TO SEE THROUGH THEIR DISGUISES ?

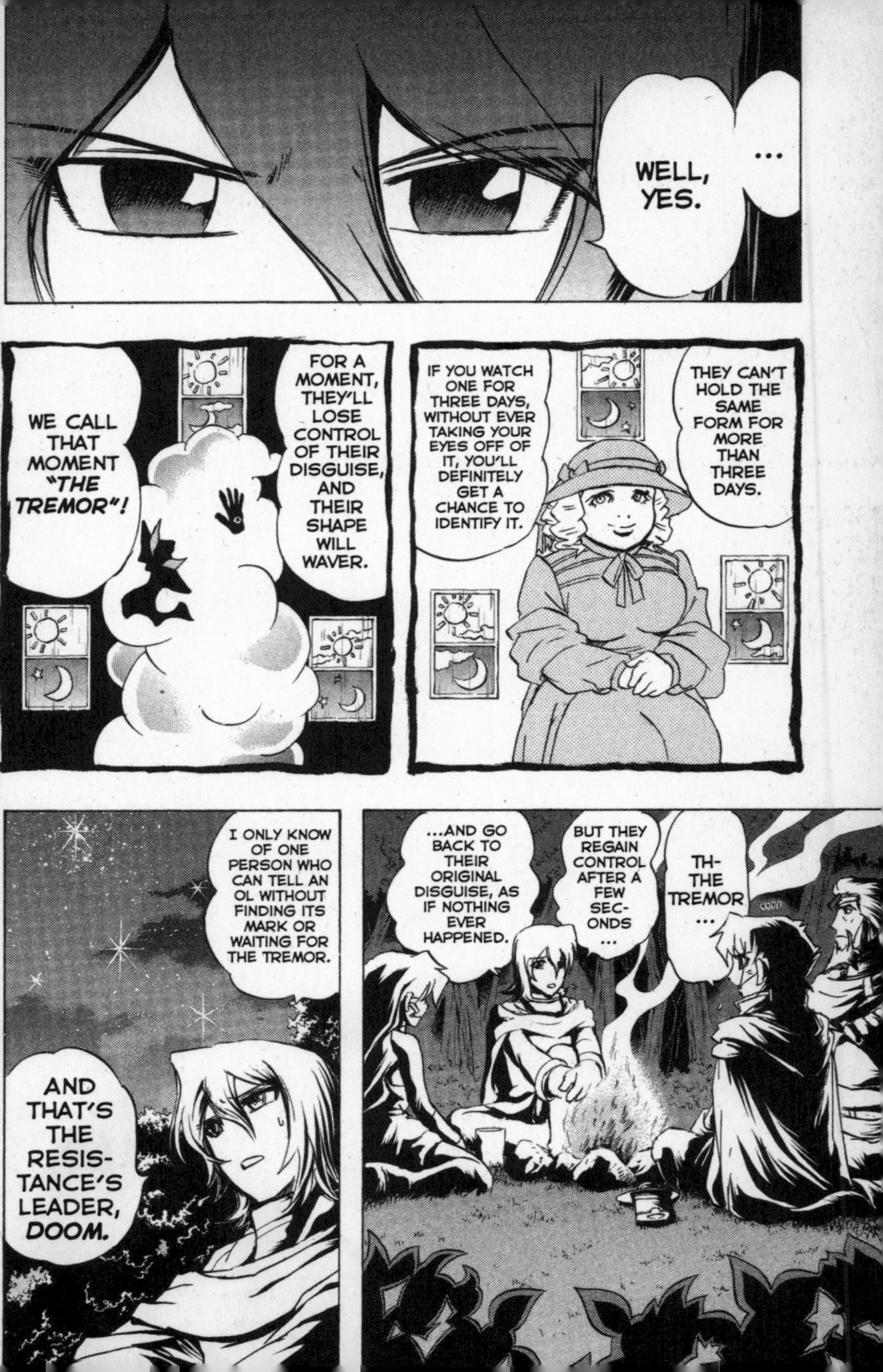
...
WELL, YES.
THEY CAN'T HOLD THE SAME FORM FOR MORE THAN THREE DAYS.
IF YOU WATCH ONE FOR THREE DAYS, WITHOUT EVER TAKING YOUR EYES OFF OF IT, YOU'LL DEFINITELY GET A CHANCE TO IDENTIFY IT.
FOR A MOMENT, THEY'LL LOSE CONTROL OF THEIR DISGUISE, AND THEIR SHAPE WILL WAVER.
WE CALL THAT MOMENT *"THE TREMOR"*!
TH- THE TREMOR...
BUT THEY REGAIN CONTROL AFTER A FEW SEC- ONDS...
...AND GO BACK TO THEIR ORIGINAL DISGUISE, AS IF NOTHING EVER HAPPENED.
I ONLY KNOW OF ONE PERSON WHO CAN TELL AN OL WITHOUT FINDING ITS MARK OR WAITING FOR THE TREMOR.
AND THAT'S THE RESIS- TANCE'S LEADER, *DOOM*.

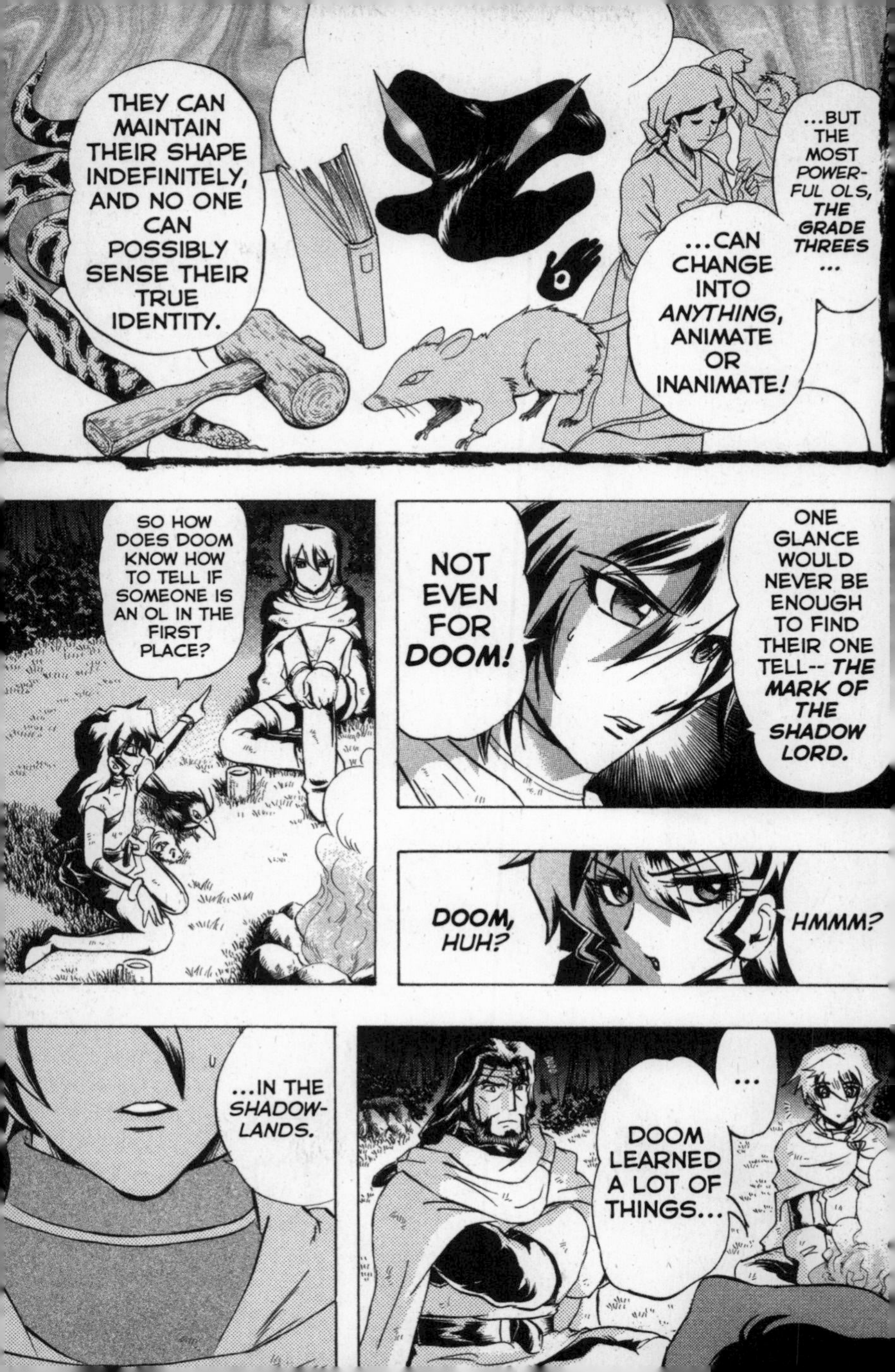
...BUT THE MOST POWERFUL OLS, THE GRADE THREES...
...CAN CHANGE INTO ANYTHING, ANIMATE OR INANIMATE!
THEY CAN MAINTAIN THEIR SHAPE INDEFINITELY, AND NO ONE CAN POSSIBLY SENSE THEIR TRUE IDENTITY.
ONE GLANCE WOULD NEVER BE ENOUGH TO FIND THEIR ONE TELL-- THE MARK OF THE SHADOW LORD.
NOT EVEN FOR DOOM!
HMMM?
DOOM, HUH?
SO HOW DOES DOOM KNOW HOW TO TELL IF SOMEONE IS AN OL IN THE FIRST PLACE?
...
DOOM LEARNED A LOT OF THINGS...
...IN THE SHADOWLANDS.

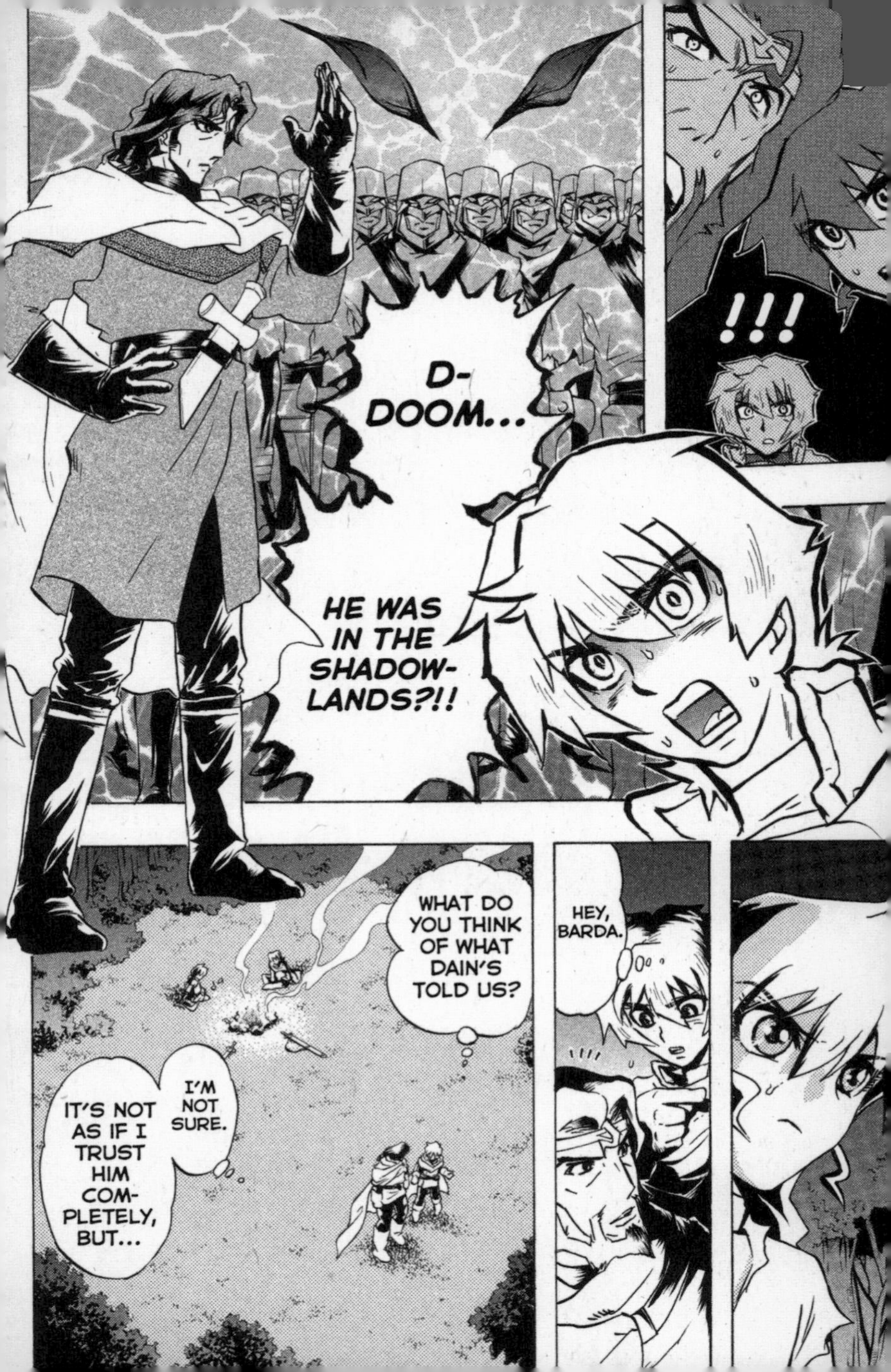
!!!
D-DOOM...
HE WAS IN THE SHADOWLANDS?!!
HEY, BARDA.
WHAT DO YOU THINK OF WHAT DAIN'S TOLD US?
I'M NOT SURE.
IT'S NOT AS IF I TRUST HIM COMPLETELY, BUT...

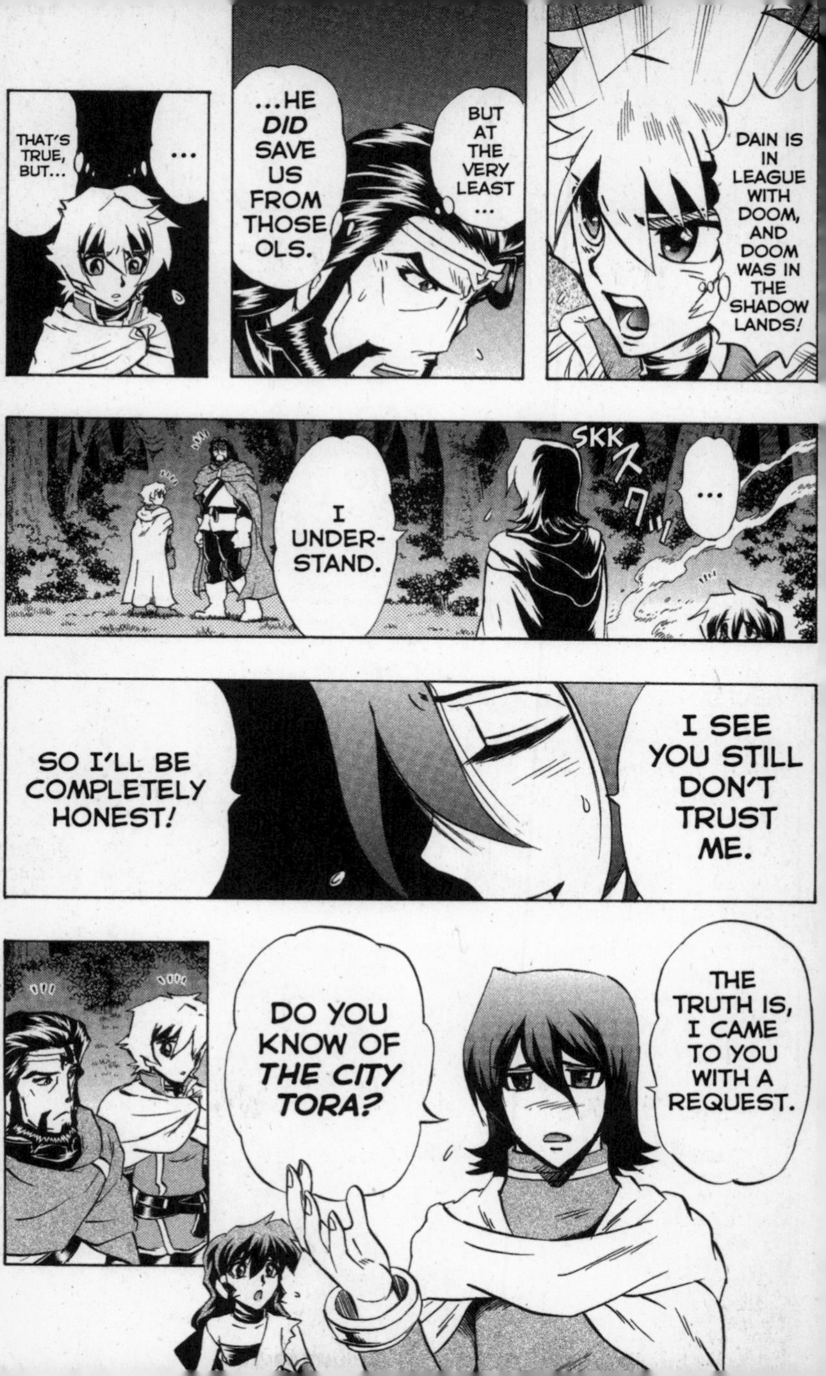
DAIN IS IN LEAGUE WITH DOOM, AND DOOM WAS IN THE SHADOW LANDS!
BUT AT THE VERY LEAST...
...HE *DID* SAVE US FROM THOSE OLS.
...
THAT'S TRUE, BUT...
...
SKK
I UNDERSTAND.
I SEE YOU STILL DON'T TRUST ME.
SO I'LL BE COMPLETELY HONEST!
THE TRUTH IS, I CAME TO YOU WITH A REQUEST.
DO YOU KNOW OF *THE CITY TORA?*

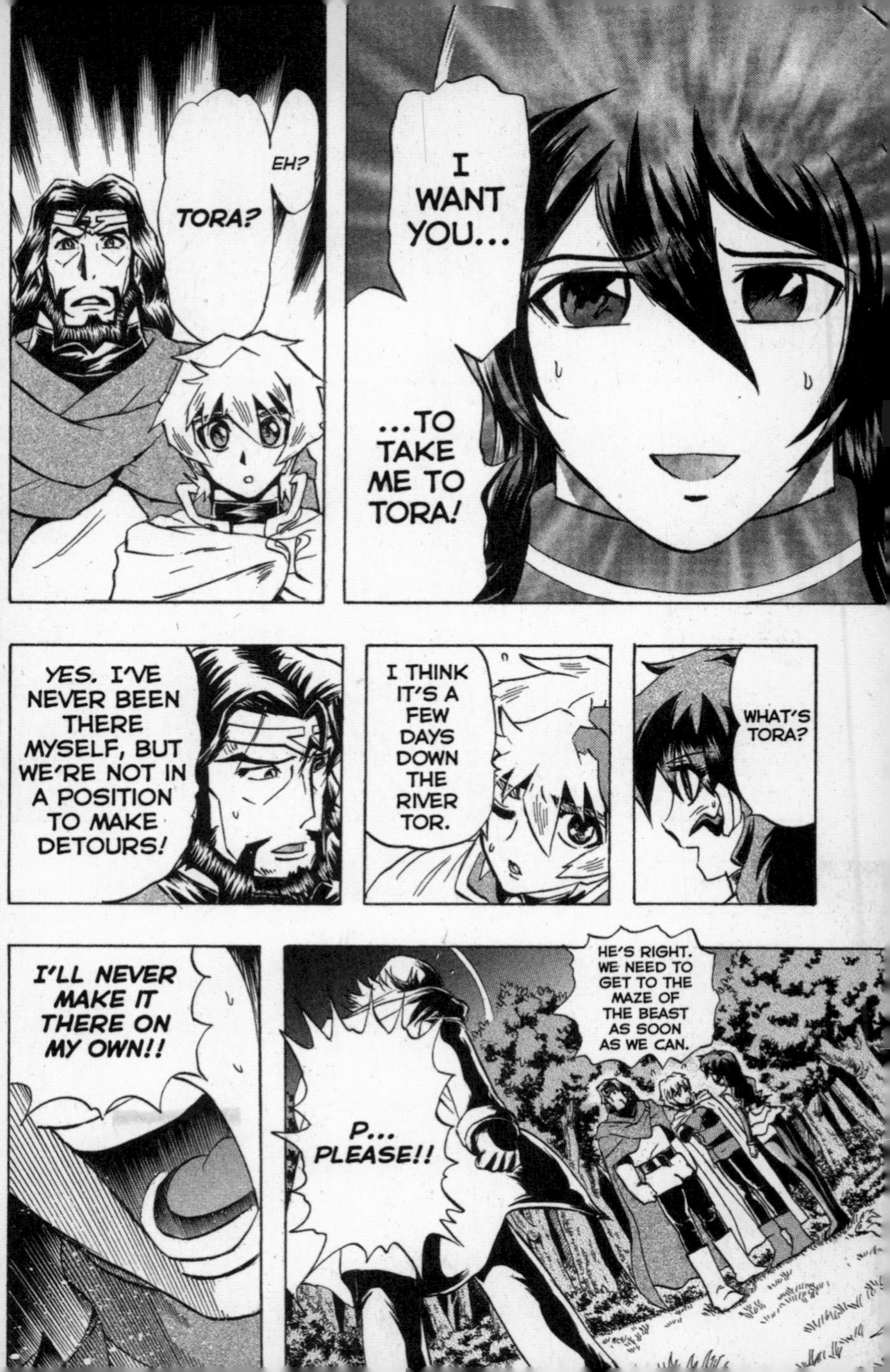
I WANT YOU...
...TO TAKE ME TO TORA!
EH?
TORA?
WHAT'S TORA?
I THINK IT'S A FEW DAYS DOWN THE RIVER TOR.
YES. I'VE NEVER BEEN THERE MYSELF, BUT WE'RE NOT IN A POSITION TO MAKE DETOURS!
HE'S RIGHT. WE NEED TO GET TO THE MAZE OF THE BEAST AS SOON AS WE CAN.
P... PLEASE!!
I'LL NEVER MAKE IT THERE ON MY OWN!!

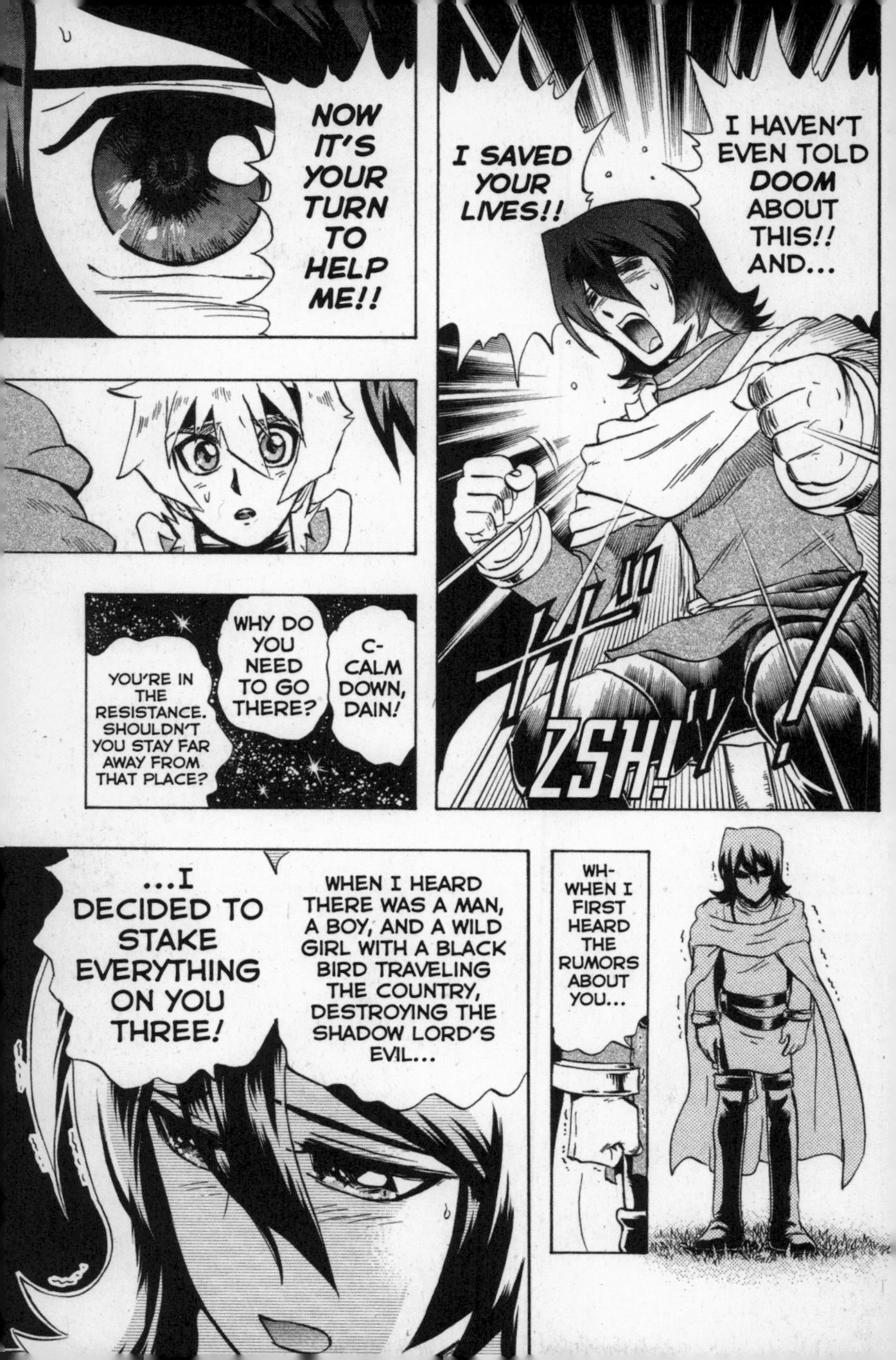
I HAVEN'T EVEN TOLD DOOM ABOUT THIS!! AND...
I SAVED YOUR LIVES!!
ZSH!
NOW IT'S YOUR TURN TO HELP ME!!
C- CALM DOWN, DAIN!
WHY DO YOU NEED TO GO THERE?
YOU'RE IN THE RESISTANCE. SHOULDN'T YOU STAY FAR AWAY FROM THAT PLACE?
WH- WHEN I FIRST HEARD THE RUMORS ABOUT YOU...
WHEN I HEARD THERE WAS A MAN, A BOY, AND A WILD GIRL WITH A BLACK BIRD TRAVELING THE COUNTRY, DESTROYING THE SHADOW LORD'S EVIL...
...I DECIDED TO STAKE EVERYTHING ON YOU THREE!

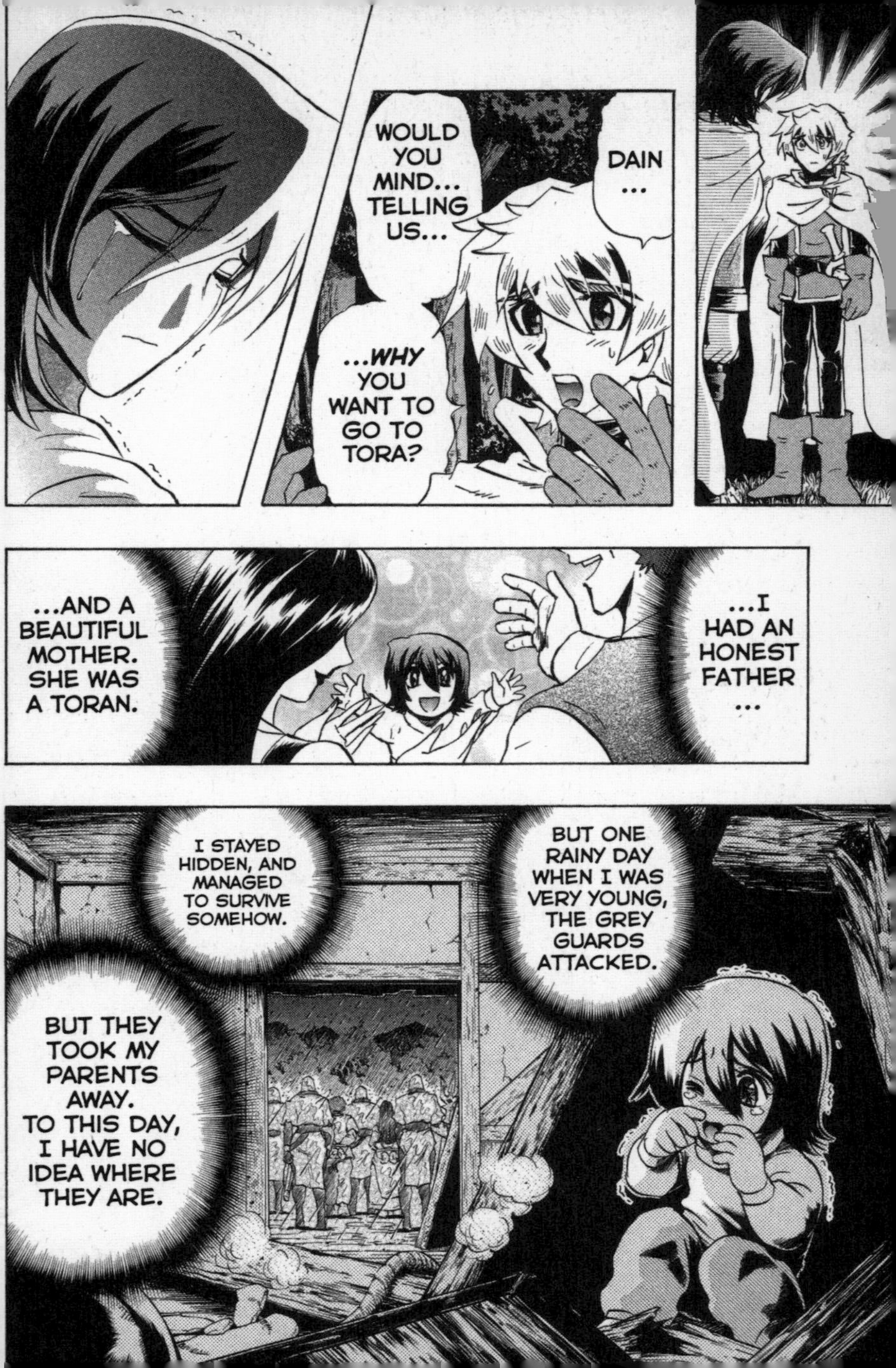
DAIN ...
WOULD YOU MIND... TELLING US...
...WHY YOU WANT TO GO TO TORA?
...I HAD AN HONEST FATHER ...
...AND A BEAUTIFUL MOTHER. SHE WAS A TORAN.
BUT ONE RAINY DAY WHEN I WAS VERY YOUNG, THE GREY GUARDS ATTACKED.
I STAYED HIDDEN, AND MANAGED TO SURVIVE SOMEHOW.
BUT THEY TOOK MY PARENTS AWAY. TO THIS DAY, I HAVE NO IDEA WHERE THEY ARE.

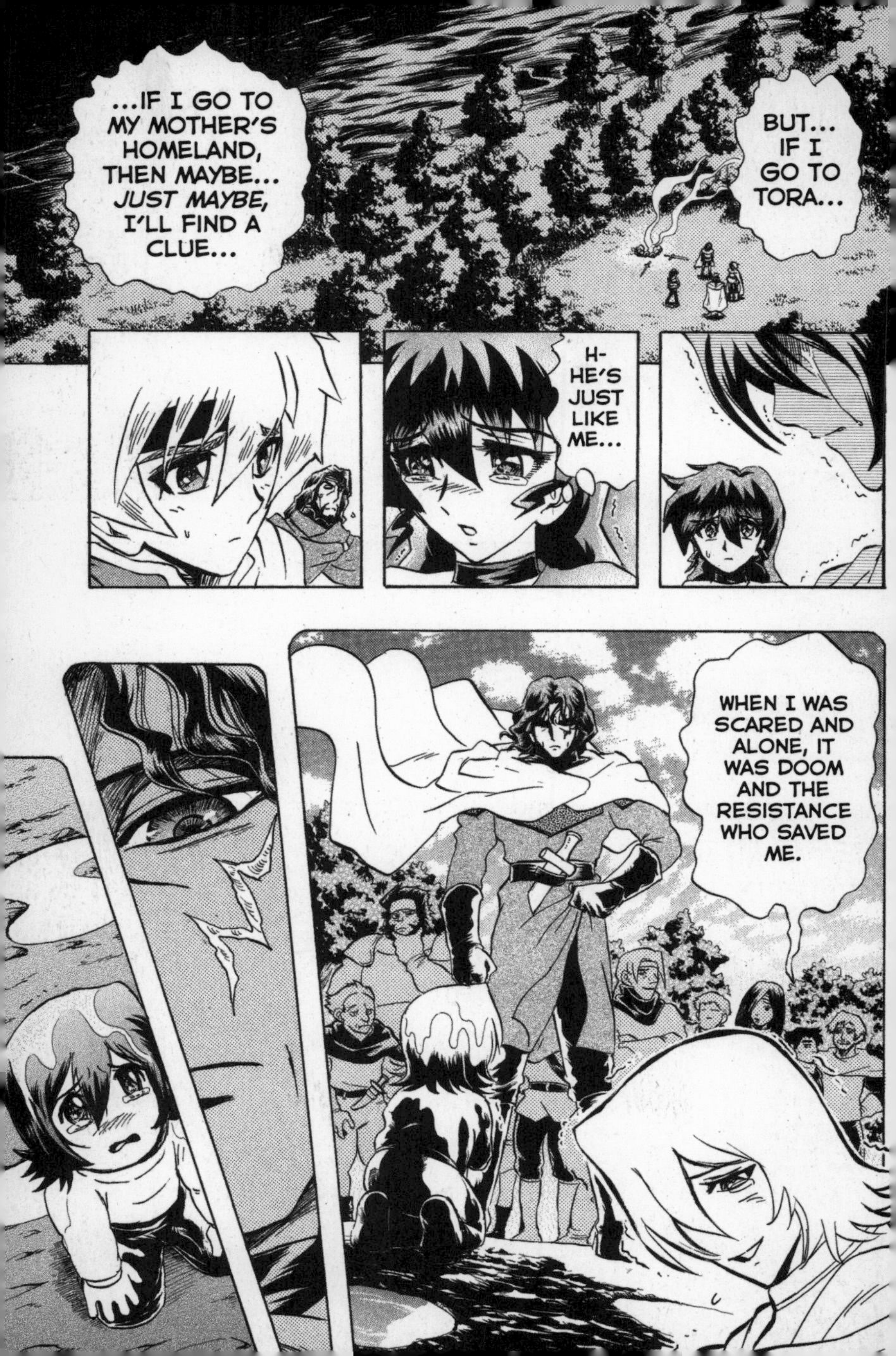
...IF I GO TO MY MOTHER'S HOMELAND, THEN MAYBE... *JUST MAYBE,* I'LL FIND A CLUE...
BUT... IF I GO TO TORA...
H- HE'S JUST LIKE ME...
WHEN I WAS SCARED AND ALONE, IT WAS DOOM AND THE RESISTANCE WHO SAVED ME.

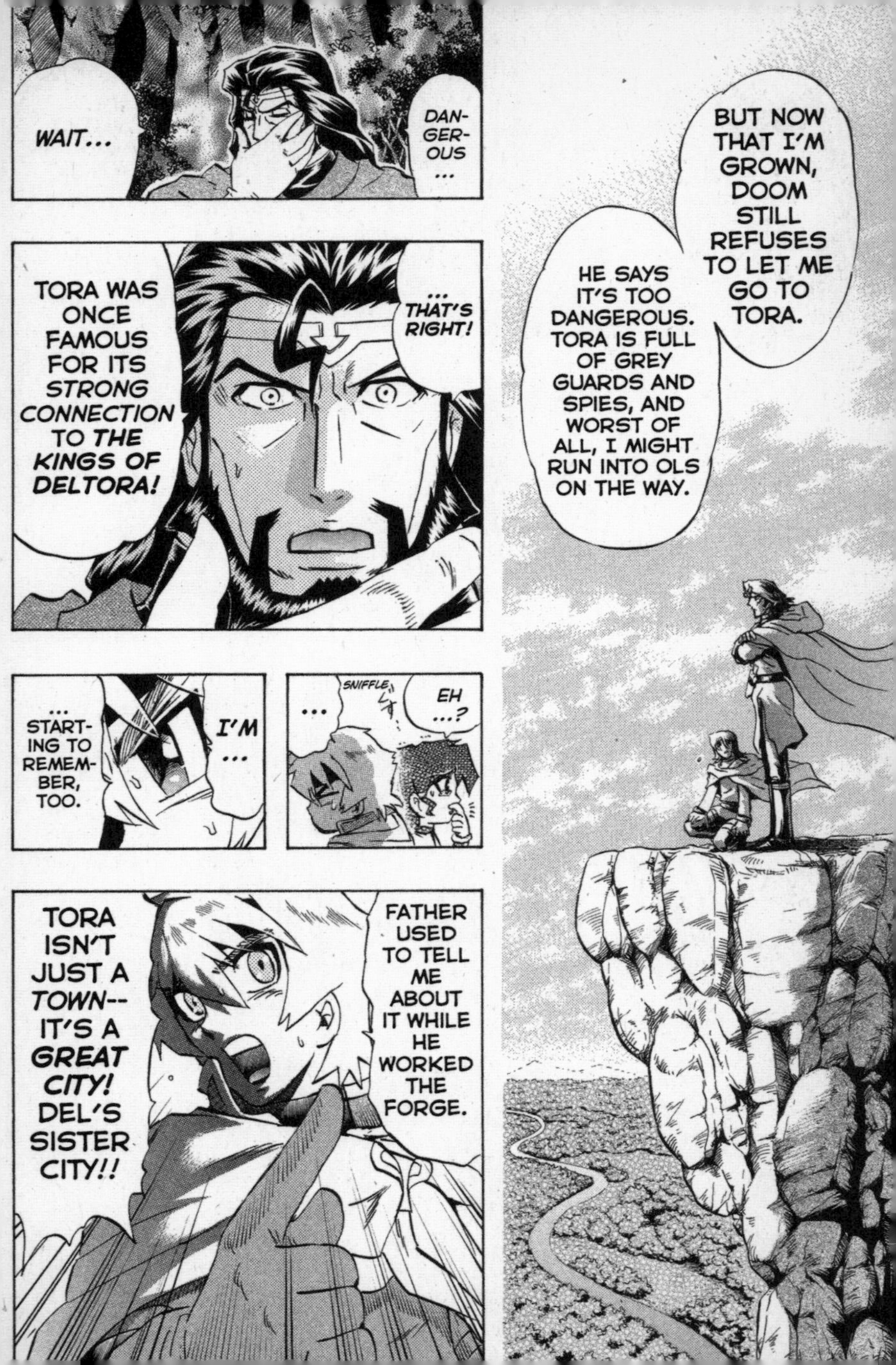
BUT NOW THAT I'M GROWN, DOOM STILL REFUSES TO LET ME GO TO TORA.
HE SAYS IT'S TOO DANGEROUS. TORA IS FULL OF GREY GUARDS AND SPIES, AND WORST OF ALL, I MIGHT RUN INTO OLS ON THE WAY.
DAN-GER-OUS...
WAIT...
...THAT'S RIGHT!
TORA WAS ONCE FAMOUS FOR ITS STRONG CONNECTION TO THE KINGS OF DELTORA!
EH ...?
SNIFFLE
...
I'M ...
...STARTING TO REMEMBER, TOO.
FATHER USED TO TELL ME ABOUT IT WHILE HE WORKED THE FORGE.
TORA ISN'T JUST A TOWN-- IT'S A GREAT CITY! DEL'S SISTER CITY!!

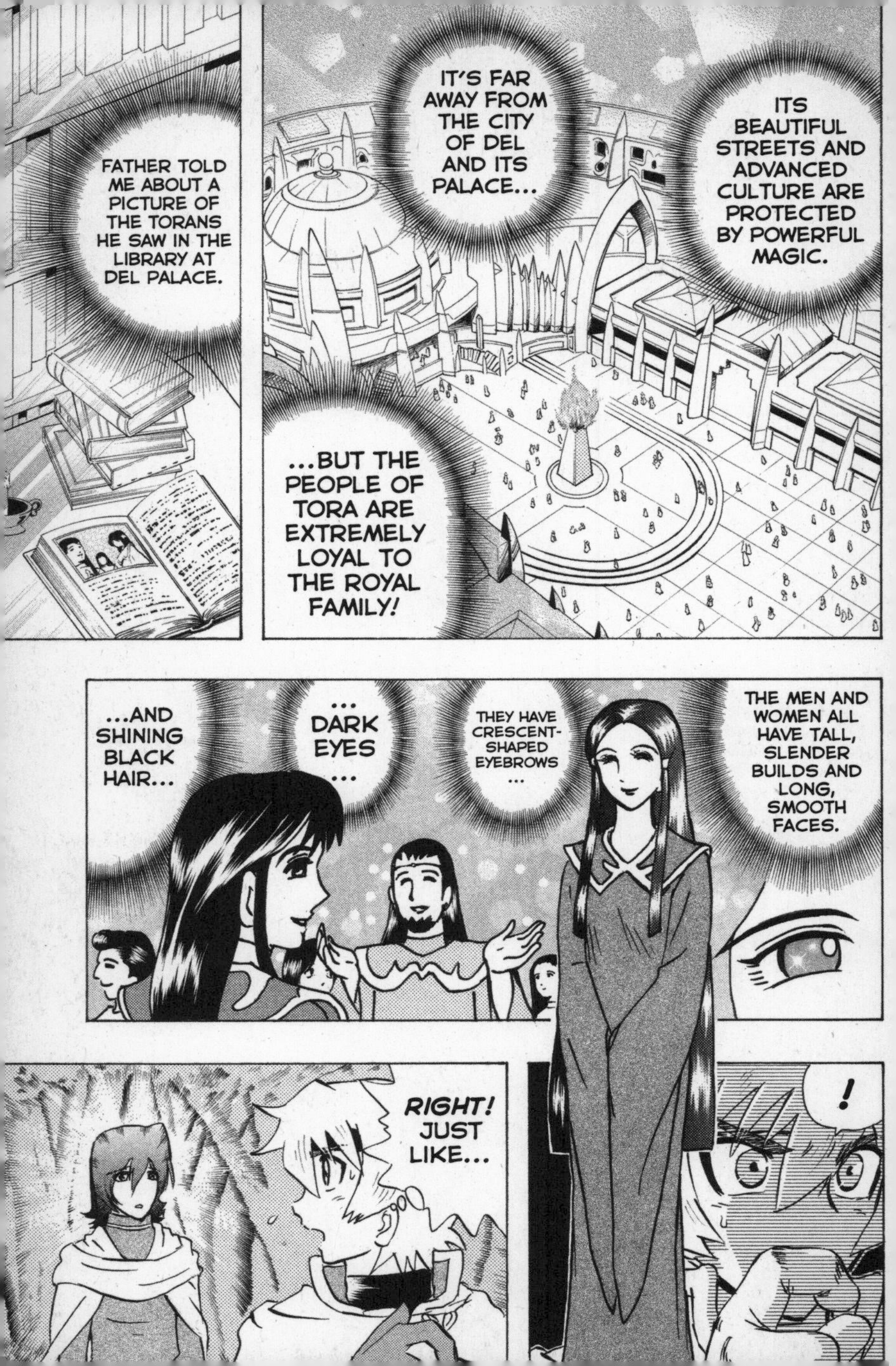
IT'S FAR AWAY FROM THE CITY OF DEL AND ITS PALACE...
ITS BEAUTIFUL STREETS AND ADVANCED CULTURE ARE PROTECTED BY POWERFUL MAGIC.
...BUT THE PEOPLE OF TORA ARE EXTREMELY LOYAL TO THE ROYAL FAMILY!
FATHER TOLD ME ABOUT A PICTURE OF THE TORANS HE SAW IN THE LIBRARY AT DEL PALACE.
THE MEN AND WOMEN ALL HAVE TALL, SLENDER BUILDS AND LONG, SMOOTH FACES.
THEY HAVE CRESCENT-SHAPED EYEBROWS ...
... DARK EYES ...
...AND SHINING BLACK HAIR...
!
RIGHT! JUST LIKE...

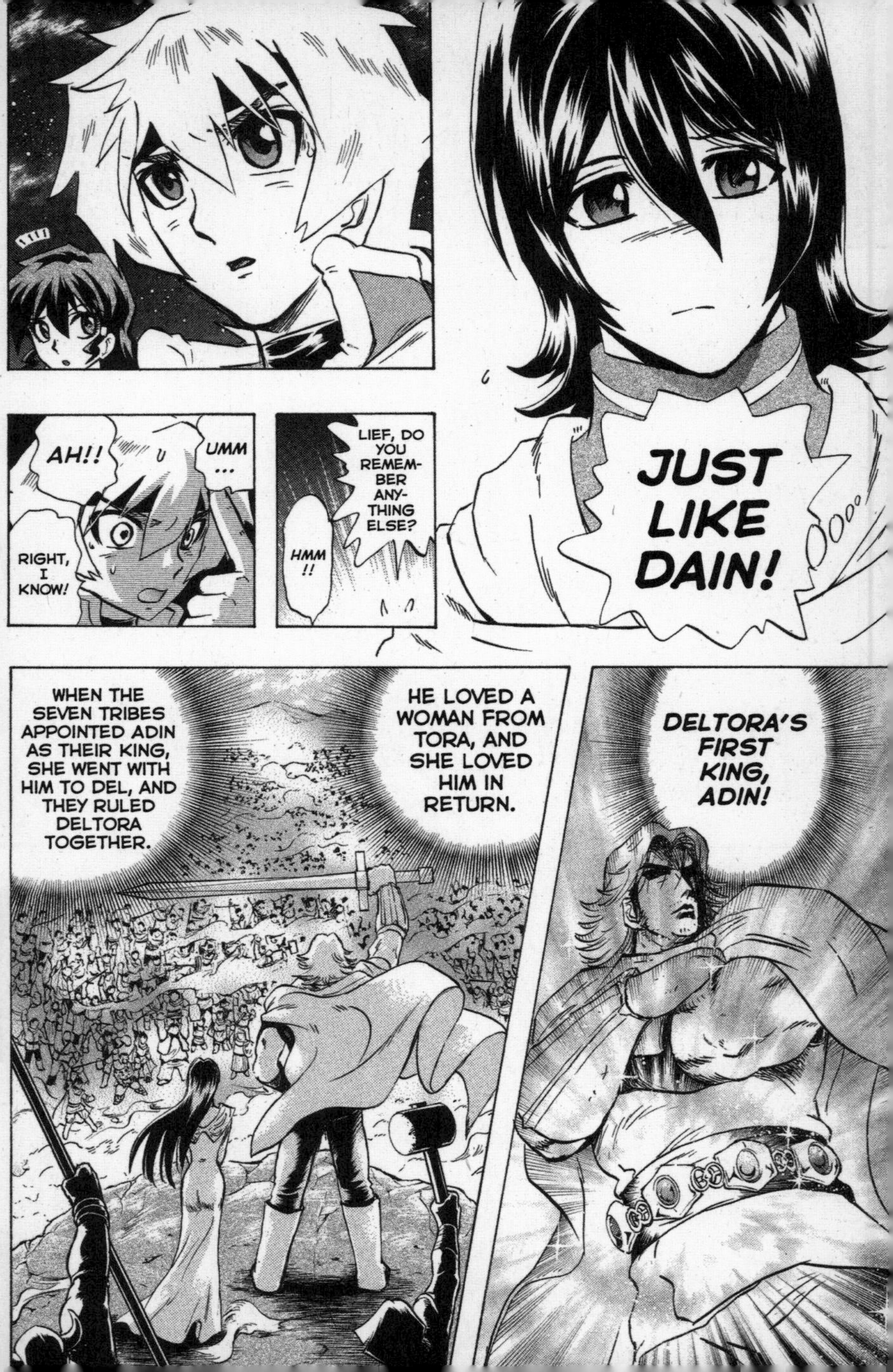
JUST LIKE DAIN!
LIEF, DO YOU REMEMBER ANYTHING ELSE?
HMM !!
UMM ...
AH!!
RIGHT, I KNOW!
DELTORA'S FIRST KING, ADIN!
HE LOVED A WOMAN FROM TORA, AND SHE LOVED HIM IN RETURN.
WHEN THE SEVEN TRIBES APPOINTED ADIN AS THEIR KING, SHE WENT WITH HIM TO DEL, AND THEY RULED DELTORA TOGETHER.

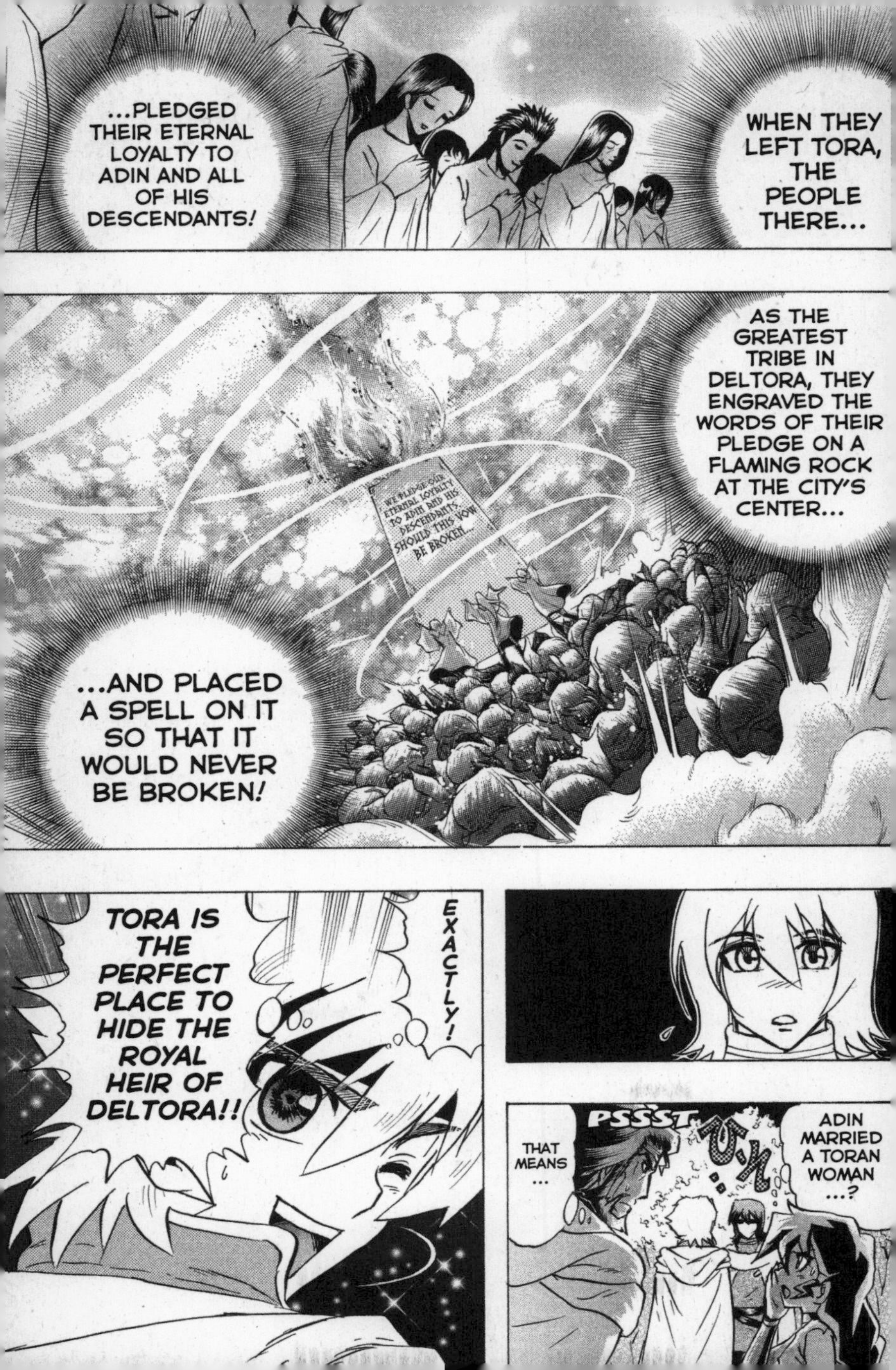
WHEN THEY LEFT TORA, THE PEOPLE THERE...
...PLEDGED THEIR ETERNAL LOYALTY TO ADIN AND ALL OF HIS DESCENDANTS!
AS THE GREATEST TRIBE IN DELTORA, THEY ENGRAVED THE WORDS OF THEIR PLEDGE ON A FLAMING ROCK AT THE CITY'S CENTER...
WE PLEDGE OUR ETERNAL LOYALTY TO ADIN AND HIS DESCENDANTS. SHOULD THIS VOW BE BROKEN...
...AND PLACED A SPELL ON IT SO THAT IT WOULD NEVER BE BROKEN!
ADIN MARRIED A TORAN WOMAN ...?
UH
PSSST
THAT MEANS ...
EXACTLY!
TORA IS THE PERFECT PLACE TO HIDE THE ROYAL HEIR OF DELTORA!!

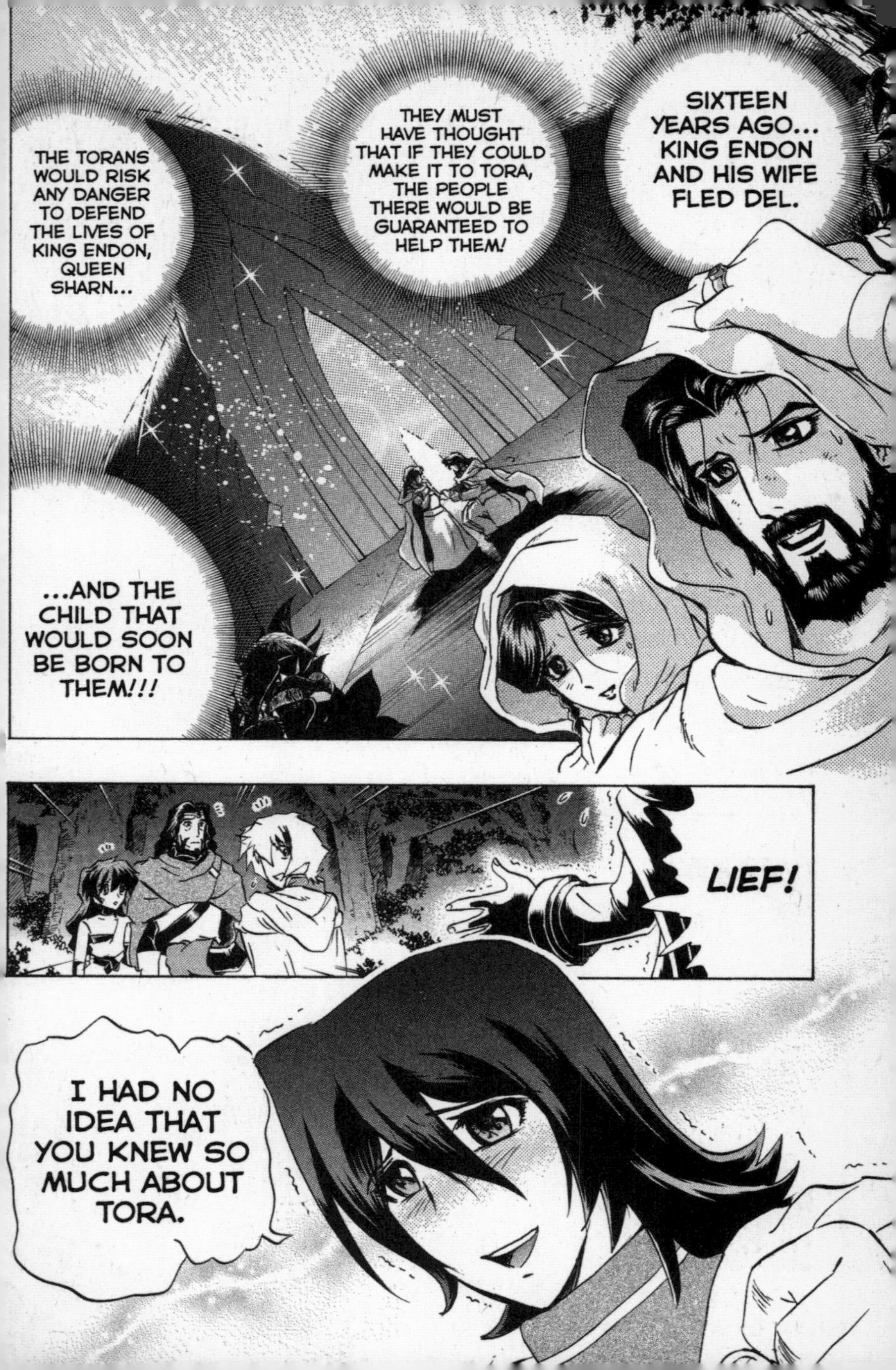
SIXTEEN YEARS AGO... KING ENDON AND HIS WIFE FLED DEL.
THEY MUST HAVE THOUGHT THAT IF THEY COULD MAKE IT TO TORA, THE PEOPLE THERE WOULD BE GUARANTEED TO HELP THEM!
THE TORANS WOULD RISK ANY DANGER TO DEFEND THE LIVES OF KING ENDON, QUEEN SHARN...
...AND THE CHILD THAT WOULD SOON BE BORN TO THEM!!!
LIEF!
I HAD NO IDEA THAT YOU KNEW SO MUCH ABOUT TORA.